KNIGHTHOOD AND SOCIETY IN THE HIGH MIDDLE AGES

MEDIAEVALIA LOVANIENSIA
SERIES I / STUDIA XLVIII

KU LEUVEN
INSTITUTE FOR MEDIEVAL AND RENAISSANCE STUDIES
LEUVEN (BELGIUM)

In memory of Pieter De Leemans (1973–2019)
our colleague and friend,
and for many years a most dedicated editor and inspirer of this series.

The editorial board of the Mediaevalia Lovaniensia

KNIGHTHOOD AND SOCIETY
IN THE HIGH MIDDLE AGES

Edited by

David CROUCH and Jeroen DEPLOIGE

LEUVEN UNIVERSITY PRESS

ISBN 978 94 6270 170 0
eISBN 978 94 6166 275 0
https://doi.org/10.11116/9789461662750
D/2020/1869/56
NUR: 684

Cover design: Friedemann Vervoort
Cover illustration: Miniature illustrating the *Prose Lancelot*. New Haven (CT), Yale University, Beinecke Rare Book & Manuscript Library, MS 229, fol. 94v detail (*ca.* 1275–1300).

GPRC
Guaranteed
Peer Reviewed
Content
www.gprc.be

CONTENTS

ILLUSTRATIONS

ACKNOWLEDGEMENTS

The present volume is the result of two research projects: "The Sacralisation of Knighthood," directed by Jeroen Deploige (Special Research Fund, Ghent University, 2012–16), and "The Genesis of Chivalry: Conduct in Western European Society 1000–1350," granted to David Crouch (Leverhulme Trust, 2013–16). Its actual impetus came from the small conference entitled "Noble Warriors or Warring Nobles? The Complications of Knightly Identity in the High Middle Ages," which we organised in Ghent in December 2015 with the generous support of the Flemish Research Foundation (FWO) and the Henri Pirenne Institute for Medieval Studies. The chapters by Dominique Barthélemy, David Crouch, John Hosler, Jean-François Nieus, Eljas Oksanen, Nicholas Paul and Nicolas Ruffini-Ronzani, included in this collection, were first presented as draft papers at the Ghent conference. The conference also taught us, however, that there were still various aspects of the construction of the high medieval chivalric identity that were escaping our attention. Thanks to the willingness of Jörg Peltzer, Sara McDougall, Louise Wilkinson and Claudia Wittig to join us in this publication project, we were able to bring more coherence and balance to this collection. We are grateful to Martin Aurell, Xavier Baecke, Matthew Bennett and Peter Hoppenbrouwers, who shared with us their expertise at the conference in Ghent and who have indirectly enriched the present volume. We also thank Frederik Buylaert, Erika Graham-Goering and Jeroen De Gussem, as well as the anonymous peer reviewers of this publication and the editorial team of Leuven University Press, for their feedback and advice. Our deepest gratitude goes to our authors for their commitment, their intellectual generosity and their patience.

The editors

David CROUCH and Jeroen DEPLOIGE*

TAKING THE FIELD:
KNIGHTHOOD AND SOCIETY
IN THE HIGH MIDDLE AGES

In popular imagination few phenomena are as strongly associated with medieval society as knighthood and chivalry. At the same time, and due to a long tradition of differing national perspectives and ideological assumptions, few phenomena have continued to be the object of so much academic debate. The volume Knighthood and Society in the High Middle Ages *explores various aspects of chivalric identity formation, taking into account both commonalities and peculiarities across Western Europe. This introductory chapter first provides a historiographical frame in which any consideration of chivalric identity has to be set. It then attempts to clarify the most important assumptions and points of view about the interwovenness of nobility and knighthood. Finally, it briefly introduces what the various essays collected in this volume have to offer individually, and what they might tell us collectively about how, between the eleventh and the early thirteenth centuries, knighthood evolved from a set of skills and a lifestyle that was typical of an emerging elite habitus, into the basis of a consciously expressed and idealised chivalric code of conduct.*

Few historical icons are as strongly associated with the Middle Ages as the knight. Yet it is striking how difficult it remains unambiguously to define terms such as knighthood and chivalry. We can safely say that these have been very fluid concepts since the Middle Ages themselves, to which we can trace back the origins of the long historical process of the idealisation of the chivalric ethos. The interpretations given to concepts such as knighthood and chivalry often tell us more about the time and the environment in which they were developed than about their actual meaning for medieval society. The representation of the knight thus functioned through the ages as a *pars pro toto*, so to speak, for how popular images of the Middle Ages—as either an idealised world or a caricature of primitiveness—were used for con-

* While this introduction is the unanimous result of fruitful conversation between its two authors, the reader may recognise David Crouch's hand in the sections on historiography and nobilisation, and Jeroen Deploige's in the introductory paragraphs and the last two sections.

temporary agendas.[1] Even apart from such appropriation of the past, and apart from his central place in the long history of "medievalism," the knight has become a kind of timeless cultural icon which continues to appeal to the imagination, both in the popular culture of fantasy and in contemporary art.[2]

At the same time, there are few phenomena that have remained so strongly, and for so long, the object of historiographic effort and debate. For most of the twentieth century knighthood has mainly been studied either from a social-historical perspective or through the lens of literary history. In past decades, however, views on high medieval knighthood have profoundly changed. Historians have increasingly stressed that knights should not be considered a newly emerging social class defined by their common knightliness, but rather be seen as a complex and variable cultural construct. Certainly, knights were intrinsically related to the martial practice of mounted combat, but the idea of knighthood had come to signify more than that, even as early as in the eleventh century. In the subsequent centuries, the idea of knighthood, and chivalry, grew more complex and diverse. Knights did not merely perceive themselves as professional horseback warriors, but increasingly associated their martial practice with prowess and a noble status as even the highest aristocracy, kings and princes, embraced their martial ideals. Knights became noble warriors and knighthood gained many new dimensions in the course of the twelfth and thirteenth centuries. Knightly identity was influenced by Christian concepts of violence and spiritual warfare and by ideals of *preudommie*, it was expressed at tournaments which developed an elaborate etiquette, it became closely connected to the courtly festivities of princes and monarchs, and it served as a marker of nobility and even as a legitimation for the privileged aristocratic status. However, knightly and chivalric ideology often stood in sharp contrast to the actions of those who were considered knights. The idealised image of a noble warrior often masked the pragmatic reality of a warring noble.

---

1. For a collection of case studies see Barbara Gribling and Katie Stevenson, eds., *Chivalry and the Medieval Past* (Woodbridge: Boydell, 2016).

2. See e.g. the exhibition, organised in 2017 in Gaasbeek Castle (Belgium) and devoted to contemporary artists paying homage to the spirit of chivalry and to the knight as a cultural icon, with works by artists such as Marina Abramovic, Jan Fabre, Damien Hirst, Kubra Khademi, Eleni Mylonas and many others. The exhibition catalogue is published as Joanna De Vos et al., *The Artist/Knight* (Veurne: Hannibal Publishing, 2017).

Although the different aspects of knighthood have been widely studied in recent historiography, the global impression resulting from it is still one of much discussion and conceptual disarray. One of the main reasons for this is definitely the fact that our understanding of chivalry continues to be encapsulated in national approaches and traditions, which still do not sufficiently manage—partly due to linguistic barriers—to enter into dialogue with each other and fully recognise the commonalities and particularities of the phenomenon across Europe. It is also striking that far too few real collaborations are being pursued between the various disciplines and subfields that have taken an interest in the phenomenon of chivalry, such as political, military and literary history. We cannot in this volume aim to offer a global synthesis of the topic. This book can therefore not be placed next to Richard W. Kaeuper's recent and erudite *Medieval Chivalry*, for example.[3] Our purpose is different. What is presented here is a varied collection of essays by leading scholars from different national and disciplinary backgrounds who are currently addressing in their research different aspects of the relationship between knighthood and society in the High Middle Ages, and who have been willing to reflect more specifically on the way in which their particular research might contribute to a new and better understanding of the different markers of a growing chivalric identity in the West.

The wonderful complexity of the movement of the medieval mind we call "chivalry" is thus explored in the chapters that follow, but to begin with we must provide in this introduction a historiographical frame in which any consideration of chivalric identity has to be set. We then attempt to clarify the most important assumptions and points of view about the interwovenness of nobility and knighthood.[4] Finally, we briefly introduce what the various essays collected in this volume have to offer individually, and what they might tell us collectively about chivalry in relation to the process of noble identity formation.

3. Richard W. Kaeuper, *Medieval Chivalry* (Cambridge: Cambridge University Press, 2016). See also Robert W. Jones and Peter Coss, eds., *A Companion to Chivalry* (Woodbridge: Boydell & Brewer, 2019).

4. Some of these insights have also been further elaborated and recently published in David Crouch, *The Chivalric Turn: Conduct and Hegemony in Europe before 1300* (Oxford: Oxford University Press, 2019), 9–12, 252–300.

Chivalry as a Historiographical Construct

The words and ideas of Maurice Keen (1933–2012) inform several of the contributions which follow, and his own position on medieval chivalry is a good point from which to track backwards to find the assumptions which have guided the historiographical debate over more than three centuries and formed his own views. Keen believed chivalry to be an essentially intellectual movement first fully visible in the early thirteenth century which arose out of a new articulation of existing military and religious ethics, and which was in part characterised by the unreal degree of moral expectation it imposed on the male social elite which professed to embrace it, of which the knight (Old French *chevaler*) was the defining figure. Keen's conclusion was not by any means a new departure. It has in fact been customary since the mid-eighteenth century to treat chivalry as a moral programme, and as a programme still relevant to contemporaries. Mark Girouard entertainingly and learnedly demonstrated in 1981 how present views of chivalry remain coloured by its adoption in the nineteenth century by numerous writers of several nations interested in employing its cachet of antiquity, nobility and authority to fit several differing— but usually conservative—moral and educational agendas.[5] They all believed chivalry could be described as a moral and ethical phenomenon because, as far as they understood it, chivalry always had been, even in the remote past. One of its earliest and better British students, Charles Mills (1788–1826), persuasively argued just that point before his tragically early death.[6]

The nineteenth-century understanding of chivalry as essentially a moral-ethical programme rooted in Christian theology was inherited from an earlier generation of scholarship. It ultimately derives from the French Enlightenment. It owed most to Jean-Baptiste de la Curne de Sainte-Palaye's (1697–1781) popular *Mémoires de l'ancienne chevalerie* (first published in 1759), a work compiled in large part from his own preliminary essays on the subject from the 1740s. Charles Nodier's (1780–1844) introduction to the 1826 edition of the *Mémoires* took some space to assess its long-term significance, and concluded

5. Mark Girouard, *The Return to Camelot: Chivalry and the English Gentleman* (New Haven, CT: Yale University Press, 1981).
6. Charles Mills, *The History of Chivalry or Knighthood and its Times*, 2 vols. (London: Longman, Hurst, Rees, Orme, Brown and Green, 1825).

broadly—as had also Charles Mills in England the previous year—
that La Curne had established chivalry by his great work as being an
essentially moral and improving phenomenon in an otherwise primitive age: "il est certain qu'on y retrouve la peinture exacte et fidèle
des moeurs et des usages des siècles simples et grossiers où la chevalerie étoit une institution importante."[7] For Mills, chivalry evolved
into "the most beautiful form of manners ... that has ever adorned the
history of man."[8] Much the same verdict on La Curne's work was to
be found in contemporary Germany, where in 1823 Johann Gustav
Gottlieb Büsching (1783–1829) presented the Frenchman's ideas to
a new public, adding his own rather florid and rambling observations
drawn from medieval German literature.[9] Büsching's ideas were to
be influential too: his work was to provide the intellectual scenery for
Richard Wagner's medieval Teutonic fantasy, *Parsifal*.

However, La Curne himself had predecessors in his views, not
least the prolific Jesuit antiquary, Claude-François Menestrier (1631–
1705), whose *Chevalerie ancienne et moderne* was published in 1683.
Some of the basic ideas on chivalry were thus formulated in the age of
Louis XIV, in whose father's lifetime the last courtly jousts had been
staged in France—festivities which Menestrier himself had chron-
icled. Menestrier modestly contended in his work that no previous
writer had ever truly understood chivalry the way he did, and so had
confused the word's several meanings, which he would clarify for his
readers. But dubious modesty aside, he was indeed a pioneer in a new
intellectual field and so had good reason to assert the importance of
his analysis. *Chevalerie*, he was the first to say, was a complicated
phenomenon to analyse because it comprehended numerous senses
in French: the profession of the horseback warrior; an estate of lesser
nobility; the holders of fiefs and membership of chivalric and religious
associations. In all its senses and in his discussion, however, Menestrier related chivalry to nobility, and to superiority in society. As far

7. Jean-Baptiste de La Curne de Sainte-Palaye, *Mémoires de l'ancienne chevalerie con-
sidérée comme un établissement politique et militaire*, 2nd ed., introd. and notes Charles
Nodier, 2 vols. ([1759]; Paris: Girard, 1826), 1: 2.

8. Mills, *The History of Chivalry*, 11. He may have been quoting Montesquieu's positive verdict on "le système merveilleux de la chevalerie" which the great man believed
had no match in any earlier society. See Charles Montesquieu, *De l'esprit des lois*, 5 vols.
([1748]; Paris: Dabo, 1824), 3: 205.

9. Johann Gustav Gottlieb Büsching, *Ritterzeit und Ritterwesen*, 2 vols. (Leipzig: F.A.
Brockhaus, 1823).

as he was concerned, the idea of *chevalerie* was a constant in society wherever there were aristocratic warriors, and he harked back as far as the order of *Equites* in Republican and Imperial Rome. He dealt with the moral demands on the medieval knight only briefly, under the heading of the oaths that knights must take on entry into their order:

> ... on void par ce serment que l'ordre du S. Esprit tient beau-coup des manières et des usages de toutes les anciennes che-valeries, de celle de Religion et de Profession, puis qu'on y fait des voeux; de celle des hommages liges, par les engagemens que l'on se fait auprés du Souverain, des fraternitez d'armes, et des adoptions, des societez d'amitié, interest et de service.[10]

Menestrier thus brought the profession of arms, social status and com-mitment to moral excellence together under the heading of *chevalerie* and argued that as a phenomenon it was timeless. Under the heading of moral excellence, he was keen to emphasise the value of the bene-diction of arms and the ceremony of inauguration of a medieval knight at the altar as it developed in the later Middle Ages, a ritual on which there is still much to say, as Dominique Barthélemy illustrates in this volume. Menestrier was not a man much enamoured of fiction, and despised the Arthurian romances as sources for his reconstruction of chivalry; he preferred legal and institutional evidence. His chivalry naturally therefore gravitated to grants of nobility and the Rules of the curial and ecclesiastical orders of knights, of which he regarded the Order of the Hospitallers as the most noble and superior, so to that extent he acknowledged some link between chivalry and crusading endeavour, which is explored here in the chapters by John Hosler and Nicholas Paul.

The many inadequacies of Menestrier's reasoning were system-atically dissected soon after his death by the Carmelite friar, Blaise Vauzelle (1651–1729), otherwise known as the Père Honoré de Sainte-Marie, who published in 1718 his *Dissertations historiques et critiques sur la chevalerie*, in which he took apart many of Menes-trier's proofs and categories. But, as often happens with controver-sialists, a fierce and austere desire to point out the inadequacies in the reasoning of someone else's theories was not coupled with the

---

10. Claude-François Menestrier, *De la chevalerie ancienne et moderne avec la manière d'en faire les preuves* (Paris: De la Caille, 1683), 325.

imagination to find adequate new ones. If anything, the good father took Menestrier's approaches further than he had. On the matter of chivalry's origins, he took it for granted that wherever there had been noble warriors there had always been *chevalerie*, of which "Christian chivalry" was but the latest episode. In the universalising manner of Enlightenment scholarship, he even found reason to believe the Aztec empire had possessed a knighting ceremony.[11] He did not quibble with Menestrier's linking of chivalry with nobility, though he did allow here that there had been occasional historical exceptions. For him, as also for Menestrier, Christian chivalry owed something to crusading fervour. He even pursued and expanded upon Menestrier's eccentric argument—for which he had found material in Gilles-André de la Roque's *Traité de la Noblesse* (1678)— that *chevalerie* extended to women who embraced the crusading orders, and that there was a degree of *chevaleresse* corresponding to the *chevaler*. The interaction between women and chivalric ideals is a subject that has resurfaced only in our generation and is explored in this volume by Louise Wilkinson and Nicolas Ruffini-Ronzani.[12]

Unlike Menestrier however, Father Honoré deployed a mass of medieval chronicles and romances in his support, and as a result his portrayal of the later stages of Christian chivalry in Europe, as he would have looked at it, is much more vivid and evocative than that of his predecessor. This was the approach which was employed rather more rigorously and thoroughly by Jean-Baptiste de la Curne de Sainte-Palaye in the next generation, to produce a more familiar analysis of chivalry, one that was located in the European—or rather, French— Middle Ages, and was reconstructed laboriously and self-consciously from the analysis of literary remains as much as legal texts. He was willing to credit Menestrier with being one of his forerunners in doing this, but not Father Honoré. La Curne was a pioneering student of medieval French literature, and his edition of Froissart was to be the standard for over a century. So he was well equipped to reconstruct from his reading the training and ideals of the young medieval knight and the course of a typical career, a historical exercise which was the subject of his preliminary essays of the 1740s before he republished

---

11. Père Honoré de Sainte-Marie, *Dissertations historiques et critiques sur la chevalerie, ancienne et moderne seculière et regulière* (Paris: Giffart, 1718), 337.

12. See also, recently, Sophie Cassagnes-Brouquet, *Chevaleresses: une chevalerie au féminin* (Paris: Perrin, 2013).

them in *Mémoires de l'ancienne chevalerie*. La Curne located chivalry entirely in the French Middle Ages and, since he saw the ceremony of the reception of arms as an indicator of *chevalerie* (in the sense of knighthood), he was happy to believe that it was a reality in the time of Charlemagne. Indeed, he was ready to accept that it might have been a characteristic of the Germanic warbands described by Tacitus, who reported that they practised delivery of arms. But the "Golden Age of Chivalry," as he called it, was for him the later Middle Ages when there were romances and tracts to describe and exalt the virtues of the true *chevalier*. If such tracts commenced for Maurice Keen with the *Ordene de Chevalerie*, they began for La Curne with the *Roman des Eles*, which he believed dated from the 1250s. In fact, we now know that both tracts are much older, dating to the 1210s.

It is in the 1740s therefore that we find the first fully-articulated historical model of chivalry as we expect it to be: a pattern of exalted moral conduct which was expected of the military nobility of the western European centuries following the twelfth. La Curne's model rapidly passed into the European intellectual mainstream, and had already been absorbed in England by the 1760s, where it filtered into the minds of the early thinkers of the Romantic movement.[13] It held the field throughout the nineteenth century when, as has been said, his intellectual model of chivalry was adopted uncritically as the basis for programmes of conservative social reform. This reformist and literary approach reached its culmination in 1884 with the remarkably erudite but historically tone-deaf polemic, Léon Gautier's *La Chevalerie*. The book preached a restoration of chivalry as a panacea for all the problems and corruption of Third Republic France, in particular its secularity and modernism. It took a century for academics to return to a subject made so comprehensively ridiculous by its most accomplished and ardent devotee.

This largely shared historiography between the Francophone and Anglophone historian on the subject of chivalry and knighthood is not the only story however. As Jörg Peltzer comprehensively demonstrates in this volume, German scholarship subsequent to Büsching

---

13. Peter Burke, "Origins of Cultural History," in *Varieties of Cultural History* (Ithaca, NY: Cornell University Press, 1998), 15–16. See also, for the reception of these ideals in the Holy Roman Empire, Martin Wrede, *Ohne Furcht und Tadel—für König und Vaterland. Frühneuzeitlicher Hochadel zwischen Familienehre, Ritterideal und Fürstendienst. Studien zu Beharrungswillen und Anpassungsvermögen einer traditionalen Elite*, Beihefte der Francia 75 (Ostfildern: Thorbecke, 2012), esp. 372 ff.

has found divergence as much as similarity in the study of the medieval development of knighthood and the chivalric ethos within the Empire when compared with the western lands. One obvious sticking point has long been the anomalous position of the ministerial knight of the Empire, who shared the vocation of the free knight of the West but not necessarily his status or ideals. But a more recent epistemological divergence has been in the attention given in German historiography to the concept described in the Latin word *curialitas*.[14] In the twentieth century there has been a realisation which has filtered by various routes into Anglophone thinking that "courtliness" (Occitan: *cortesia*; Old French: *cortoisie*; Middle High German: *Hövescheit*) operated as a behavioural code of superior conduct for many years, perhaps centuries, before the "chivalric turn."[15] Some of the consequences of this realisation are explored in David Crouch's chapter below.

The restoration of the study of chivalry within the social history of the Middle Ages was brilliantly accomplished by Maurice Keen. His *Chivalry* (1984) has none of the Francocentricity of earlier studies, including Sidney Painter's (1902–60) disappointing 1940 essay, *French Chivalry*. Nor does it have the purblindness of earlier British scholarship on the subject of knightly aristocratic life, all too often determined to pinpoint the extent and numbers of knights' fees, and laboriously trace their descent from the surveys and feodaries that survive in such numbers in the English medieval record. It is striking how the seventeenth-century antiquaries of England in pursuit of the knight, beginning with the generation of John Selden (1584–1654) and William Dugdale (1605–86), were seduced by the copious surviving legal records from the English Middle Ages. Their French counterparts, by contrast, pursued the knight through the richer fields of their native medieval literary inheritance. Maurice Keen possessed neither form of insularity. Instead he focussed on the cultural turn which La Curne had long before identified as the "Golden Age of Chivalry,"

14. Most comprehensively summed up in the essays in Josef Fleckenstein, ed., *Curialitas. Studien zu Grundfragen der höfisch-ritterlichen Kultur*, Veröffentlichungen des Max-Planck-Instituts für Geschichte 100 (Göttingen: Vandenhoeck und Ruprecht, 1990).

15. Principally propagated by: C. Stephen Jaeger, *The Origins of Courtliness: Civilizing Trends and the Formation of Courtly Ideals, 939–1210* (Philadelphia, PA: University of Pennsylvania Press, 1985); Joachim Bumke, *Courtly Culture: Literature and Society in the High Middle Ages* (Woodstock NY: Overlook Press, 2000), translated by Thomas Dunlap from *Höfische Kultur: Literatur und Gesellschaft im hohen Mittelalter* (Munich: Deutscher Taschenbuch Verlag, 1986). For the "chivalric turn," see Crouch, *The Chivalric Turn*, 7–8, 301–6.

the consequences and developments of which Keen pursued across
Europe in a work of humanism and a scholarship both formidable and
graceful. This volume is a conscious attempt to take up and further
pursue his insights.

Knighthood and Nobilisation

In the second half of the twentieth century there was a developing critical consciousness of assumptions made unthinkingly by Menestrier
and his eighteenth-century successors: that knights, by being knights,
were noblemen and constituted a noble class. They have been challenged within two national historiographies. Dissent appears in Britain before the Second World War. A senior British medievalist writing
in 1984 saw this challenge as unnecessary and unwelcome revisionism, but in doing so offered a study of the emergence of what to him
was a heresy. In British historiography he dated it to the observation
of Sir Frank Stenton (1880–1967) in 1929 that the Latin term *miles*
in England was not used in any honorific sense before 1166, which
he backed up by detailing the meagre resources commanded by many
Anglo-Norman *milites*.[16] Stenton's pragmatic observation was later
to be pursued in some detail in 1970 by Sally Harvey in her metic-
ulous study of the *milites* who appear in *Domesday Book* and other
contemporary and subsequent eleventh- and twelfth-century English
land surveys. She arrived at the view that the *milites* of 1086 occupied a variety of economic levels, some eminent, some modest and
some lowly. Some were clearly landed vassals of good family, some
men commanded only the resources comparable to a free peasant,
and others were no more than retained warriors, with the word *miles*
intended in their case to evoke no more than the generalised sense of
"soldier."[17] Her analysis relied perhaps too much on the assumption
that when a Latin source called a person a *miles* we should assume
that the French *chevaler* was what was meant. But that Anglo-Norman
knights formed a continuum of wealth and status—from men of little
standing other than what they drew from their profession to high-born

16. Reginald Allen Brown, "The Status of the Norman Knight," in *War and Government
in the Middle Ages: Essays in Honour of J.O. Prestwich*, ed. John Gillingham and James C.
Holt (Woodbridge: Boydell, 1984), 18–32.
17. Sally Harvey, "The Knight and Knight's Fee in England," *Past & Present* no. 49
(1970), 3–43.

associates of princes—was an unexceptionable deduction from her mass of evidence and it implicitly challenged the idea of knights as a homogenous social group. Harvey followed up her deduction with the suggestion that what was true of the knight in 1100 was not necessarily true of the knight in 1200. Over the century those poorer men fell out of consideration as the dignity of knight was increasingly confined to the elite, though the explanation she offered relied on a less than convincing argument about the increase in the cost of knightly equipment and monetary inflation in twelfth-century society.[18] Nonetheless, her fine work still informs the general understanding of the English knight in the Anglo-Norman period, that is until 1154.[19]

Allen Brown (1924–89), the reactionary of 1984, was at least reassured by the continuing orthodoxy of his French colleagues on the subject of the status of the eleventh-century knight. He found in Georges Duby's landmark study of the Maconnais a welcome assertion that *miles* and *nobilis* were synonymous before 1100, though he failed to appreciate that Duby's theory also insisted that knights were no more than military henchmen to princes who rose in status as their masters threw their society into feudal chaos in their violent competition for power. Brown was however disturbed to find that the eminent Norman historian Lucien Musset (1922–2004)—who appreciated Duby's ideas rather better than he did—was a backslider and was willing to admit that early Norman knights might have been in fact humble men and had found an able disciple in the young British historian, David Bates. Bates's *Normandy before 1066* was a unique book at the time for a British Anglophone (though not for an American) in its full engagement with continental historiography and primary sources, and it expressed and sustained the view of "the relative insignificance of some *milites*" before 1066.[20] Bates was rather more *au fait* with French historiography than was Brown. He had absorbed the emerging criticism of the model of social change proposed by Duby for the Maconnais and the "transformation of the year 1000," the supposed effects of which Dominique Barthélemy continues to critique in his chapter in this book.

18. Harvey, "Knight and Knight's Fee," 39–42.
19. David Crouch, *The English Aristocracy, 1070–1272. A Social Transformation* (New Haven, CT: Yale University Press, 2012), 3–61.
20. Brown, "Status of the Norman Knight," 19–20; David Bates, *Normandy before 1066* (London: Longman, 1982), 109–11.

Barthélemy in his many works has offered his own view of the status of the knight. It is the logic of his rejection of mutationism that there would then have been no rise of a knighthood forged in the heat of violence that accompanied the final social breakdown of Carolingian society and social ideals. He sees rather a continuity in the idea of the noble warrior from the tenth through to the twelfth century. He rejects any idea that a new subordinate military class arose in the tenth or eleventh century which colonised the mentality of the magnates and castellans who employed it with its military ethic.[21] He has therefore in effect returned to a much earlier French idea of knighthood, the one that Menestrier, Father Honoré and La Curne de Sainte-Palaye would have recognised, that the profession of the elite horseback warrior had its own universal nobility. Unusually for a French historian, he cites in his support a school of Anglophone thinking on the subject, the views of John Gillingham (in his day also a critic of Duby) on the eleventh-century emergence of a battlefield ethic of ransom (rather than massacre) offered in solidarity by knights to others of their profession; an ethic Gillingham calls "chivalry," meaning simply "status-specific" warrior behaviour.[22] Along with Barthélemy he sees this chivalry as a shared élite male ideology from kings through magnates to knights of varying degrees.

There is a divergence between ideas of nobilisation in knighthood in Dominique Barthélemy's reconstruction and the German tradition,

21. As developed in Dominique Barthélemy, *La société dans le comté de Vendômois de l'an mil au XIVe siècle* (Paris: Fayard, 1993), 507–13, cf. p. 511: "le *miles* n'est rien d'autre que le membre à part entière, adulte et légitime, de la 'société féodale:' chevalier régnant et chevalier servant tout à la fois. La chevalerie, c'est le pouvoir noble, et en elle il y a toujours eu quelque chose de royal." His views were subsequently summarised in idem, *La chevalerie: de la Germanie antique à la France du XIIe siècle* (Paris: Fayard, 2007), see esp. p. 11 (rev. ed., Paris: Perrin, 2012).

22. His first such statement was in John Gillingham, "Kingship, Chivalry and Love: Political and Cultural Values in the Earliest History Written in France: Geoffrey Gaimar's *Estoire des Engleis*," *Anglo-Norman Political Culture and the 12th-Century Renaissance*, ed. C. Warren Hollister (Woodbridge: Boydell, 1997), 33–58, esp. 38–39. There have been a number of subsequent restatements of which the more important include: John Gillingham, "1066 and the Introduction of Chivalry into England," in *The English in the Twelfth Century: Imperialism, National Identity and Political Values* (Woodbridge: Boydell, 2000), 209–31; and idem, "Fontenoy and After: Pursuing Enemies to Death in France between the Ninth and Eleventh Centuries," in *Frankland: The Franks and the World of the Early Middle Ages*, ed. Paul Fouracre and David Ganz (Manchester: Manchester University Press, 2008), 242–65. For a recent iteration see idem, "Surrender in Medieval Europe—An Indirect Approach," in *How Fighting Ends: A History of Surrender*, ed. Holger Afflerbach and Hew Strachan (Oxford: Oxford University Press, 2012), 55–72.

where the idea of a rise in the status of knights as a social group within the Empire has been established since the work of Karl Bosl (1908–93) began appearing in the 1940s. This divergence is a consequence of the phenomenon that Bosl analysed over several decades: the existence of ministerial knights within the Empire, and the indisputable fact that these "serf-knights" indeed rose socially during the eleventh and twelfth centuries on the back of their usefulness to their lords, until their descendants became the majority of the German *Ritterstand* of the thirteenth century.[23] In the 1960s, the Dutch historian Johanna Maria van Winter came to a similar view, especially for the county (and later duchy) of Guelders, although according to her research nobles and ministerial knights were not amalgamated there until the end of the sixteenth century.[24] Some reflection on the historiographical divergence between the national historiographies is in Karl Ferdinand Werner's (1924–2008) work on nobility, when he turned his attention to knighthood. In pursuit of a Franco-German insight into the subject Werner used the work of Michel Parisse (1936–2020) on the Franco-Germanic borderland of Upper Lotharingia, which found that the French areas could be tied into the dominant historiography of his day, where knighthood rose on the backs of the territorial ambitions of the local ecclesiastical and lay magnates. By contrast, in the Germanic region where knighthood was ministerial it was difficult to find it deployed in the description of landowners, and its social impact came rather later than in the French lands.[25] This Franco-Germanic divergence in the status of knights is still very much a given in historiography. The German side of the question is dealt with in this book by Jörg Peltzer and Claudia Wittig, who explore the various ways in which it was acted out and the complications and tensions caused by

23. See the summary in Werner Hechberger, *Adel, Ministerialität und Rittertum im Mittelalter*, Enzyklopädie deutscher Geschichte 72 (Munich: R. Oldenbourg Verlag, 2010), 27–37.

24. Johanna Maria van Winter, *Ministerialiteit en ridderschap in Gelre en Zutphen*, Bijdragen van het Instituut voor middeleeuwse geschiedenis der Rijksuniversiteit Utrecht 21, 2 vols. (Groningen: J.B. Wolters, 1962). See also idem, "The Ministerial and Knightly Classes in Guelders and Zutphen," *Acta historiae Neerlandica* 1 (1966): 171-86. For a brief overview of recent research on the Low Countries see Arie van Steensel, "Origins and Transformations. Recent Historiography on the Nobility in the Medieval Low Countries I," *History Compass* 12 (2014): 263–72.

25. Karl Ferdinand Werner, *Naissance de la noblesse. L'essor des élites politiques en Europe* (Paris: Fayard, 1998), 472-76.

the complicated status of those knights of the Empire who were *minis-teriales*.

One major unresolved question regarding the nobilisation (or not) of knighthood is what precisely was the origin and significance of the noble ethic that was developed to justify it, that is, Maurice Keen's sense of chivalry. The question features early in both French and German historiographies. The long-standing German tradition is that the Imperial *Ritterstand* was subject throughout the twelfth century to a defining *Tugendsystem*, derived from the schools, an idea which is still very much a current topic in German scholarship, as Claudia Wittig demonstrates in this book.[26] In France one of Duby's pupils, Jean Flori (1936–2018), identified an "idéologie de la glaive," a moral-theological programme defining the rightful use of the secular power represented by the sword in a series of studies centred on the early rituals of the blessing of arms about to be conferred on princes.[27] His argument takes it as given that this ethic travelled downwards in society in the Sombartian mechanism of "cultural diffusion" subscribed to by Georges Duby, from expectations of righteous kingship to princely and magnate power and finally to the agents of that power, the knights.[28] He naturally deferred to Duby's now-unfashionable ideas about knighthood and its supposed feudal mutation, and assumed with Duby and others—back to La Curne and Menestrier—that what might have been true of the inauguration of the thirteenth-century knight was true of his predecessor in the tenth or eleventh century. His idea that northern France was the region which saw the birth and growth of *chevalerie* may not now be "de l'avis de tous."[29] Nonetheless it is one of Flori's most powerful arguments that a well-defined set of Biblical principles, deriving ultimately from Carolingian expectations of righteous kingship, had travelled downwards by the eleventh century to be employed in inauguration rituals of non-royal princes and lords. Well before the twelfth century, as Jörg Peltzer notes in this volume, these

26. The idea can be traced to Gustav Ehrismann, "Die Grundlagen des ritterliches Tugendsystem," *Zeitschrift für deutsches Altertum und deutsches Literatur* 56 (1919), 137–216.

27. Jean Flori, *L'idéologie de la glaive: préhistoire de la chevalerie* (Geneva: Droz, 1983); idem, *L'Essor de la chevalerie, XIᵉ–XIIIᵉ siècles* (Geneva: Droz, 1986); idem, *Chevaliers et chevalerie au Moyen Âge* (Paris: Hachette Littératures, 1998).

28. For an overview see David Crouch, *The Birth of Nobility: Constructing Aristocracy in England and France, 900–1300* (Harlow: Longman, 2005), 207–13.

29. Flori, *L'Essor de la chevalerie*, 2.

principles—the defence of the Church and the solace of the representative defenceless, the poor, the widow and orphan—are expected of
the *miles* in the writings of the Empire, and they will turn up in the
twelfth-century literature specifically addressed to the moral formation of the knight. This was part of what Flori called an "élévation
idéologique de la *militia*."[30] By the thirteenth century this "Davidic
ethic," as David Crouch calls it, was absorbed into early chivalric literature, not least in Maurice Keen's Urtext framed around the inauguration of the knight, the *Ordene de Chevalerie*.

Whatever position one adopts on the status of knighthood and
whether or not one believes that knights constituted a social class
before 1150, there is no doubt that knighthood was a profession that
after that date was increasingly defined in moral and ethical terms, and
since true nobility was virtue, then knights were by definition becoming noble.[31] It remains a given in French and German historiographies,
rooted as both still are in the vision of the knight in contemporary
literature, that by 1200 the knight properly lived in a courtly world of
noble pursuits and festivals.[32] In the more materialist terms of British
historiography, knights were defined as noble in the second half of the
twelfth century by the expectation that they would adopt as much as
they could of a lifestyle that the magnates of their time rejoiced in: the
possession of a great seal, a hall, a household, elite clothing and the
pursuit of beasts of the chase.[33] By 1200 the old comprehensive category of knight was as a result contracting severely. Knights for hire
were categorised as *routiers*, mercenaries who were not bound by any
ethic of loyalty and righteous conduct and who had little status as a
result.[34] Whatever *adoubement* had been in 1100, it was by the time of
the *Ordene* associated with the embrace of Keen's hyper-moral form

30. Ibid., 290.
31. For the social use of that tag see Guido Castelnuovo, "Juvénal et la noblesse au
Moyen Âge ou les avatars d'une citation," in *Des plats pays aux cimes alpines. Hommages
offerts à François Bertrandy*, ed. Fabrice Delrieux and François Kayser, Sociétés Religions
Politiques 17, 2 vols. (Chambéry: Université de Savoie, 2010), 2: 13–27.
32. Thomas Zotz, "Ritterliche Welt und höfische Lebensformen," in Josef Fleckenstein,
Rittertum und ritterliche Welt, coll. Thomas Zotz (Berlin: Siedler Verlag, 2002), 173–229;
Joseph Morsel, *L'aristocratie médiévale, V^e–XVe siècles* (Paris: Armand Colin, 2004),
240–52.
33. David Crouch, *The Image of Aristocracy in Britain, 1000–1300* (London, 1992),
132–48.
34. David Crouch, "William Marshal and the Mercenariat," in *Mercenaries and Paid
Men: the Mercenary Identity in the Middle Ages*, ed. John France (Leiden: Brill, 2008),
15–32.

of conduct, which we can call chivalry because by now it fit the definition that Enlightenment historians gave it. Knights had risen in society by 1200 because the qualifications for knighthood had been morally as much as materially exalted to a new place. Such a conclusion encourages a return to the question of how and why it was that the knight came to be "nobilised" across Europe during the twelfth century. This collection of essays is intended to contribute to just such a debate.

Knighthood and Society

Throughout the five parts of this collection, we gradually move from the level of knighthood in its social-historical meaning to the more abstract, idealistic understanding of chivalry as a code of conduct. Part I contains broad discussions of the development and geographical variants of knighthood in France, the German Empire and the Anglo-Norman *regnum*. Central to these discussions are the significance of knighthood as a specific, culturally modelled form of military service, and its relationship to the history of nobility. Taken together, the essays in Part I provide us with the contours of the insights that are fleshed out in the subsequent parts.

In the first chapter, Dominique Barthélemy brings a critical synthesis of his most recent insights into the development of chivalry, based on French source material. Implicitly present in his argument remains his refutation, discussed above, of the thesis of a *mutation féodale* in the decades around the year 1000, once so influential in French historiography in the wake of George Duby's work. For Barthélemy, the development of knighthood in France since the ninth century is, as we have seen, a purely noble phenomenon. Yet, unlike most knighthood studies, particularly in Anglophone scholarship, he does not consider chivalry as the new kind of hyper-morality, surfacing only in the late twelfth and early thirteenth centuries in chivalric romance. He regards the decades around 1100 as the crucial period in which chivalric behaviour found its origin. Significant in this respect is the simultaneous emergence around that time of both the crusade ideal propagated by the Church and the tournament phenomenon cherished by the lay world. Compared to the traditional service relationships and kin obligations that were so typical of "feudal society," these new phenomena implied, at least on the surface, a certain material disinterestedness, in which personal salvation and prowess were at stake. Nevertheless, Barthélemy argues, the reality of knighthood also showed an obvious continuity before and after this *mutation chevaleresque* of around 1100.[35] Also in the tenth and eleventh centuries feudal warfare was more focused, limited and rational than traditional ideas about pre-chivalric feudal anarchy suggest. And phenomena such as the dubbing ceremony and the tournament, so strongly associated with the refinement of chivalric culture and the display of prowess, found their roots precisely in the feudal interactions and warfare of the second half of the eleventh century. All in all, noble knights remained tied to their traditional vassalic obligations, even after the emergence of "classic chivalry."

Jörg Peltzer, in the second chapter, elucidates how the development of knighthood in the German Empire differed from that in France. In the high medieval German territories, the Latin term *miles* did not necessarily imply a social distinction since it could be used in the sense of both vassal and warrior to designate simultaneously members of the high aristocracy and simpler soldiers. However, the specific vernacular German term for knight, *Ritter*, was used initially, and until well into the twelfth century, to denominate almost exclusively warriors of lower rank, such as the unfree *ministeriales* who functioned as administrators and men at arms in the service of the higher aristocracy. Originally, knighthood as a social function was thus anything but an exclusively noble phenomenon, even though unfree *ministeriales*, for example, could enjoy significant power and prestige and be bestowed with heritable fiefs.[36] Only in the second half of the twelfth century, under the influence of both Church and court, was the chivalric ethos gradually aspired to by men across the ranks, including the king and the highest aristocracy. But knighthood in the Empire kept its particularities. The girding with the sword, for

35. Barthélemy does not use this specific French expression in his contribution to the present volume, but it is a leading idea in several of his publications such as Dominique Barthélemy, "Les chroniques de la mutation chevaleresque en France (du Xe au XIIe siècle)," *Comptes rendus des séances de l'Académie des Inscriptions et Belles-Lettres* 151 (2007), 1643–65; idem, *La chevalerie*, 11; idem, *Nouvelle histoire des Capétiens, 987–1214* (Paris: Seuil, 2012), 224 ff.
36. The Anglophone reader may be most familiar with this phenomenon through Benjamin Arnold, *German Knighthood 1050–1300* (Oxford: Clarendon Press, 1985), but Peltzer also relies upon more recent German scholarship, such as Jan Ulrich Keupp, *Dienst und Verdienst. Die Ministerialen Friedrich Barbarossas und Heinrichs VI.*, Monographien zur Geschichte des Mittelalters 48 (Stuttgart: Hiersemann, 2002).

example, obtained a different meaning in German history from that at the French noble courts. While for the nobleman it did not immediately mean an important privilege, for the successful *ministerialis* it constituted a rite that entailed greater social appreciation, and association with the world of the free-born and lower aristocracy. Finally, after 1200, knightly birth started to take precedence over personal qualities. *Ritterschaft*, as a common denominator, began to play a crucial role in slowly merging successful *ministeriales* and the low-ranked freeborn knights with the lower aristocracy, and in distinguishing them from counts and barons.

With Eljas Oksanen's contribution we shift our attention to the high medieval Anglo-Norman *regnum* and look specifically at the phenomenon of paid military forces between the late eleventh and early thirteenth centuries. While the use of mercenaries was not an exclusive Anglo-Norman phenomenon, it played an important role in the consolidation of power in England after the Norman conquest. English kings relied increasingly on paid military service in exchange for both wages and money fiefs. The organisational changes in warfare were facilitated by economic growth, urbanisation, commercial expansion and the intensified circulation of physical currency from the second half of the twelfth century onwards. Mercenaries may have been considered as genuine *milites* and knights, but since their commitment was not based on traditional loyalty they were increasingly viewed in a derogatory way for not meeting the true chivalric ideal that began to develop in the decades around 1200. Oksanen illustrates this process of chivalric identity formation and its negative mirror by looking at two classes of foreign fighters who have played an important role in England's military history: the Welsh and the Flemish. One could say, Oksanen argues, that the image of the mercenary developed as the sinister twin to that of the chivalric knight.

In Part II, then, we explore what is traditionally regarded as the life-blood of the noble habitus and the chivalric identity, namely lineage. Social elites secured and consolidated their power, property and prestige mainly through inheritance. For them, family awareness was thus a crucial thing. Post-war historiography on this topic has long been dominated by, once more, Duby's influence. Building on previous scholarship of Marc Bloch (1886–1944) and Karl Schmid (1923–93), Duby developed the influential thesis that the alleged political *mutation féodale* of around the year 1000 was also accompanied by a new form of family organisation among social elites.[37] Before that time, Duby argued, horizontal, clan-based forms of kinship prevailed among the traditional aristocracy. Yet from the eleventh century onwards, noble families supposedly started to foster the formation of vertical lineages to preserve their lordships. Those lineages would have been pre-eminently agnatic, that is patrilineal, and would even have privileged primogeniture up to the end of the twelfth century. Daughters were, at best, married off, or were destined for a life in the convent, while younger sons were denied marriage and inheritance.

In recent decades, Duby's assumptions have met with various objections, not least because of their dependence on obsolete sociological theories rather than on empirical research.[38] Regional studies showed convincingly that medieval family structures and inheritance practices were far more contingent and complex than Duby's model of agnatic lineages and primogeniture suggests.[39] They pointed out, for example, the role of maternal blood relatives and the importance of co-lordship in noble families. In her chapter on the "chivalric family," Sara McDougall amplifies these criticisms and proposes a definition of aristocratic families with less emphasis on either blood or paternal descent. She approaches such families as broadly conceived and fluid kin-groups, with a shared sense of both paternal and, even primarily, maternal ancestry, who aimed at the acquisition and retention of properties, territories and titles in both the world and the Church. McDougall distinguishes three avenues that can be further explored in future research into medieval family structures and consciousness, and that recognise more thoroughly the essential role of both maternal lineage and women in medieval noble families. She argues in favour of looking at noble marriages first and foremost in the light of the property transactions between families. She invites scholars to examine more closely the motivations behind practices of remarriage and divorce and the arrangements made in such situations with regard to child custody and inheritance. Finally, she shows that more research

37. Georges Duby, "Lignage, noblesse et chevalerie au XIIᵉ siècle dans la région mâconnaise: une révision," in *Hommes et structures du Moyen Âge* (Paris-The Hague: Mouton, 1973), 395–422.

38. Crouch, *The Birth*, 101–10.

39. See e.g. Theodore Evergates, *The Aristocracy of the County of Champagne* (Philadelphia, PA: University of Pennsylvania Press, 2007), esp. 82–100, and Hélène Débax, *La seigneurie collective. Pairs, pariers, paratge: les coseigneurs du XIᵉ au XIIIᵉ siècle* (Rennes: Presses universitaires de Rennes, 2012).

is required to uncover the diversity of prevailing high medieval inheritance standards, which often respected the rights of all kin as heirs, including siblings and even "bastard" children born outside marriage.

While McDougall's programmatic contribution is mainly illustrated with examples from higher noble echelons, Jean-François Nieus presents an empirical case study that homes in on the strata of local lordship and knighthood. Central to his chapter is the late tenth- and early eleventh-century history of the family of Choques in the Artois region in the southern part of the county of Flanders. Nieus's careful analysis corroborates different insights presented in the earlier chapters of this volume. He endorses Barthélemy's statement that in this northern part of the French kingdom knighthood and military service constituted a noble responsibility both before and after the turn of the millennium. He illustrates Oksanen's discussion of Flemish knights who sold their military skills in the Norman conquest and colonisation of England. Finally, he shows, just like McDougall, that primogeniture was not a dominant practice in such families and that marriages also offered matrilineal opportunities.

Research on chivalry and the crusade is, to this day, still much divided between two distinct historiographical traditions. However, the two phenomena are strongly related. Crusading experiences and memories have had a great impact on the shaping of chivalric ideals. Part III therefore contains two contributions in which the Levant forms the locus for the further elaboration of the image and expectations of knightly prowess and noble virtue in the West.

John Hosler focuses on the famous siege of Acre (1189–91) during the Third Crusade, as reported by four different eyewitnesses. Through their texts he studies how contemporaries used knightly performance in actual combat situations to gauge the extent to which knights actually met the chivalric expectations and norms imposed on them. Inspired by Richard W. Kaeuper's analysis of the main chivalric qualities discerned in medieval Europe,[40] Hosler discusses how his chroniclers and authors linked military prowess to status, honour and piety, or, more specifically, to leadership, behaviour and virtue. This approach is relevant not only to gaining insight into existing judgements, but also to examining how the developments and outcomes of real warfare, through the dissemination of such coloured eyewitness

---

40. As developed in Richard W. Kaeuper, *Chivalry and Violence in Medieval Europe* (Oxford: Oxford University Press, 2001).

reports, may have impacted on the further definition and future expectations of the chivalric ideal.

Nicholas Paul, in his particularly rich case study, shows how also local authors in the West, who had never travelled to the Levant, could use the crusading frontier as the stage for the glorification of knightly reputation and prowess. Paul studies a number of little-known but particularly fascinating texts from the Benedictine abbey of Brogne in the diocese of Liège. They date, just like the ones studied by Hosler, from the late twelfth and early thirteenth centuries—the crucial period in the codification of aristocratic conduct. The narratives seem at first sight to commemorate the acquisition by the abbey of a fragment of the True Cross, known as the "Holy Cross of Antioch." On closer inspection, however, they mainly offer a chivalric biography of the twelfth-century local lord Manasses of Hierges. On his deathbed in 1177, he had promised the abbey the cross he had brought with him from the Holy Land after an eventful career in the entourage of his niece Queen Melisende of Jerusalem. The texts from Brogne, where the recently acquired Cross soon began to take a central place in the community's propagation of its identity, present Manasses as a model of nobility and knightly prowess. Most striking in this discursive construction of knightliness is precisely the emphasis on his participation in the Crusade and on his performance of noble virtue in the Eastern Mediterranean.

The essays in Part IV explore how the development of a chivalric identity also influenced the expectations placed on aristocratic women and how, at the same time, the representation of courtly women contributed again to that same chivalric identity.

In her richly documented and illustrated synthesis, Louise Wilkinson looks at how chivalric values informed and permeated the female aristocratic culture of the High Middle Ages. Even though they were excluded from martial practice and military ethos, women participated with their male consorts and relatives in the same noble conduct, practices of lordship and family consciousness. The chivalric woman had to excel in noble virtue and moral superiority. Physical beauty, if worn without vanity, could be an indicator of inner beauty; that is also why in medieval culture so many virtues were allegorically represented by beautiful noblewomen, sometimes even in military dress. Wilkinson scrutinises chronicles and literary sources for the information they provide about the expectations regarding the education, marriage and lifestyle of aristocratic women. Just like McDougall she also shows the concrete agency of women in these fields.

The literary and poetic representation of aristocratic women could, moreover, also contribute to the reproduction, and thus reinforcement, of male chivalric stereotypes. That is what Nicolas Ruffini-Ronzani shows in his informative case study about the composition of the satirical poem *Tournoiement des dames*, written in the late 1180s by Hugh III of Oisy, a nobleman from the North-French Cambrésis. The *Tournoiement* belongs to a tradition of light-hearted poems in which gender roles are reversed and women are represented as the competitive participants in a fictional tournament. From a historical perspective the *Tournoiement* is interesting as testimony to the increased literary creativity among lay lords from the second half of the twelfth century onwards, and to how topsy-turvy mirrors of male and female behaviour humorously enhanced existing cultural norms. However, by analysing the protagonists of the *Tournoiement* Ruffini-Ronzani also manages to expose the political subtext of the poem.

Finally in Part V we look at how chivalry was taught as a consciously cultivated ideal and code of conduct. Even though around 1200 the term "chevalerie" was still primarily understood as "knightliness"—that is the condition, skills or deeds of the horseback warrior—there was, as we have noted, an undeniable tendency among the aristocracy gradually to associate itself with a new kind of hyper-morality. But just as knighthood cannot be defined in its socio-historical sense as an unambiguous and uniform phenomenon within the western European context, and must be placed in a complex prehistory of various influencing factors, we notice that the same applies in no lesser degree to the modelling of the chivalric ideal. This is shown by the chapters on the didactics of chivalry by Claudia Wittig and David Crouch, focusing respectively on the Empire and on the French and Anglo-Norman world.

Wittig's discussion builds further on what we learn from Peltzer's contribution. Like elsewhere in Europe, the chivalric culture in the Empire started to be elaborated in terms of new behavioural ideals and aristocratic self-representation from the second half of the twelfth century onwards. Wittig analyses how this cultural movement also became attractive to lower-ranked men of service. She deploys a close reading of a selection of popular didactic texts such as the thirteenth-century *Der Welsche Gast* by the Friulian canon Thomasin von Zerclaere and the anonymous *Der Winsbecke*. Most of these were written by clerical authors and expound the guidelines for, and benefits of, an exemplary chivalric life. Wittig clearly shows how this behavioural literature was particularly directed to the lower nobility, who by that time had absorbed the most successful *ministeriales*, and to whom such treatises were instructional to strengthening its position between service and lordship.

However, the gradual emergence of a chivalric code of conduct, fully articulated by the beginning of the thirteenth century, was not a phenomenon with purely clerical roots. That is also one of David Crouch's arguments in the concluding essay. Whereas Wittig mainly looks at the unambiguous didactics of knighthood after 1200, Crouch dissects three traditions of conduct literature that in the course of the twelfth century must have formed the seedbed of what was to become the ideal of chivalry. The first tradition is called "Catonian" and is indebted to the popularity in the high medieval classroom of antique proverbial wisdom. The second tradition is biblical in origin and derived from the typical Solomonic wisdoms which were spread from the pulpit. The third tradition, however, is represented by conduct books by and for the elite. Crouch focuses here on the genre of the *enseignement* which we mainly know from Occitania, but which goes back to Latin examples from the eleventh century. A century before the sublimation of the ideal of knighthood we find the earliest vernacular articulation of "courtliness" in these texts, not yet specifically intended for knights as such but as an ideal of superior lay conduct for the *preudomme* and the *preudefemme*. Only around 1200, Crouch argues, was it the figure of the knight who became the repository of a distinct hyper-moral form of conduct.

From Knightly/Courtly Habitus to Chivalric Identity Formation

Precisely because this collection offers such a varied range of research pathways that are currently being explored in various countries and subfields of historical scholarship, it is inevitable that in the essays collected here the reader will also be confronted with differences of emphasis, and even apparent contradictions. The challenging aspect of this collection lies in this confrontation. It is clear, for instance, that the juxtaposition of the chapters by Dominique Barthélemy and

Jörg Peltzer suggests more than just the coexistence of a French and
a German narrative about the origins of chivalry. It clearly indicates
that there are still major challenges for further research informed by
both traditions, for example for frontier regions such as the southern
Low Countries, where the imperial and French spheres of influence
met and competed with each other. It also shows the lack of insight
into the development of chivalry in regions that are even less explicitly present in this collection. While the geographical emphasis of this
book can be situated mainly in north-western Europe, and despite the
glimpses of texts and persons from Italy or the Iberian peninsula in
various chapters, it would certainly be worth developing comparisons
with, for example, the meaning and ethos of chivalry in the context
of the Italian city-states or among the Castilian *caballeros villanos*.[41]

An apparent contradiction which cannot be denied either, and which
has already been touched upon above, concerns the chronology of the
development of chivalry. *Mutation chevaleresque* around 1100, or a
"Chivalric Turn" around 1200? While Barthélemy sees the decades
of the end of the eleventh and the early twelfth centuries as the period
in which the characteristics of so-called "classic chivalry" begin to
manifest themselves, we can observe that in several of the other essays
in this book the development of chivalric norms is regarded as a typical phenomenon of the late twelfth and early thirteenth centuries.
This second chronology is, as we have seen, also the one established
by Maurice Keen, of which David Crouch analyses the seedbed in
this volume. Remarkably, in their previous work, both Barthélemy
(2007) and Crouch (2005; 2019) have used the concept of "habitus,"
as coined by the French sociologist Pierre Bourdieu (1930–2002), as
a tool to clarify their analyses. In its classical Bourdieuian definition,
a habitus is a socially constituted and ingrained set of skills, habits,

---

41. On knighthood in the Italian cities see e.g. Jean-Claude Maire-Vigueur, *Cavaliers
et citoyens: guerre, conflits et société dans l'Italie communale, XIIᵉ–XIIIᵉ siècles*, Civilisations et sociétés 114 (Paris: Fondation de l'École des hautes études en sciences sociales,
2003); Paulo Grillo, *Cavalieri e popoli in armi: Le istituzioni militari nell'Italia mediev-
ale* (Bari: Laterza, 2008); Peter Hoppenbrouwers, "An Italian City-State Geared for War:
Urban Knights and the Cavallata of Todi," *Journal of Medieval History* 39 (2013): 240–53;
Aldo D. Scaglione, Knights at Court: Courtliness, Chivalry, and Courtesy From Ottonian
Germany to the Italian Renaissance (Berkeley, CA: University of California Press, 1991),
esp. 169–87. On Castilia see e.g. Carlos Astarita, "Caracterización económica de los cabal-
leros villanos de la Extremadura castellano-leonesa, siglos XII-XV," *Anales de historia
antigua y medieval* 27 (1994): 11–83; Jesús D. Rodríguez-Velasco, *Order and Chivalry:
Knighthood and Citizenship in Late Medieval Castile*, trans. Eunice Rodríguez Ferguson
(Philadelphia, PA: University of Pennsylvania Press, 2010).

values, sensitivities, tastes, etc. which, on a more or less unconscious level, is specific to those people who occupy a more or less similar place in the "social field."[42] Barthélemy discerns a "knightly habitus" among noble warriors as early as in the Carolingian era, manifested in shared norms of sociability and interaction, also during private warfare. With the rise of "classic chivalry" around 1100, this unarticulated habitus would have evolved into a more explicit sensitivity to prowess, an aesthetic and moral embellishment of war, and a feeling of adherence, through birth and heritage, to a delocalised social class.[43] Crouch, on the other hand, equates "courtliness," as it has developed at least since the eleventh century, with the widespread habitus of the high-medieval lay elites. It is this "courtly habitus" that, towards the end of the twelfth century, is transformed into a new ideal of self-conscious noble conduct and is exclusively associated with noble knightliness.[44] For Crouch, as for Keen, this is the moment when chivalry takes full shape.

Contradictory as they seem, we can consider both views as also complementary, especially when we realise that they actually use the same words—habitus, chivalry—for different concepts. Barthélemy, who is less sensitive to the distinction in modern English between knighthood (skills and lifestyle) and chivalry (ideal of conduct), focuses on battlefield behaviour and public display, while Crouch deals with the codification of male elite hyper-morality. What remains absolutely crucial and revealing in this history is that between the late eleventh and early thirteenth centuries a unique cultural-historical process of noble identity formation took place, in which the shifting meaning of knightliness was instrumental. The attempt to retrace and map out this complex, gradual development of a "chivalric identity" is exactly what this book is all about. The fact that it recurs throughout the book's individual chapters as a common thread arguably makes it a shared and important concern to which all its individual authors below subscribe.

This culturally constructed identity is not an absolute or essentialistic given, but, indeed, subjected to an ongoing process of social categorisation, identification and comparison, and as such the product of

42. Pierre Bourdieu, *Outline of a Theory of Practice*, trans. Richard Nice ([1972]; Cambridge: Cambridge University Press, 1977), 78–86; idem, *Distinction: A Social Critique of the Judgement of Taste*, trans. Richard Nice ([1979]; London: Routledge, 1984), 169–225.
43. Barthélemy, *La chevalerie*, 478–82.
44. Crouch, *The Birth*, 46–56; idem, *The Chivalric Turn*, 3–17, 116–46.

collective imagination.[45] As Martin Aurell recently argued, this process of noble identity formation involves expectations: the expectations of the group with regard to the social actor, and the expectations of the actor with regard to the group. It also involves a connection with the group that must be recognised by the other, hence the importance of recognisable markers and attributes.[46] The five parts of this volume aim at analysing a number of important factors that can be distinguished in this process, such as martial practices and knightly rituals, the role of lineage, the cultivation of memories, the gendering of noble roles and, finally, the development of chivalric didactics. In their sequence, they help us to understand how, between the eleventh and the early thirteenth centuries, knighthood evolved from a set of skills and a lifestyle that was typical of an emerging elite habitus into the basis of a consciously expressed and idealised chivalric code of conduct. But it was not important just that the image and self-image of knighthood were articulated with increasing accuracy. At the same time, this process was also accompanied by the accentuation of differences—differences from those who did not live up to the chivalrous ideal, but who thereby validated it. These forms of stereotyping are also dealt with across the chapters of this book: think of the image of the mercenary, of the mischievous knight, of the Muslim warrior.[47] And so we witness the gradual maturation of the idea of chivalry as not only an ideal of conduct, but, certainly from the late twelfth century onwards, a distinct *ordo* and a synonym of noble virtue.[48]

45. Social identity as a process of categorisation, identification and comparison has been elaborated in the work of social psychologists such as Henri Tajfel and John C. Turner. See e.g. their "The Social Identity Theory of Intergroup Behavior," in *Political Psychology: Key Readings*, ed. John T. Jost and Jim Sidanius, Key Readings in Social Psychology ([1986]; New York: Psychology Press, 2003), 276–93. See also Bourdieu, *Distinction*, 440, 479, 482, and for a more recent introduction Richard Jenkins, *Social Identity*, 4th ed. (London: Routledge, 2014).

46. Martin Aurell, "La Noblesse au XIIIᵉ siècle: paraître, pouvoir et savoir," in *Discurso, memoria y representación. La nobleza peninsular en la Baja Edad Media (Actas de la XLII Semana de Estudios Medievales de Estella-Lizarra. 21 al 24 de julio de 2015)* (Pamplona: Fondo de Publicaciones del Gobierno de Navarra, 2016): 7–32, at 12–13.

47. On the Muslim warrior see also Catalina Girbea, *Le Bon Sarrasin dans le roman médiéval, 1100–1225*, Bibliothèque d'histoire médiévale 10 (Paris: Classiques Garnier, 2014).

48. Max Lieberman, "A New Approach to the Knighting Ritual," *Speculum* 90 (2015): 391–423, *passim*; Crouch, *The Chivalric Turn*, 273–99.

— Part I —

NOBLE WARRIORS, WARRING NOBLES

Dominique BARTHÉLEMY*

CHIVALRY IN FEUDAL SOCIETY ACCORDING TO FRENCH EVIDENCE

Feudal conflicts were not as harsh and bloody as previous scholars used to believe. That is why, instead of imagining a complete shift from barbarity to chivalry—a kind of French or Christian miracle in the heart of medieval darkness— this chapter argues that the feudal habit of sparing enemies of the same social status has been at the root of classical chivalry, as studied by Maurice Keen, John Gillingham and Matthew Strickland. The invention of the tournament can therefore be seen as the culmination of chivalric ideals and practices. Instead of being a result of feudal violence restrained by the Peace of God movement—as argued, until recently, by many scholars— the tournament may well appear to have been intended to give more occasions to young nobles to display prowess. Once they were dubbed as knights, such a display of prowess would have been difficult in the normal course of prudent feudal campaigns. Originally part of feudal life and sociability, and allowing the launch of small wars and legal actions, dubbing ceremonies thus tended to become the incentive of a series of displays of prowess in tournaments, or even in feudal wars, in accordance with the new chivalric ideal and behaviour, marked by vanity and narcissism. Hence also the simultaneous emergence of another ideal of chivalry, deeply serious and altruistic, in the service of Church or State. In reality, however, most of the knights were expected to be chivalrous in both ways, alternately, while at the same time they continued to act and think like traditional vassals.

The final years of the eleventh century in France witnessed the emergence of the tournament and the crusade, all but simultaneously. Both phenomena marked a break with the materialistic and vengeful spirit of an earlier stage of lordship, and they can be considered as two opposing poles of chivalric society as classically conceived. The tournament

* I am most grateful to David Crouch and Jeroen Deploige for including the present contribution with its numerous references to works of mine from 1997 on. These are provided not because I ascribe to them any particular importance, but in the hope that such references and others may prove useful: since the majority of my work is in French, it remains largely unknown or known only superficially outside the Francophone world. The reader may wish also to consult the works of Jean Flori, similarly in French, from especially his *L'essor de la chevalerie, XIᵉ–XIIᵉ siècles* (Geneva: Droz, 1986) to his *Chevaliers et chevalerie au Moyen Âge* (Paris: Hachette, 1998), from which it will be possible to compare our two approaches.

was a sort of game, not inexpensive but without any serious stake other than that of showing one's mettle in an elegant display. In it the enemy was respected; his life was spared and he might therefore spread the fame of the winner's prowess. The crusade, on the other hand, was in principle an opportunity for a knight to abandon his patrimony and leave all behind in the service of a greater cause; to put his life in obvious danger and fight in a righteous war for the sake of his soul's salvation. The seriousness of the crusade strongly contrasted with the frivolity of the tournament, and it is easy to understand why the Church condemned the one and recommended the other. Twelfth- and thirteenth-century knights might very well participate in both activities, going on crusade in order to expiate the sin of the tournament. Both activities had in common that they were disinterested, in contrast to the service owed to a lord and the support owed to one's family in feudal life and warfare, which was rewarded by a fief. This appearance of disinterestedness led very soon to a certain idealisation of "chivalry," loosely understood and not entirely coherent, and "tonal rather than precise in its implications" as Maurice Keen has nicely put it.[1]

In fact, this idealised knighthood always differed, to a greater or lesser extent, from real life. It was soon enough being represented—with all the nostalgia attributed to a past golden age—as an ideal in decay. Many a knight would declare, long before Edmund Burke, that "the age of chivalry is gone."[2] Historians of the eighteenth and nineteenth centuries, basing their judgements to a large extent on medieval literature, therefore often took it for granted that "chivalry" was something quite alien to "feudal society" and was marvellously opposed to it, or superimposed upon it, around the year 1100, as something that challenged its harshness and materialism and could be attributed to the preaching of the Church and the civilising influence of women.

However, advances in historical scholarship as well as the increasing influence of sociology with its aversion to simple explanations and its tendency to pick apart social constructs, have steadily changed the game. Historical scholarship does not always follow a direct path, and is not averse to detours, such as the so-called "Transformation of the Year One Thousand" advocated by Georges Duby and some other

---

1. Maurice H. Keen, *Chivalry* (New Haven: Yale University Press, 1984), 2.
2. Edmund Burke, *Reflections of the Revolution in France*, ed. Conor Cruise O'Brien ([1790]; Harmondsworth: Penguin, 1986), 169.

historians.[3] Fortunately, however, English scholarship led by Maurice Keen and further exemplified by Matthew Strickland and John Gillingham has sidestepped over-concentration on the evidence of the medieval cartulary and the traps of nominalism. Employing chronicles, they discovered a twelfth-century knighthood that was contingent and shifting in nature,[4] and in the two preceding centuries—the tenth and eleventh—found some intriguing forerunners[5] of chivalric culture that might surprise those who believe *a priori* that feudal society was typified by extreme and disordered violence. And what if classic chivalry was no more than a natural offshoot of feudal conflict? What if, even in the twelfth century, it simply helped conflict to continue while overlaying it here and there with a civil veneer? For years these two questions have driven my research. In this essay, I would therefore like to launch several observations and suggestions in the wake of my recently revised *La chevalerie: de la Germanie antique à la France du XIIe siècle.*[6]

3. See the critique in my *The Serf, the Knight, and the Historian*, trans. Graham Robert Edwards (Ithaca: Cornell University Press, 2009). [Translation with revisions of my *La mutation de l'an mil a-t-elle eu lieu? Servage et chevalerie dans la France des Xe et XIe siècles* (Paris: Fayard, 1997).]

4. Matthew Strickland, *War and Chivalry. The Conduct and Perception of War in England and Normandy, 1066–1217* (Cambridge, Cambridge University Press, 1996); idem, "Killing or Clemency? Ransom, Chivalry and Changing Attitudes to Defeated Opponents in Britain and Northern France, 7th–12th Centuries," in *Krieg im Mittelalter*, ed. Hans-Henning Kortüm (Berlin: Akademie-Verlag, 2001), 94–122; idem, "Provoking or Avoiding Battle? Challenge, Duel and Single Combat in Warfare of the High Middle Ages," in *Armies, Chivalry and Warfare in Medieval Britain and France*, ed. Matthew Strickland, Harlaxton Medieval Studies n.s. 7 (Stamford: Paul Watkins, 1998), 317–43.

5. John Gillingham, "1066 and the Introduction of Chivalry into England," in *Law and Government in Medieval England and Normandy: Essays in Honour of Sir James Holt*, ed. George Garnett and John Hudson (Cambridge: Cambridge University Press, 1994), 31–55; idem, "Fontenoy and After: Pursuing Enemies to Death in France between the Ninth and Eleventh Centuries," in *Frankland: The Franks and the World of the Early Middle Ages: Essays in Honour of Dame Jinty Nelson*, ed. Paul Fouracre and David Ganz (Manchester: Manchester University Press, 2008), 245–65; idem, "Holding to the Rules of War (*bellica iura tenentes*): Right Conduct before, during, and after Battle in North-Western Europe in the Eleventh Century," *Anglo-Norman Studies* 29 (2006): 1–15.

6. See my *La chevalerie: de la Germanie antique à la France du XIIe siècle* (Paris: Fayard, 2007; rev. ed., Paris: Perrin, 2012); idem, "The Chivalric Transformation and the Origins of Tournament as seen through Norman Chroniclers," *The Haskins Society Journal: Studies in Medieval History* 20 (2008): 141–60.

Towards Classic Chivalry

The concept of "feudal society" has several disadvantages. It fed many of the prejudices of nineteenth- and twentieth-century authors, and is obviously reductionist if it encourages an impression that vassalage, or private alliances and powers, held sway over the whole of France after 877, when the great Carolingians went into decline. But in my opinion, the concept has other disadvantages which require a more nuanced approach.[7] One reason is that in the post-Carolingian world the charismatic allegiance of counts, barons, or vavassors to their lord was now openly flaunted, and negotiated in courts of justice and in every social interaction. It did, of course, imply an engagement to serve the lord in arms as a knight, if necessary killing or dying on his behalf, and it guaranteed the right to hold and retain a patrimonial fief.[8] But it could often also simultaneously define itself within the same world, by means of lawsuits or even combat, through the rights and dues of kinship, through Christian morality, or by the public interest.

Karl Ferdinand Werner has done much to convince historical orthodoxy, once and for all, of the importance and public nature of post-Carolingian principalities and the social longevity of their elites, in contrast to antiquated notions of feudalism as being unstable and disorderly. But it is unfortunate that at the same time he resolutely dismissed the idea of a "feudal society" and attributed to "knighthood" a Roman definition and "origin."[9] His views have been improved upon and nuanced by Jean Dunbabin.[10] In my opinion, they inescapably demonstrate that there never was in the French kingdom during the

7. See my "La théorie féodale à l'épreuve de l'anthropologie. Note critique sur *Fiefs and Vassals* de Susan Reynolds," *Annales. Histoire, sciences sociales* 52 (1997): 321–41 and "Vassaux et fiefs dans la France de l'an mil," in *Feudalism: New Landscapes of Debate*, ed. Sverre Bagge, Michael H. Gelting, and Thomas Lindkvist (Turnhout: Brepols, 2011), 57–75.

8. *Vassal* or, in Latin, *vassus, vassallus*, was still current term. Dudo of Saint-Quentin, like the author of the *Chanson de Roland*, uses it absolutely, to connote a warrior of noble status, i.e., a knight. *Miles* was a synonym, and its spread around 1000 (as in Richer of Reims's work, charters, and notices) is probably traceable to educational reform after Dudo's own training, which is studied in a fine article by Leah Shopkow, "The Carolingian World of Dudo of Saint-Quentin," *Journal of Medieval History* 15 (1989): 19–37, at 22.

9. Karl Ferdinand Werner, "Du nouveau sur un vieux thème: les origines de la *noblesse* et de la *chevalerie*," *Comptes-rendus des séances de l'Académie des inscriptions et belles-lettres* 129 (1985): 186–200.

10. Jean Dunbabin, *France in the making, 843–1180*, 2nd ed. (Oxford: Oxford University Press 2000).

tenth and eleventh centuries any autonomy among castellans, any unleashing of violence, or any serious questioning of social hierarchies. I suggested in a recent monograph that we should recognise the political system of the time as essentially one of viscosity, common to so many feuding societies.[11]

Feudal warfare, that is, castle warfare among counts (rather than against the king) and among barons, however brutal, was in fact relatively focused, limited, and rational. Great skill was exercised by the kings, the counts, and the barons, ever sensitive to social demands, so as to alternate fighting with compromise and clemency. In feudal "warfare," the tendency was always towards indirect "revenge," by hitting the adversary's peasants (through pillaging) and vassals (by ambushes and sieges), before eventually negotiating with the enemy.[12]

There had long been a "chivalrous" tendency in feudal society. It may not have been chivalry as classically understood, since it lacked both the demonstration of tourneying prowess and the associated expectation of gracious treatment due to each knight from his peer. But when it came to open warfare or covert connivance among noble adversaries, the development of classic chivalry followed lines that were already evident in feudal conflict. There was no sudden change of direction.

The *Life of Gerald of Aurillac*, written by Odo of Cluny around 940, bears valuable witness to the compromises, even the contradictions, inherent in feudal warfare from its very beginnings, that is, from Gerald's generation (*ca.* 855–909). For all the author's hagiographic agenda, he nonetheless worked from testimonies that he selected and interpreted. He is therefore able to depict a castle lord, occasionally described as a "count," making war for only just causes, defending his peasants against neighbouring lords whose aim is to attack him through them.[13] In defending them, he is also defending his own honour. Moreover he does so without bloodshed, with an admirable clemency that offers a contrast with the bad lord, the malignant knight (the "lone wolf") who oppresses his dependents.[14] It is all the easier

11. See my *Nouvelle histoire des Capétiens, 987–1214* (Paris: Seuil, 2012).

12. See my "Feudal War in Tenth-Century France," in *Vengeance in the Middle Ages: Emotion, Religion and Feud*, ed. Susanna A. Throop and Paul Hyams (Farnham: Ashgate, 2010), 105–13.

13. Odo of Cluny, *Vita sancti Geraldi Auriliacensis*, 1.7, ed. Anne-Marie Bultot-Verleysen (Brussels: Société des Bollandistes, 2009), 142–44.

14. Odo of Cluny, *Vita Geraldi*, 1.40, 190.

to credit this portrayal since it chimes with what all the protagonists of feudal wars did according to the annals of the tenth century and around the turn of the millennium: they made peace after an exchange of indirect hostilities such as pillage, or after attacks on castles.[15]

It sufficed for Odo to play down such acts of war as were committed or endorsed by Gerald of Aurillac, to make plain that Gerald fought without vengeful aims, always preferring to arrive at an accommodation,[16] a fact that made him a man of peace and justice.[17] The hagiographer even attributes to Gerald's peaceful character his concession to his enemy's vassals of what would later be called a "conditional truce,"[18] a phenomenon that would eventually become regular practice—not to mention his allusion to "drawing back the blades of swords," a phrase which has occasioned much comment.[19]

When examined closely, the feudal conflict proper to counts and castle lords supported by their vassals is clear from the end of the ninth century, and in a generally moderate form. By this we mean conflicts over castles and territory which rarely led to a fight to the death but were resolvable through compromise. In general the protagonists, supported or restrained by their superiors, were of equal or almost equal rank, interrelated or linked to common heiresses. They often left the action on the ground to lesser vassals who had their own quarrels and were trying to win over various others to their side. Hostilities between parties alternated with negotiations. Such hostilities comprised pillaging raids, ambushes, fairly brief sieges of castles, or rather blockades ending in capitulation, the capture of a castle through treachery, or a retreat to avoid a blockade-busting battle. In all such activities, *exchanges* (in every sense of the word) took place among the opponents. These could be brutish, for although defeated parties

15. For the finest example, in 954, see: *Les Annales de Flodoard*, ed. Philippe Lauer (Paris, 1905), 140.

16. Odo of Cluny, *Vita Geraldi*, 1.7–8, 142–44.

17. Dudo of Saint-Quentin says something similar about "duke" Richard I: *De moribus et actis primorum Normanniae ducum*, 4.127, ed. Jules Lair, Mémoires de la Société des Antiquaires de Normandie 23.2 (Caen: Le Blanc-Hardel, 1865), 293–94; translated as Dudo of Saint-Quentin, *History of the Normans*, trans. Eric Christiansen (Woodbridge: Boydell, 1998), 168.

18. Odo of Cluny, *Vita Geraldi*, 1.36, 184–86.

19. Ibid., 1.8, 144, lines 15–16: "precepit, mucronibus gladiorum retro actis, hastas inantea dirigentes pugnarent" ("He ordered them to fight with the blades of their swords drawn back and directing their lances forward.") Some have too readily seen this as revealing the origins of the tournament: see Anne-Marie Bultot-Verleysen's explanation of the passage in her edition of Odo of Cluny, *Vita Geraldi*, 291–92 n. 16.

might be spared, they were not always well treated in captivity. But on the whole there was no extreme or unchecked violence.

Such at least is the scene we glimpse through a small number of particularly detailed, not to say densely packed sources. At the level of a large district (*pagus*) like Poitou between 1007 and 1028, we have the valuable *Conventum Hugonis*.[20] At the inter-regional level, we have the complete Book One of William of Poitiers' *History* of William the (future) Conqueror recounting his early years of warfare between 1042 and 1066, which, as we shall see, was already taking on some chivalrous aspects.[21]

In all of this, the impression that one has is of a kind of social game between great lords that allowed their vassals, knights, to undertake a few warlike actions but also, and perhaps chiefly, to pillage peasants. Was not that the essential, underlying purpose of feudal warfare?

When, in addition to proscribing attacks on churches and clerics, the millennial councils of peace forbade plunder by indirect vengeance in a number of bishoprics, were they, we may ask, taking a sideswipe at feudal warfare? Such an intention is indeed evident, but only fitfully in certain dioceses, particularly in the eastern part of the Capetian kingdom. The prohibition on looting was applicable only to internal conflict within the diocese; it largely ignored the inter-provincial warfare that was considered "public." The principalities in the west (the duchy of Normandy and the counties of the Loire Valley) were little affected. But the bid by bishops to control local warfare was not an enterprise to limit it to particular times as is sometimes said. Modern historians have insufficiently grasped that it almost always entailed the formation of companies of peace-keepers under episcopal control, and that the term "peace movement" is therefore somewhat deceptive.[22] That said, this "movement" still did not have the scope and impact (produc-

20. See the *Conventum inter Guillelmum Aquitanorum comitem et Hugonem chiliarchum*, ed. Jane Martindale, *English Historical Review* 84 (1969): 528–53, reproduced with introduction and postscript, in her *Status, Authority and Regional Power: Aquitaine and France, Ninth to Twelfth Centuries*, Variorum Collected Studies Series 488 (Aldershot: Ashgate, 1997), chap. 7 and 8.

21. William of Poitiers, *The Gesta Guillelmi of William of Poitiers*, ed. and trans. Ralph H. C. Davis and Marjorie Chibnall, Oxford Medieval Texts (Oxford, 1998), 49.

22. See my "The Peace of God and Bishops at War in the Gallic Lands from the Late Tenth to the Early Twelfth Centuries. R. Allen Brown Memorial Lecture," in *Proceedings of the Battle Conference, 2009*, ed. Christopher P. Lewis, Anglo-Norman Studies 32 (Woodbridge: Boydell and Brewer, 2010) 1–23 and "Paix de Dieu et communes dans le royaume capétien, de l'an mil à Louis VI," *Comptes-rendus des séances de l'Académie des inscriptions et belles-lettres* 158.1 (janvier-mars 2014): 207–41.

ing "knighthood") which is sometimes credited to it.[23] Taken in total, the struggle against "enemies of the peace" increasingly took on the likeness of a crusade, and it allowed the arming of peasants.

In this sense, if "chivalry" is understood as warfare for a holy cause, with no restraint shown towards the enemy, the "peace movement"— or rather, "war for the sake of peace"—is in effect its early form. But to me it seems that the meaning of chivalry is to be located rather in the ritualised conflicts between noblemen, whose brutality was tempered by codes of behaviour formulated at princely courts, and particularly in the western principalities.

The greater princes were already in the early period (*ca.* 980 to 1060) better resourced for their wars than were mere castle lords or barons. Detectable in the works of chroniclers such as Richer of Reims,[24] William of Jumièges[25] and William of Poitiers[26] are indications of stipendiary knights coming from neighbouring regions being welcomed into larger princes' households and periodically swelling their troops. Dudo of Saint-Quentin, writing between 1015 and 1026, reflecting ideas or tensions that were contemporary to him, imagines the dukes of Normandy in the tenth century with knights arriving from elsewhere to be given "palms of valour," and also zealous barons arriving, among whom were those that were prudent in warfare and likewise young noblemen in quest of daring exploits.[27] Was not journeying to the outer reaches of Christendom (Spain or Italy) the finest way to bring back those sorts of stories and trophies?

Even warfare involving kings, princes, and counts in France seems generally not to have been that brutal.[28] There were few pitched battles:

23. Among others, see Charles T. Wood, *The Age of Chivalry: Manners and Morals, 1000–1450* (London and New York, 1970).

24. Richer of Reims, *Historiae*, 4.90, ed. Harmut Hoffmann, Monumenta Germaniae Historica, Scriptores (in Folio) 38 (Hanover: Hahn, 2000), 293. On the degree to which the term is appropriate, see Marjorie Chibnall, "Mercenaries and the *familia regis* under Henry I," *History* 62 (1977): 15–23; reprinted in her *Piety, Power and History in Medieval England and Normandy*, Variorum Collected Studies Series 683 (Aldershot: Ashgate, 2000), no. 18.

25. *The* Gesta Normannorum Ducum *of William of Jumièges, Orderic Vitalis and Robert of Torigni*, ed. and trans. Elisabeth Van Houts, 2 vols., Oxford Medieval Texts (Oxford: Clarendon Press, 1992–95), 2: 103.

26. William of Poitiers, *Gesta*, 22–24.

27. Dudo of Saint-Quentin, *History*, 3.44, 187. Dudo regularly distinguishes between *tirones* and *maiores natu* in the Norman duke's entourage, e.g., ibid., 4.106, 145.

28. Action could nevertheless be rougher against certain rebels, see Richer of Reims, *Historiae*, 4.78, 285.

Hugh Capet, for instance, took care not to engage with Charles of Lorraine. Otherwise there were abortive battles in which some of the potential combatants were hesitant about fully committing themselves or choosing between rival camps with which they had links, and so adopted a wait-and-see policy.[29] At the same time, some battles written up by the chroniclers as epics of bloodletting, no less so than those fought in earlier days to defend the land (and gain fiefs) in the face of "pagan incursions," were pure invention, like that between Franks and Aquitanians shortly after 987 described by Ademar of Chabannes.[30] Others were not, and we need to take seriously the brutality of the victories won by Count Fulk Nerra of Anjou at Conquereuil in 992 over the count of Rennes[31] and at Pontlevoy in 1016 over the Count of Blois, when Fulk was aided by the Count of Maine, who dropped his policy of wait-and-see in time to help him. Several sources attest that, in the second of these battles, not only men on foot were killed, but also many knights (vassals).[32]

Pontlevoy perhaps makes it reasonable to modify John Gillingham's distinction regarding Fontenoy-en-Puisaye in 841 and distinguish between "Pontlevoy and after."[33] Perhaps the trauma of such a massacre encouraged, obliged even, Fulk's son Geoffrey Martel to seek two much less bloody victories. At Mont-Couer in 1035[34] and Nouy in 1044,[35] he captured the opposing count so as to obtain ransom and concessions. Thereafter, in 1049, he faced a coalition grouped around King Henry I, with the duke of Normandy and the count of Blois ral-

29. Odo of Saint-Maur, *Vie de Bouchard le Vénérable, comte de Vendôme, de Corbeil, de Melun et de Paris (X^e et XIe siècles)*, ed. Charles Bourel de la Roncière (Paris: Picard, 1892), p.19.

30. Ademar of Chabannes, *Chronicon*, ed. Pascale Bourgain, Richard Landes, and Georges Pon, Corpus Christianorum Continuatio Mediaevalis 119 (Turnhout, Brepols: 1999), 150–51.

31. Richer of Reims, *Historiae*, 4.81–86, 287–90. Rodulfus Glaber, *Historiarum libri quinque*, 2.3, ed. John France, in Rodulfus Glaber, *Opera*, ed. and trans. John France, Neithard Bulst, and Paul Reynolds, Oxford Medieval Texts (Oxford: Clarendon Press, 1989), 56–60.

32. *Chronica de gestis consulum Andegavorum*, in *Chroniques des comtes d'Anjou et des seigneurs d'Amboise*, ed. Louis Halphen and René Poupardin (Paris: Picard, 1913), 51–53; *Historia sancti Florentii Salmurensis*, in *Chroniques des églises d'Anjou*, ed. Paul Marchegay and Emile Mabille (Paris: Renouard, 1869), 274–75.

33. Gillingham, "Fontenoy and after," 264, posits that men on foot were more readily killed from the time that prisoners were no longer reduced to slavery.

34. *La chronique de Saint-Maixent*, ed. and French trans. Jean Verdon, Les classiques de l'histoire de France au Moyen Âge 33 (Paris: Belles Lettres, 1979), 116.

35. Rodulfus Glaber, *Historiarum*, 5.19, 242–44; *Chronica de gestis consulum Andegavorum*, 56–57.

lying to him through sworn loyalty, in a battle-free campaign. In this the royal army or "host" laid siege to the castle of Mouliherne without engaging with the Angevin force directly in front of it. It is remarkable how much William of Poitiers makes of the personal rivalries within the royal army and its contacts with the opposing Angevin "host".[36] This is the first occasion—and in a source that abounds in circum-stantial proof—where we are able to suspect the vying for position or rivalry amongst the lords' vassals that was characteristic of classic chivalry. William of Poitiers' account, composed around 1075, gives a good illustration of how a genuinely chivalric parallel could appear within the context of feudal warfare.

The siege of Mouliherne was an unimpassioned business. The for-ty-year-old King Henry, himself a celebrated knight, bade his vassal, Duke William of Normandy, not to take risks in his service. It is fine testimony to a concern that the vaunted ideal of dying for one's lord (as William's own great-great-grandfather, William Longsword, was said to have done according to later legend) should not become a battlefield tactic.[37] But did the future Conqueror really risk getting killed? His biographer makes clear that the king's chief dread was that William might show off his prowess on a horse and make use of a pointed lance, presumably similar to those used in tournaments. And that is indeed what happened, for, according to the obliging account given by William of Poitiers, the young duke wielded the lance with great skill. It led to a falling-out between William and his lord, the king, because William had thereby earned excessive honour; even Geoffrey Martel, the enemy, was free with his admiration, as if to win William over to himself. Everything here speaks of feudal interaction: the vassal had served his lord without truly obeying him, and there had been no end of mutual observation and communication between adversaries; it was as if there had been advance preparation of the balance that would be drawn up, once the truce arrived, of wrongs endured or caused by each.

Are we not entitled to view this account in William of Poitiers' *His-tory*, like other references in his work,[38] as moving towards the ideal and practices of classic chivalry?

---

36. William of Poitiers, *Gesta*, 14–18.

37. On the formation of the legend representing William Longsword as a vassal dying for his lord, see my *Chevaliers et miracles: la violence et le sacré dans la société féodale* (Paris: Colin, 2004), chap. 1.

38. See my observations in *La chevalerie*, rev. ed. (2012), 233–35.

Dubbing and Tournament in a Continuing Feudal Context

It would be good to know whether the beginning of William of Poitiers' work, which is missing in the only known surviving manuscript, included an account of Duke William's dubbing, which William of Malmesbury in a later reworking of the material attributed to King Henry I.[39] Such is not impossible, for a series of references to dubbing (though lacking a true description of the rite) are soon evident shortly after 1060 in Loire Valley notices and Norman chronicles.[40]

The development of the rite is significant. Yet it has not always been convincingly interpreted by modern historians. There is nothing, for instance, to encourage the view that it was some sort of spectacular means to effect or consecrate the social rise of modest ranking warriors. Rather it concerned noble heirs who had been trained and encouraged in arms according to certain techniques and codes in order to conserve their rank. Although the earliest witnesses to dubbing date from the same time as those testifying to typically chivalrous rites and gestures—as in tournaments and the civil treatment of prisoners—the link between them and a new ethic is not wholly clear.[41] It is rather to the growing authority of counts and suzerain dukes that they appear to attest.

There are especially detailed notices from the Loire Valley regarding the history of lands granted to monks and monastic relationships with the heirs or vassals of the donors which reveal far more about vassalic relationships and knighthood in the eleventh century than, for example, do the documents of the Mâcon region used by Georges Duby. They also provide valuable insights on dowry, liege homage, or the horse granted to the monastery by a knight preparing for death and

---

39. William of Malmesbury, *Gesta Regum Anglorum*, vol. 1, ed. and trans. R.A.B. Mynors, R.M. Thomson, and M. Winterbottom, vol. 2, R. M Thomson and H. Winterbottom, *General Introduction and Commentary*, Oxford Medieval Texts (Oxford: Clarendon Press, 1998–99), 1: 427–29; the editors argue (2: 220) that this "information, unique to William," might be "derived from the lost beginning of William of Poitiers," but it may be simply an elaboration from William of Poitiers, *Gesta*, 7.

40. See my "La cour du prince et l'essor de l'adoubement chevaleresque, en Normandie aux XIᵉ et XIIᵉ siècles," in *Guerre et Société au Moyen Âge, Byzance-Occident, VIIIᵉ–XIIIᵉ siècle*, ed. Dominique Barthélemy and Jean-Claude Cheynet, Monographies 31 (Paris: ACHCByz, 2010), 153–60.

41. A recent article oddly presents this basic data as the fruit of research: Max Lieberman, "A new Approach to the Knighting Ritual," *Speculum* 90 (2015): 391–423.

used by the monks in their negotiations with his relatives.[42] Suddenly, around 1060, there appear references to dubbing, not described as such, but communicated through expressions like *miles factus* (having received the arms of knighthood). The notices say no more about the rite and rarely mention its performer, but here and there one glimpses a count and a court without ever discovering if the lord concerned actually made a gift of arms. By thus evoking dubbing these notices were drawing attention to a noble heir's coming of age. When he came into possession of his inheritance, the recipient would have claims to enter into agreements and pursue issues concerning the land. He might cast doubt on the grant made to the monks, and only be placated with small gifts, finery, equipment, even a mount.

Paradoxically, dubbing hardened a knight; it could make him vindictive and ill-disposed towards the Church. He could unleash feudal warfare on close relations when, freshly dubbed, he bore a grudge against a paternal uncle who despoiled him of his castle. Thus the young Bouchard of L'Isle Bouchard seized his own uncle, without shrinking from setting alight the priory of Tavant.[43] And what are we to make of the Limousin youth who raped his aunt in public?[44] Anthropology encourages us to see that the violence in these two cases was targeted and meaningful; we can, at a pinch, hear the "message" being conveyed. But such men would hardly win awards for civility and moderation, and even their contemporaries were able to perceive the hand of God in their early deaths. In general, around 1100, there was no shortage of young knights who, around the time they were dubbed, were a source of much violence and expense. They drew regular criticism from Orderic Vitalis.[45]

Among literary sources, it is not to the romances of the twelfth century, like those of Chrétien de Troyes, with their avowedly chivalrous

42. See my "Économie monastique et société féodale: les cadeaux ou 'charités' des moines aux chevaliers, en France de l'Ouest au XIe siècle," in *Richesse et croissance au Moyen Âge*, ed. Dominique Barthélemy and Jean-Marie Martin, Monographies 43 (Paris: ACHCByz, 2014), 183–224, at 211–18.

43. Act edited by Charles Métais, *Cartulaire de l'abbaye cardinale de la Trinité de Vendôme*, 5 vols. (Paris: Picard, 1893–1900), 2 (1894): no. 359. See my "Les comtes, les sires et les 'nobles de châteaux' dans la Touraine du XIe siècle," in *Campagnes médiévales: l'homme et son espace. Études offertes à Robert Fossier* (Paris: Publications de la Sorbonne, 1995), 439–53.

44. Geoffrey of Vigeois, *Chronicon*, ed. Philippe Labbe, in *Novae bibliothecae manuscriptorum librorum*, 2 vols. (Paris: Cramoisy, 1657), 2: 291.

45. Orderic Vitalis, *The Ecclesiastical History of Orderic Vitalis*, ed. and trans. Marjorie Chibnall, 6 vols., Oxford Medieval Texts (Oxford: Clarendon Press, 1969–80), 6: 241.

spirit, that we need to look for the greatest number of dubbings. Rather they are to be found in *chansons de geste* devoted to the claims of a despoiled heir or the avenging of a dead hero, obligatory elements for those wanting their inheritance.

It was rare for a father to dub his own son.[46] Dubbing pertained to a lord, after a period of apprenticeship serving him as a squire.[47] However, dubbing was not a purely vassalic ritual; it was commonly mentioned without the man who dubbed being named, as it modified the relationship the one being dubbed was to have with his entire social environment. That said, it seems not to have been simply the "conferment of a grade" without the identity of the man who orchestrated it mattering. Often, in Orderic Vitalis's *Ecclesiastical History*, what causes it to be mentioned is the disappointment or revenge of a ducal conferrer, William the Conqueror or his son Henry Beauclerc, against one or more ungrateful conferees who had betrayed him and rebelled.[48] Their punishment would be all the harsher in light of it.

The most suggestive hint, from the pen of Orderic Vitalis, is to be found in one of those shrewd and clever remarks of which Helias de la Flèche was master, and which marked his attempt between 1095 and 1100 to secure for himself the splendid inheritance of the county of Maine. To gain his end he had to make homage to the duke of Normandy, at the time a principality controlled by William Rufus. Despite being around thirty he proposed as a stratagem to recommence his career by entering into the ducal mesnie, as if he were an aspirant to knighthood and a lordship, so as to gain arms and the fief he desired.

It may be supposed, therefore, that for vassals in the largest part of western France, under princes who in the eleventh century were already strong and aggressive overlords,[49] a period spent in a prince's household was a necessity. And it is not unreasonable to imagine that,

46. So it was said later of Tancred of Hauteville: see below, note 56. And although Orderic Vitalis cites Archbishop Lanfranc as the man who dubbed Henry Beauclerc (Orderic Vitalis, *Ecclesiastical History*, 4: 120), other sources say that it was in reality his father, William the Conqueror. Marjorie Chibnall suggests in her *The World of Orderic Vitalis* (Woodbridge: Boydel & Brewer, 1996), 144, that Orderic must have confused him with William Rufus.

47. Orderic Vitalis, *Ecclesiastical History*, 2: 40, 126, 138. One effect of dubbing seems to have been to clarify downward the status of squire, proscribing participation in knightly combats.

48. Orderic Vitalis, *Ecclesiastical History*, 3: 12 and 6: 190, 332.

49. The example of Fulk Nerra, count of Anjou is very ably drawn by Bernard Bachrach from mentions in notices, "Enforcement of the Forma Fidelitatis: The Techniques Used by Fulk Nerra, Count of the Angevins (987–1040)," *Speculum* 59 (1984): 796–819.

as in the twelfth century, the suzerain would delay the young man's dubbing as long as possible and sometimes determine the young man's marriage.[50] Better documented is the case where a young nobleman was enabled by his dubbing to begin a lawsuit and warfare against a close kinsman (generally the paternal uncle) who had deprived him of his inheritance. He would then rely on the suzerain who had dubbed him—thus Bouchard of L'Isle Bouchard relied on the count of Blois in the 1060s—at the risk of his adversary's relying on a different suzerain (as this Bouchard's uncle Geoffrey Fuel did on the count of Anjou, an enemy of the count of Blois).

This aspect of dubbing, rooted as it was in the Early Middle Ages, has tended to escape modern historians. This is partly because they fail to see feudal society as being one of routine inheritance,[51] and therefore a society of quarrels over inheritance and of matrimonial competition—something that to my mind was its fundamental problem. There has, moreover, been a tendency among historians toward excessively abstract preconceptions, overlooking the fact that knighthood concerned creatures of flesh and blood.

That said, there is a question whether the relationship between new knight and the man who dubbed him was entirely defined by all that dubbing implied, both before it happened and after. In some cases, it mattered little. To be dubbed was, in itself, formally, more honourable than to pledge homage. King Philip I and King Louis VI were both dubbed on occasions other than their royal consecration.[52] During his stay in a princely household, a young knight rubbed shoulders with contemporaries and might form with them one of those bands

50. Gilbert of Mons, *La chronique de Gislebert de Mons*, 48, ed. Léon Vanderkindere (Brussels: Kiessling, 1904), 85. Eng. trans. by Laura Napran as *The Chronicle of Hainaut by Gilbert of Mons* (Woodbridge: Boydell, 2005), here 49–50.

51. Such would tend to be shown by, among other studies, Georges Duby's *La société aux XIᵉ–XIIᵉ siècles dans la région mâconnaise* (Paris: Colin, 1953), had he not thought to make it more exciting (and to meet 1950s readers' expectations) by presuming an "upsurge of violence" alongside social change between 980 and 1030, which he deduced too readily from poorly relativised documentary sources and mishandling of contemporary semantics.

52. Philippe I, anointed king in 1059 at the age of seven, reigned after his father's death in 1060 under a sort of tutelage accorded to Count Baldwin V of Flanders "de Lille," who dubbed him in 1067 at the age of 15, as Baldwin's son proudly recalled in 1087: see act cited by Maurice Prou, *Recueil des actes de Philippe Ier roi de France* (Paris: Klincksieck, 1908), xxxii n. 5. Louis VI did not succeed him before he was 27, and nothing would be known of his dubbing by the Count of Ponthieu in 1098, were it not mentioned in a bishop's letter, printed in Jacques-Paul Migne, ed., *Patrologiae cursus completus: series Latina*, 221 vols. (Paris, 1847–67), 162 (1854): col. 664 (epistle 43).

of restless young bloods who inspired Georges Duby's pen[53] and of whom Orderic Vitalis gives us the first examples in Robert Curthose's entourage between 1075 and 1077, rebelling against their lord and father.[54] The households of dukes, counts, and barons did not simply contain in their courts the sons of vassals with origins in their lands; they contained also, as Marjorie Chibnall properly worked out from Saint Anselm and Orderic Vitalis,[55] a whole knightly society milling around from one court to another in search of glory and gain—and of heiresses, too. It was a society of vying and striving, one of whose early deployment Dudo of Saint-Quentin already around 1015 to 1026 gives glimpses, but which by 1100 seemed time-hallowed.[56]

The echoes we have of this society of civil one-upmanship, much given to glorying in its acts of prowess in combat and dispute, suggest that such prowess counted more than dubbing itself. Although the man who conferred the honour could pretend to having a hold over the one dubbed, the latter rarely boasted of him; an exception occurred when, by dubbing him, an uncle or father-in-law might appear to have chosen him as heir.[57] What gave a knight prestige was not so much his assumption of arms as what he did with them afterwards. It was as if dubbing finally let him off the leash to allow him to win renown. Ansold, lord of Maule, who experienced a good death in 1106, mentioned that he had spent 53 years as a knight; although he said nothing of his dubbing, he spoke of having started out as a knight errant,

---

53. See Georges Duby, "Les jeunes dans la société aristocratique dans la France du Nord-ouest au XIIᵉ siècle," *Annales. Économies, sociétés, civilisations* 19 (1964): 835–46; reproduced in idem, *Hommes et structures du Moyen Âge* (Paris and The Hague: Mouton, 1973) 213–25. However, as was often the case, Duby worked quickly and did not get to the heart of the matter: here no analysis was done by him of specifically the world of competitions and tournaments in the twelfth century.

54. Orderic Vitalis, *Ecclesiastical History*, 3: 110–12.

55. Chibnall, "Mercenaries."

56. According to Geoffrey Malaterra, Tancred of Hauteville, father of Robert and Roger Guiscard, had in his youth, i.e., during the first half of the eleventh century, participated in *exercitiis militaribus* ("knightly exercises," i.e., tournaments) and frequented the courts of princes and kings: *De rebus gestis Rogerii, Calabriae et Siciliae comitis, et Roberti Guiscardi ducis fratris eius, auctore Gaufredo Malaterra*, ed. Ernesto Pontieri, Rerum Italicarum scriptores 5.1 (Bologna: Zanichelli, 1927–28), fasc.1: 40; English translation by Kenneth Baxter Wolf as: Geoffrey Malaterra, *The Deeds of Count Roger of Calabria and Sicily and of his brother Duke Robert Guiscard* (Ann Arbor: University of Michigan Press, 2005). I prefer the translation "knightly" for *militaribus* to Wolf's "military."

57. Thus Count Fulk le Réchin of Anjou prided himself on having been dubbed by his uncle, Geoffrey Martel, *Fragmentum historiae Andegavensis*, in *Chroniques des comtes d'Anjou et des seigneurs d'Amboise*, ed. Louis Halphen and René Poupardin (Paris: Picard, 1913), 236.

on a probationary excursion, a *tirocinium*, undertaken in Sicily with the Norman conquerors.[58] The biography of Roger the Great Count, written about 1097 by Geoffrey Malaterra, was able to describe the earth-shattering career of an élite knight without mentioning an initial dubbing.[59]

As for the epic *Chanson de Roland* (contemporary with Malaterra's work), when the eponymous hero grieves over his sword, he says only in an artificial manner that he received it from Charlemagne, and there has been much modern debate over whether Charlemagne actually dubbed him.[60] Be that as it may, what Roland himself prizes are all the conquests he achieved in wielding it.

For knights who lived when the *Chanson* was written, Sicily, the journey to Jerusalem, and the route to Santiago de Compostella provided plenty of opportunities for them to show their courage. The Church, overlooking somewhat the canon of Clermont that rejected feudal motivation for the first crusade (i.e., that they should go "without seeking glory or gain"), did not hesitate to urge them to imitate their forefathers. But would they ever return? And would people credit their stories?[61] Simply to have opportunities to gain distinction at home in France might not be too bad. But did feudal warfare offer enough? Or was it risk-free for the chivalric class?

58. Orderic Vitalis, *Ecclesiastical History*, 3: 192: "Predictus miles tirocinii sui tempore probis actis emicuit."

59. Geoffrey Malaterra, *De rebus gestis Rogerii*, 1.4, speaks immediately of *militaribus disciplinis* (knightly exercises). Marie-Agnès Avenel, currently working on an edition and French translation of Geoffrey's biography nevertheless informs me that the anonymous *Historia sicula*, written in 1148, says that Tancred dubbed his own sons: *Anonymi historia Sicula a Normannis ad Petrum Aragonensem*, ed. Lodovico Muratori, Rerum Italicarum scriptores 1.8 (Milan: Societas Palatinae, 1726), cols. 745–80.

60. See *Chanson de Roland*, laisses 171–72, ed. Cesare Segre, trans. Madeleine Tyssens, 2nd ed. (Geneva: Droz, 2003). Jean Flori has maintained that this was simply a bestowal of arms in a technical sense: see his "La notion de chevalerie dans les chansons de geste du XIIᵉ siècle: étude historique du vocabulaire," *Le Moyen Âge* 81 (1975): 211–44 and 407–45. Excellent criticism of these analyses of vocabulary is to be found in Michel Stanesco, *Jeux d'errance du chevalier médiéval: Aspects ludiques de la fonction guerrière dans la littérature du Moyen Âge flamboyant*, Brill's Studies in Intellectual History 9 (Leiden: Brill, 1988), 51: "What we need to take into account is not an inventory of words supposedly closer to the truth because verging on the exhaustive, but the intentional meaning into which they are inserted."

61. See my "Des légendes chevaleresques dans une *Histoire ecclésiastique*: Orderic Vital et les captifs de l'Orient," in *Rerum gestarum scriptor. Histoire et historiographie au Moyen Âge. Mélanges Michel Sot*, ed. Magali Coumert, Marie-Céline Isaïa, Klaus Krönert, and Sumi Shimahara (Paris: Publications de l'Université Paris-Sorbonne, 2012), 177–89.

Around 1100, a tale was written by Ralph Tortaire in book 8 of the *Miracles of Saint Benedict* that could be seen as cruel and stimulating—it is at least no fabrication. It told of Burgundian horsemen with men on foot who boldly crossed the Loire to pillage the Berry region, going so far as to raid Saint Benedict's livestock. To embolden them they had a jongleur go before them intoning the great deeds of their forefathers. As they wearily returned to their boats, they were chased by peasants led by a monk, and when the latter called with a loud voice on the saint to curse them, the pillagers panicked in a way that epic poetry only ever ascribed to serfs. A good few were drowned in the river and prisoners were taken, whom the abbot lectured before they were released so that they could tell the countryside around how great was the power of Saint Benedict.[62] Whether or not the story was exaggerated, it reminds us that the knights did not go unchallenged on the ground by fighters who, though less well armed, were numerous, determined, and in some regards less fastidious.[63] From the 990s onwards, knights who did not co-operate with diocesan peace movements or went back on their word were regularly harassed by the large hosts that supported them.[64] Although such miscellaneous armies suffered defeats, the diocesan communes were re-energised after 1096 by the Crusade,[65] and one such gathering of communes, led not long after, in 1111, by King Louis VI, captured the castle of Le Puiset.[66]

An increasingly important development in the warfare of princes was archery. In 1098, horses belonging to Norman knights and installed in front of the royal castle at Chaumont-en-Vexin were brought down by arrows shot from the fortress—the archers were ordered not to shoot at the knights themselves.[67] In 1119, it was the King of England who used this tactic to defeat the French king's cavalry at the battle

62. *Les miracles de saint Benoît,* ed. Eugène de Certain (Paris: Société de l'histoire de France, 1858), 336–39. See my *Chevaliers et miracles,* 124–25.

63. See Ralph of Caen, *Tancredus,* ed. Edoardo D'Angelo, Corpus Christianorum Continuatio Mediaeualis 231 (Turnhout: Brepols, 2011), 54. For an English translation: *The Gesta Tancredi of Ralph of Caen: A History of the Normans on the First Crusade,* trans. Bernard S. Bachrach and David Steward Bachrach (Aldershot: Ashgate, 2005), 81.

64. See my "The Peace of God and Bishops at War in the Gallic Lands from the Late Tenth to the Early Twelfth Centuries," *Anglo-Norman Studies* 32 (2009): 1–32.

65. Orderic Vitalis, *Ecclesiastical History,* 5: 230 (Diocese of Rouen, 1096) and 6: 44 (Dioceses of Laon and Noyon, 1119).

66. Suger, *Vie de Louis VI le Gros,* chap. 19, ed. Henri Waquet, Les classiques de l'histoire de France au Moyen Âge 46 (Paris: Les Belles Lettres, 1929), 139.

67. Orderic Vitalis, *Ecclesiastical History,* 5: 218.

of Brémule,[68] thereby chivalrously sparing their lives while stopping them from showing knightly prowess. The same thing happened again at Rougemontier (Bourgthéroulde) in 1124 to crush the rebellion of what was described as "the flower of the knighthood."[69]

It seems to me that in such a context the earliest tournaments arrived on cue. They were fights among gentlemen. They were in principle managed in line with conventions, and were technically designed to minimise (without totally eliminating) the dangers attendant on displaying prowess. They excluded archers, which allowed young knights to show their skill and valour in the way that the future William the Conqueror had, as he gripped his lance at Mouliherne in 1049 in the absence of any formal organisation.[70]

Modern historians have noted the earliest evidence for tournaments in France and Lorraine (as far as the Rhineland) between 1110 and 1130, shortly before the earliest (and ineffective) formal condemnation by a council of such "loathsome fairs."[71] They have however shown mistrust of some earlier texts,[72] refusing above all to recognise as tournaments what Orderic Vitalis among others regularly called "knightly exercises" (exercitia militaria) and Galbert of Bruges even termed tornationes, since they constituted whole episodes in feudal wars.[73]

But the fact that the earliest dubbings known to us make sense largely in feudal interaction has never led to our excluding them from studies of the later culture of knighthood. Why, then, should we exclude the earliest tournaments?[74] I recently argued this point, proposing that we should interpret the observation of these "knightly exercises," notably

---

68. Ibid., 6: 238.

69. Ibid., 6: 350: "Ecce militaris flos totius Galliae et Normanniae hic consistit."

70. And at the price of something approaching flight: see above, note 21.

71. See Flori, *Chevaliers et chevalerie*, 133; David Crouch, *Tournament* (London: Hambledon and London, 2005), 2–8.

72. Especially of the coded confrontation between Normans before Mileto in 1062: Geoffrey Malaterra, *De rebus gestis*, 2.23, 37. See my "Les origines du tournoi chevaleresque," in *Agôn. La compétition, Vᵉ–XIIᵉ siècle*, ed. François Bougard, Régine Le Jan, and Thomas Lienhard, Haut Moyen Âge 17 (Turnhout: Brepols, 2012), 111–29.

73. Galbert of Bruges, *De multro, traditione et occisione gloriosi Karoli comitis Flandriarum*, ed. Jeff Rider, Corpus Christianorum Continuatio Mediaeualis 131 (Turnhout: Brepols, 1994), 13; English translation by Jeff Rider as: Galbert of Bruges, *The Murder, Betrayal, and Slaughter of Glorious Charles, Count of Flanders* (New Haven and London: Yale University Press, 2013), 11. See also *De multro*, 131 and 162 ("tot militiae, tot tornationes exercitabant milites"), and cf. in deed, if not in word: ibid., 119, 154.

74. See my discussion of "feudal interaction," and how it engendered both the ritual of dubbing and the tournament, in *Nouvelle histoire des Capétiens*, 224–34.

in evocative paragraphs of Orderic Vitalis,[75] as truly explaining the origins of tournaments.

The very term "knightly exercises," soon to be interchangeable with *tornationes*, generally meant something precise that could also be described factually without using that label. Such were confrontations before a castle, where one group of knights, assailants, fought another, the besieged, who had come out specifically for that reason.

These were not decisive combats, unless they degenerated[76] or if the group of assailants got carried away and pursued their advantage, using the lance to impede the closing of the castle gates behind those they were chasing.[77] Horses of the opposing party might be taken instead of being killed, though this did not mean that swords were not drawn.[78] But it was enough to capture the adversary bodily, if possible, once he had been thrown off his horse by use of the lance. Implied was a series of sharp changes of direction (or "turns") that make it unnecessary for us to look (as in the case of "dubbing") for a Germanic etymology for "tournament." Thus it seems that what took place in 1098 was above all a show, a performance, when, instead of going for a bloody assault, those besieging Le Mans watched some of their men turn round against some of the besieged: "renowned champions" from the two camps showed their strength and reaped the praise of their princes and peers.[79] Everyone desired to be thought the best.[80] And the best of all shone by his generosity.[81] What did gaining the castle or keeping it matter? Especially as all of this failed to stop the hosts from continuing to pillage round about.

Doubtless such rash and dangerous exercises regularly resulted in fatalities that were deplored. At Falaise in 1106 they caused one nota-

75. There are no mentions of tournaments in Loire Valley notices that are otherwise peppered with dubbings, although a later text does attribute the invention of the tournament to the Touraine district in the 1060s, on which see my "Les origines du tournoi." Yet why should such notices mention them, when they bore no relation to monastic property?

76. Orderic Vitalis, *Ecclesiastical History*, 5: 204.

77. Ibid., 5: 182.

78. Ibid., 6: 246–48 and 232 ("lanceis ac mucronibus insignes ictus vicissim miscebant.")

79. Ibid., 5: 242: "Famosi nempe pugiles nitebantur utrinque suas ostentare vires et promereri a principibus suis atque commilitonibus sanguinolentas laudes" ("Indeed renowned champions on each side strove to display their strength and earn bloodstained praise from their princes and fellow knights.")

80. Ibid., 6: 232.

81. Ibid., 6: 246.

ble death.[82] At Breteuil in September 1119 the Flemish champion, defeated by Ralph de Gael and captured by him after a hard fight, died of his wounds.[83] And it is understandable that the monk Orderic Vitalis more than once distanced himself from the "bloodstained praise"[84] of which the participants in tournaments were fond, as indeed he did from all the shallowness they encouraged, which ended in the extravagant and indecent festivities of young noblemen.

All the same, from time to time the ecclesiastical chronicler's reluctance abates. Orderic has nothing but admiration for Ralph de Gael's exploits. Here, as on another occasion in his own work, as in Suger's on one occasion, the vivid colour of knighthood seemingly broke through all the cloister's defences. Yet neither Orderic Vitalis nor Suger would probably have been present at any of these fine performances. So what accounts for such a specific tone? It is worth noting that on each of these three occasions the originator of the feat is the very lord who claims the place (like Ralph de Gael) or is defending it against his prince in spite of the latter's effort to treat him as a public enemy and thereby threaten to disinherit him (as in the cases of Hubert of La Ferté in 1083 and Hugh of Crécy in 1108).[85] Accounts of knightly prowess are therefore not indifferent; they are feudally significant. They tell of a way to gain recognition of one's rights that is more elegant than burning down a church or raping a noblewoman. Even the knights' behaviour, good or bad, on crusade ended up being interpreted in a biased manner, according to the hazards of feudal interactions, as Suger's *Life of Louis VI* testifies.[86]

In the east, nobles risked death and torture. But in France, as the twelfth century dawned, in spite of sometimes very bitter kinship hatreds and repeated betrayals of vassalic homage, the move from 1119 on was towards the organisation of tournaments that were in principle

---

82. Ibid., 6: 78–80.

83. Ibid., 6: 248.

84. Ibid., 5: 242; cf. Orderic's sentiment expressed in 4: 232–33: "Sic frequens exercitium feri Martis multum cruorem effundit, et vita speciosis iuvenibus crudeliter extorta lugubre damnum pluribus ingerit" ("Thus the frequent exercise of wild Mars [=fighting] spills much blood, and the life bloodily wrenched from beautiful young men inflicts sorrowful loss on even more.")

85. Suger notes both his skill and valour in combat: *Vie de Louis VI*, chap. 15, 94.

86. Suger evaluates the crusaders from the royal region according to their later fidelity to Louis VI, ibid., 36, 38, 44.

sporting events.[87] Meanwhile captive prisoners were well treated, their word tended to be trusted, and Orderic's very dense narrative suggests that knights dealt with one another on a basis of mutual respect.[88] Such good manners, the latest version of noble honour, would protect them from the severity of a prince like Henry Beauclerc—though not always, of course.

Conclusion

Practices we may consider chivalrous enjoyed an ambiguous relationship with the advance of princely power. On the one hand, the princes seemed to be largely the sponsors of the courts and tournaments in which they were extolled, even if they were respected only imperfectly and the vassal's devotion was always insisted on.[89] On the other, such practices tended to protect knights at fault or in disgrace, thereby limiting their ardour and the risks they took in warfare on the prince's behalf.

That is why I detect, from the twelfth century on, the development of controversy over what chivalry really meant or what injunctions should be given to novice knights when they were dubbed. Thus it was possible for Henry Plantagenet to have read to him both John of Marmoutier's history of his father Geoffrey of Anjou and John of Salisbury's *Policraticus*. In the first, the prince is praised for having always treated each of his knights with kindness and elegance. His son ought surely to emulate him. Straight away the picture of Geoffrey Plantagenet's splendid dubbing at Rouen in 1127 *before* Henry Beauclerc rather than *by* him[90] seeks to idealise the young man's integration, with that of those dubbed with him, into the chivalrous society whose good manners uphold narcissism and regarding which John of Marmoutier

87. Orderic Vitalis, *Ecclesiastical History*, 6: 230, but here the tournament is used as a bait to entice opponents away from their role as defenders.

88. Such is clear enough in the interaction and feudal wars in Maine from 1098 to 1100, where William Rufus treats captive knights very well and takes them at their word, Orderic Vitalis, *Ecclesiastical History*, 5: 238 and 244, and among foes jokes alternate with threats, ibid., 302.

89. Personal loyalty to a suzerain was at the heart of *militaris disciplina* as Orderic saw it, ibid., 6: 158 and 288. According to him, Roman discipline had not allowed pillage, ibid., 472.

90. John of Marmoutier, *Historia Gaufredi ducis Normannorum et comitis Andegavorum*, in *Chroniques des comtes d'Anjou*, ed. Louis Halphen and René Poupardin (Paris: Picard, 1913), 177–80.

even forgets to prescribe some effort to defend churches and the poor. It is almost as if Geoffrey Plantagenet were a courtly version of Gerald of Aurillac! The picture given makes for a striking contrast with several recommendations of John of Salisbury, who in some passages of his *Policratus* would like to see a royal army recruited from the best from every social class and disciplined Roman-style[91]—something utterly incompatible with the feudal and properly chivalric spirit.

The feudal class would long resist John of Salisbury's type of project. Even the Crusades did not put it into practice; crusading activity continued to be characterised by voluntary devotion. Even the dubbing liturgies of the thirteenth century enjoined service to the king, the Church and justice, only in general terms, without in any way providing, for example, a means whereby knights who perjured their oaths might be deprived of their lands. All in all, they continued to see their duty toward the king as one of vassals rather than as conforming to the idea of a chivalric militia, a notion that belongs only to modern minds.

91. John of Salisbury, *Policraticus*, 6, ed. Clement C. J. Webb (Oxford: Methuen, 1909).

Jörg PELTZER*

KNIGHTHOOD IN THE EMPIRE

This chapter looks at the formation of knighthood, the significance of knighting and the role of the court in shaping the knights as a group in the Holy Roman Empire between the eleventh and thirteenth centuries. The formation of knighthood was a lengthy process pre-conditioned by the role of the miles *as warrior and vassal in the eleventh century and subsequently shaped by Church (crusades) and court (chivalric values). At the end of the twelfth century the idea of chivalry provided the framework for a way of life to which men of different ranks could aspire. Mainly based on personal qualities, it offered the opportunity to gain honour for both the king and the unfree* ministerialis *alike. The knightly investiture had no single specific meaning. Its significance depended on the social and legal status of the individual. In the thirteenth century, knightly birth became the decisive criterion for determining knightly status. For the upper nobility this was of secondary importance, but further down the social scale it demarcated the difference between noble and non-noble. Consequently, "knight" became the collective term for members of the lower aristocracy and thus became a term of aristocratic rank. In the late Middle Ages the term* miles *had two very different meanings: that of the* chevalier *as a way of life aspired to by aristocrats across the ranks and that of the knight as a member of the lower aristocracy.*

In 1976, the German medievalist Arno Borst published an anthology of important texts on the history of knighthood.[1] In his introduction, he emphasised that knighthood was a European phenomenon, the analysis of which could be achieved only by a collective common effort of scholars across Europe and across academic disciplinary boundaries.[2] Since then research has significantly enhanced our understanding of medieval knighthood, but a comprehensive history of this phenomenon in a European perspective remains a desideratum. The present volume is a step towards filling that gap, yet there is still a good way to go. The evidence is anything but clear-cut and regional variations are to be expected. This is further complicated by different research tradi-

* I am very grateful to Jan Keupp (Münster) whose critical reading improved this text.
1. In what follows the term knighthood refers to the status of a knight, while the term chivalry refers to a certain way of life associated with knighthood.
2. Arno Borst, ed., *Das Rittertum im Mittelalter*, Wege der Forschung 349 (Darmstadt: Wissenschaftliche Buchgesellschaft, 1976), 16.

tions. In France, for example, the theme of "feudal anarchy" framed for a very long time the discussion on the origins of knighthood, as Dominique Barthélemy observes in his contribution to this volume.[3] In German scholarship, this was not the case. Here, the history of the *ministeriales*, men of unfree status who made their careers in the service of their lords as administrators and warriors, played an important role.[4] Consequently, the history of knighthood in Europe can and probably needs to be told in different ways to account for the various findings. This also holds true for the analysis of knighthood in the vast lands of the Empire, but the advances made by scholars over the past four decades allow for a sketching out of some major developments.[5] In what follows, I will look at the formation of knighthood (that is, what it meant to be a knight and who considered themselves or were considered knights), the significance of knighting, and the role of the court in shaping the knights as a group. The chronological focus is on the period between the eleventh and thirteenth centuries.

3. An overview is provided by Werner Hechberger, *Adel im fränkisch-deutschen Mittelalter. Zur Anatomie eines Forschungsproblems*, Mittelalter-Forschungen 17 (Ostfildern: Thorbecke, 2005), 420–23. See also Dominique Barthélemy, "Chivalry in Feudal Society According to French Evidence" in this volume.

4. On the emergence of the *ministeriales*, see Thomas Zotz, "Die Formierung der Ministerialität," in *Gesellschaftlicher und ideengeschichtlicher Wandel im Reich der Salier*, ed. Stefan Weinfurter, 3 vols., Die Salier und das Reich 2 (Sigmaringen: Thorbecke, 1991–92), 3: 3–50; their role in the second half of the twelfth century was recently analysed in depth by Jan Ulrich Keupp, *Dienst und Verdienst. Die Ministerialen Friedrich Barbarossas und Heinrichs VI.*, Monographien zur Geschichte des Mittelalters 48 (Stuttgart: Hiersemann, 2002); cf. Benjamin Arnold, *German Knighthood, 1050–1300* (Oxford: Clarendon Press, 1985). The legal status of the *ministeriales* varied from court to court. Eike von Repgow noted in his *Sachsenspiegel* (written between 1220 and 1235) that they existed in such manifold forms that if one tried to describe them one would never come to an end, Eike von Repgow, *Sachsenspiegel. Landrecht*, III, chap. 42.2, ed. Karl August Eckhardt, Monumenta Germaniae Historica, Fontes iuris Germanici antiqui N.S. 1.1 (Göttingen: Musterschmitt-Verlag, 1973), 223.

5. The historiography is analysed by Hechberger, *Adel im fränkisch-deutschen Mittelalter*, 417–48; Werner Hechberger, *Adel, Ministerialität und Adel im Mittelalter*, Enzyklopädie deutscher Geschichte 72 (Munich: Oldenbourg, 2010), 34–37, 99–106; Werner Paravicini, *Die ritterlich-höfische Kultur des Mittelalters*, Enzyklopädie deutscher Geschichte 32 (Munich: Oldenbourg, 1994). A recent, well documented and richly illustrated summary for a general readership is provided by Sabine Buttinger and Jan Ulrich Keupp, *Die Ritter* (Stuttgart: Theiss, 2013).

The Formation of Knighthood

"You are speaking of knights. What are they? ... and tell me: who is bestowing knighthood (*"du nennest ritter: waz ist daz? ... sô sage mir, wer gît ritterschaft?"*) the squire asks the knight in Wolfram of Eschenbach's *Parzival*. King Arthur, replies the knight, is making knights.[6] The historian's answer, unfortunately, would not be that straightforward. The roots of the knightly image in the Empire around 1200 were manifold. Some of them reached back to the tenth century. Looking at the term *miles*, Josef Fleckenstein and Franz-Reiner Erkens have shown the significance of its two meanings: vassal and warrior.[7] Occasionally used to denominate vassals in the tenth century, *miles* became more regularly deployed in this sense in the eleventh century. It could refer to men of the upper aristocracy as well as to men of lower rank. Consequently, in its meaning of vassal, the term *miles* carried little value in terms of social distinction. It was not an attribute the upper echelons of the aristocracy considered necessary to emphasise.[8]

Like vassal, the second meaning of *miles*, warrior, was also socially inclusive. The king, as well as the ordinary soldier, could be named *miles*. Adalbero of Laon or Gerard of Cambrai grouped *milites* together as warriors in their schematic classification of society in the eleventh century.[9] As warriors they could and should distinguish themselves in battle, when they fought together for victory while facing the threat of

6. Wolfram von Eschenbach, *Parzival. Studienausgabe*, chap. 123, vv. 4–7, ed. Karl Lachmann, Peter Knecht, and Bernd Schirok (Berlin, New York: De Gruyter, 2003), 126.

7. Josef Fleckenstein, "Die Entstehung des niederen Adels und das Rittertum," in *Herrschaft und Stand. Untersuchungen zur Sozialgeschichte im 13. Jahrhundert*, ed. Josef Fleckenstein, Veröffentlichungen des Max-Planck-Instituts für Geschichte 51 (Göttingen: Vandenhoeck und Ruprecht, 1977), 17–39; Josef Fleckenstein, "Über den engeren und weiteren Begriff von Ritter und Rittertum (*miles* und *militia*)," in *Person und Gemeinschaft im Mittelalter. Karl Schmid zum fünfundsechzigsten Geburtstag*, ed. Gerd Althoff, Dieter Geuenich, Otto Gerhard Oexle, and Joachim Wollasch (Sigmaringen: Thorbecke, 1988), 379–92; Franz-Reiner Erkens, "Militia und Ritterschaft. Reflexionen über die Entstehung des Rittertums," *Historische Zeitschrift* 258 (1994): 623–59.

8. Erkens, "Militia und Ritterschaft," 633.

9. Adalberon of Laon, *Poème au roi Robert*, ed. Claude Carozzi, Les classiques de l'histoire de France au Moyen Âge 32 (Paris: Belles Lettres, 1979), 22–23; *Gesta pontificum Cameracensium*, ed. Ludwig Bethmann, Monumenta Germaniae Historia, Scriptores (in Folio) 7 (Hanover: Hahn, 1846), 402–89, at 485. Cf. Otto Gerhard Oexle, "Deutungsschemata der sozialen Wirklichkeit im frühen und hohen Mittelalter. Ein Beitrag zur Geschichte des Wissens," in *Mentalitäten im Mittelalter. Methodische und inhaltliche Probleme*, ed. František Graus, Vorträge und Forschungen 35 (Sigmaringen: Thorbecke, 1987), 65–117; Otto Gerhard Oexle, "Die funktionale Dreiteilung als Deutungsschema der sozialen Wirklichkeit in der ständischen Gesellschaft des Mittelalters," in *Ständische Gesellschaft*

humiliation and even death. Yet, even though *miles*/warrior had greater potential than *miles*/vassal to create a group identity and, during battle, probably achieved that for a moment, it was not sufficient to create the chivalric ethos aspired to by men across the ranks, including the king, in the second half of the twelfth century. It is telling that, far into the second half of the twelfth century, the German term for *miles*, *Ritter*, referred almost exclusively to mounted warriors of lower rank.[10] Thus *miles* in its socially inclusive meanings of vassal and warrior pre-conditioned the formation of knighthood, but more was needed to form a chivalrous identity embraced by all ranks of *milites*.

Following in the footsteps of Carl Erdmann,[11] German scholarship has turned to the Church as a key player in this process. The churchmen initiating the peace of God in France not only forbade fighting during certain periods, but also tried to protect unarmed persons against the violence of the warriors in general. Some bishops even created their own militias to enforce the rulings of the peace.[12] The malefactor thus turned protector and churchmen propagated with increasing intensity the idea that knights ought to use their military powers to protect the weak and to fight against the enemies of the church. In his *Liber de vita christiana*, written in the second half of the eleventh century, Bonizo of Sutri sketched out what he believed knights ought to do: they ought to serve their lords loyally and to protect them, if necessary, with their own lives. They should neither strive for booty nor commit perjury, but fight for the *res publica* and against schismatics and here-

---

und soziale Mobilität, ed. Winfried Schulze, Schriften des Historischen Kollegs: Kolloquien 12 (Munich: Oldenbourg, 1988), 19–51.

10. Joachim Bumke, *Studien zum Ritterbegriff im 12. und 13. Jahrhundert*, Euphorion: Beihefte zum Euphorion 1 (Heidelberg: Winter, 1977), 36–40. See also Claudia Wittig, "Teaching Chivalry in the Empire (*ca.* 1150–1250)" in this volume.

11. Carl Erdmann, *Die Entstehung des Kreuzzugsgedankens*, Forschungen zur Kirchen- und Geistesgeschichte 6 (Stuttgart: Kohlhammer, 1935), 309–25.

12. Buttinger and Keupp, *Die Ritter*, 32–33; on the peace of God, see Hartmut Hoffmann, *Gottesfriede und Treuga Dei*, Schriften der Monumenta Germaniae Historica 20 (Stuttgart: Hiersemann, 1964); Thomas Head and Richard Landes, eds., *The Peace of God. Social Violence and Religious Response in France around the Year 1000* (Ithaca, New York: Cornell University Press, 1992); Dominique Barthélemy, *L'an mil et la paix de Dieu. La France chrétienne et féodale, 980–1060* (Paris: Fayard, 1999); Hans-Werner Goetz, "Die Gottesfriedensbewegung im Licht neuerer Forschungen," in *Landfrieden. Anspruch und Wirklichkeit*, ed. Arno Buschmann and Elmar Wadle, Rechts- und staatswissenschaftliche Veröffentlichungen der Görres-Gesellschaft N. F. 98 (Paderborn: Schöningh, 2002), 31–54.

tics. Finally, they ought to defend the poor, widows and orphans.[13] The protection of the Church and the weak had traditionally been the task of kings; it was now specifically extended to knights.[14] Churchmen thus offered the warriors an important role within the society.

Crucial for the image of the term *miles* was the run-up to the First Crusade. When, in 1095, Pope Urban II launched his appeal to march eastwards and to battle for the freedom of the Church, he amalgamated the idea of pilgrimage and military campaign. By using their force to defend the Church instead of fighting among themselves and committing heinous crimes (*malitia*), the knights would become *milites Christi* and thus transform their group into a true *militia Christi*.[15] In such a way the term became acceptable for magnates and even kings.[16] The association with Christ was fitting for men of all ranks. To fight in and for his name brought honour to all.

The First Crusade was not the enterprise of knights from the Empire. Urban's assemblies north of the Alps took place in the French kingdom, not in the Empire, where Henry IV did not accept Urban's papacy. Consequently, Urban's appeal had little impact in the central regions of the Empire. The Franconian chronicler Ekkehard of Aura noted that, due to the schism, the tune of that trumpet hardly reached the eastern Franks, Saxons, Thuringians, Bavarians and Swabians.[17] But it did not remain entirely unheard. In particular, along the western marches, men were inspired by Urban's call. Godfrey of Bouillon, duke of Lower Lorraine, and Robert, count of Flanders, were the most prominent among them.[18] In any case, as important as Urban's appeal was for the image of a *miles christianus*, the spread of the underlying

13. Bonizo of Sutri, *Liber de vita christiana*, ed. Ernst Perels, Texte zur Geschichte des römischen und kanonischen Rechts im Mittelalter 1 (Berlin: Weidmann, 1930), 248–49; Erkens, "Militia und Ritterschaft," 639; Gerd Althoff, "Nunc fiant Christi milites, qui dudum extiterunt raptores. Zur Entstehung von Rittertum und Ritterethos," *Saeculum* 32 (1981): 317–33, at 330.

14. Erkens, "Militia und Ritterschaft," 639; Althoff, "Nunc fiant Christi milites," 332.

15. Baldric of Bourgueil, *The Historia Ierosolimitania of Baldric of Bourgueil*, ed. Steven Biddlecombe (Woodbridge: Boydell, 2014), 8–9; Erkens, "Militia und Ritterschaft," 645.

16. Ibid.

17. *Frutolfs und Ekkehards Chroniken und die anonyme Kaiserchronik*, ed. Franz-Josef Schmale and Irene Schmale-Ott, Ausgewählte Quellen zur deutschen Geschichte des Mittelalters 15 (Darmstadt: Wissenschaftliche Buchgesellschaft, 1972), 140.

18. Alexander Berner, "Kreuzfahrer aus dem Nordwesten des Reichs, 1096–1230," in *Die Kreuzzugsbewegung im römisch-deutschen Reich (11.–13. Jahrhundert)*, ed. Nikolas Jaspert and Stefan Tebruck (Ostfildern: Thorbecke, 2016), 13–40, at 17–21; Stefan Tebruck, "Kreuzfahrer und Jerusalempilger aus dem sächsisch-thüringischen Raum (1100–1300)," in ibid., 41–83, esp. at 45 and 77; Alan Murray, "Das erste Jahrhundert der Kreuzzugsbe-

idea of the knight deploying his heroics to protect the Church was not dependent on the range of his authority. It can be reasonably assumed that the reformed monastic houses, which enjoyed great popularity among the German aristocracy, played their part in disseminating these ideas in the Empire.[19]

Half a century after Clermont the way, therefore, had been well paved when Pope Eugenius III called for a new crusade and none other than Bernard of Clairvaux preached its necessity to the Germans. A fervent advocate of the idea of the *miles Christi,* Bernard provided the potential German crusaders with a clear image of what it meant to be a good knight. Fighting in the name of God brought true honour.[20] The disastrous outcome of the Second Crusade, however, sowed some seeds of doubt regarding this idea. One of the participants, Bishop Otto of Freising, explained its failure by the sinfulness of the crusaders themselves, implying that going on crusade was not enough to cover up past misdeeds.[21] Some theologians even wondered whether the armed pilgrimage corresponded to divine will and thus questioned the concept of the crusade as the ultimate fulfilment of knighthood.[22] At the imperial court, however, such thoughts did not

wegung im Südwesten des Reiches: Kreuzfahrer aus Franken, Schwaben und dem Elsaß im Zeitraum von 1097 bis 1204," in ibid., 85–102, at 87–89.

19. Cf. mainly for France: Althoff, "Nunc fiant Christi milites."

20. Bernard of Clairvaux, *Sancti Bernardi opera*, ed. Jean Leclercq and Henri Rochais, 8 vols. (Rome: Ed. Cistercienses, 1955–77), 8: 313–15 (no 363: Bernard's letter to the German archbishops); Jonathan Philipps, *The Second Crusade. Extending the Frontiers of Christendom* (New Haven: Yale University Press, 2007), 73; Josef Fleckenstein, "Die Rechtfertigung der geistlichen Ritterorden nach der Schrift ‚De laude novae militiae' Bernhards von Claivaux," in *Die geistlichen Ritterorden Europas*, ed. Josef Fleckenstein and Manfred Hellmann, Vorträge und Forschungen 26 (Sigmaringen: Thorbecke, 1980), 9–22, at 14–15. It must be noted that in his treatise *De laude novae militiae* Bernard addressed specifically the Knights Templars as *milites Christi* distinguishing them from other knights, even from other crusaders. In other contexts, however, he used the term *milites Christi* for crusaders in general and there is no reason to assume that he did not do so during his campaign of 1146, Fleckenstein, "Die Rechtfertigung der geistlichen Ritterorden," 14.

21. Otto of Freising, *Ottonis et Rahewini Gesta Friderici I. imperatoris,* ed. Georg Waitz, Monumenta Germaniae Historica, Scriptores rerum Germanicarum in usum scholarum separatim editi [46] (Hanover: Hahn, 1912), 93; Knut Görich, "Schmach und Ehre: Konrad III. auf dem Zweiten Kreuzzug," in *Stauferzeit—Zeit der Kreuzzüge*, ed. Alexander Beihammer, Schriften zur staufischen Geschichte und Kunst 29 (Göppingen: Gesellschaft für staufische Geschichte, 2011), 42–57, at 43.

22. Klaus Schreiner, "‚Hof' (curia) und ‚höfische Lebensführung' (vita curialis) als Herausforderung an die christliche Theologie und Frömmigkeit," in *Höfische Literatur, Hofgesellschaft, Höfische Lebensformen um 1200. Kolloquium am Zentrum für Interdisziplinäre Forschung der Universität Bielefeld (3. bis 5. November 1983)*, ed. Gert Kaiser and Jan-Dirk Müller, Studia humaniora 6 (Düsseldorf: Droste, 1986), 67–139, at 131–32.

gain the upper hand in the second half of the twelfth century. Emperor
Frederick I Barbarossa, who as a 25-year-old had taken part in the
Second Crusade (against his father's wish), had no doubts about the
role of the knight as a *miles Christi* and the crusade as the place for
the *militia Christi*. Preparing for the Third Crusade, Frederick held a
diet at Mainz in 1188. His invitation made his intentions very clear:
the assembly was Christ's court (*curia Christi*), not the usual imperial court; its beginning was scheduled for Sunday *Laetare Jerusalem*. The start of the crusade itself was fixed on 23 April 1189, Saint
George's day.[23] This perfectly clear stage-managing may have served
to persuade those who doubted the righteousness of a crusade, but first
and foremost it was a statement of Frederick's own convictions. By
taking the cross, he and his men became *milites Christi* and formed
the *militia Christi*, Christ's army; a message well understood by contemporaries.[24]

Yet as important as the ecclesiastical influence was in forming a chivalrous identity that could be embraced by men of all rank, it was not
the only force determining its characteristics.[25] The court was another
important factor. Notwithstanding the great emphasis on the Christian
values and the idea of a *miles Christi* at Frederick's court of 1188,
the court usually was the centre of the secular values of knighthood.
It created the space where men of different ranks met and associated
with each other. This conviviality fostered the competition and hence
the emergence of further criteria to distinguish between good and bad
knights. The traditional values of military prowess, loyalty and good
Christian behaviour were still of great importance, but other qualities
became significant, too. Values traditionally associated with kingship
were transferred to the *milites* in general in the course of the twelfth
century: moderation (*temperantia/moderatio*), steadiness (*constantia*)

23. "Historia de expeditione Friderici imperatoris," in *Quellen zur Geschichte des
Kreuzzuges Kaiser Friedrichs I.*, ed. Anton Chroust, Monumenta Germaniae Historica,
Scriptores rerum Germanicarum n.s. 5 (Berlin: Weidmann, 1928), 1–115, at 11–13; "Histo-
ria peregrinorum," in ibid., 116–72, at 125–26; Josef Fleckenstein, "Friedrich Barbarossa
und das Rittertum," in *Das Rittertum im Mittelalter*, ed. Borst, 392–418, at 396; Schreiner,
",Hof' (*curia*)," 131.

24. Otto of Sankt Blasien, *Ottonis de Sancto Blasio chronica*, ed. Adolf Hofmeister,
Monumenta Germaniae Historica, Scriptores rerum Germanicarum in usum scholarum
separatim editi [47] (Hanover: Hahn, 1912), 46 (*milicia Christi*); "Historia de expeditione
Friderici imperatoris," 91 (Frederick I as *miles Christi*); Fleckenstein, "Friedrich Barbarossa und das Rittertum," 407; Schreiner, ",Hof' (*curia*)," 131.

25. This point is also made by David Crouch, "When was Chivalry? Evolution of a
Code" in this volume.

and generosity (*largitas*).[26] Courtly life demanded proper manners. The knight had to know how to dress properly and how to behave at the table. Ideally, he mastered the art of courtly love (*minne*), the concept of an aristocrat serving a woman.[27]

At the courts, large and small alike, troubadours told stories that unfolded imagined worlds of ideal chivalric behaviour. The western influence on the literature spread at the German courts has long been recognised and emphasised.[28] The perhaps most vivid illustration of this cultural transfer is the journey of the *Lanzelet* from the Angevin realm to the imperial court. Around 1200, Ulrich of Zatzikhoven composed the story of the Arthurian knight *Lanzelet* in Middle High German. At the end of his work he disclosed that he owed his knowledge of this story to a certain Huc de Morville, who came as a hostage for Richard I to the court of Emperor Henry VI (*ca.* 1194) and who brought with him *daz welsche buoch* (the French book) of *Lanzelet*. At the request of his friends, Ulrich took on the task of composing this "long and strange story in German."[29] But not all was imported from

26. Heinz Krieg, "Friedrich Barbarossa und das Rittertum," in *Friedrich Barbarossa und sein Hof*, ed. Caspar Ehlers, Schriften zur staufischen Geschichte und Kunst 28 (Göppingen: Gesellschaft für staufische Geschichte, 2009), 127–54, at 131–32; Barbara Haupt, "Der höfische Ritter in der mittelhochdeutschen Literatur," in *Rittertum und höfische Kultur der Stauferzeit*, ed. Johannes Laudage and Yvonne Leverkus, Europäische Geschichtsdarstellungen 12 (Cologne: Böhlau, 2006), 170–92; Jan Ulrich Keupp, "Verhöflichte Krieger? Überlegungen zum ‚Prozeß der Zivilisation' am stauferzeitlichen Hof," in ibid., 217–45; Gerhard Lubich, "‚Tugendadel'. Überlegungen zur Verortung, Entwicklung und Entstehung ethischer Herrschaftsnormen der Stauferzeit," in ibid., 247–89; Joachim Bumke, *Höfische Kultur. Literatur und Gesellschaft im hohen Mittelalter* (Munich: Deutscher Taschenbuch-Verlag, 2008), 267–86, 381–581. For specific aspects of courtly life such as the hunt or the tournament, see e.g. Josef Fleckenstein, ed., *Das ritterliche Turnier im Mittelalter. Beiträge zu einer vergleichenden Formen- und Verhaltensgeschichte des Rittertums*, Veröffentlichungen des Max-Planck-Instituts für Geschichte 80 (Göttingen: Vandenhoeck und Ruprecht, 1985); Werner Rösener, ed., *Jagd und höfische Kultur im Mittelalter*, Veröffentlichungen des Max-Planck-Instituts für Geschichte 135 (Göttingen: Vandenhoeck und Ruprecht, 1997).

27. Bumke, *Studien zum Ritterbegriff*, 99–100.

28. Bumke, *Höfische Kultur*, 120–35.

29. Ulrich von Zatzikhoven, *Lanzelet*, ed. Florian Kragl, 2 vols. (Berlin, New York: de Gruyter, 2006), 1: 523, vv 9338–49; ibid., 2: 1272–74. The identity of Huc de Morville has long been discussed. The idea that he was Hugh Nereth, who in 1208 became bishop of Coutances, is no longer upheld. However, the more recent view that he is to be identified with Hugh de Morville, lord of Appleby and one of the Becket murderers, is also wrong, for this Hugh "was dead or in exile by the mid-1170s." In all likelihood, Huc de Morville is to be identified with his relative and namesake Hugh de Morville, lord of Burgh by Sands, who died in 1202. On the Morvilles see Nicholas Vincent, "The Murderers of Thomas Becket," in *Bischofsmord im Mittelalter*, ed. Natalie Fryde and Dirk Reitz, Veröffentlichungen des Max-Planck-Instituts für Geschichte 191 (Göttingen: Vandenhoeck und Ruprecht, 2003), 211–72, at 224–29, quote on 225; for Hugh Nereth, see Jörg Peltzer,

the west. Indigenous oral traditions were also put on parchment. The song of the Nibelungen, for example, was written down shortly before 1200.[30] German knights composed their songs of courtly love. Ulrich von Liechtenstein's *Frauendienst* (*ca.* 1255) is a famous example.[31] Finally, the *Kaiserchronik*, probably composed in the mid-twelfth century, shows that there were independent literary developments in the Empire which already at an early date used ideas of chivalric behaviour.[32] The terrain was thus well prepared when the popular culture of chivalric literature arrived at the courts in the Empire.

The history of the terms *Hövescheit/hövesch* underscores just how important the courts of the king and magnates were in shaping and defining the behaviour of their attenders. *Hövescheit/hövesch* was a mid-twelfth century neologism. Its Latin equivalent *curialitas* appeared for the first time in the second half of the eleventh century. Another more nuanced translation was offered by the term *urbanitas* which became attached to the courtly world in the course of the twelfth century. While some clerics who were critical of courtly life considered the verb *höveschen* as synonymous with *fornicare*, secular writers used *hövescheit/hövesch* to describe proper appearance, dressing and behaviour distinguishing the world of the court from the world of the rustics.[33]

Canon Law, Careers and Conquest. Episcopal Elections in Normandy and Greater Anjou, Cambridge Studies in Medieval Life and Thought 4.71 (Cambridge: Cambridge University Press 2012), 149–50.

30. Jan-Dirk Müller, *Das Nibelungenlied*, Klassiker-Lektüren 5 (Berlin: Schmidt, 2015).

31. Ulrich von Liechtenstein, *Frauendienst*, ed. Franz Victor Spechtler, Göppinger Arbeiten zur Germanistik 485 (Göppingen: Kümmerle, 2003).

32. Jürgen Wolf, "*hövesch*—Verwirrende Beobachtungen zur Genese der deutschen Hofkultur," in *Mittelhochdeutsch. Beiträge zur Überlieferung, Sprache und Literatur. Festschrift für Kurt Gärtner zum 75. Geburtstag*, ed. Ralf Plate and Martin Schubert (Berlin: de Gruyter, 2011), 356–74; Peter Somogyi and Jürgen Wolf, "Einleitung," in *Die Ritteridee in der deutschen Literatur des Mittelalters. Eine kommentierte Anthologie*, ed. Jörg Arentzen and Uwe Ruberg (Darmstadt: Wissenschaftliche Buchgesellschaft, 2011), xiii–xxxvi. A new edition of the *Kaiserchronik* is being prepared by Mark Chinca and Christopher Young (both of Cambridge), and Jürgen Wolf and Jürg Fleischer (both of Marburg).

33. On *curialitas/hövescheit* see the articles in Josef Fleckenstein, ed., *Curialitas. Studien zu Grundfragen der höfisch-ritterlichen Kultur*, Veröffentlichungen des Max-Planck-Instituts für Geschichte 100 (Göttingen: Vandenhoeck und Ruprecht, 1990), in particular Paul Gerhard Schmid, "Curia und curialitas. Wort und Bedeutung im Spiegel der lateinischen Quellen," in ibid., 15–26; Peter Ganz, "'hövesch'/'hövescheit' im Mittelhochdeutschen," in ibid., 39–54; see also Peter Ganz, "curialis/hövesch," in *Höfische Literatur, Hofgesellschaft, Höfische Lebensformen um 1200. Kolloquium am Zentrum für Interdisziplinäre Forschung der Universität Bielefeld (3. bis 5. November 1983)*, ed. Gert Kaiser and Jan-Dirk Müller, Studia humaniora 6 (Düsseldorf: Droste, 1986), 39–56; Thomas Zotz, "Ritterliche Welt und höfische Lebensformen," in *Rittertum und ritterli-*

The epitome of an imperial court in the second half of the twelfth century was Fredrick's diet held at Mainz on Pentecost 1184. At Frederick's invitation, magnates and their large retinues flocked to Mainz from all corners of the Empire north of the Alps,[34] and some, attracted by the "dignity of the Empire," may even have come from other realms.[35] The well-informed Gilbert of Mons tells us that in total 70,000 knights attended the court.[36] The figure is certainly too high, but his point is well made: this was a court of unrivalled magnitude, signalling in all its splendour the superior rank of its lord, the Emperor. Significantly, Gilbert uses the term *miles* not just to describe the nameless retinues of the great lords, but also to characterise at least some of the magnates. Thus Leopold, duke of Austria, was a *miles probus et largus* who led his 500 *milites*.[37] This is no isolated case. Joachim Bumke has shown that towards the end of the twelfth century the authors of German vernacular texts started to extend the use of the term "knight" from men of lower rank to those of the upper aristocracy, including the king.[38] The term had become *hoffähig* (acceptable at court). The festivities of Mainz make this all too clear.[39] The girding with the sword of the king's sons—their admission into the chivalric community and their public commitment to the chivalric ethos—took centre stage. It was followed by a demonstration of generosity, when

che Welt, ed. Josef Fleckenstein (Berlin: Siedler, 2002), 173–229, at 219–29; C. Stephen Jaeger, *The Origins of Courtliness—Civilizing Trends and the Formation of Courtly Ideals, 939–1210* (Philadelphia: University of Pennsylvania Press, 1991), 155–61. On the term *urbanitas* see the fundamental work by Thomas Zotz, "Urbanitas. Zur Bedeutung und Funktion einer antiken Wertvorstellung innerhalb der höfischen Kultur des hohen Mittelalters," in Fleckenstein, *Curialitas*, 295–308; Jaeger, *Origins of Courtliness*, 143–47.

34. Gilbert of Mons, *La chronique de Gislebert de Mons*, ed. Léon Vanderkindere (Brussels: Kiessling, 1904), 157–60.

35. Otto of Sankt Blasien, *Chronica*, 37.

36. Gilbert of Mons, *Chronique*, 157.

37. Ibid., 156.

38. Bumke, *Studien zum Ritterbegriff*, 92–94; Josef Fleckenstein, "Kaisertum und Rittertum in der Stauferzeit," in *Die Ritterorden zwischen geistlicher und weltlicher Macht im Mittelalter*, ed. Zenon Hubert Nowak, Ordines militares 5 (Toruń: Uniwersytet Mikołaja Kopernika, 1990), 7–20.

39. The literature on this event is vast. Of particular importance in this context are: Elsbeth Orth, "Formen und Funktionen der höfischen Rittererhebung," in *Curialitas*, ed. Fleckenstein, 128–70, who also analyses what other writers than Gilbert of Mons had to say about the festivities, in particular the knighting of Frederick's sons; Josef Fleckenstein, "Das Turnier als höfisches Fest im hochmittelalterlichen Deutschland," in *Turnier*, ed. Fleckenstein, 229–56, at 236–37; Fleckenstein, "Friedrich Barbarossa und das Rittertum;" Krieg, "Friedrich Barbarossa und das Rittertum;" Knut Görich, *Friedrich Barbarossa. Eine Biographie* (Munich: C. H. Beck, 2011), 505–14.

the magnates lavishly handed out precious gifts not just in honour of Frederick and his sons, but, as Gilbert notes, also to spread the fame of their own names. On the following two days the festivities were continued by a showing of knightly strength and elegance when, according to Gilbert, 20,000 knights began to show their prowess on horseback. Without arms and exchanging no blows, the knights raced their horses and sported their shields, lances and banners. The emperor, even though as Gilbert emphasised, "he was no greater or more becoming in body than the others," headed the group.[40] As leader of a most splendid imperial chivalry, Frederick was set in a perfect frame. Gilbert's description of the event also shows that, ideally, personal qualities, not rank, differentiated the knights. At the same time, however, though this ideal could distinguish an individual and perhaps even cause his advancement in society, it did not question the social hierarchy. Regardless of his knightly qualities, the Emperor held the foremost position. The day in Mainz, however, ended in chaos. In the evening, a heavy storm flattened the Emperor's chapel and some of the houses which had been built just for the occasion, as well as a number of tents. Some people even died in the ruins. A tournament scheduled for neighbouring Ingelheim was cancelled. Gilbert provides no reason for it, but another chronicler, Otto of Sankt Blasien, had a clear opinion. The storm was a divine signal that the behaviour of the "sons of this world" had been far too vain and some of the more prudent men understood this.[41] In light of the prohibition of tournaments by Pope Alexander III at the Lateran Council only five years earlier,[42] some of the bishops may indeed have had second thoughts about the appropriateness of the tournament and may have advised Frederick to cancel it.[43] Ecclesiastical elements were not absent at the festivities at Mainz. After all, the framework was the feast of Pentecost.[44] None-

40. Gilbert of Mons, *Chronique*, 156–57.
41. Otto of Sankt Blasien, *Chronica*, 38.
42. *The General Councils of Latin Christendom. From Constantinople to Pavia-Siena (869–1424)*, ed. Antonio Garcia y Garcia et. al., Conciliorum oecumenicorum generaliumque decreta 2.1 (Turnhout: Brepols, 2013), 142, chap. 20. Cf. the efforts made by Archbishop Wichmann of Magdeburg to prevent knights from participating in tournaments after sixteen had died at tournaments within one year, *Chronicon Montis Sereni*, ed. Ernst Ehrenfeuchter, Monumenta Germaniae Historica, Scriptores (in Folio) 23 (Hanover: Hahn, 1974), 130–226, at 155–56.
43. Krieg, "Friedrich Barbarossa und das Rittertum," 136.
44. The knighting of the king's sons may also have contained ecclesiastical elements, Orth, "Formen und Funktionen," 151. Gilbert used the verb *ordinare* to describe the girding with the sword of the king's sons. Orth, "Formen und Fuktionen," 158 and n. 123,

theless, compared to the diet of 1188, the dominance by the secular aspects of chivalry is obvious. It is therefore no surprise to see Arnold of Lübeck commenting on Frederick's crusade a couple of years later that the Emperor went off *quam pro deo tam pro honore temporali* and that, when they were received by the king of Hungary, they organised a tournament.[45] At the end of the twelfth century, the ideals of chivalry were firmly rooted in ecclesiastical as well as secular values. These ideals provided the framework for a way of life to which men of different ranks could aspire, because it was mainly based on personal qualities. It thus offered the opportunity to gain honour for the king and the unfree *ministerialis* alike. For the latter in particular, the emphasis on personal virtue opened the way for social climbing. In principle this did not by any means challenge the existing social order. Firstly, the climbing took place within the accepted framework of rules and values. Instead of weakening it, the successful knight thus strengthened the existing social and political order. Secondly, loyalty (*fidelitas*), a key element in stabilising hierarchically-structured societies, was also a key value of true chivalric behaviour—it reminded the ambitious knight to respect the social hierarchy. Chivalry was thus able to create the sense of a community and the chance of personal advancement without automatically levelling the differences in social and sometimes even legal status of its members.

The Significance of Knighting

Entry to this chivalrous community was granted through a ritual: the girding with the sword. There is not enough evidence to trace its history in detail in the Empire in the eleventh and twelfth centuries.[46] Only

provides an analysis of Gilbert's use of the verb *ordinare*. In this context it probably means "promoted to knighthood according to the proper form." But it is noteworthy that Gilbert saw at least parallels to ecclesiastical ordination. See also Crouch, "When was Chivalry?" on the meaning of *Ordene de Chevalerie*, below.

45. Arnold of Lübeck, *Chronica Slavorum*, ed. Johann Martin Lappenberg, Monumenta Germaniae Historica, Scriptores rerum Germanicarum in usum scholarum separatim editi [14] (Hanover: Hahn, 1868), 127–28 (Frederick's motivation), 131 (tournament in Hungary).

46. What follows is based on the fundamental article by Orth, "Formen und Funktionen;" see also Bumke, *Studien zum Ritterbegriff*, 101–18; Bumke, *Höfische Kultur*, 318–41; Zotz, "Ritterliche Welt," 198–99; Karl Leyser, "Early Medieval Canon Law and the Beginnings of Knighthood," in *Institutionen, Kultur und Gesellschaft im Mittelalter. Festschrift für Josef Fleckenstein zu seinem 65. Geburtstag*, ed. Lutz Fenske, Werner Rösener, and Thomas Zotz (Sigmaringen: Thorbecke, 1984), 549–66; Hechberger, *Adel im*

for the second half of the twelfth century do the sources allow a closer look, and it is certainly significant that the German term *Schwertleite* appears in the vernacular sources only from the mid-twelfth century onwards.[47] They portray the girding as a ritual in which ecclesiastical elements were increasingly integrated.[48] It thus visualised the twin roots of chivalry. For members of the aristocracy, the legal significance of the ritual of knighting became less and less important.[49] The original close link between the granting of arms and majority existed only loosely by the mid-twelfth century. Occasionally the girding could mean reaching the age of majority, but it was not a necessary rite of passage. Aristocrats could exercise their lordship and engage in warfare without having been girded.[50] The ritual could thus be used with some flexibility and it was often combined with other important moments of transition in life such as marriage or the enfeoffment with one's lordship.[51] Even if the aristocrat could choose the moment of the knighting, the knighting was a social obligation he could hardly avoid. Men of high standing were expected to be girded with the sword eventually.[52] In the literary world, it was King Arthur who made knights, and at the courts of the twelfth century this was a matter for the great lords, ideally the king himself.[53] The public effect of the knighting of high-born sons could be increased by promoting a number of other young men to knighthood on the same occasion.[54] They thus formed a knightly entourage for the new knight, possibly their (future) lord and certainly their social superior. Such mass promotions were not limited to courtly feasts. They could also be performed on military cam-

---

fränkisch-deutschen Mittelalter, 436–41. An older work is Wilhelm Erben, "Schwertleite und Ritterschlag. Beiträge zu einer Rechtsgeschichte der Waffen," *Zeitschrift für historische Waffen- und Kostümkunde* 8 (1917–20): 105–68.

47. Bumke, *Studien zum Ritterbegriff*, 101.
48. Orth, "Formen und Funktionen," 143–53, esp. at 150–52.
49. Ibid., 155; Bumke, *Studien zum Ritterbegriff*, 107; and see below.
50. Orth, "Formen und Funktionen," 155, 157.
51. Ibid., 156.
52. Ibid., 157–58. A much later example provides the chronicler John of Viktring, who claimed in the early fourteenth century that the daughter of King Conrad IV, Elisabeth, had stipulated that, in order to marry her, Meinhard of Görz had first to become a knight: John of Viktring, *Iohannis abbatis Victoriensis Liber certarum historiarum*, ed. Fedor Schneider, 2 vols., Monumenta Germaniae Historica, Scriptores rerum Germanicarum in usum scholarum separatim editi [36.1–2] (Hanover and Leipzig: Hahn, 1909–10), 1: 194.
53. Orth, "Formen und Funktionen," 156–57.
54. Ibid., 162–64; Bumke, *Studien zum Ritterbegriff*, 115–18.

paigns, thereby strengthening the morale of the troops.[55] Among the
men promoted on such occasions, we should expect a good number
of *ministeriales*. However, the individual girding with the sword was
not necessarily a privilege of the aristocrat or the freeborn. In his *Vita*,
Arnold of Selenhofen (d. 1160), archbishop of Mainz, is said to have
girded Meingot, son of his *ministerialis* Meingot, with the sword.[56]

Given that men of very different background could be girded with
the sword there is little reason to believe that the ritual had a single specific meaning. What knighting meant to the individual differed
according to his social and legal status. We have already seen that for
an aristocrat the knighting was part of his life style, and something
to be done eventually. It was an occasion to celebrate entry into the
chivalrous community. For the father of the knighted man, it could
be used to manifest his and his family's rank. For a *ministerialis*, the
situation was different. From his point of view, the girding with the
sword was not just an expected rite of passage that one eventually
went through, but a chance to improve his position in society. The
knighting was an important way to associate with free and noble men.
He was now a knight just like them. In the mid-twelfth century, the
Ebersheimer Chronicle noted that the members of the courtly *familia
ministerialis* had become so noble (*nobilis*) and bellicose that they
appeared like free men.[57] The knighting blurred the legal differences
beyond recognition. Behaving like an aristocratic knight, a *ministerialis* stood a good chance of being treated like one.[58] This explains why
the knighting of Meingot was described as a special favour granted to
him by Archbishop Arnold. For the author of the *Vita*, it was a means
by which the archbishop could express his affection for his *ministerialis*.[59] In addition, Arnold provided him and his brother with fiefs[60]—an
important indicator that knighting alone was no guarantee of social
advancement; it also needed landed substance.

---

55. E.g. *Chronica Slavorum*, 131.
56. *Vita Arnoldi archiepiscopi Moguntinensis. Die Lebensbeschreibung des Mainzer
Erzbischofs Arnold von Selenhofen*, ed. and trans. Stefan Burkhardt, Klöster als Innovation-
slabore 2 (Regensburg: Schnell und Steiner, 2014), 74–75. The thesis that the *Vita* is a modern forgery no longer stands. Following the forgery-thesis Bumke disregarded this evidence
in his discussion of the girding with the sword, Bumke, *Studien zum Ritterbegriff*, 105–6.
57. *Chronicon Eberheimense*, ed. Ludwig Weiland, Monumenta Germaniae Historica,
Scriptores (in Folio) 23 (Hanover: Hahn, 1874), 427–53, at 433.
58. Cf. Keupp, *Dienst und Verdienst*, 82–98.
59. *Vita Arnoldi*, 74–75.
60. Ibid.

The Role of the Court in Shaping the Knights as a Group

As far as the sources allow us to tell—and we do not know how many people were actually knighted—knighting was generally perceived to be a good and desirable act across the ranks of warriors in the second half of the twelfth century. In the course of the thirteenth century, however, we can observe a more nuanced perception of the ritual. In particular among the sons of simple knights, we see a number of people who were not knighted and, apparently quite deliberately, remained squires (*armigeri, Edelknechte*).[61] This development was due to processes of social differentiation that reshaped the hierarchy of the aristocracy in the Empire. These processes are more clearly visible at the top where towards the end of the twelfth century the imperial princes began to emerge as the new elite group.[62] But they can also be observed at the bottom end of the aristocracy. The reign of Frederick Barbarossa not only witnessed the great staging of chivalry as a specific way of life common to men of different ranks, it also saw the first measures to restrict the entry to knighthood. In 1186 or 1188, Frederick decreed that sons of priests, deacons and peasants should not obtain the *cingulum militare*; a serf should be deprived of all knightly rights.[63] It is telling that this was decided during the years in which the Emperor celebrated chivalry most intensively. The splendid courts and their feasts provided the opportunity of association and social promotion, but they also increased the pressure of social differentiation. Precisely because on these occasions a great number of men came together, it became necessary to emphasise differences in rank. Precisely because these courts fostered the idea of a chivalric identity and the association

61. See, e.g., Volker Rödel, *Reichslehenswesen, Ministerialität, Burgmannschaft und Niederadel. Studien zur Rechts- und Sozialgeschichte des Adels in den Mittel- und Oberrheinlanden während des 13. und 14. Jahrhunderts*, Quellen und Forschungen zur hessischen Geschichte 38 (Darmstadt: Historische Kommission für Hessen, 1979), at 432–511; Volker Rödel, "Multi ignobiles facti milites. Zur Entstehung des Niederadels als Stand," *Jahrbuch für westdeutsche Landesgeschichte* 41 (2015): 7–32; Fleckenstein, "Die Entstehung des niederen Adels und das Rittertum," 31–39.

62. The starting point is still: Julius Ficker, *Vom Reichsfürstenstande. Forschungen zur Geschichte der Reichsverfassung zunächst im 12. und 13. Jahrhunderte*, 2 vols. (Innsbruck: Wagner, 1861–1923; repr. Aalen: Scientia, 1961); more recently, Jörg Peltzer, *Der Rang der Pfalzgrafen bei Rhein. Die Gestaltung der politisch-sozialen Ordnung des Reichs im 13. und 14. Jahrhundert*, RANK. Politisch-soziale Ordnungen im mittelalterlichen Europa 2 (Ostfildern: Thorbecke, 2013).

63. *Die Urkunden Friedrichs I. Teil 4. 1181–1190*, ed. Heinrich Appelt, Monumenta Germaniae Historica, Diplomata F I.4 (Hanover: Hahn, 1990), 273–77, no. 988.

of knighthood and aristocracy, the identification of who belonged to this group and who did not became more pressing.

The integrating nature of the great twelfth-century courts and their assemblies and the intensifying of the processes of social differentiation were no contradictions, but two sides of the same coin.[64] Around 1200, these processes were still very much in flux, and as to chivalry, it was not yet entirely clear what was the decisive criterion for membership. The regulations of a public peace for the county of Hainaut, agreed on by Count Baldwin VI and members of the regional aristocracy in 1200, stated that those sons of knights who, by their twenty-fifth birthday had not been knighted, should be treated like peasants in the context of the peace.[65] According to this line of thought, knightly birth alone was not enough to enjoy knightly treatment. For this, the girding with the sword was required. However, in the long run, this view combining dynastic and personal qualities did not prevail in determining the difference between knights and peasants. Knightly birth became the decisive criterion, even though the king retained the prerogative to promote to knighthood men from non-knightly backgrounds.[66] For the dukes, counts and most of the barons (*Herren*) this development was of secondary importance. But further down the hierarchy, the impact was much more profound. Due to the close association of knighthood and aristocracy in the second half of the twelfth century, the differences between knighthood and aristocracy became blurred. Being a knight became almost synonymous with being an aristocrat. Consequently, for the mass of knightly *ministeriales* who did not have stellar careers like Markward of Annweiler (who was freed and promoted

64. On the important role of the court in shaping the political and social hierarchy, see Hans-Werner Goetz, "Der ‚rechte' Sitz. Die Symbolik von Rang und Herrschaft im Hohen Mittelalter im Spiegel der Sitzordnung," in *Symbole des Alltags—Alltag der Symbole. Festschrift für Harry Kühnel*, ed. Gertrud Blaschitz, Helmut Hundsbichler, Gerhard Jaritz, and Elisabeth Vavra (Graz: Akademische Druck- und Verlagsanstalt, 1992), 11–47; Karl-Heinz Spieß, "Rangdenken und Rangstreit im Mittelalter," in *Zeremoniell und Raum. 4. Symposium der Residenzen-Kommission der Akademie der Wissenschaften in Göttingen veranstaltet gemeinsam mit dem Deutschen Historischen Institut Paris und dem Historischen Institut der Universität Potsdam. Potsdam, 25. bis 27. September 1994*, ed. Werner Paravicini, Residenzenforschung 6 (Sigmaringen: Thorbecke, 1997), 39–61; Karl-Heinz Spieß, "Kommunikationsformen im Hochadel und am Königshof im Spätmittelalter," in *Formen und Funktionen öffentlicher Kommunikation im Mittelalter*, ed. Gerd Althoff, Vorträge und Forschungen 51 (Stuttgart: Thorbecke, 2001), 261–90; Keupp, *Dienst und Verdienst*, 381–88; Peltzer, *Rang der Pfalzgrafen bei Rhein*, 336–419.

65. *Thesaurus novus anecdotorum*, ed. Edmond Martène and Ursin Durand, 5 vols. (Paris: Delaulne, 1717), 1: cols. 765–69; Fleckenstein, *Rittertum und ritterliche Welt*, 167.

66. Rödel, "Multi ignobiles facti milites," 26–27.

to ducal dignity by his Emperor Henry VI[67]) but also for simple free-born knights and even impoverished barons (*Herren*), knightly birth became the decisive marker of aristocracy.[68] Whether or not they were girded with the sword was of only secondary importance to their status. It was down to individual circumstances (their ambitions, career paths and wealth) whether the knighting was performed or not.

The poem "The Two Squires" composed by Stricker in the first half of the thirteenth century nicely illustrates this situation.[69] Two squires argued over the need to become knighted. One of them saw no necessity to undergo the ritual. He argued that a knightly life cost too much, the service demanded from knights by their lords was too harsh, and the lords did not honour them as they had done in the past. Finally, it made no difference to the social standing of his family. His wife and his children would be as noble as if he were a knight. The other squire took a very different and seemingly more traditional view: (knightly) birth, reason, (powerful and elegant) body and land were conditions for knighthood, which, if a squire possessed all of this thanks to divine mercy, almost compelled him to become a knight. Otherwise, he would act against God's wish. In addition, becoming a knight honoured the squire's family. This reasoning finally prevailed in the debating contest, but in reality quite a few squires decided against being knighted. Their thoughts may well have been similar to the argument developed by Stricker's reluctant squire.

As a common denominator, knightly birth played a crucial role in merging the *ministeriales* and the low-ranked freeborn knights to the lower aristocracy, a slow and regionally diverse process going on into

67. Burchard of Ursberg, *Die Chronik des Propstes Burchard von Ursberg*, ed. Oswald Holder-Egger and Bernhard von Simson, Monumenta Germaniae Historica, Scriptores rerum Germanicarum in usum scholarum separatim editi [16] (Hanover: Hahn, 1916), 72–73. His remarkable career has often been treated by scholarship, see, e.g., Keupp, *Dienst und Verdienst*, 250–85; Jan Ulrich Keupp, "Der Ruf des Südens: Pfälzer Ritter in Italien (12. bis 14. Jahrhundert)," *Mitteilungen des Historischen Vereins der Pfalz* 108 (2010): 381–97, at 382–89.
68. Rödel, "Reichslehenswesen," 432–511; Rödel, "Multi ignobiles facti milites," 7–32; Karl-Heinz Spieß, "Ständische Abgrenzung und soziale Differenzierung zwischen Hochadel und Ritteradel im Spätmittelalter," *Rheinische Vierteljahrsblätter* 56 (1992): 181–205.
69. *Die Kleindichtung des Stricker*, ed. Wolfgang Wilfried Mölleken, Gayle Agler, and Robert E. Lewis, 5 vols, Göppinger Arbeiten zur Germanistik 107 (Göppingen: Kuemmerle, 1973–78), 1: 92–115, no. 4; Stephen L. Wailes, *Studien zur Kleindichtung des Stricker*, Philologische Studien und Quellen 104 (Berlin: E. Schmidt, 1981), 197–209.

the fourteenth century.[70] Knight(s) became the collective term for members of this layer to distinguish them from the counts and barons. It thus became a denominator of a certain rank within the aristocracy. Yet, it did not quite transform into a personal title like duke or count. While those titles were borne by men and women alike, *miles* was almost exclusively reserved for men. The Alheit, who called herself a young "knightess" in 1342, remained an exception.[71] The functional connotations of the term knight remained strong.

Conclusion

The formation of knighthood was a lengthy process pre-conditioned by the role of the *miles* as warrior and vassal in the eleventh century and subsequently shaped by the church (crusades) and the court (chivalric values). At the end of the twelfth century, the idea of chivalry provided the framework for a way of life to which men of different ranks could aspire. Mainly based on personal qualities, it offered the opportunity to gain honour for the king and the unfree *ministerialis* alike. The knightly investiture had no specific single meaning. Its significance depended on the social and legal status of the individual. In the thirteenth century knightly birth became the decisive criterion to determine knightly status. For the upper nobility this was of secondary importance, but further down the social scale it demarcated the difference between noble and non-noble. Consequently, "knight(s)" became the collective term for members of the lower aristocracy and thus became a term of aristocratic rank. The association of the term "knight" with the lower aristocracy did not mean the exclusive appropriation of the term by that social group. The chivalric idea as a specific way of life to be aspired to by all members of aristocracy remained very powerful. In fact, the Late Middle Ages developed the chivalric orders into an institution emphasising chivalry as a noble, personal virtue and hence not bound to a specific aristocratic rank. Created at first in Western Europe in the fourteenth century, the idea was later also adopted in the Empire. It seems significant however, that this was not the only form in which chivalric life was organised

70. See the works quoted above [n. 64] and the articles in Fleckenstein, ed., *Herrschaft und Stand*.
71. Rödel, "Multi ignobiles facti milites," 22–23.

in the Empire. Besides the orders organised at the courts of the magnates, the members of the lower aristocracy, the knights, created their own associations, in which they mostly stayed among themselves.[72] As different as they were in their origins, both organisations offered their members the opportunity to feel like a *chevalier* and to adopt a chivalric identity. In the later Middle Ages, the term *miles* thus had two very different meanings: the *chevalier* as a way of life aspired to by aristocrats across the ranks and the knight as a member of the lower aristocracy. This, however, was by no means an exclusive characteristic of the situation in the Empire, but appears to have been a much more widespread phenomenon. Research into knighthood remains a task of European scope.

---

72. It should be noted that the chivalric orders in the Empire could be much more independent from the princely courts than in Western Europe and that quite a few of them were organised by the lower aristocracy, Andreas Ranft, *Adelsgesellschaften. Gruppenbildung und Genossenschaft im spätmittelalterlichen Reich*, Kieler historische Studien 38 (Sigmaringen: Thorbecke, 1994); Tanja Storn-Jaschkowitz, *Gesellschaftsverträge adliger Schwureinungen im Spätmittelalter—Edition und Typologie* (Berlin: Logos, 2007); Holger Kruse, Werner Paravicini and Andreas Ranft, eds., *Ritterorden und Adelsgesellschaften im spätmittelalterlichen Deutschland. Ein systematisches Verzeichnis*, Kieler Werkstücke: Reihe D, Beiträge zur europäischen Geschichte des späten Mittelalters 1 (Bern, Frankfurt, New York, and Paris: Lang, 1991); Jörg Peltzer, "Rang und Performanz. Die Signifikanz des Tuns und Lassens für den eigenen Rang," in *Die Performanz der Mächtigen. Rangordnung und Idoneität in höfischen Gesellschaften des späten Mittelalters*, ed. Klaus Oschema, Cristina Andenna, Gert Melville, and Jörg Peltzer, RANK. Politisch-soziale Ordnungen im mittelalterlichen Europa 5 (Ostfildern, Thorbecke, 2015), 55–72, at 67–72. Another, less formalised, area of chivalric behaviour across the ranks were the Prussian crusades in the Late Middle Ages, Werner Paravicini, *Die Preussenreisen des europäischen Adels*, so far 2 vols., Beihefte der Francia 17 (Sigmaringen: Thorbecke, 1989–); and his papers in Jan Hirschbiegel, Andreas Ranft, and Jörg Wettlaufer, eds., *Werner Paravicini, Edelleute und Kaufleute im Norden Europas, gesammelte Aufsätze* (Ostfildern: Thorbecke, 2007), and Ulf Christian Ewert, Andreas Ranft, and Stephan Selzer, eds., *Werner Paravicini, Noblesse. Studien zum adligen Leben im spätmittelalterlichen Europa. Gesammelte Aufsätze* (Ostfildern: Thorbecke, 2012).

Eljas OKSANEN

KNIGHTS, MERCENARIES AND PAID SOLDIERS: MILITARY IDENTITIES IN THE ANGLO-NORMAN *REGNUM*

The economic transformations of the High Middle Ages profoundly influenced the emergence of chivalric culture and knightly identity. During the twelfth and thirteenth centuries western Europe witnessed unprecedented commercial expansion, urban growth and the monetisation of society. New fiscal revenues, together with the administrative advances linked to the so-called renaissance of the twelfth century, strengthened the hand of royal administrations and altered the economics of warfare. Paid soldiers had probably always been a presence on medieval battlefields, but now stipendiarii *emerged as an increasingly distinct social and military category of armed service. For the Anglo-Norman kings these fighters, many of whom were foreigners, represented a flexible and often logistically superior alternative to traditional forms of service owed by their landed vassals. In consequence the creation of an Anglo-Norman chivalric culture during the late twelfth century was substantially informed by the aristocratic elite's need to secure their political position in the face of encroachment from other social classes. With specific reference to Welsh and Flemish paid soldiers in Anglo-Norman service, this paper explores how the development of stereotyped images of the mercenary—greedy, lowborn, treacherous, uncontrollably violent—paralleled and defined the concurrent birth of knightly identity.*

Soon you could have heard Flemings from Flanders, and French and Picards shouting aloud: "We have not come to this country to hang around but to destroy the king, Henry, the old warrior, and to get for ourselves the wool of England that we so much desire." My lords, the truth is that most of them were weavers, they do not know how to bear arms like knights, and why they had come was to pick up plunder and the spoils of war...[1]

---

1. "Tost i purrïez oïr e bien en halt crier entre Flamens de Flandres et Franceis e Puier: 'Nus n'eimes pas en cest païs venuz pur sujorner, mes pur lu rei destruire, Henri, le vielz guerier, e pur aver sa leine, dunt avum desirier.' Seignurs, ço est la verité: li plus furent telier, ne sevent porter armes a lei de chevalier, mes pur ço furent venuz, pur aver guain e guerre..." Jordan Fantosme, *Jordan of Fantosme's Chronicle*, ed. and trans. R.C. Johnston (Oxford: Oxford University Press, 1981), 72.

> Still, he [King Henry II] made all the resistance against them
> that he possibly could: for he had with him 20,000 Brabanters,
> who served him faithfully, but not without the large pay which
> he gave them.[2]

The above lines give two perspectives on the use of paid soldiers
during the Angevin civil war of 1173–74: one is an imagined scene
described by the courtly poet Jordan Fantosme, condemning soldiers
brought over to England by rebel magnates as unworthy opponents
to the kingdom's knightly defenders; the other is a laconic remark by
the king's clerk Roger of Howden, recording in his political chronicle
the victorious monarch's reliance on the very same class of mercenary
hirelings. These attitudes preserve contemporary concerns and opin-
ions on the increasing use of paid soldiers in late twelfth-century thea-
tres of war and, taking its cue from them, this paper will approach the
question of chivalry and knightly identity from a decidedly unchiv-
alrous perspective. Rather than directly investigating the chivalrous
knight, I will examine the social and cultural spaces around him, for
these excluded regions were just as crucial in defining knightly identity. The focus will be on the image of the mercenary and the paid
soldier from the end of the eleventh century to the beginning of the
thirteenth in the Anglo-Norman world and its environs in north-western Europe, and how its development helped to define the social and
military identity of Anglo-Norman knighthood.

Mercenaries have historically had a bad reputation. In popular imagination and in the works of political philosophy alike venal soldiers of
fortune represent the antithesis to combatants whose motivations are
construed along the lines of loyalty to God, king or country.[3] Various
forms of financial support in return for military service have been historically ubiquitous, however, and the distinction between a grasping
mercenary and a loyal retainer in receipt of a cash salary may be a

---

2. "Sed ipse in quantum potuit resistebat illis. Habuit enim secum viginti millia Braban-
cenorum, qui fideliter servierunt illi, et non sine magna mercede, quam eis dedit." Roger of
Howden, *Chronica magistri Rogeri de Houedene*, ed. William Stubbs, 4 vols., Rolls Series 51
(London: Longman, 1868–71), 2: 47; Roger of Howden, *The Annals of Roger de Hoveden*,
trans. Henry T. Riley, 2 vols. (London: Bohn, 1853; repr., Felinfach: Llanerch, 1996), 1: 368.

3. Sarah Percy, *Mercenaries. The History of a Norm in International Relations* (Oxford:
Oxford University Press, 2007), 68–93 for a historical overview of the use of mercenaries
in Europe. See also a wide-ranging selection of papers on medieval mercenaries in John
France, ed., *Mercenaries and Paid Men. The Mercenary Identity in the Middle Ages* (Boston and Leiden: Brill, 2008).

matter of perspective or propaganda. The word "mercenary" itself is thus problematic, and in this paper my general preference is to use either the less charged term "paid soldier" to mean persons whose term of service was temporary and who received primarily monetary compensation, or else the terminology with which the contemporaries themselves designated specific groups of fighters. As will be discussed a complication of terms was very much part of the history of how "knightly" and "mercenary" identities interacted in the Anglo-Norman period. Chivalry, here understood as a self-conscious code and culture among the secular elite, emerged during the decades on both sides of the year 1200.[4] One powerful dynamic that drove its emergence was the older military elite's desire to distinguish itself from soldiers of lower-class background with whom they served and competed for patronage. In order to examine this topic, this paper will first discuss the history of paid military service in the Anglo-Norman realm, and then investigate English attitudes towards paid soldiers with particular reference to two classes of foreign fighters: the Welsh and the Flemish.

Paid Military Service in the Anglo-Norman *Regnum*

Perhaps the most influential early Anglo-Norman text to guide the ranking of military service by virtue is Archbishop Anselm of Canterbury's (d. 1109) sermon on the ties that bound together lords and their followers, as related by his biographer Eadmer. The highest form of service is one performed by men who hold land from their lord, compared to angels in their loyalty; next are those who seek to recover their rightful inheritance through service, likened to monks aspiring to Heaven; and those who serve for wages are relegated to the lowest rung, for service in expectation of material rewards lacks the hallmarks of the true and faithful loyalty properly owed to worldly princes and the heavenly Lord alike.[5] But even though his preferences were clear, Anselm did not claim waged service to be immoral as such. This judgement, for certain categories of paid soldiers, would not be made until later in the twelfth

4. David Crouch, *The Birth of Nobility. Constructing Aristocracy in England and France, 900–1300* (Harlow: Pearson/Longman, 2005), 80–88, and see his chapter "When was Chivalry? Evolution of a Code" in this volume.

5. Eadmer, *The Life of St Anselm*, ed. R.W. Southern, Oxford Medieval Texts (Oxford: Clarendon Press, 1972), 94–96; Stephen Brown, "Military Service and Monetary Reward in the Eleventh and Twelfth Centuries," *History* 74 (1989): 36–37.

century. Responding to recent spasms of warfare, and the accompanying looting of Church property and attacks against non-combatants,
the Third Lateran Council of 1179 excommunicated Brabanters (*Bra-
bançons*) and other *routiers*, which by then were general terms designating paid soldiers of lower class origin.[6] Walter Map, another courtly
author writing in the late twelfth century, attributed to them heresy
and other evils.[7] Jordan Fantosme's views on the Flemish "weavers"
were shared by many contemporary and near-contemporary authors
who wrote of such fighters as being nothing but rapacious, greedy and
untrustworthy villains.[8] These qualities served to distinguish them from
those espousing emergent chivalric mores such as the concept of largesse, or liberality with one's worldly wealth, which created a strong
contrast to a mercenary's primarily financial terms of service.[9]

Yet, this rhetoric flies in the face of the realities of warfare. Paid
soldiers had no particular monopoly over wartime pillaging, although
they were made convenient scapegoats by ecclesiastical and courtly
authors.[10] And since at least the classic study of the finances of war in
the Anglo-Norman realm by J.O. Prestwich it has been commonplace
to contextualise paid service as its integral feature.[11] Narrative sources
show that there is an unbroken continuity in the use of all types of
paid soldiers including paid knights—in Latin usually called *solidarii,
stipendiarii* and *milites stipendiarii*—by the rulers of England since
the Norman Conquest.[12] William the Conqueror (1066–87) used paid
knights from the earliest stages of his consolidation of the kingdom.
In 1068 he discharged *solidarios milites* from his service with liberal
rewards, and in 1069–70 gathered another force for campaigning in

6. *Decrees of the Ecumenical Councils*, ed. Norman P. Tanner, 2 vols. (Georgetown:
Georgetown University Press, 1990), 1: 224–25, § 27; H. Géraud, "Les routiers au XIIe
siècle," *Bibliothèque de l'École des Chartes* 3 (1841): 125–47.

7. Walter Map, *De Nugis Curialium. Courtiers' Trifles*, ed. M. James, C.N.L. Brooke
and R.A.B. Mynors, Oxford Medieval Texts (Oxford: Clarendon Press, 1983), 118.

8. Michael Prestwich, *Armies and Warfare in the Middle Ages. The English Experience*
(New Haven: Yale University Press, 1996), 152–53.

9. Crouch, *Birth of Nobility*, 68–71.

10. John France, *Western Warfare in the Age of the Crusades, 1000–1300* (Ithaca: Cornell University Press, 1998), 70–76.

11. J.O. Prestwich, "War and Finance in the Anglo-Norman State," *Transactions of the
Royal Historical Society* 5th Series 4 (1954): 19–43.

12. Ibid.; C. Warren Hollister, *The Military Organisation of Norman England* (Oxford:
Clarendon Press, 1965), 178–86 and for a more recent overview Michael Prestwich,
"Money and Mercenaries in English Medieval Armies," in *England and Germany in the
High Middle Ages*, ed. Alfred Haverkamp and Hanna Vollrath (Oxford, 1996), 129–50.

the northern and eastern parts of the country.[13] Again in 1085, threatened by a Danish invasion, William called up an army of paid soldiers from the continent.[14] His son William Rufus (1087–1100) was criticised by William of Malmesbury for his open-handedness with his men: "sellers sold to him at their own prices and knights fixed their own rate of pay."[15] Abbot Suger called Rufus a merchant of knights.[16] The Anglo-Norman kings sought the cooperation of neighbouring princes in the search for military auxiliaries: the treaties of 1101, 1110 and 1163 concern a deal that obliged the count of Flanders to provide 500 or 1,000 mounted soldiers to the king of England in return for an annual money fief.[17] Narrative sources refer to several similar accords going back to the reign of William the Conqueror.[18] As will be discussed in more detail below, paid foreign soldiers arrived to England in large numbers during the civil wars of Stephen's reign (1135–54), and formed an important part of the armies of the Angevin kings from Henry II (1154–89) to John (1199–1216).

The ubiquity of paid knightly service is best illustrated by the fact that it was a common feature of the *familia regis*, the royal household, of the English kings—that most central institution of royal power and government. As Marjorie Chibnall's study of the military household of Henry I has shown, it brought together men from both high aris-

13. Orderic Vitalis, *The Ecclesiastical History of Orderic Vitalis*, ed. and trans. Marjorie Chibnall, 6 vols., Oxford Medieval Texts (Oxford: Clarendon Press, 1969–80), 2: 220, 236.

14. *Chronicon Monasterii de Abingdon*, ed. Joseph Stevenson, 2 vols., Rolls Series 2 (London: Longman, 1858), 2: 11; John of Worcester, *The Chronicle of John of Worcester. Vol. III: The Annals from 1067 to 1140 with the Gloucester Interpolations and the Continuation to 1141*, ed. and trans. P. McGurk, Oxford Medieval Texts (Oxford: Clarendon Press, 1998), 42; William of Malmesbury, *Gesta Regum Anglorum*, vol. 1, ed. and trans. R.A.B. Mynors, R.M. Thomson, and M. Winterbottom, vol. 2, R. M Thomson and H. Winterbottom, *General Introduction and Commentary*, Oxford Medieval Texts (Oxford: Clarendon Press, 1998–99), 1: 482.

15. "... cui pro libito venditor distraheret mercimonium, et miles pacisceretur stipendium." William of Malmesbury, *Gesta Regum*, 556.

16. Suger, *Vie de Louis VI Le Gros*, ed. Henri Waquet, Les classiques de l'histoire de France au Moyen Âge 46 (Paris: Belles Lettres, 1964), 8.

17. *Diplomatic Documents Preserved in the Public Records Office*, ed. Pierre Chaplais (London: H.M. Staionary Office, 1964), 1–12; "The Anglo-Flemish Treaty of 1101," trans. Elisabeth van Houts, *Anglo-Norman Studies* 21 (1999): 169–174; François-Louis Ganshof, Raoul Van Caenegem, and Adriaan Verhulst, "Note sur le premier traité Anglo-Flamand de Douvres," *Revue du Nord* 40 (1958): 245–57; Renée Nip, "The Political Relations between England and Flanders (1066–1128)," *Anglo-Norman Studies* 21 (1998): 145–67; Eljas Oksanen, *Flanders and the Anglo-Norman World, 1066–1216* (Cambridge: Cambridge University Press, 2012), 54–72.

18. Oksanen, *Flanders and the Anglo-Norman World*, 56–57.

tocratic families and common backgrounds. Their rewards included wages and money fiefs.[19] In early Anglo-Norman England there was nothing inherently wrong about monetary reward in itself.[20] In an often-quoted passage by Orderic Vitalis the *milites stipendiarii* who were tricked into capitulating by the regular castle garrison at the siege of Bridgnorth in 1102 "called the whole army to witness the tricks of these plotters, so that their downfall might not bring contempt on other paid soldiers."[21] As Orderic saw it, there was a sense of professional pride in being a paid knight. "Mercenary" identity could even be deployed tactically on the field of politics. In his contemporary account of the death of Count William Clito of Flanders at the siege of Aalst in 1128, Galbert of Bruges was careful to state that William was at that time performing military service to Duke Godfrey of Lorraine not as a vassal but as a paid soldier: "He was the duke's knight in this matter and died there not for his own county but for the duke's welfare and honor, just like any other *solidarius*."[22] The misapprehension that Godfrey possessed lordship over Flanders was thereby avoided, and the status and the character of the count left undiminished. Irregular or paid service has been associated in particular with the *juvenes*, or young knights who sought advancement and opportunities on the tournament fields and in the service of great households.[23] Yet the

19. Key studies are: Marjorie Chibnall, "Mercenaries and the *Familia Regis* under Henry I," in *Anglo-Norman Warfare. Studies in Late Anglo-Saxon and Anglo-Norman Military Organisation and Warfare*, ed. Matthew Strickland (Woodbridge: Boydell, 1992), 84–92 and J.O. Prestwich, "The Military Household of the Norman Kings," *English Historical Review* 94 (1981): 1–35. For Henry I's household see also Stephen Morillo, *Warfare under the Anglo-Norman Kings, 1066–1135* (Woodbridge, Boydell & Brewer, 1994), 60–66; R.W. Southern, *Medieval Humanism and Other Studies* (Oxford: Basil Blackwell, 1970), 214–20.

20. Brown, "Military Service," 37–44.

21. "coram omni exercitu ne talis eorum casus aliis opprobrio esset stipendiariis complicum dolos detegebant." Orderic Vitalis, *Ecclesiastical History*, 6: 28.

22. "Ducis enim miles in hoc fuerat, nec ibidem pro comitatu proprio sed pro salute et honore ducis, velut alius quislibet solidarius, mortuus est." Galbert of Bruges, *De multro, traditione, et occasione gloriosi Karoli comitis Flandriarum*, ed. Jeff Rider, Corpus Christianorum. Continuatio Mediaeualis 131 (Turnhout: Brepols, 1994), 167; Jeff Rider, *The Murder, Betrayal and Slaughter of the Glorious Charles, Count of Flanders*, trans. Jeff Rider (New Haven and London: Yale University Press, 2013), 186; Brown, "Military Service," 35.

23. Georges Duby, "Au XIIe siècle: les "jeunes" dans la société aristocratique," *Annales. Économies, sociétés, civilisations* 19 (1964): 835–46 is the classic study on this topic, but for a more modern revision of his underpinning themes see David Crouch and Claire de Trafford, "The Forgotten Family in Twelfth-Century England," *Haskins Society Journal* 13 (1999): 41–63.

"youth" of one of the most famous knights of the era, William Marshal (1146/7–1219), who would become the regent of England during the minority of Henry III (1216–72), lasted into his forties. Despite the inherent precariousness of relying on a lord's favour Marshal did well out of household service, and he later saw that a similar career path could benefit one of his younger sons.[24]

Ultimately, paid military service was common because the wealthy and the powerful saw great benefit in it. The late twelfth-century administrative treatise *The Dialogue of the Exchequer* stated that scutage (the commutation of military service obligations by cash payment) was collected as "the prince prefers to expose *stipendiarios*, rather than his own people, to the hazards of war."[25] Such a high-minded attitude obfuscates the fact that the utility of paid military service was founded on a simple matter of logistics. Based on the number of knights' fees assessed, the theoretical ceiling for knight service in England at the end of the twelfth century was some 6,500 men.[26] In practice this figure would have been lower, and not everyone could have been called at the same time: Robert of Torigny wrote that Henry II was served during his 1157 procession through Wales by only 2,000 knights, which in itself is an uncertain and possibly exaggerated figure.[27] Moreover, the traditional term of military service for land-holding vassals was forty or sixty days.[28] This was an inadequate system in the face of the realities of twelfth-century warfare, and particularly problematic for the Anglo-Norman kings owing to the geographic spread of their dominions. Transport alone from England to the continent, or vice versa, could eat up the term of service, and there were objections to being forced to discharge it abroad in the first place.[29] When Richard I prepared for war in 1198 he did not order his chief justiciar to call up a grand if temporary host, but to find him

24. David Crouch, *William Marshal*, 3rd ed. (London and New York: Routledge, 2016), esp. 31–59 on Marshal's early career.

25. "Mauult enim princeps stipendarios quam domesticos bellicis opponere casibus." Richard fitz Neal, *Dialogus de Scaccario: the Dialogue of the Exchequer*, ed. Emilie Amt (Oxford: Oxford University Press, 2007), 78–80.

26. Thomas Keefe, *Feudal Assessments and the Political Community under Henry II and His Sons* (Berkeley: University of California Press, 1983), 52–59.

27. Robert of Torigny, *The Chronicle of Robert of Torigni*, ed. Richard Howlett, vol. 4 of *Chronicles of the Reigns of Stephen, Henry II, and Richard I*, Rolls Series 82 (London: Longman, 1889), 193.

28. C. Warren Hollister, "The Annual Term of Military Service in England," *Medievalia et Humanistica* 13 (1960): 40–7.

29. Prestwich, "Money and Mercenaries," 135.

either 300 knights to serve for a year or the money to hire an equal number at the rate of three shillings per day.[30]

It has been argued that a critical shift in the Crown's preference for supplementing the military strength of the royal household with a large body of paid soldiers—in particular foot soldiers—took place in the second half of the twelfth century.[31] This clearly built on a long continuity of paid service, but a significant milestone along the path was Henry II's expedition to Toulouse in 1159. Robert of Torigny noted that Henry preferred not to trouble his townsmen and country knights (*agrarii milites*) and instead raised scutage to hire a countless host of paid soldiers (*solidarios vero milites innumeros*).[32] Jacques Boussard's classic article on the armies of Henry II cleared the path for appreciating the effectiveness of large bodies of paid infantry soldiers in western European warfare. As he stated, Henry "clearly owed his military power to his Brabanter and Welsh mercenaries."[33] More recent scholarship has preferred to locate the adoption of large armies of hired soldiers as a permanent feature of Anglo-Norman warfare to the reigns of Richard I and John. It is nevertheless recognised that Henry, like his sons, made great use of paid soldiers because of their skill in battle and, in particular, sieges, because their own nobles were often uninterested in war, and because silver could be a more reliable procurer of manpower than a baronial elite whose loyalties were suspect in that one eventuality every twelfth-century king had to deal with: rebellion and civil war.[34]

Here the logistics of warfare, and consequently the political and social position of the medieval warrior, cannot be disentangled from the great economic growth that was gathering pace. Twelfth- and thirteenth-century England witnessed an extraordinary period of urban growth and commercial expansion. This economic transformation was arguably the single most important factor in shaping the devel-

30. Roger of Howden, *Chronica*, 4: 40.
31. Steven Isaac, "The Problem with Mercenaries," in *The Circle of War in the Middle Ages. Essays on Medieval Military and Naval History*, ed. Donald J. Kagay and L.J. Andrew Villalon (Woodbridge: Boydell, 1999), 102; Michael Mallett, "Mercenaries," in *Medieval Warfare. A History*, ed. Maurice Keen (Oxford: Oxford University Press, 1999), 213; France, *Western Warfare*, 66–67.
32. Robert of Torigny, *Chronicle*, 202.
33. Jacques Boussard, "Henri II Plantagenêt et les origines de l'armée de métier," *Bibliothèque de l'École des Chartes* 106 (1945–46): 189–224, at 202.
34. John Hosler, *Henry II. A Medieval Soldier at War, 1147–1189* (Leiden and Boston: Brill, 2007), 119–23; Prestwich, *Armies and Warfare*, 149–50.

opment of medieval society before the Black Death. The urban landscape of England (as on the neighbouring continent) would assume its
pre-modern shape through the expansion of old towns and the founding of new ones. The most intense period of development fell between
the mid-twelfth and the mid-thirteenth centuries, when some 230
new boroughs were established in England and Wales.[35] Commercial
expansion in the countryside was witnessed by the founding of weekly
markets, which connected the rural population to networks of interre-
gional and even international trade. We have records of 239 markets in
all of England by the time Henry II became king in 1154. By 1250 the
total number of market events chartered or attested had nearly quadru-
pled to 922. Not all markets may have existed at the same time, as old
institutions withered and new ones were founded, but a sense of their
density and accessibility is given by the fact that the vast majority of
settlements south of the line from the River Severn to the Humber
were within 10 km of at least three such sites.[36]

It is doubtful if any of this would have been possible without the
accompanying expansion of money economy that penetrated ever
more deeply into society.[37] The importance of economic growth in the
twelfth century, especially the ability of the Crown to extract cash for
its military undertakings by rents and taxes, is well understood.[38] Less
attention has been paid to the sheer scale in the increase of the physical
currency in circulation. Based on single coin finds, mint and hoard evidence it has been estimated that there were between 3.5 and 7 million
silver pennies in circulation in England around the time of Henry II's
first monetary reform in 1158. This was probably not dissimilar to the
number of coins that circulated at the eve of the Norman Conquest in
1066. But by Henry II's second reform in 1180 the upper end of the

35. Maurice Beresford, *New Towns of the Middle Ages. Town Plantation in England,
Wales and Gascony* (London: Lutterworth Press, 1967), 319–47; Samantha Letters, *Online
Gazetteer of Markets and Fairs in England and Wales to 1516* (London: Institute of Historical Research, 2002; last updated 16 September, 2013), http://www.history.ac.uk/cmh/
gaz/gazweb2.html, accessed 1 March, 2018.
36. Letters, *Online Gazetteer*. On the development of the rural market economy, see
James Masschaele, *Peasants, Merchants and Markets: Inland Trade in Medieval England,
1150–1350* (New York: St Martin's Press, 1997).
37. Jim Bolton, "What Is Money? What Is a Money Economy? When Did a Money
Economy Emerge in Medieval England?," in *Medieval Money Matters*, ed. Diana Wood
(Oxford: Oxbow, 2004), 1–15; Diana Wood, *Money in the Medieval English Economy,
973–1489* (Manchester: Manchester University Press, 2012), 141–52.
38. Cf. Hollister, *Military Organisation*, 169–71; J.O. Prestwich, *The Place of War in
English History, 1066–1214*, ed. Michael Prestwich (Woodbridge: Boydell, 2004), 57–70.

estimate had doubled to 14 million, and then the total surged by 1210 to between 24 and 72 million, afterwards increasing more gradually to around 115 million by 1247.[39] Going by the mean estimates, the first five decades from 1158 saw an over nine-fold increase in the volume of English currency.

It has been argued, and the numismatic evidence supports it, that the period of most rapid and transformative commercial growth began in the latter part of the twelfth century.[40] The royal administration sought to adapt its fiscal and military policies in response to the challenges and opportunities the changing situation presented. John's exactions for his political and military efforts on the continent, part of the background for the Magna Carta, are infamous. Yet as Henry II's Brabanter armies and Richard's attempt to finance the pay of 300 knights show, John was blazing no new trail. Contemporaries were well aware of the trajectory the economy had taken. In its discussion of the history of royal rents, the *Dialogue of the Exchequer* linked the push by the royal administration to collects its estate rents in cash rather than in kind to the financial demands of overseas warfare.[41] It is important to locate the emergence of chivalry against this background of rapid economic development and change in the manner warfare was organised. The use of paid armies must have been facilitated by the greater and ever increasing amount of silver in circulation, with the overall monetisation of the economy lubricating the wheels of exchange and making it easier to use cash in all manner of transactions.

Foreign Soldiers: the Welsh and the Flemings

The interplay between the logistics of warfare and the emergence of a new aristocratic culture can be seen in the images and identities that came to be associated with various classes of foreign soldiers. Of the reservoirs of foreign military manpower that the Anglo-Normans tapped into from the mid-twelfth century onwards, Wales was

39. Martin Allen, *Mints and Money in Medieval England* (Cambridge: Cambridge University Press, 2012), 318–24, 344.

40. James Masschaele, "Economic Takeoff and the Rise of Markets," in *The Companion to the Medieval World*, ed. Carol Lansing and Edward English (Chichester: Wiley-Blackwell, 2009), 89–109.

41. Richard fitz Neal, *Dialogus de Scaccario*, 62–64.

among the most important.[42] We know from narrative sources that Welsh troops were employed during the troubles of Stephen's reign by Angevin partisans: Earl Robert of Gloucester called them to his service in 1139, and three Welsh kings led contingents at the battle of Lincoln in 1141.[43] More is known from the reign of Henry II onwards. The Welsh first appear in Angevin continental conflicts in 1167, when Henry II deployed Welshmen at the siege of Chaumont in France.[44] He again relied on the Welsh during the civil war of 1173–74, and they played a key role in the final and decisive battle at Rouen.[45] In the Pipe Rolls of Henry's, Richard's and John's reigns the Welsh contingents raised were upwards of several hundred men in size, with the single largest known mustering being the 2,100 men called up by Richard in 1196.[46] It is possible larger numbers served on the field: the French chronicler William the Breton wrote that 3,400 Welshmen were killed at Les Andelys that same year, and Richard of Devizes claimed John brought in 4,000 Welsh during his 1191 coup.[47] The terms of employment of these Welsh troops are not always known. It is easy to assume that it involved cash compensation (and a promise of plunder), and Pipe Rolls certainly account for Welshmen serving for the king's coin. But at times they could have also been political auxiliaries as vassals to the English crown or allies among the Anglo-Norman marcher bar-

---

42. I.W. Rowlands, "'Warriors Fit for a Prince': Welsh Troops in Angevin Service, 1154–1216," in *Mercenaries and Paid Men. The Mercenary Identity in the Middle Ages*, ed. John France (Boston and Leiden: Brill, 2008), 207–30 is the key study on the employment of Welsh soldiers during this period.

43. *Gesta Stephani*, ed. and trans. K.R. Potter and R.H.C. Davis, Oxford Medieval Texts (Oxford: Clarendon Press, 1976), 110–11; Henry of Huntingdon, *Historia Anglorum*, 726, 734; Orderic Vitalis, *Ecclesiastical History*, 6: 542, 536, 540.

44. Stephen of Rouen, "The 'Draco normannicus' of Etienne de Rouen," ed. Richard Howlett, vol. 2 of *Chronicles of the Reigns of Stephen, Henry II, and Richard I*, Rolls Series 82 (London: Longman, 1885), 681–86; John Hosler, "Revisiting Mercenaries under Henry fitz Empress, 1167–1188," in *Mercenaries and Paid Men. The Mercenary Identity in the Middle Ages*, ed. John France (Boston and Leiden: Brill, 2008), 35–36.

45. Robert of Torigny, *Chronicle*, 265; Roger of Howden, *Gesta Regis Henrici Secundi Benedicti Abbatis*, ed. William Stubbs, 2 vols., Rolls Series 49 (London: Longman, 1867), 1: 74; Rowlands, "Warriors," 212–13; Hosler, "Revisiting Mercenaries," 37–38.

46. *The Chancellor's Roll for the Eighth Year of the Reign of King Richard the First, Michaelmas 1196*, ed. Doris Stenton, Publications of the Pipe Roll Society n.s. 4 (London: Pipe Roll Society, 1930), xvii–xviii; Rowlands, "Warriors," 212–18.

47. Richard of Devizes, *The Chronicle of Richard of Devizes of the Time of King Richard the First*, ed. John T. Appelby (London: Thomas Nelson, 1963), 33; William the Breton, *Philippides*, ed. H.-François Delaborde, vol. 2 of *Œuvres de Rigord et de Guillaume le Breton: Historiens de Philippe-Auguste* (Paris: Rebouard, 1885), 135–36.

ons.[48] It should be noted, of course, that lordship and cash compensation are not in practice mutually exclusive categories.

William of Newburgh's account of the engagement at Rouen in 1174 shows that Welsh troops excelled as skirmishers: travelling through the woods under cover of night, they fell upon the unprepared French supply train and administered a material and moral upset that in the end broke the enemy's will to offer battle.[49] The perception of the Welsh as foot soldiers comfortable with ambush tactics is perhaps what led Jacques Boussard call them "mi-soldat, mi-brigand."[50] This is a regrettable characterisation, not the least because it obviates a fundamental aspect of Welsh military organisation: the *teulu*, or the princely warband. Even more so than the Anglo-Norman aristocratic household, the late twelfth-century *teulu* was principally a military force and a gathering of mounted soldiers.[51] While there is little reason to believe a *teulu* was at the heart of every Angevin deployment of Welsh troops, we do catch occasional glimpses of princes leading their men in England or the continent. This was so in 1174 when Rhys ap Gruffudd of Deheubarth participated in the siege of Tutbury and lent the services of his son Hywel to Henry II in France.[52] The Welsh warrior-aristocracy availed themselves of the wider European lessons in the technologies of war, including castle building and siege-craft.[53] The destruction of the strategic fortress of Damville and several towns on the Norman border by Welsh troops in 1188 cannot have been the act of marauding woodsmen but of soldiers who knew what they were about.[54]

The story of the Welsh soldier in the Anglo-Norman world is entangled with the development of chivalry through a shared social and

48. Matthew Bennett, "The Impact of 'Foreign' Troops in the Civil Wars of King Stephen's Reign," in *War and Society in Medieval and Early Modern Britain*, ed. Diana Dunn (Liverpool: Liverpool University Press, 2000), 106–8; Rowlands, "Warriors," 209–10.

49. William of Newburgh, "The Fifth Book of the 'Historia rerum Anglicarum' of William of Newburgh," ed. Richard Howlett, vol. 2 of *Chronicles of the Reigns of Stephen, Henry II, and Richard I*, Rolls Series 82 (London: Longman, 1885), 195–96.

50. Boussard, "Henry II," 218.

51. A.D. Carr, "*Teulu* and *Penteulu*," in *The Welsh King and His Court*, ed. T.M. Charles-Edwards, Morfydd E. Owen, and Paul Russell (Cardiff: University of Wales Press, 2000), 63–81.

52. Ralph of Diceto, "Ymagines Historiarum," ed. William Stubbs, vol. 1 of *The Historical Works of Master Ralph de Diceto, Dean of London*, Rolls Series 68 (London: Longman, 1876), 384; *Brut y Tywysogyon: or, The Chronicle of the Princes. Peniarth ms. 20 Version*, trans. Thomas Jones (Cardiff: University of Wales Press, 1952), 69; Rowlands, "Warriors," 223.

53. Carr, "*Teulu* and *Penteulu*," 69–71.

54. Roger of Howden, *Chronica*, 2: 345; Roger of Howden, *Gesta*, 2, 46–47.

cultural context. A considerable body of scholarship sees the twelfth century as a period of the invention of a new English identity that successfully combined Anglo-Saxon and Norman heritage.[55] The trauma of the Conquest was overcome by a sense that it was only a milestone on the continuing journey of the English people: in the end it benefited them through exposure to a more civilised continental culture. John Gillingham has argued that this historiographical construct, seen in the works of Anglo-Norman chroniclers, leaned on juxtaposing the neighbouring Welsh, Scottish and Irish peoples as uncivilised barbarians. They were seen as primitive in their social organisation, scandalous in their marital practices and—here most pertinent—brutally savage in their conduct of warfare.[56] The reception of these images can be somewhat finessed. Deplorable savagery is also a close cousin to admirable ferocity and bravery, for which Henry II praised the Welsh in his letter to Emperor Manuel I Komnenos.[57] But broader views of the Welsh in late twelfth-century western European court culture took after the English chroniclers. "*Galois sont tot par nature / Plus fol que bestes en pasture*," mocked Chrétien de Troyes in his Arthurian romance *Perceval*, written by 1190.[58] The fact that the Welsh military elite did not adopt the mainstream chivalric culture of the late twelfth century played into their image as outsiders.[59] The Welsh were clearly a very considerable addition to the fighting capacity of the Angevin kings. In the context of the Anglo-Norman society at war, however, they were significant not only as a consistent component of its military machine but as a convenient stereotype of savagery that helped to define the aristocracy's image of itself as civilised and chivalrous.

55. Cf. David Carpenter, *The Struggle for Mastery. Britain, 1066–1284* (London: Penguin, 2003), 1–25; Michael Clanchy, *England and Its Rulers* (3rd ed., Oxford: Blackwell, 2006), 228–45; Ian Short, "Tam Angli quam Franci: Self-Definition in Anglo-Norman England," *Anglo-Norman Studies* 18 (1995): 153–75; Hugh Thomas, *The English and the Normans: Ethnic Hostility, Assimilation, and Identity, 1066–c. 1220* (Oxford: Oxford University Press, 2003), 56–82.

56. John Gillingham, "Conquering the Barbarians: War and Chivalry in Twelfth-Century Britain," *Haskins Society Journal* 4 (1992): 67–84; John Gillingham, "The Beginnings of English Imperialism," *Journal of Historical Sociology* 5 (1992): 392–409.

57. Gerald of Wales, "Itinerarium Kambriae et Descriptio Kambriae," ed. James F. Dimock, vol. 6 of *Giraldi Cambrensis Opera*, Rolls Series 21 (London: Longman, 1868), 181.

58. Chrétien de Troyes, *Le Roman Perceval ou Le Conte du Graal*, ed. Keith Busby (Tübingen: Niemeyer, 1993), 12, lines 243–44; Rowlands, "Warriors," 218–19.

59. David Crouch, *The Image of Aristocracy in Britain, 1000–1300* (London & New York: Routledge, 1992), 159–63.

The processes by which an out-group is invented in order to help define the identity of an in-group are equally present in writings about Flemish soldiers in Anglo-Norman service. This is seen across two generations of English authors: the chroniclers of King Stephen's reign, writing principally in the 1140s, and the chroniclers of the reigns of Stephen's successors Henry II and Richard I writing between the 1170s and 1190s. Medieval Flanders and England shared a variety of connections and exchanges as neighbouring realms, separated only by the narrows of the English Channel which, of course, served as much as a superhighway of travel and communications as a boundary. Flemish soldiers had helped William the Conqueror to secure his kingdom, and, as the Anglo-Flemish treaties demonstrate, a high level of military and political cooperation was possible between the kings and the counts.[60] When the involvement of Flemish soldiers in Anglo-Norman conflicts reached its apogee during the intermittent warfare of King Stephen's reign it built on well-established precedents. In *ca.* 1143 the sense of closeness between the two realms is suggested by the northern chronicler Alfred of Beverley, who wrote of the Flemings "thronging on the island up to this day."[61] He considered them the sixth nation of Britain.

What kind of fighters were these Flemings who arrived to serve in England? High-status members of the Flemish aristocracy had been coming for some time, as Jean-François Nieus demonstrates elsewhere in this volume for the Conquest period.[62] The best known is undoubtedly William of Ypres, the grandson of Count Robert I of Flanders. William could fairly be called King Stephen's chief general and right-hand man. He commanded a contingent of Flemish soldiers and his military and political support was crucial in keeping Stephen's cause alive in 1141 after the king had been imprisoned by his enemies.[63] Stephen's position as the count of Boulogne, a mari-

---

60. Oksanen, *Flanders and the Anglo-Norman World*, 179–218.

61. "Qui hoc usque in insulam catervatim confluentes … Quorum crebra in insulam confluencia et inter Normannos cohabitacio quousque procedat sequens aetas videbit." Alfred of Beverley, *Aluredi Beverlacensis Annales, sive Historia de Gestis Regum Britanniae*, ed. Thomas Hearne (Oxford: e theatro Sheldoniano, 1716), 10.

62. Jean-François Nieus, "Sigard's Belt: The Family of Chocques and the Borders of Knighthood (*ca.* 980–1100)."

63. Isaac, "The Problem with Mercenaries," 103–6; Oksanen, *Flanders and the Anglo-Norman World*, 226–31; and more broadly on his career see Jean-François Nieus, "The Early Career of William of Ypres in England: A New Charter of King Stephen," *English Historical Review* 130 (2015): 527–45; Ernest Warlop, "Willem van Ieper, een

time principality across the Channel from Dover and adjacent to Flanders, probably helped him to attract fighters from the southern Low Countries to his service.[64] Neither were his opponents strangers to retaining Flemings. Robert fitz Hubert, a Flemish relative of William of Ypres, brought a retinue to England on the side of Stephen's rival, Empress Matilda, serving briefly under her half-brother Earl Robert of Gloucester. This relationship did not end well: fitz Hubert fell out with Gloucester in 1139 and opportunistically seized the castle of Devizes for himself. He did not long enjoy his spoils and was soon captured and hanged.[65] Other high-status individuals from the southern Low Countries include William of Ypres's half-brother Fromold of Ypres and Queen Matilda's kinsman Pharamus of Boulogne, who was to survive the regime change and received lands in Buckinghamshire from Empress Matilda's son, King Henry II.[66] William of Ypres had been exiled from Flanders in the early 1130s by Count Thierry, and like him many Flemish leaders may have arrived to England as a result of the count's slow-burning hostility towards factions that had opposed him during the civil war of 1127–28. Though dispossessed, they would have been men of rank and valuable connections.[67] Much less is known of the unnamed but clearly very large numbers of less exalted Flemish fighters: William of Malmesbury simply states that "knights of all kinds made a rush to him [King Stephen], men who served in light harness also, especially from Flanders and Brittany."[68] In narrative sources of Stephen's reign Flemish soldiers are sometimes denounced for their individual deeds but, unlike the Welsh, they did not suffer from invidious characterisations based on their origin or perceived lack of culture. Flemish aristocrats shared in the general

Vlaams condottiere (vóór 1104–1164)," *De Leiegouw* 6 (1964): 167–92 and ibid. 7 (1965): 197–218.

64. On Stephen's continental domain, see Edmund King, "Stephen of Blois, Count of Mortain and Boulogne," *English Historical Review* 115 (2000): 271–96.

65. *Gesta Stephani*, 104–8; John of Worcester, *Chronicle*, 3: 284–90; William of Malmesbury, *Historia Novella. The Contemporary History*, ed. Edmund King, trans. K.R. Potter, Oxford Medieval Texts (Oxford: Clarendon Press, 1998), 62, 74–76; Oksanen, *Flanders and the Anglo-Norman World*, 223–24.

66. Bennett, "The Impact of "Foreign" Troops," 106; J.H. Round, "Faramus of Boulogne," *The Genealogist* 12 (1896): 145–51; Ernst Warlop, *The Flemish Nobility before 1300* (Kortrijk: G. Desmet-Huysman, 1975), 1.1: 213; Warlop, "Willem van Ieper," 202.

67. Isaac, "The Problem with Mercenaries," 106–7.

68. "Currebatur ad eum ab omnium generum militibus, et a levis armaturae hominibus, maximique ex Flandria et Britannia." William of Malmesbury, *Historia Novella*, 32.

character of the Anglo-Norman members of their class, and those of lower rank were of little interest to the chroniclers.

A radically different view emerged a generation after Stephen's death. In the writings of William fitz Stephen (*ca.* 1173–74), Ralph of Diceto or "of Diss" (after *ca.* 1181), Gervase of Canterbury (after *ca.* 1188) and William of Newburgh (*ca.* 1198), the Flemings of Stephen's reign were depicted as predatory wolves or low-class weaver-bandits who were cast out from the kingdom at the accession of Henry II in 1154.[69] But Flemings, as a nation, had never been so described in sources contemporary to Stephen's reign, nor had they ever been called *routiers* or by other terms designating a lower class status.[70] Many Flemings continued to prosper in England after Henry's accession, and even William of Ypres—surely near the top of Henry's political hit list—was shuffled from the royal estates he held only after a gentlemanly grace period of three years. Together with the false association of Flemings exclusively with Stephen's faction, these descriptions are rhetorical ploys: the inauguration of the new king was celebrated by the banishing of a villainous representative of the old regime.[71]

Such revisionism in the Flemish contribution to recent English history encapsulates the shared processes by which national identities and social hierarchies came to be imagined in the later decades of the twelfth century. This connection is particularly explicit in Jordan Fantosme's verse chronicle of the 1173–74 Angevin civil war, quoted at the beginning of this chapter. His work was the first text to identify Flemish soldiers as "weavers" (*telier*). Flanders was noted for its textile industries and was a major consumer of English wool, so it is no wonder that this designation resonated with the audiences.[72] Its

69. Gervase of Canterbury, "Gesta Regum," ed. William Stubbs, vol. 2 of *The Historical Works of Gervase of Canterbury*, Rolls Series 73 (London: Longman, 1880), 73; Ralph of Diceto, "Ymagines Historiarum," 297; William fitz Stephen, "Vita Sancti Thomae, Canturiensis Archiepiscopi et Martyris," ed. James Craigie Robertson, vol. 3 of *Materials for the History of Thomas Becket*, Rolls Series 67 (London: Longman, 1877), 18–19; William of Newburgh, *Historia rerum Anglicarum*, ed. Richard Howlett, vol. 1 of *Chronicles of the Reigns of Stephen, Henry II, and Richard I*, Rolls Series 82 (London: Longman, 1884), 101–2.
70. Isaac, "The Problem with Mercenaries," 109.
71. Emilie Amt, *The Accession of Henry II in England. Royal Government Restored, 1149–1159* (Woodbridge: Boydell, 1993), 82–98; Oksanen, *Flanders and the Anglo-Norman World*, 241–48.
72. T.H. Lloyd, *The English Wool Trade in the Middle* Ages (Cambridge: Cambridge University Press, 1977), 1–24; Oksanen, *Flanders and the Anglo-Norman World*, 152–55; Adriaan Verhulst, "La laine indigène dans les Pays-Bas entre le XIIe et le XVIIe siècle.

function, however, was not simply descriptive. Fantosme's poem was composed with an aristocratic audience in mind shortly after the rebellion of Henry II's oldest son and heir, Henry, called the Young King, against his father. The civil war exposed fault lines among the Angevin political elite, and after Henry II's triumph there remained the difficult task of reconciling the victorious and defeated factions. Fantosme's solution was to retell history less as an internal Angevin dispute than an invasion of England by foreign forces. The poem declines to concentrate on the activities of either the older or the younger Henry, but focuses instead on the invasion of northern England by the latter's ally King William the Lion of Scotland. An interlude in East Anglia, where an army of foreign soldiers brought in by the rebel Earl Robert of Leicester was routed, introduced the Flemish weavers. It was the defeat of these two foreign forces that affirmed the cathartic, unifying message of the work.[73] Parallels can be drawn with Henry of Huntingdon's account of the Battle of Standard in 1138, which saw the Anglo-Saxons and the Normans merge as the new nation of the English in their struggle against David I of Scotland.[74] In a refrain common to twelfth-century depictions of the "Celtic" peoples, Fantosme saw King William's Scottish troops as savages more interested in plunder than battle. Flemish soldiers also served William and accounted well for themselves, which only served as contrast to the general barbarism of the Scottish troops.[75] Those in East Anglia, however, were declared to hail from *Flandres la salvaga* and made plunderers by their own admission. These Flemings were a mixed force and the presence of "many noblemen" (*maint gentil hum*) is noted in passing.[76] But the

Mise en œuvre industrielle, production et commerce," *Revue historique* 248 (1972): 281–322.

73. Laura Ashe, *Fiction and History in England, 1066–1200* (Cambridge: Cambridge University Press, 2007), 80–120; Matthew Strickland, "Arms and the Men: War, Loyalty and Lordship in Jordan Fantosme's *Chronicle*," in *Medieval Knighthood: Papers from the Fifth Strawberry Hill Conference 1990*, ed. Christopher Harper-Bill and Ruth Harvey, Medieval Knighthood 4 (Woodbridge: Boydell, 1992), 187–220.

74. Henry of Huntingdon, *Historia Anglorum. The History of the English People*, ed. and trans. Diana Greenway, Oxford Medieval Texts (Oxford: Clarendon Press, 1996), 712–18; John Gillingham, "Henry of Huntingdon and the Twelfth-Century Revival of the English Nation," in *Concepts of National Identity in the Middle Ages*, ed. Simon Forde, Lesley Johnson, and Alan Murray (Leeds: University of Leeds, 1995), 75–101.

75. Gillingham, "Conquering the Barbarians," 70–71.

76. Jordan Fantosme, *Chronicle*, 63. The use of the word *salvage* by the poet was a considered choice: it can be equally translated as "savage," "strange" or "foreign," and underlined the association between the barbarism and the alien character of the enemy. See

final battle scene between the opposing armies is imagined as a fervent
nationalistic contest between English aristocratic chivalry and foreign
working-class banditry, in which the latter were utterly crushed. The
poet's closing statement: "They would be better off hanging from a
rope in Flanders."[77] Chivalry was reserved for the elite.

Knights, Mercenaries and Social Identities

Fantosme's account suggests that the war of 1173–74 provoked not
only political soul-searching among a factionalised Anglo-Norman
elite but reflections on military identity. As has been discussed, since
the 1159 Toulouse campaign Henry II had employed large numbers of
paid soldiers. The relations between the kings of England and France
would not recover from the fallout of the expedition, and in *ca.* 1198
the chronicler William of Newburgh wrote of it as the beginning of
a period of conflicts that had lasted to his day.[78] The situation in late
twelfth-century France has been compared to that in Italy during the
era of the Condottieri: political fragmentation combined with increasing wealth leading to endemic warfare that nurtured the formation
of mercenary companies.[79] Contemporary concerns over the use of
paid soldiers are evident in the excommunication of *routiers* and
their employers in Lateran III in 1179, and in the 1171 treaty between
King Louis VII of France and Emperor Frederick Barbarossa of Germany that sought to limit the use of Brabanters and Cotarelli (another
generic term for mercenaries) in their territories.[80] But Henry II took a
more pragmatic stance, and the outcome of the civil war vindicated his
employment of Brabanters and the Welsh. It confirmed, if it had not

---

DMF: *Dictionnaire du Moyen Français*, version 2015 (ATILF – CNRS & Université de
Lorraine), http://www.atilf.fr/dmf/, accessed 1 March, 2018.

77. "Miel lur vendreit en Flandres pendre a une hart." Jordan Fantosme, *Chronicle*, 77.

78. William of Newburgh, "Historia rerum Anglicarum," vol. 2 of *Chronicles*, 491.

79. John France, "Introduction," in *Mercenaries and Paid Men. The Mercenary Identity
in the Middle Ages*, ed. John France (Boston and Leiden: Brill, 2008), 3–4.

80. *Friderici I. Diplomata inde ab a. MCLXVIII. usque ad a. MCLXXX.*, ed. Heinrich
Appelt, Monumenta Germaniae Historica, Diplomata Regum et Imperatorum Germaniae
10.3 (Hannover: Hahnsche Buchhandlung, 1985), 46–47. In so far as Louis was concerned,
the fact that the French king commanded inferior fiscal resources compared to those of
his Angevin rival may have motivated the attempt to shut down *routier* employment. For
a comparative overview of their finances at the start of the thirteenth century, when more
documentary evidence is available, see John Gillingham, *The Angevin Empire* (2nd ed.,
London: Arnold, 2001), 95–100.

been signalled clearly enough already, the trend towards the crown's increasing use of paid contingents of foreign soldiers.

It was in this period that formal distinctions consolidated around different classes of mounted combatants. In the sources of Henry I's reign the words *milites* and *equites*, knights and merely mounted soldiers, could be used interchangeably.[81] At that time the term *serviens* likewise covered an ambiguous range of mounted or lightly armed troops.[82] During the reign of Henry II the English royal administration began to develop a more typologically refined approach. It first acknowledged *miles* as a distinct rank in the Assize of Clarendon of 1166.[83] Financially the distinction between knights and other mounted soldiers was made explicit in the royal payroll records of the 1173–74 conflict.[84] The Assize of Arms in 1181 listed the minimum equipment that each holder of a knight's fee should possess.[85] Further regimentation is suggested by the 1194 tournament charter of Richard I, which separated landed and landless knights into different categories.[86]

Elite identity, such as that which knighthood presumed, required something to contrast itself with. In the second half of the twelfth century the secular landed elite faced increasingly stiff competition for power and patronage from groups of people whose fortunes had been lifted by the socio-economic forces of the twelfth-century renaissance. These included urban merchants and the developing administrative profession, and the new norms of warfare opened novel avenues for advancement for military men of non-knightly origin. As being a knight began to accrue an increasingly specific administrative, social and cultural meaning the internal divisions within the community of military professionals were thrown into sharper relief. The verse biography *History of William Marshal* recounts the career of its titular hero

81. See for instance the Anglo-Flemish treaties, *Diplomatic Documents*, 1–12.
82. Chibnall, "Mercenaries," 87–88.
83. William Stubbs, *Select Charters and Other Illustrations of English Constitutional History*, revised by H.W.C. Davis (9th ed., Oxford: Clarendon Press, 1913), 173; Crouch, *The Image of Aristocracy*, 141.
84. *The Great Roll of the Pipe for the Nineteenth Year of the Reign of King Henry the Second, A.D. 1172–3*, Publications of the Pipe Roll Society 19 (London: Wyman, 1895), 97, 101–2; *The Great roll of the Pipe for the Twentieth Year of the Reign of King Henry the Second, A.D. 1173–1174*, Publications of the Pipe Roll Society 21 (London: Wyman, 1896), 34, 94, 139; *The Great Roll of the Pipe for the Twenty-First Year of the Reign of King Henry the Second, A.D. 1174–1175*, Publications of the Pipe Roll Society 22 (London: Wyman, 1897), 127–28.
85. Stubbs, *Select Charters*, 183.
86. Howden, *Chronica*, 3: 268.

in the princely households of western Europe of the late twelfth and early thirteenth centuries, and it offers many examples of the snobbery of the aristocratic knighthood towards their lower-class colleagues. Written *ca.* 1224–26, in a time when courtly chivalry had accumulated a full complement of manners and mores, the work offers a stinging retrospective assessment of the *routier* commanders Sancho de Savannac, Mercadier and Lupescar, employed respectively by Young King Henry, Richard I and John. These men are painted as greedy, grasping, incompetent and cruel in their conduct towards non-combatants. The author's argument is plain: only proper knights, such Marshal himself, could be trusted to offer honourable and genuinely loyal military service to a lord or a king—and by extension enjoy their confidence and munificence.[87]

These portrayals placed the knight and the mercenary in opposition to each other. Like the image of the English *chevalier* laying low the foreign *telier* in Jordan Fantosme's chronicle, they combined narratives from ongoing debates about national identity, social identity and class identity. In the Anglo-Norman world of the later twelfth century the development of knightly identity drew strength from contrasting notions of civilised behaviour and barbarism that had defined discussions of national identity in the preceding generation. The concept of the uncivilised Welshman or Scot provided a ready model for the Flemish bandit. But if foreigners provided a readily definable out-group for medieval authors concerned with forging such images, the paid soldier was a concept less easy to manage. The structures of military service were shot through with different types of monetary reward, whether it took the form of wages to a *routier* captain or a stipend to a household knight. Ultimately all competed for the same limited pool of financial and patronage opportunities. In his critique of *routier* commanders, William Marshal's biographer sought to assuage the unease created by this link between people from different social backgrounds. But if chivalry was how the later twelfth-century knightly elite maintained a socially competitive edge, what should one make of the fact that paid knightly service continued to be a common phenomenon—could a *miles stipendarius* still be a *gentil hum*?

---

87. David Crouch, "William Marshal and the Mercenariat," in *Mercenaries and Paid Men. The Mercenary Identity in the Middle Ages*, ed. John France (Boston and Leiden: Brill, 2008), 15–32.

An example of this contemporary debate arrives from a Franco-German principality closely tied to the Anglo-Norman political world. The social politics of accepting payment for military service much engaged Gilbert of Mons in his early thirteenth-century chronicle of the deeds of the counts of Hainaut. Gilbert's former patron Count Baldwin V (1171–95) had been energetically involved in the political and military conflicts of north-western Europe, and curating his conduct in service to other princes was important in the memorialisation of the count's life. Laura Napran has shown that, in a manner reminiscent of Saint Anselm's hierarchies of service a hundred years earlier, Gilbert squared the circle by implicitly grading military service to foreign magnates into different categories. First, paid soldiers, who fought for profit. Second, auxiliary knights, who had their expenses covered by their employer but who did not take additional payment. Finally, and most prestigiously, those who fought only as loyal friends to their allies, accepting no payment and shouldering their own expenses. Gilbert was very specific that Baldwin had always occupied the last category. By contrast, Baldwin's regional rival Duke Henry of Brabant was described as not only insisting that his expenses be covered but reaping handsome profits from his military alliances and adventures. Such conduct was to be considered degrading to a nobleman and, as Gilbert could be suspected of implying, turned him into a mere mercenary.[88] A similar transmutation had befallen William of Ypres, the first among King Stephen's Flemish retainers. During his lifetime William's one-time leadership of presumably paid and certainly foreign soldiers had not imperilled his elite station, but the succeeding generations found it easy to paint William as little better than a *routier* captain.[89]

It appears that Gilbert of Mons sought to further refine categories of paid service by differentiating the typically synonymous terms *stipendarius* and *solidarius*; he used the former to describe anonymous contingents of paid soldiers and knights, and the latter only in reference to named paid knights with high-status family connections.[90] As former chancellor of Hainaut, Gilbert would have been well versed in

88. Laura Napran, "Mercenaries and Paid Men in Gilbert of Mons," in *Mercenaries and Paid Men. The Mercenary Identity in the Middle Ages*, ed. John France (Boston and Leiden: Brill, 2008), 292–95.

89. Oksanen, *Flanders and the Anglo-Norman World*, 241–45.

90. Gilbert of Mons, *La Chronique de Gislebert de Mons*, ed. Léon Vanderkindere (Brussels: Kiessling, 1904), 100–1; Napran, "Mercenaries and Paid Men," 291–92.

administrative minutiae and more sensitive than most chroniclers to
the gradations of military service. This typology seems to have been
particular to Gilbert, but like the broader themes of his writing on the
finances of war it points to the thorny issues that paid service opened
among an elite engaged in redefining its social and cultural identity.
As S.D. Church has shown, in King John's household receiving wages
and money fiefs was considered less prestigious than payment in the
form of gifts, preferential loans, and patronage through land grants
and marriage arrangements.[91] From a strictly economic perspective
the results may have been very similar, but these practices expose the
norms of social expectation.

Conclusion

Knighthood and chivalry arose in the context of economic transformations that profoundly reshaped European society during the Central
Middle Ages. New fiscal revenues, together with the administrative
advances linked to the so-called renaissance of the twelfth century,
strengthened the hand of royal administrations and altered the logistics of warfare. Paid soldiers had probably always been a presence on
the medieval battlefields, but now *stipendiarii* emerged as an increasingly distinct, even self-conscious, category of armed service. For the
Anglo-Norman kings these fighters, many of whom were foreigners,
represented a flexible and often logistically superior alternative to
traditional forms of service owed by their landed vassals. For members of the established military and baronial elite the new avenues of
warfare could provide political and financial opportunities, but also
presented potential challenges to their social status and privileged
relationship with the ruler. The creation of an Anglo-French chivalric
culture during the late twelfth century was substantially informed by
the aristocratic elite's need to secure its political position in the face
of encroachment from other social classes. In its development it drew
colour and vigour from existing discourses on national identity. Yet
the search for any simple solution to this dilemma was foiled by this
self-same elite's involvement in, even dependence on, the financial
rewards of paid military service.

91. S.D. Church, "The Rewards of Royal Service in the Household of King John: A
Dissenting Opinion," *English Historical Review* 110 (1995): 277–302.

An echo of this debate is heard in the difficulty of applying the modern term "mercenary" to this period. Various defining characteristics that would separate the mercenary from other soldiers in receipt of cash compensation have been suggested: a mercenary lacked the personal ties of lordship, had complete ownership of arms and equipment, had to be recruited outside his employer's dominion, or was distinctively a foreigner.[92] All of these capture aspects of medieval military service that were no doubt important to contemporaries, but no single definition has risen above the others. The condition they seek to describe remains ambiguous. The image of the mercenary developed as the sinister twin to that of the chivalric knight, and this dual evolution is critical to the story of medieval knighthood. While the complexities of knightly identity will not yield to a single explanation—as the other chapters in this volume amply demonstrate—the growth of chivalric mores was fuelled by the emerging knightly elite's desire to distinguish itself from lower-class soldiers. One way of achieving this was to divide the complicated realities and complex gradations of military service into discrete categories. The consequent destabilisation of the status of paid soldiers served the broader programme of building up an exclusive knightly identity for the nobility: it is axiomatic that when defining what one is one must define what one is not, in other words constantly reinforce a difference between the self and the other. The overall moral and social question of paid knightly service, however, was not so easy to solve, and the practicalities of the growing money economy and the demands of warfare made it a matter impossible to ignore. It introduced a creative instability at the very foundation of knightly identity.

---

92. Richard Abels, "Household Men, Mercenaries and Vikings in Anglo-Saxon England," in *Mercenaries and Paid Men. The Mercenary Identity in the Middle Ages*, ed. John France (Boston and Leiden: Brill, 2008), 144–45; Brown, "Military Service," 49–50; France, "Introduction," 5–12; Isaac, "Problem with Mercenaries," 102; Mallett, "Mercenaries," 209; Prestwich, *Armies and Warfare*, 147; Prestwich, "Money and Mercenaries," 136; Rowlands, "Warriors," 223–24.

— Part II —

KNIGHTHOOD AND LINEAGE

Sara MCDOUGALL

THE CHIVALRIC FAMILY

This chapter proposes a new understanding of the aristocratic family in the eleventh and twelfth centuries, with a focus on Northern France and its near neighbours and with comparisons to Iberian, Imperial German and Southern Italian examples. Drawing upon recent scholarship, it challenges traditional accounts of knightly society as bound by laws of patriline, primogeniture and patriarchy. Medieval aristocratic families and the family law of the eleventh and twelfth centuries were not those of later centuries, nor did they function in compliance with the rules imagined by structuralist scholars. There was no rigid system of inheritance bound by rigid rules about legitimate marriage and legitimate succession. Inheritance from a father to his eldest son repeated over generations was a preferred and lauded ideal, but it was not the rule. It did not define family structure or succession. Families included far more kinds of kin than those related by paternal blood alone. Succession practices could favour maternal over paternal, female over male, and even the kinds of children anachronistically described as "illegitimate." Legitimate birth, in fact, had yet to become a status indicator that determined inclusion or exclusion. Marriage was too fluid an institution to offer such clear demarcations. Status, power and lineage, maternal as well as paternal, mattered more than did any concept of legitimate marriage or legitimate birth.

Who medieval aristocrats considered to be their kin, how they conceived of family, what they felt they owed their relations, and how this family structure related to "the birth of Europe," to the rise of states governed largely by hereditary rulers, are all questions that have generated a good deal of scholarly interest. Alongside and as a result of this research, there is an image of the noble, chivalric family that has long held sway in both scholarly and popular representations of medieval Europe. It is the image of a patrilineal clan, represented by a proud family tree of male ancestors and constituting a grand male lineage. It is the image of a family following the laws of primogeniture, with all lands and titles passing to the eldest son. Each new generation saw this eldest son knighted and married, recognised as the sole heir. Younger sons were sent off to seek lands of their own by conquest or relegated to the Church, effectively severing ties with their natal kin. Daughters, meanwhile, were either enclosed in convents or married off and absorbed into new families. Any woman, be she wife, mother, daughter, or sister, had only a supporting role in her family, though the honour of her male kin depended upon her chastity. If she had sex with anyone other than her husband she deserved death and sometimes got it. Aside from chaste fidelity to her spouse, a wife's value was measured primarily by her procreative powers, her ability to produce a male heir. This burdensome obligation meant that a wife often died young in childbirth. Failure to produce this essential heir would mean the loss of her husband, who would repudiate her in favour of a more fertile spouse.

This image of medieval aristocratic families has a long pedigree, but it is largely false. It is the chief purpose of this chapter to dispel these notions. Recent scholarship has provided a wealth of information that can be assembled to present a very different picture. These new findings showcase a diversity of regional practices, but nevertheless we can still identify an essentially consistent account of the "chivalric family," that is, medieval noble family structure and family consciousness.

This chapter takes as its geographic focus Northern France and its near neighbours, with comparisons to Iberian, Imperial German and Southern Italian examples. Its chronological focus is on the eleventh and twelfth centuries, in part because of this moment in time's essential role in the history of chivalry, but also because it is my contention that our understanding of medieval aristocratic families in this period, and family law of the time in particular, both suffer from anachronism. In their work on the eleventh and twelfth centuries, scholars have all too often fallen into the trap of projecting back from the thirteenth century and beyond. As Constance Bouchard has so astutely argued in her work on incest prohibitions and noble marriages in Northern France, we should not assume that eleventh-century noble families exploited incest rules in the same ways that twelfth-century nobles did.[1] This point can be extended beyond incest: we cannot assume that noble families of the eleventh and twelfth centuries adhered to the same values and rules as those found in thirteenth-century sources. We must try to understand their ideas and practices of marriage and inheritance on their own terms.

1. Constance Bouchard, "Consanguinity and Noble Marriages in the Tenth and eleventh Centuries," *Speculum* 56 (1981): 268–87. For a similar reading of the term chivalry, see also her *Strong of Body, Brave and Noble: Chivalry and Society in Medieval France* (Ithaca NY: Cornell University Press, 1998), 104.

To that end, it is first of all important to recognise all the things that these families were not. Here some long-beloved scholarly forefathers must be acknowledged but ultimately rejected on this topic. Above all, on the subject of noble families and marriage, this author would urge that one read the eloquent French historian Georges Duby (1919–96) as one reads historical fiction, not as a guide to anything like what we now understand medieval families to have been. Indeed, the older, fictitious image of the medieval noble family offered at the beginning of this chapter is due largely to his persuasive and pervasive scholarship. Drawing on the work of Karl Schmid (1923–93), Duby simplified and elegantly presented a history of structural change in French noble and royal families linked to other changes in political and social structure, a "feudal transformation," at around the year 1000. In the midst of these other transformations, Schmid and Duby identify a shift in family structure from horizontal and clan-based kinship including both maternal and paternal kin to a vertical patrilineal noble family structure that marginalised and even excluded women and younger sons.[2] The writing is so deliriously good, the structuralist binaries so enticingly straightforward, the misogyny of the medieval society so deliciously horrible, that the reader is helplessly drawn in, but at a cost. Over the past several decades, generations of scholars have pointed to ever more problems with Duby's ideas, both for medieval Europe in general and for the Mâconnais and Northern France that served as the chief sites for Duby's research.[3] It is my contention

2. Karl Schmid, "Zur Problematik von Familie, Sippe und Geschlecht, Haus und Dynastie beim mittelalterlichen Adel," *Zeitschrift für die Geschichte des Oberrheins*, 105 (1957): 1–62; Georges Duby, *The Chivalrous Society* trans. Cynthia Postan (London: Edward Arnold, 1977).
3. Karl Leyser, "The German Aristocracy from the Ninth to the Early Twelfth Century: A Historical and Cultural Sketch," *Past & Present* 41 (1968): 25–53; idem, "Debate: Maternal Kin in Early Medieval Germany: A Reply," *Past & Present* 49 (1970): 126–34; Anita Guerreau-Jalabert, Régine Le Jan, and Joseph Morsel, "De l'histoire de la famille à l'anthropologie de la parenté," in *Les tendances actuelles de l'histoire du Moyen Âge en France et en Allemagne*, ed. Otto Gerhard Oexle and Jean-Claude Schmitt (Paris: Publications de la Sorbonne, 2002), 433–46; Anita Guerreau-Jalabert, "Sur les structures de parenté dans l'Europe médiévale," *Annales. Économies, sociétés, civilizations* 36 (1981): 1028–49; Benjamin Arnold, *Princes and Territories in Medieval Germany* (Cambridge: Cambridge University Press, 1991), chap. 8; David Crouch, *The Image of Aristocracy in Britain 1000–1300* (London: Routledge, 1992), esp. 10–11; Elisabeth Van Houts, *Memory and Gender in Medieval Europe, 900–1200* (Toronto: University of Toronto Press, 1999); Theodore Evergates, *The Aristocracy of the County of Champagne* (Philadelphia: University of Pennsylvania Press, 2007), 119–40; Amy Livingstone, *Out of Love for my Kin. Aristocratic Family Life in the Lands of the Loire 1000–1200* (Ithaca: Cornell University

that we must continue to challenge the ideas about patriarchy, patriline, and primogeniture in marriage and in families and more found
in Duby's beautiful tomes. We must shake free of the various deeply
misleading notions that we owe to Duby: notions of how nobles married and divorced, how they thought of themselves, and the nature
of their relationships with their clerical kinsmen.[4] Briefly put, noble
marriage and succession practices did not develop as a result of a competition between two opposing classes of persons, clergy and nobility,
who each had their own ideas about how families could be made and
unmade. No strict canon law inflicted upon nobles by a stern class of
clergy forced any transformation in family marriage structure or inheritance practice. Instead, over the eleventh and twelfth centuries, men
and women together, clergy and lay alike, formulated an ideal of marriage as monogamous and indissoluble. The strategic use and abuse of
this ideal in marriage law, exploited by laity as well as clergy, served
as the underpinnings of a system that allowed powerful families to
continue in their efforts to rule over western Europe.

Redefining Chivalric Families

Recent scholarship has suggested definitions for a noble family such
as "a group of blood relatives conscious of their close ties with each
other and their ancestors,"[5] thus emphasising blood and a shared
sense of ancestry. We can also find as a definition for medieval families in general, "a unit with offspring produced by a married couple
and by the husband with mistresses or concubines,"[6] thus emphasising shared descent from one man. I would argue that we need to
adopt a definition that is more wide-ranging and flexible, and with less
emphasis on either blood or paternal descent. I suggest we define a

Press, 2010); Constance Bouchard, *Rewriting Saints and Ancestors: Memory and Forget-
ting in France, 500–1200* (Philadelphia: University of Pennsylvania Press, 2014), 107–8.
    4. Sara McDougall, "The Making of Marriage in Medieval France," *Journal of Family
History* 38 (2013): 103–21.
    5. Constance Bouchard, "The Origins of the French Nobility: A Reassessment," *Ameri-
can Historical Review* 86 (1981): 501–32, at 502. Scholarly ideas of family have expanded
a great deal since 1981, and particularly at the hands of Constance Bouchard, so it is
unlikely that she would still endorse this definition. See most recently Bouchard, *Rewriting
Saints.*
    6. Stephanie Christelow, "The Division of Inheritance and the Provision of Non-Inher-
iting Offspring Among the Anglo-Norman Elite," *Medieval Prosopography* 17:2 (1996):
1–44, at 7.

noble family, instead, as a very broadly conceived kin-group, made up of people with a shared sense of not just paternal but also, or even primarily, maternal lineage. Their sense of family included not just blood relations but also marital kin. It reached back via ancestors on both sides to some celebrated ancestor or ancestors of legendary origins, such as Trojan or Arthurian. They also claimed descent from less legendary imperial or royal stock, if the claim was still sometimes quite fictive in their connections to the ancestor in question. Aristocratic identity was also associated with certain territories or titles. But we should not imagine a static society. New marriages and new generations, new political achievements and military losses constantly shifting the boundaries and membership of this fluid group, whose centre also shifted depending on the particular circumstances of the kindred. Membership of such a group was neither exclusive nor necessarily lifelong. One constant, however, is that the goal, the collective vision, of this group centred on the acquisition and retention of property and titles, on the advancement of its members in both secular and holy spheres, at home and abroad, in crusading enterprises or less exalted forms of conquest and colonisation.

While the vagueness of such a definition may annoy some readers, it offers a far more accurate assessment of our current understanding of these people and how they thought of themselves and functioned as a unit. Adopting this sense of what counted as kin also facilitates our efforts to uncover commonalities throughout various regions of western Christian Europe.

Making use of this working definition of the "chivalric family," this chapter is divided into three sections: marriage, remarriage and divorce, and inheritance. It aims to elaborate on several points central to the understanding of medieval aristocratic families that I propose, relying heavily on the excellent recent prior scholarship cited above and below. One key aspect that will not be dealt with in detail below, but has absolute pride of place in any understanding of noble families, is the centrality of lineage. As demonstrated most recently by Constance Bouchard, we now know that from the time of the rise and fall of the Carolingian Empire we can find sources that demonstrate powerful people's shared sense of family consciousness. We learn of an obsession with ancestry and an eagerness to prove noble status by claiming descent from the Emperor Charlemagne and his family or another venerable lineage such as the Visigothic rulers of Iberia,

the Lombard kings of Italy or the Wessex in England.[7] They made
such claims, we know, because membership of these kin-groups could
mean great power and wealth, the kind of connections that made a
career. In doing so, as recent scholarship has emphasised, they made
use of not just paternal but also maternal ancestry, as well as some
artistic licence.

As what follows will address in detail, the acquisition or retention
of property and influence was the business of these men and women,
and it was very much a family business, drawing upon both near and
quite distant kin. One of the main means by which a family's holdings
transferred was, of course, inheritance, a system that valued kin, but
one that had fewer rules, I argue, than has often been assumed. The
establishment of rigid rules begins only in the late twelfth century;
application of these rules, of course, remains another matter entirely.
Both long before and after the establishment of this inheritance law,
marriage served as an essential means for perpetuating the family and
furthering its efforts at enrichment. Marriage deserves pride of place
in any understanding of medieval noble families, therefore, but it must
be properly contextualised. We should recognise that nobles made use
of a wide range of connections with kin beyond the natal family. We
should recognise as well that marriage was not necessarily a one-time
event for those who did marry. Remarriage following death or divorce
played a fundamental role in the structure, and the constant restructur-
ing, of medieval families. At the same time, we should not overstate, or
at least not misunderstand, the role of marriage in noble family structure. Not all medieval nobles made good by means of marriage, nor
had they to marry to make good. They participated in a broad network
system that could also profit from the activities and connections of
men and women who did not marry or produce children. Churchmen
and women had their uses for the larger group, as did bachelor uncles.
Also, while the children born of marriages had certain advantages,
it was not necessarily always a requirement that a child be born of
marriage to succeed as a medieval nobleman or woman. It is clear that
children born outside legitimate marriage did have a place, if some-

7. Bouchard, *Rewriting Saints*; Ian Wood, "Genealogy Defined by Women: The Case of
the Pippinids," in *Gender in the Early Medieval World: East and West 300–900*, ed. Leslie
Brubaker and Julia M. H. Smith (Cambridge: Cambridge University Press, 2004), 234–56;
Helmut Reimitz, "Geschlechterrollen und Genealogie in der fränkischen Historiographie,"
in *Frauenbild und Geschlechterrollen bei antiken Autoren an der Wende von der Spätantike
zum Mittelalter* (Cologne: Böhlau, 2007), 335–54.

times tenuous, in noble families. We should recognise too, as I have argued elsewhere, that the term "bastard" requires careful definition if we are to avoid anachronism.[8]

While the role of marriage has not been properly contextualised, the role of women has become increasingly appreciated in recent scholarly literature. We can go further still in recognising the essential role of both maternal lineage and women, as wives, heiresses, widows, and as divorcées, in medieval noble families. In our understanding of a noblewoman's lifecycle, additionally, we should recognise, as recent scholarship has highlighted, that it was within the realm of the possible in some regions that many women outlived their husbands. Indeed, despite the difficulties of calculating the age of people whose year of birth we usually do not know, scholars such as Theodore Evergates have determined that more than a few noblewomen of the Champagne probably lived into their 60s and 70s, sometimes having had many children with successive husbands.[9]

All this leaves us with a very broad and complex understanding of kin, and a broad and interrelated kin-group. This does not mean, of course that all members of a kin-group acted in concert, far from it. Brothers could be enemies as easily as could stepmothers, uncles, or husbands, not to mention ex-husbands or ex-fathers-in-law.[10] This reliance on broad kin-groups did not bring peace to Europe, far from it.[11] It did, though, serve as the primary vehicle by which the chivalric noble, or noblewoman, made his or her way in the world.

Making Chivalric Families: Getting Married

Unlike the fairy tales of yore that often end with a marriage, both the medieval chivalric tales of Chrétien de Troyes and also scholarly histories of the chivalric family often begin with marriage. Marriage, legal marriage, had different meaning, implications, and practices from those found in the thirteenth century. Even canon law, the law

8. Sara McDougall, *Royal Bastards: the Birth of Illegitimacy, c. 800–c. 1230* (Oxford: Oxford University Press, 2017), 171–73.

9. See Evergates, *Aristocracy*.

10. Constance Bouchard, "Conclusion: The Future of Medieval Kinship Studies," in *Verwandtschaft, Name und Soziale Ordnung (300–1000)*, ed. Steffen Patzold and Karl Ubl (Berlin: De Gruyter, 2014), 303–13.

11. On violence as socially constructive and cohesion-building see Max Gluckman, "The Peace in the Feud," *Past & Present* 8 (1955): 1–14.

of the Church, had a good deal of fluidity and flexibility well into the thirteenth century. Most importantly, as will be addressed in the section on inheritance, marriage or its absence did not have ramifications for children and their inheritance rights found in the thirteenth century and beyond.

Marriage, even first marriage, could be a rather late moment to encounter a chivalric aristocrat on the make. Matrimony marked, often, a man's transition to adulthood and sometimes his initial stepping into the role of ruler of whatever lands or titles his family or that of his wife had bestowed upon him in the course of their efforts to organise the prospects of the next and later generations of their families. It could also, however, have been arranged for him before his birth, promised as the son of one lineage to the daughter of another, born or unborn.

Let us therefore begin with marriage. Age at the time of an arrangement to marry varied tremendously.[12] The norm seems to have been for nobles to marry spouses from a similar social ranking, more or less, and around the same age, though men often had ten years or more on their wives, and women sometimes married much younger men. If the union was agreed to when the intended spouses were quite young, the daughter might be raised alongside her future husband, or she might stay at home or with natal kin; an abbess-aunt in a convent might provide for her education. Some children could be promised, as the Trencavel example considered below suggests, before birth. Other men and women might marry in their fifties or beyond.

Among the families considered here parents or guardians arranged the marriages of their children, and could, in fact, arrange first marriages well into that "child's" adult years. When men and women reached their majority, particularly when widows or widowers remarried, they could sometimes choose the most desirable mate for themselves, as seems often to have been the case in the Champagne, or might require royal or comital permission, as sometimes happened in other parts of France, and in Iberia, England, Sicily and Jerusalem.[13] Some who wished to remarry, it should be added, needed the assent

---

12. Evergates, *Aristocracy*, 101–18; Jonathan Lyon, *Princely Brothers and Sisters: The Sibling Bond in German Politics, 1100–1250* (Ithaca: Cornell University Press, 2012), 53.

13. Evergates, *Aristocracy*, 101; Simon Barton, *The Aristocracy in Twelfth-Century León and Castile* (Cambridge: Cambridge University Press, 1997), 51; Joanna Drell, *Kinship and Conquest: Family Strategies in the Principality of Salerno During the Norman Period, 1077–1194* (Ithaca: Cornell University Press, 2002), 60–61; eadem, "The Aristo-

of religious authorities and needed to appease as well any potentially aggrieved kinsmen, as they had first to find some way to get themselves unmarried from their current spouse. In any case, the marriages, at least as we can reconstruct them, all share some sort of property transaction. As all this suggests, these marriages took place for a range of reasons that cannot always be explained by a desire to perpetuate the family dynasty, as the Duby-Schmid model assumed.[14]

To take one example from the South of France, in 1110, Bernard Aton IV Trencavel and his wife Cecilia of Provence promised their daughter Ermengard in marriage to Gausfred, the son of Girard of Roussillon, and included in their offer four local fiefs, two castles and all that came with them. They promised that if Ermengard died Gausfred could marry one of their other daughters instead. Bernard and Cecilia also promised that if they died without male issue Gausfred could have, along with the daughter he married, at least Béziers and Agde, and if they had no other children surviving them, also everything else they had.[15] This was a match of enormous local political significance. A depiction of the matrimonial arrangements was included among the illustrations of the late twelfth-century Catalan cartulary, the *Liber feudorum maior* (Fig. 5.1). Ermengard and Gausfred would eventually marry, but not for quite a few years. This example demonstrates how impersonal these arrangements could be. A daughter of one family was to marry the heir of another family. It need not matter which daughter, but somehow that property, and a woman born to that family, was to unite with the heir of the other family, and could in principle eventually inherit all that the Trencavel family had. Things went another way. In the end, the Trencavel family carried on its rule in the south via Ermengard's brother. After the death of Ermengard's and Gausfred's son, Roussillon passed into the hands of the House of Barcelona to the exclusion of Gausfred's children with another woman.[16]

cratic Family," in *The Society of Norman Italy*, ed. Graham A. Loud and Alex Metcalfe (Leiden: Brill, 2002), 98–113, at 112.

14. The importance of desire for offspring will be considered in more detail below, in the discussion of motivations for annulments.

15. *Liber feudorum maior: cartulario real que se conserva en el archivo de la corona de Aragon*, ed. Francisco Miquel Rosell, 2 vols. (Barcelona: Consejo Superior de Investigaciones Científicas, 1945), 2: 269–70, no. 786.

16. Martin Aurell, *Les noces du comte: mariage et pouvoir en Catalogne (785–1213)* (Paris: Publications de la Sorbonne, 1994), 350–51; McDougall, *Royal Bastards*, 171–73.

Fig. 5.1—Bernard Aton IV Trencavel and his wife Cecilia of Provence promise their daughter Ermengard to the future Gausfred III of Roussillon. Barcelona, Archivo de la Corona d'Aragon, *Liber Feudorum Maior*, fol. 78v (late twelfth century). © age fotostock, Spain.

Remarriage and Divorce

Theodore Evergates makes a significant point when he calls for attention to the role of remarriage and what he calls blended families in medieval noble society.[17] In his Champagne, women frequently remarried and often had children with both of their spouses, acting, as Evergates describes it, as the "linchpin" between two families. The implications for child custody and inheritance are dauntingly complex, but potentially of the greatest importance for our understanding of medieval noble concepts of family and of their inheritance succession practices.

In Champagne, Evergates found noblewomen living long lives, often with two marriages, and often with multiple children born to each. Sometimes they brought the children with them to the new marriage, and this might also include children from the husband's first marriage; sometimes the children were left behind to be raised by their paternal kin. That could mean an end to the relationships between mother and children and her first husband's lineage.[18] The sources at least offer few traces of any ongoing connections between Eleanor of Aquitaine and her daughters with Louis VII following her divorce and remarriage to Henry II. More often, however, Evergates sees the women as the linchpin between two families, acting to perpetuate both lineages, lineages within which children with the same mother but a different father, or the reverse, nevertheless referred to each other as siblings. Evergates offers as an example Geoffroy IV of Joinville's referring to Hugh III of Broyes as his brother. Both men were the sons of Felicity of Brienne, but with different fathers.[19] The *Acts and Letters of the Marshal Family* provide as well the image of the 1248 funeral of Matilda Bigot, countess of Norfolk and Warenne, with the four sons born to her and her two successive husbands, acting as her pallbearers.[20] To this we can add the voice of Jonathan Lyon on the Staufen court: "At the royal court, the distinction between full siblings and half siblings

17. Evergates, *Aristocracy*, 148–50.

18. Ibid., 151–52.

19. Ibid., 150, 354 n. 57: "Ego Gaufridus, dominus Jonisville, frater Hugonis, dominus Brecensis."

20. *The Acts and Letters of the Marshal Family, Marshals of England and Earls of Pembroke, 1145–1248*, ed. David Crouch (London: Cambridge University Press for the Royal Historical Society, 2015), 39 and notes.

seems not to have been a significant one."[21] That said, half siblings had various advantages or disadvantages that their combination of lineage provided, the different mix of paternal or maternal blood provided different kinds of ties and opportunities and assets.

Less frequent than remarriage following the death of a spouse, but also deserving of careful scholarly analysis, is what medieval sources often call divorce but what we might think of as an annulment, the dissolution of a marriage. While we know surprisingly little about the consequences of annulments, scholars have made more effort to understand what led medieval noblemen and women to seek to dissolve their—in principle—indissoluble marriages.

We should first of all recognise that noble families of the eleventh and twelfth centuries did not have quite the same ideas about legitimate marriage and its consequences for inheritance found only in later centuries. To be sure, contemporary Christian marriage law norms urged above all, and with greatest consistency, monogamous and indissoluble marriage, privileging only the children born to such unions. Noblemen and women did generally restrain themselves to one legally wed spouse at a time, but they did not necessarily stay with that spouse for life. Duby judged motivations wrongly here too. He assumed that men changed wives above all in search of male heirs, and this is once again misleading. When noblemen and women did obtain annulments and remarry—or simply remarry without bothering with any niceties of divorce—desire for offspring does not appear to be the primary motivation. Men did change wives, and women changed husbands, but new political circumstances, or what we might call personal differences, most consistently explain these actions.

Indeed, childlessness may not have necessarily mattered as much as we might assume. Research into noble families in Iberia, for example, has suggested that as many as one in three noble families did not have any children who survived them.[22] Other families certainly managed many, even astonishingly many children. Those who did not, however, did not necessarily seek to annul their marriages. Some marriages, some partners, were too politically useful to set aside. This may explain, for example, the Flemish count Philip of Alsace's score of

21. Lyon, *Princely Brothers*, 95.

22. Reyna Pastor de Togneri, "Historia de las familias en Castille y León (siglos X–XIV) y su relación con la formación de los grandes dominios eclesiásticos," *Cuadernos de Historia de España* 43–44 (1967): 88–118 at 103; Barton, *Aristocracy*, 46.

years as husband to Elisabeth of Vermandois. Philip remained married to Elisabeth until her death in 1183 despite their having no issue, and despite as well a salacious story of his executing her lover by hanging him upside down above a latrine.[23] The usefulness of a wife's political identity and connections does not, however, explain why the childless Emperor Henry II remained with his wife Cunigunde of Luxembourg, whom he married before he became emperor, a shift in fortunes that could well have inspired another man to upgrade to a more politically important and potentially fertile spouse.

As for those men and women who did end one marriage in favour of another, we can point to a range of motivations. Some sought to profit from new opportunities, or not to lose any more time on a union that had ceased to prove useful. What remains baffling to us is the consequences of these ruptures.

In principle, if a marriage was dissolved with both spouses granted the right to remarry, which was most often the outcome in these cases, the spouses no longer had any rights to any property that was exchanged as part of the marriage contract. We know far less than we would like about the details of how the presumably herculean task of resolving who should get what got sorted out. Some papal letters and canon law texts urge that church courts might have oversight and could punish failure to return a dowry, for example, with ecclesiastical sanctions. On the whole this was probably a matter of private settlement or of secular litigation. Evergates suggests that as long as a husband returned the dowry there was no need for litigation, and indeed suggests that many families found a way to handle the dissolution of a union and all its implications for property and any issue with some ease, or at least without major crisis. We would of course still like to know a great deal more.[24]

23. Benedict of Peterborough, *The Chronicle of the reigns of Henry II and Richard I, A.D. 1169–1192*, ed. William Stubbs, 2 vols., Rolls Series 49 (London: Longman, 1867) 1: 99–101; Ralph of Diceto, *The Historical Works of Master Ralph de Diceto, Dean of London*, ed. William Stubbs, 2 vols., Rolls Series 68 (London: Longman, 1876), 1: 402; Roger of Howden, *Chronica magistri Rogeri de Houedene*, ed. William Stubbs, 4 vols., Rolls Series 51 (London: Longman, 1868–71), 2: 83. For a refutation of this alleged adultery and execution see Ruth Harvey, "Cross-Channel Gossip in the Twelfth Century," *Harlaxton Medieval Studies* 8 (2000): 48–59.

24. Looking to England and to the thirteenth century, Paul Brand has unearthed a handful of cases of annulments on the grounds of precontract, that is an annulment on the grounds that a man or woman already had a living spouse at the time of the subsequent, and therefore illegal, marriage. Brand has found traces of litigation that address the property implications of these annulments, which suggest that English common law courts

To examine noble divorce practice in some detail I offer two examples. In both cases property and political interests motivated noblewomen and men to change spouses. It is also important to recognise
that these shifting marital alliances did not result in the dispossess-
ion of the children born to the ruptured union. As this suggests, both
Duby's ideas on the primary motivation for changing wives (dynastic)
and his ideas on the role of the canon law of marriage in determi-
nations of succession and inheritance, at least before the thirteenth
century, require careful reconsideration. For our first example I would
like to point to the family of the knight William Marshal (d.1219).[25] In
around 1145, John Marshal, father of the great chivalric hero William
Marshal, married William's mother, Sibyl, the sister of Patrick Earl of
Salisbury. Patrick had got the better of John in their local feuding, and
this marriage was to bring peace between the warring families. John
already had a wife and two sons at this time, but this proved no problem for the new union. Somehow, we know not how, that first marriage was brought to an end so John could marry Sibyl. John's former
wife Adelina then married Stephen Gay. One of her sons with John,
Gilbert, later made an agreement with this Stephen Gay concerning
Gilbert's inheritance from his mother, which seems to have survived
the rupture of the marriage to Gilbert's father.

However it was that the first marriage of John and Adelina came
to an end, this rupture had no bearing on the rights of their sons as
heirs. Their eldest son died before his father, but the second, Gilbert,
briefly held his father's office and also his mother's lands, despite the
fact that both parents remarried and had additional children. William
Marshal inherited his father's office and lands only in 1194 after the
death of his half-brother Gilbert and that of his elder full-brother. In
this case, and in every other example I know of, the annulment of a
marriage deemed illegal—if we can hope that John and Adelina in fact
obtained an annulment before remarriage—had no negative impact
on the standing of their children. Certainly stepmothers on occasion,
the stepmother of the Ottonian Liudolf of Swabia, or the stepmother

may have seen fit to punish the spouse who belatedly discovered precontract with the loss
of some marital property. See Brand, "Secular Consequences of Annulment of Marriage
for Precontract in England," in *Texts and Contexts in Legal History: Essays in Honor of
Charles Donahue*, ed. John Witte, Sara McDougall, and Anna di Robilant (Berkeley: University of California Press: 2016) 209–21.

25. On Marshal see above all David Crouch, *William Marshal*, 3rd ed. (London: Routledge: 2016).

of Bohemond of Taranto, made sure of the success of their sons and deprived their stepsons of their fathers' titles.[26] That is not, however, the same thing as being born to an illegal marriage necessarily harming the inheritance prospects of a noble child.

We can tell much the same story as found with William Marshal's parents if we turn to one of the noble divorces featured in Theodore Evergates' research into aristocratic families of Champagne. In 1189, Thibaut of Briey, a 29-year-old widower with a young daughter, married a woman at least ten years his senior, Hermesend of Bar-sur-Seine, widow of Anselm II of Traînel, whom she had married in 1159 and who had died in 1184. Hermesend and Anselm had a son and daughter together; the son inherited Traînel.[27] As part of the 1189 marriage agreement, Thibaut promised Hemersend as dower his castle of Briey, the possibility of another castle if his inheritance prospects improved, and half of all he acquired after their marriage. Thibaut's prospects did indeed improve. His brother died in 1190 and he became count of Bar-le-Duc, and Hermesend his countess. Despite Hemersend's relatively advanced age—according to Evergates she could have been in her mid-forties—they had a son and two daughters together.

This marriage came to an end, however, in 1196.[28] Cynics might assume that the older wife had lost her charms for her husband, the new count, and this could have played a role in Thibaut's decision. What we know for certain, however, is that it was the death of the count of Luxembourg, leaving behind a vulnerable young heiress, which seems to have prompted Thibaut to act. We do not know what action he took as no trace of any annulment survives, but it seems probable that he obtained one on some valid grounds or other.[29] Free, in any case, he took up the cause of his vulnerable neighbour, whom he married. Once victorious, he ruled Luxembourg in her name. Hemersend, meanwhile, lost her dower lands promised by Thibaut in the marriage contract, and settled instead in her dower lands of Traînel, where she lived with her son and daughter-in-law until her

26. McDougall, *Royal Bastards*, 100, 132–36.

27. Evergates, *Aristocracy*, 116, 214–15.

28. Ibid., 366–67, cites Michel Parisse, "Thiébaut comte de Bar et de Luxembourg," in *Ermesinde et l'affranchissement de la ville de Luxembourg: études sur la femme, le pouvoir et la ville au XIIIᵉ siècle*, ed. Michel Margue (Luxembourg: CLUDEM, 1994), 161–78, at 168–69.

29. Michel Parisse, "Les Trois Mariages du comte de Bar Thiébaut Ier," *Annales de l'Est*, 19 (1967): 57–61, at 59–60.

death in 1211.[30] As for Hemersend's children with Thibaut, their two
daughters married local nobles and their son, Henry, succeeded to his
father's county of Bar after Thibaut's death at the Battle of Bouvines
in 1214.

Inheritance

In this culture of acquisition and deal-making, inheritance norms had
no real rigidity. There was, however, a remarkably strong and shared
sense that kin had a right to inherit titles from other kinsmen, and that
parents could bestow lands and titles on their children, or not; but that
children, and nephews and nieces, had in principle rights to what had
belonged to their ancestors. One child might take up the chief title, but
other children could expect to be provided for, by their parents and by
the sibling given charge of the title and of their wellbeing. In Iberia,
meanwhile, impartible inheritance would continue well beyond our
period, with younger sons and daughters born in and out of marriage
alike favoured.[31]

The rights of kin as heirs, particularly of direct descendants, but
also those of siblings or nieces, were, by and large, recognised. Medieval romance denounced kings who did not respect such principles
as fomenters of civil war.[32] Young children could inherit, regencies
worked effectively to preserve governance intact until a child reached
the age of majority. To be sure, sometimes a powerful neighbour or
overlord might take advantage of a young and vulnerable heir's circumstances to invade or force a marriage and assume power via these
means. A late ruler's brothers, too, might not leave a young niece or
nephew in peace. But it was generally considered right that children
inherit titles from their parents, that parents should be able to pass
their lands and titles on to their children or other close kin.[33]

---

30. Evergates, *Aristocracy*, 118, 215.

31. Barton, *Aristocracy*, 39–42; McDougall, *Royal Bastards*, see esp. chap. 10.

32. Sarah Kay, ed. and trans., *Raoul de Cambrai* (Oxford: Clarendon Press, 1992). See
also Stephen White, "Disinheritance," in *Law and Government in Medieval England and
Normandy: Essays in Honour of Sir James Holt*, ed. George Garnett and John Hudson
(Cambridge: Cambridge University Press, 1994), 173–97.

33. The Empire to a large extent offers an exception to this, with some titles in the gift
of the emperor, and the title of emperor itself contested, often passing only with difficulty
from father to son.

Recognition of the importance of a kin-group's right to rule can be found most obviously, perhaps, in the case of the kingdom of Jerusalem, in which rule over the kingdom passed to nephews, brothers, daughters, and sisters over and over, in the absence of any consistent ability to produce direct male heirs. We can see this as well in parents' decisions to name as sole heir to a title their daughter, keeping her at home with her father's title while marrying off the son, as in the case of the succession of Duke Conan III of Brittany's daughter Bertha.[34] We see the value of these lineages, the degree to which their rights received respect, in the successful assumption of power by a very young heir via a regency. Other examples of this are found when we consider the successful temporary removal of a monk and an abbess from their monastic retreats so they could marry, have children and, having perpetuated the dynasty, return to religious life.[35]

As this suggests, we cannot imagine medieval social order as governed by the kind of male-dominated legalism imagined by Duby. Noble families did not operate according to the logic of a strict primogeniture.[36] Even the narrower idea of a lineage as a patriline is rather misleading. Take, for example, the early succession to Hainaut. With the chronicler Gilbert of Mons as our guide, we begin, in the eleventh century, with Count Hermann, who had Hainaut "by hereditary right" and managed to acquire as well neighbouring Valenciennes, once he bought off the siblings of the late count, who had died without direct heirs. Count Hermann and his wife Richilde produced two children, a son and a daughter. If for the county of Hainaut succession operated according to strict primogeniture or even a rougher sense of paternal lineage, we could not imagine what happens next. Rather than having Hainaut pass from father to son, we find that after Hermann's death his widow, Richilde, ruled Hainaut as her dower and as guardian for her young children. But then Richilde remarried, to Baldwin of Flanders, son to Count Baldwin V, a mighty dynast who, along with his wife Adela of France, imparted to their extremely well-married children Carolingian, Capetian, and Lombard ancestry. Richilde and Baldwin, who inherited Flanders from his father, had two sons together. At this

34. Melissa Pollock, "Duchesses and Devils: The Breton Succession Crisis (1148–1189)," *French History* 23 (2009): 1–22.

35. McDougall, *Royal Bastards*, chap. 6.

36. See also the case elaborated in Jean-François Nieus, "Sigard's Belt: The Family of Chocques and the Borders of Knighthood (*ca.* 980–1100)" in this volume.

point, though possibly already before, Richilde's children with Hermann, the two heirs to Hainaut, became a nun and a bishop, and the son
was maligned as allegedly "lame" or having some "defect of body."
Richilde and Baldwin meanwhile retained Hainaut and Valenciennes
for themselves and for their sons.[37] These sons and Richilde failed to
hold on to Flanders, the paternal inheritance, after Baldwin's death,
but they retained Hainaut, which they had claim to only via Richilde's
first marriage. Needless to say, none of this can be explained by reference to some supposed rule of primogeniture or even an exclusive
focus on paternal lineage.

Let us now turn briefly to Baldwin V of Flanders and Adela of
France's two other children, Baldwin VI's siblings. Here we can see
again how differently succession operated from what those who adhere
to Duby's ideas might expect. Their daughter Matilda married that
most famous of bastards, William of Normandy, in around 1050, and
William and Matilda had to pay a great deal for this union of Norman
power with some of the best lineage on offer, as this union violated
the then-pope's ideas on incest prohibitions. As for Robert, Baldwin
and Adela's younger son, he married another widow acting as regent,
Gertrude of Saxony, formerly the wife of the Count of Holland. Robert
nicknamed himself "the Frisian" after his marital connections again,
as with his brother Baldwin, this was a family connection to power
only accessible to him via his wife's first marriage. On his elder brother's death, however, Robert claimed Flanders for himself, making war
on the widow and young heir that his late brother had commended to
his protection. In the end Robert won, passing Flanders on to his son
Robert, who married yet another woman of the best lineage, Clemence
of Burgundy. To be sure, these marriages would not result in peace or
smooth succession for Flanders. In none of them, in any case, can we
say that any strong rule of paternal inheritance was being adhered to.
Nor did these families practise strict primogeniture, excluding all but
the eldest son from inheriting undivided title and lands. Indeed, as
Amy Livingstone writes: "Individual circumstance and family need
dictated the dispersal of family resources rather than a dedication to

37. Gilbert of Mons, *La chronique de Gislebert de Mons*, ed. Léon Vanderkindere
(Brussels: Kiessling, 1904), 2–17, 34, 43, 47; *The Chronicle of Hainaut by Gilbert of
Mons*, trans. Laura Napran (Woodbridge: Boydell, 2005) 3–11, 21–31. See also Karen
Nicholas, "Countesses as Rulers in Flanders," in *Aristocratic Women in Medieval France*,
ed. Theodore Evergates (Philadelphia: University of Pennsylvania Press, 1999), 111–37,
at 115.

the idea that one method of distribution was in some way superior to all others. Inheritance was thus, diverse, fluid, and far from monolithic…" In the Loire Valley she has researched so extensively, we can find inheritance practices that include "collective, impartible, partible, and primogenitary" modes.[38]

There is, therefore, little evidence for a rejection of cognatic family structure in favour of agnatic at around the year 1000, and we must continue to seek better ways to understand how these families in fact functioned.[39] Clearly, they did not forget maternal kin or mothers, nor did they exclude daughters. Moreover, to take on another of Duby's all-too-dominant ideas, they did not operate in opposition to a competing class of clergy. Important clerics and prominent laymen both often had noble ancestry, or soon joined its ranks, and did not forget their kin. As for those nobles in secular life, no fear of the clergy, who were in fact their "brother monks," compelled them to modify their marriage or inheritance practices.[40]

Nor did nobles necessarily exclude from their families "bastards," children born to their kin but outside "lawful marriage," treating them as without any claims on the family's resources. Indeed, it is worth considering in some detail that most famous alleged outsider to the chivalric family: the bastard. We should recognise, first of all, that Duby and others' ideas about the role of Christian marriage law have once again misled scholars, and profoundly. To be sure, children born to illicit unions had a harder time of it than any half-siblings born of a marital union. "Illicit unions" is a broad umbrella, but we can think most obviously of the children of priests, once priests were required to live as celibates, and also of the children born to non-marital relationships such as concubinage or a secret affair, as having weaker claims as heirs to what their parents wished to pass down to them.

That does not mean, however, that all children born outside legal marriage suffered. Children born to illegal marriages made between

38. Livingstone, *Out of Love*. See also eadem, "Climbing the Tree of Jesse: Aristocratic Marriage in the Lands of the Loire, 1050–1150," in *Les stratégies matrimoniales (IXᵉ–XIIIᵉ siècle)*, ed. Martin Aurell (Turnhout: Brepols, 2013), 101–15.

39. David Crouch, *The Birth of Nobility. Constructing Aristocracy in England and France, 900–1300*, (Harlow: Pearson, 2005): 112 "the Duby-Schmid thesis has been found by historians to perform badly under testing in northern Europe."

40. McDougall, "Making of Marriage;" Amy Livingstone, "Brother Monk: Monks and their family in the chartrain, 1000–1200," in *Medieval Monks and Their World: Ideas and Realities. Studies in Honor of Richard E. Sullivan*, ed. Richard Eugene Sullivan, David R. Blanks, and Michael Frassetto (Leiden: Brill, 2006), 93–115.

parents of similar (high) status retained their value as heirs even if
their parents' marriage was denounced as illegal or annulled. If parents
did bring their union to an end, separate, and remarry, a step-parent
might find an opportunity to cut them out in favour of their own children, but the illegality of the union did not (yet) bastardise children.
Children born to illegal marriages needed no help asserting their rights
as potential heirs until late in the twelfth century, the very moment in
which popes began to provide legitimacy to these children via various
legal mechanisms.[41]

As this suggests, the presence or absence of a legitimate marriage,
by which I mean a union generally recognised as valid and binding,
did not determine a child's worth as heirs. Instead, the status and political situation of the father and mother were the determining factors,
and determined both if the couple engaged in something resembling a
legitimate and public union with some property transferred, and also
what the relative value of their children could be. If a nobleman had
children with two different women in succession, it was the children of
the higher status woman, or the woman with more political influence,
generally through her natal kin, who had the best chance of inheriting
the best of what their father had. The illegality of a marriage, meanwhile, if the union was contracted between two high status persons,
had no bearing on the rights of their issue. Well into the late twelfth
century, the children of countless marriages deemed illegal by churchmen or statesmen alike inherited, and usually without any known
challenges to their rights as heirs. Indeed, it is anachronistic to apply
the word "bastard" to eleventh- and twelfth-century children of high
status parents whose marriage was considered illegal. Only in the final
decades of the twelfth century do we find such children described by
contemporaries as *bast* or *bastart* in French, *bastardalha* in Occitan,
or *bastardo* in Castilian. Until then, the most consistent usage for the
Latin term *bastardus* and for its variants such as *nothus* or *spurius* or
the newly-coined term for illegitimate issue *illegitimus* had its foundations in considerations of the parents' social status, not their marital
status.[42]

41. McDougall, *Royal Bastards*, esp. chap. 6.
42. See further McDougall, *Royal Bastards*, 44–48, 157–58. One possible exception
is found with a Roman council presided over by Gregory VII in 1074–75 which sought
to exclude from ordination the children of priests and of adultery and all who were in any
way bastards: *Acta ponticum romanorum inedita*, ed. Julius von Pflugk-Harttung, 2 vols.

As for those *bas* children born to less formal unions, to misalliances between a higher status parent with a lower status partner, they too did not necessarily count for nothing. Certainly their prospects were not likely to be good if their father refused to acknowledge them, but that "defect" could on occasion be corrected even against a father's wishes. Robert Curthose evidently did not want to recognise some children as his, but the alleged mother forced the issue by successfully undergoing the ordeal. Other men, most notably Robert's prolific brother King Henry I, freely acknowledged children born to their extramarital liaisons as their own, provided for them, and either helped with their upkeep in the care of the mother and her family, or had the child reared by a member of the father's own kin-group, or even at their own court.

Whatever the circumstances of their upbringing, some bastards were certainly considered members of their families. Northern French charter evidence shows that those granting a part of the family property to a religious institution asked for the consent of men referred to in these documents as "bastards"—as in "Johannes Bastardus." That they did so indicates that they recognised these "bastards" as potential claimants to the property whose assent was needed for the transfer to take place unchallenged.[43] To keep those born outside marriage from seeking titles in competition with "legitimate" half-siblings western European nobles did not evidently feel the need to go so far as to castrate the son of a ruler and his concubine to ensure his exclusion, as happened to Byzantine bastard Basil Lekapenos in the tenth century.[44] Excluded kin, like other political rivals in medieval Europe, whatever their quality of birth, died in battle or in prison, and in some cases found themselves blinded and enclosed in monasteries, but this could happen to a man regardless of any sense that he was or was not of legitimate birth. In any case, bastards could not be "counted out." In addition to the charter evidence just mentioned, we can find some bastards enjoying impressive success in claiming an inheritance, whether or not designated as heirs by their parents. William of Normandy succeeded in obtaining both the duchy of Normandy left to him by his father and eventually, by conquest, the English kingdom ruled

(Stuttgart: W. Kohlhammer, 1884), 2: 126, XIX: "filius presbyteri et adulter et quicumque bastardus non ordinetur…"

43. Dominique Barthélemy, *La société dans le comté de Vendôme de l'an mil au XIVᵉ siècle* (Paris: Fayard, 1993), 536–40.

44. Michael Psellos, *Chronographia*, 1.3, ed. E.R.A. Sewter (New Haven: Yale University Press, 1953), 11.

by his kinsman. The bastard Eustace of Breteuil, in principle excluded by his own father in favour of a nephew, nevertheless managed to take possession of what had belonged to his father and he probably could have kept his father's title had he behaved better. William of Ypres made a good couple of tries to claim Flanders despite being born outside marriage, and he did so with the support of an extremely powerful aunt, Clemence of Burgundy.[45] Teresa, the daughter of Emperor Alfonso VI of Castile-León and one of his concubines, obtained Portugal as a hereditary gift. She and her Burgundian husband—Clemence's brother—succeeded in establishing dynastic rule over a new kingdom. Bad behaviour, on occasion, cost bastards like Eustace of Breteuil their inheritances, as did bad luck, but the same can be said for their "betters."

Our sources are most detailed on the bastard children of noblemen, but with some effort we can recognise that noblewomen also had bastard children, and this did not stay quite the secret or have quite the consequences that we often mistakenly imagine. This is worth considering, and would merit further scholarship, not just for what it suggests about illegitimate birth, but also for the circumstances of women who had children out of wedlock. Take, for example, the many mistresses of Henry I of England. As Kathleen Thompson explains, they included "daughters or wives of those with a tradition of service to the crown" and represented a wide range of possible social statuses from bottom to rather high.[46] Ede of Greystoke had at least one or two children with Henry, presumably but not necessarily before her marriage to Robert d'Oilly, the constable of Oxford. These and many more children were recognised as Henry's, who also had a relationship of some kind with "Isabel, daughter of the count of Meulan and great-granddaughter of King Henry I of France." While Thompson assumes that it was "rare for those ladies to become respected matriarchs and dowagers" as happened with Isabel of Meulan, there is in fact no evidence that any of Henry's mistresses suffered a decline in status or marital prospects as a result of their extramarital relations. Certainly it is possible they did, but it is also possible they did not. We have no idea what it meant for these women to have had sex and children with a king or nobleman despite not being his wife. We do not know much about their relations

45. Nicholas, "Countesses," 119.
46. Kathleen Thompson, "Affairs of State: The Illegitimate Children of Henry I," *Journal of Medieval History* 29 (2003): 129–51, at 140.

with their children, or how their families and husbands treated these children, all matters that would benefit from extensive investigation. As this suggests, women's sexual activity, while surely subject to greater scrutiny and condemnation than that of men, did not necessarily meet with the harsh consequences so often imagined.

Conclusion

While discussions of medieval family structure by necessity often focus on marriage, this is to a certain extent misleading. Not all children of higher-status unions were born within a recognised marriage arrangement. Nor did all members of chivalric families marry or, if they did marry, remain married. Families included first of all wives and their maternal kin, siblings and cousins. But they also included half-siblings, the product of remarriage after death or divorce, or extra-marital relationships. Noble parents with lands and titles to pass on to their children might choose to keep the bulk of what they had intact, but had no absolute obligation to do so, or necessarily to favour a first-born son at all costs, though it is certainly true that first-born sons, from one marriage or from another, generally had the greatest likelihood of finding favour as heirs. Other children, far from being totally excluded, obtained property or lands via dowry or smaller inheritances, and also benefitted from family connections to obtain positions in royal or ecclesiastical households, or as knights.

Perhaps most important of all, we should recognise the ephemeral quality of these families. Their membership shifted not just with every generation but with every new marriage or remarriage, with death in battle or childbirth, and with the vicissitudes of shifting political fortunes. We imagine paternal dynastic continuity when in fact what we discover are practices that provided at best a fiction of patrilineal continuity. We should recognise instead that medieval noble families included far more kinds of kin. Marriage in particular could create more tangible bonds than typically found even today in modern western ideas of family and inheritance. If we can recognise all this, we come much closer to what seems to have been family as understood and as lived by these noble knights and ladies.

Jean-François NIEUS

SIGARD'S BELT: THE FAMILY OF CHOCQUES
AND THE BORDERS OF KNIGHTHOOD (*CA*. 980–1100)

Starting from the remarkable late tenth-century mention of one Sigardus militaris cingulo laboris innexus *in the* liber traditionum *of St Peters Abbey in
Ghent, which seems to acknowledge the early presence of "knightly" profiles
in the entourage of Count Arnulf II of Flanders (965–88), this chapter aims
to provide new insight into the Flemish aristocracy and its involvement with
warfare during the tenth and eleventh centuries. After discussing the literary
and social context of Sigard (I)'s mention in the* liber, *this case study moves
to the identification and characterisation of his eleventh-century descendants,
who settled in the Artois region—especially Sigard (III) of Chocques (attested
between 1065 and 1096), whose prominent career in Flanders, Hainaut and
England can be fairly well reconstructed. By shedding light on Sigard (I)'s
descendants, on their achievements, involvement with local lordship, aristocratic networks, princely patronage and, ultimately, the "high politics" of their
time, this study also sheds retrospective light on the status of their tenth-century ancestor. This man, considered in previous scholarship to be a lowly individual because of his supposedly subordinate military activities, must in fact
have been a very prominent member of the Flemish nobility of his day.*

The counts of Flanders have a reputation of being ambitious and
powerful princes whose successes relied upon their extensive military resources. Count Arnulf I, styled "the Great" (918–65), indeed
made considerable—though in part ephemeral—southward territorial
expansion by warfare.[1] A century later, his successors were routinely
awarded an ample money fief by the Anglo-Norman monarchs in
exchange for the service of hundreds of knights: the oldest recorded
agreement, in 1101, stipulates that no fewer than 1,000 knights or

---

1. Anton C.F. Koch, "Het graafschap Vlaanderen van de 9ᵈᵉ eeuw tot 1070," in *Algemene
geschiedenis der Nederlanden*, 15 vols. (Haarlem: Fibula-van Dishoeck, 1977–83), 1
(1980): 354–83, at 367–69; Jean-François Nieus, "Montreuil et l'expansion du comté de
Flandre au Xᵉ siècle," in *Quentovic. Environnement, archéologie, histoire. Actes du colloque international de Montreuil-sur-Mer, Étaples et Le Touquet et de la journée d'études
de Lille sur les origines de Montreuil-sur-Mer (11–13 mai 2006 et 1ᵉʳ décembre 2006),*
ed. Stéphane Lebecq, Bruno Béthouart, and Laurent Verslype (Lille: Éditions du Conseil
scientifique de l'Université de Lille 3, 2010): 493–505, at 494–98; Fraser McNair, "The
Young King and the Old Count: Around the Flemish Succession Crisis of 965," *Revue
belge de philologie et d'histoire* 95 (2017): 145–62.

mounted soldiers (*milites, equites*) were to be supplied within forty days of a summons.[2] The mobilisation of such an impressive force was only conceivable in a very deeply militarised society. However, the military organisation of tenth- and eleventh-century Flanders, as well as its politically, socially and culturally correlated features, remains effectively beyond the reach of today's historians.[3] Extremely scarce evidence even makes the simple study of the noble class, which must have been the backbone of Flemish armies, difficult before the twelfth century.[4] In this context, investigating the early relationship between aristocratic status and military practice in this part of Europe sounds like an impossible challenge; however in one case at least something can be said.

This case study starts from the examination of a high-ranking *miles* (although that particular substantive was not applied to him) in the entourage of Count Arnulf II (965–88), before moving on to the identification and characterisation of his descendants in the eleventh century. By shedding light on his descendants' achievements in this period, on their involvement with local lordship, aristocratic networks, princely patronage and, ultimately, "high politics" of their time, this study also sheds retrospective light on the status of their tenth-century ancestor. Very few great noblemen came out of nowhere in the Middle Ages. They were the beneficiaries of generations of local competition and acquisitions. This man, then, considered in previous scholarship to be a low-profile individual because of his supposedly subordinate military activities, must in fact have been a very prominent member of the Flemish nobility of his day.

2. Pierre Chaplais, ed., *Diplomatic Documents Preserved in the Public Record Office. Vol. 1: 1101–1272* (London: H.M. Stationery Office, 1964), 1–4, no. 1. See Eljas Oksanen, *Flanders and the Anglo-Norman World, 1066–1216* (Cambridge: Cambridge University Press, 2012), 54–68.

3. This early period is virtually absent from the classical study by Jan-Frans Verbruggen, *Het leger en de vloot van de graven van Vlaanderen vanaf het ontstaan tot in 1305* (Brussels: Koninklijke Vlaamse Academie van België voor Wetenschappen en Kunsten, 1960). Only sporadic pre-1100 evidence surfaces in Dirk Heirbaut, "De militaire rol van de feodaliteit in het graafschap Vlaanderen gedurende de 11de en 12de eeuw," *Revue belge d'histoire militaire* 29 (1992): 311–18, and Jean-François Nieus, "Avouerie et service militaire en Flandre au XIe siècle," in *Nouveaux regards sur l'avouerie. Les avoués des abbayes et des sièges épiscopaux entre Loire et Rhin (fin XIe–milieu XIIIe siècle). Acte du colloque de Namur, 4–5 février 2016*, ed. Nicolas Ruffini-Ronzani (Turnhout, Brepols: forthcoming).

4. As exemplified by the monumental study by Ernest Warlop, *De Vlaamse adel vóór 1300*, 3 vols. (Handzame: Familia et Patria, 1968). English translation: *The Flemish Nobility Before 1300*, 4 vols. (Kortrijk: G. Desmet-Huysman, 1974–76).

The Question of Sigard's Belt

The earliest mentions of *milites* in Flemish charter material are relatively late and inconsistent. They increase slowly from the 1040s and 1050s onwards,[5] in contexts where they seem to refer more to vassalic dependence than to a personal or corporate status focused on martial activities.[6] Narrative sources such as the much-studied *Miracula sancti Ursmari* (*ca.* 1060) and *Vita sancti Arnulfi Suessoniensis* (after 1087) may well throw slightly more light on early "knighthood" or warring elites in Flanders, yet they do not predate the second half

5. An isolated, though interesting, exception is provided by a 1016 charter in which appears a *Walonem quendam nobilem militem*, apparently a substantial landowner in the region of Saint-Omer. This charter has long been suspect (mainly because of its very unusual vocabulary), but its authenticity has been confirmed in recent scholarship: Benoît-Michel Tock, "Les mutations du vocabulaire latin des chartes au XIᵉ siècle," *Bibliothèque de l'École des chartes* 155 (1997): 119–48, at 142–48 (with an edition); Laurent Morelle, "Pratiques médiévales de l'écrit documentaire. Conférences de l'année 2014–2015," *Annuaire de l'École pratique des Hautes études. Résumés des conférences et travaux* 147 (2016): 155–60 (draws on a lecture given by Jean-Charles Bédague, who completed a Ph.D. on the archive of Notre-Dame of Saint-Omer in 2014). It is now established that the 1016 charter was copied in a now-lost eleventh-century hagiographical manuscript of Notre-Dame. According to Bédague, the charter may have been composed by the author of a *vita* once preserved in this manuscript, hence its unusual, "literary" vocabulary.

6. A preliminary search through the charter texts encoded or calendared in *Diplomata Belgica. The Diplomatic Sources from the Medieval Southern Low Countries*, ed. Thérèse de Hemptinne, Jeroen Deploige, Jean-Louis Kupper, and Walter Prevenier (Brussels: Royal Historical Commission, since 2015), accessed 1 March 2018, http://www.diplomata-belgica.be, suggests that, apart from an isolated case in 1016 (see above, n. 5), the earliest reliable mention of *milites* is to be found in a 1042 comital charter for Saint-Bertin, whose witness list ends with the names of five men, each styled *miles*, who were vassals of the local advocate: J.-F. Nieus and Steven Vanderputten, "Diplôme princier, matrice de faux, acte modèle. Le règlement d'avouerie du comte Baudouin V pour Saint-Bertin (1042) et ses réappropriations sous l'abbatiat réformateur de Lambert (1095–1123)," *The Medieval Low Countries* 1 (2014): 1–59, at 50–53. Later on, in 1051, the Count of Saint-Pol (in the southern part of Flanders) is reported to have enfeoffed land *cuidam suorum militum*: Daniel Haigneré, ed., *Les chartes de Saint-Bertin d'après le grand cartulaire de Dom Charles-Joseph Dewitte*, 4 vols. (Saint-Omer: Société des Antiquaires de la Morinie, 1886–99), 1: 26, no. 73. In 1051 again, Robert, subadvocate of Saint-Amé in Douai, is styled *miles* in a witness list to his own charter, which possibly refers to his being a vassal of both the castellan of Douai and the Count of Flanders: Lille, Archives départementales du Nord, 1 G 194, no. 1004 (see Cédric Giraud, Jean-Baptiste Renault, and Benoît-Michel Tock, eds., *Chartes originales antérieures à 1121 conservées en France* (Nancy: Centre de médiévistique Jean Schneider/Orléans: Institut de recherche et d'histoire des textes, 2010), accessed 1 March 2018, http://www.cn-telma.fr/originaux, no. 374). Robert's probable predecessor *Witselinus* also appears as the castellan's *miles* in an undated deed: Lille, Archives départementales du Nord, 1 G 194, no. 1005 (see Giraud, Renault, and Tock, eds., *Chartes originales*, no. 372). Further *milites* sporadically pop up in the entourages of the bishops of Thérouanne and Cambrai during the 1060s.

of the eleventh century.[7] Therefore, the remarkable appearance of a
certain *Sigardus, militaris cingulo laboris innexus,* in a Flemish diplomatic document dating back to the late tenth century deserves our
special attention. The celebrated *liber traditionum* of St Peter's Abbey
in Ghent, a unique source for the history of Flanders at the turn of the
tenth and eleventh centuries, actually mentions this Sigard on three
occasions.[8] In what appears to be a shortened version of a solemn
charter dated 982, we can see this Sigard, "equipped with the belt of
military duty," giving the monks his allodial *villa* of Boëseghem with
its dependencies, including a church, a mill and several tenants, in the
presence of Count Arnulf II.[9] Thirteen years later, in 995, Sigard, presumably the same man, donated another estate located in the eastern
part of the county, in Bambrugge.[10] And finally, in 1002, Sigard, then
styled *vir quidam divę memorię* (hence probably on his deathbed),
added to his previous gifts a church in Terdeghem, with the consent of
his three sons Ermenfrid, Adam and Erluin.[11] Terdeghem, designated
as Sigard's *hereditas,* is located near Cassel, some fifteen kilometres
north of the aforementioned *villa* of Boëseghem (Fig. 6.1).

7. For the *Miracula Ursmari*, see now Paulo Charruadas, "Principauté territoriale, reli-
ques et Paix de Dieu. Le comté de Flandre et l'abbaye de Lobbes à travers les *Miracula S.
Ursmari in itinere per Flandriam facta* (vers 1060)," *Revue du Nord* 89 (2007): 703–28;
Jehangir Malegam, "No Peace for the Wicked: Conflicting Visions of Peacemaking in an
Eleventh-Century Monastic Narrative," *Viator: Medieval and Renaissance Studies* 39
(2008): 23–49. The *Vita Arnulfi* has been recently republished: Lisiardus and Hariulfus,
*Vitae, Miracula, Translatio et alia Hagiographica sancti Arnulphi episcopi Suessonien-
sis*, ed. Renée I.A. Nip, Corpus Christianorum. Continuatio Mediaevalis 285 (Turnhout:
Brepols, 2015).
8. Arnold Fayen, ed., *Liber traditionum Sancti Petri Blandiniensis* (Ghent: F. Mey-
er-Van Lood, 1906), 90, no. 91 (982); 96, no. 102 (995); 100, no. 106 (1002). This is
actually St Peter's second *liber traditionum*, compiled in the 1040s: Georges Declercq,
"Monastic Cartularies, Institutional Memory and the Canonization of the Past. The Two
Libri Traditionum of St Peter's Abbey, Ghent," in *Manuscript and Memory in Religious
Communities in the Medieval Low Countries*, ed. Jeroen Deploige and Renée Nip (Turnhout: Brepols, 2015—special issue of *The Medieval Low Countries* 2 (2015)), 37–72, at
56–62; idem, "La mise en livre des archives du haut Moyen Âge: le cas du second *liber
traditionum* de l'abbaye de Saint-Pierre-au-Mont-Blandin (milieu du XIᵉ siècle)," *Bibliothèque de l'École des chartes* 171 (2013, published 2017): 327–64.
9. Fayen, ed., *Liber traditionum*, 90, no. 91. For the identification of *Busingim* with
Boëseghem (Fr., dép. Nord, arr. Dunkerque, cant. Hazebrouck): Maurits Gysseling, *Top-
onymisch woordenboek van België, Nederland, Luxemburg, Noord-Frankrijk en West-
Duitsland (vóór 1226)*, 2 vols. (Tongeren: Belgisch Interuniversitair Centrum voor Neerlandistiek, 1960), 1: 157.
10. Fayen, ed., *Liber traditionum*, 96, no. 102. Bambrugge: Belg., prov. East Flanders,
arr. Aalst.
11. Ibid., 100, no. 106. Terdeghem: Fr., dép. Nord, arr. Dunkerque, cant. Wormhout.

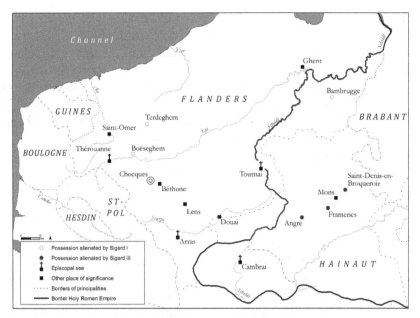

Fig. 6.1—Possessions of the family of Chocques (Map: Hans Blomme).

This man and his "belt of military duty" have attracted some (super-ficial) scholarly attention. Ernest Warlop, in his comprehensive study of the Flemish nobility, mentioned him only for observing that he was certainly not a noble, for St Peter's *liber traditionum* does not tell us he was.[12] Warlop deduced from the epithet *militaris* (which he erro-neously considered as referring to *Sigardus* himself) that Sigard was an early (and rich) knight. The French medievalist Régine Le Jan, for her part, has commented that Sigard's designation as a man "equipped with the belt of military duty" is one of the earliest examples of a positive appreciation of the "military profession" (*le métier militaire*) north of the river Seine, a "profession" practised in this case by a "rich allodial landowner."[13] Le Jan's understanding of warfare as a "pro-fessional" performance may of course need reassessment in this con-text, yet several objective conclusions can indeed be drawn from the Ghent *liber traditionum*. Firstly, Sigard can be described accurately as a substantial landowner. He did possess estates in several parts of the County of Flanders, although his core patrimony, with his allods and

12. Warlop, *De Vlaamse adel*, 1: 101 and 105 n. 369.
13. Régine Le Jan, *Famille et pouvoir dans le monde franc (VIIe–Xe siècle). Essai d'an-thropologie sociale* (Paris: Presses universitaires de la Sorbonne, 1995), 151.

inherited lands, seems to have been concentrated in the southern part
of the county, within the future castellany of Cassel. Secondly, Sigard
must have been closely connected to the comital authority. Count
Arnulf attended the ceremony when he gave Boëseghem to St Peter in
982, and the beneficiary of his repeated donations was a major Benedictine monastery in Flanders which enjoyed a privileged relationship
with the prince.[14] And finally, to the eyes of St Peter's monks, he was a
man whose social identity was intimately associated with his commitment to warring activities.

Can we go further? On Sigard's account *stricto sensu,* without any
further information in surviving records, the answer is no. It can only
be added that the wording *militaris cingulo laboris (innexus)* was certainly not invented by St Peter's monks. It appears in a letter from
Alcuin of York to Charlemagne, in an opposite formulation (*militaris cingulo laboris deposito*) metaphorically applied to Abbot Alcuin
himself, and meaning something like "now in a retired veteran's
life."[15] What we can read here is thus a learned reference looking back
to the Carolingian era. More broadly, this deliberate and thoughtful
expression ostensibly echoed the antique *cingulum militiae,* worn by
those entrusted with military responsibilities and somehow committed
to public (or princely) service.[16] But how should we interpret it in
this case? In Warlop's mind, it makes Sigard a socially obscure knight
in service to Count Arnulf II. Indeed, Warlop, writing in the 1960s,
shared the then mainstream view that tenth- and eleventh-century
milites—a term he mechanically associated with knighthood—were
dependent, lower rank "professional" mounted warriors, as opposed to
the count's *proceres,* i.e. the nobility, whose ostensible participation in
warfare resulted from its social superiority, not from necessity.[17] This
traditional view has been widely challenged in recent historiography.

14. See Steven Vanderputten, *Monastic Reform as Process. Realities and Representations in Medieval Flanders, 900–1000* (Ithaca-London: Cornell University Press, 2013),
passim. One can add that Sigard also occurs among Count Arnulf's followers in a 983
document, where he is listed in a fairly prominent position: Fayen, ed., *Liber traditionum,*
91, no. 92.
15. *Alcuini sive Albini epistolae,* ed. Ernst Dummler, Monumenta Germaniae Historica, Epistolae Karolini Aevi 2 (Berlin: Weidmann, 1895), 385–86, no. 240: "Ecce Flaccus
effeto corpore militaris cingulo laboris deposito." See Christiane Veyrard-Cosme, "Les
motifs épistolaires dans la correspondance d'Alcuin," *Annales de Bretagne et des Pays de
l'Ouest* 111 (2004): 193–205, at 199.
16. Jean Flori, *L'essor de la chevalerie, XIᵉ–XIIᵉ siècles* (Geneva: Droz, 1986), 46–48.
17. Warlop, *De Vlaamse adel,* 1: esp. 33–34 and 95–108.

Dominique Barthélemy and others have emphasised both the polysemy of the *militia* lexical register and the persistent social importance of military action for all noblemen, from kings to petty lords, which implied an overall prevalence of the nobility in warfare.[18] Accordingly, the Carolingian-style expression used in the Ghent *liber traditionum* might well have been intended to describe Sigard as a high-ranking military commander in service to the Count of Flanders.

This hypothesis can be indirectly substantiated. We have seen that Sigard had three sons, who were still alive in the early years of the eleventh century. Starting from this key information, it is possible to reconstruct Sigard's descent up to the early twelfth century. This is quite fortuitous, since Flemish sources do not usually allow us to discover biological continuities across the Year 1000.[19] Nor do they otherwise unveil the identities of most of the aristocrats cited in comital documents—generally using a single name—well up to the mid-eleventh century. Exploring Sigard's offspring is the business of the rest of this paper. By reconstructing Sigard's family and the territories and interests it commanded throughout the eleventh century, we can get a retrospective view of Sigard's own place in his world, and what sort of a man might be a *miles* at the court of Arnulf I.

Sigard's Inheritance

"Sigard" (*Sigardus, Segardus*) appears to be an extremely rare name in Flanders, which obviously facilitates the genealogical side of the investigation.[20] A man called Sigard surfaces in two mid-eleventh

18. See especially Dominique Barthélemy, "Qu'est-ce que la chevalerie, en France aux Xᵉ et XIᵉ siècles?," *Revue historique* 290 (1993): 15–74; idem, "Note sur le 'titre chevaleresque', en France au XIᵉ siècle," *Journal des savants* (1994): 101–34; and the relevant chapters in idem, *La mutation de l'an mil a-t-elle eu lieu? Servage et chevalerie dans la France des Xᵉ et XIᵉ siècles* (Paris: Fayard, 1997), and idem, *La chevalerie, de la Germanie antique à la France du XIIᵉ siècle*, 2ⁿᵈ ed. (Paris: Perrin, 2012). For a recent state of the debate: Richard W. Kaeuper, *Medieval Chivalry* (Cambridge: Cambridge University Press, 2016), 63–84.

19. Despite exhaustive research, Ernest Warlop only found two or three ascertainable tenth-century ancestors of Flemish noble families: Warlop, *De Vlaamse adel*, 1: 38–54.

20. The only "Sigard" mentioned in Warlop's dissertation is our Sigard I: ibid., 101 and 105. A certain canon of Thérouanne named *Seigardus* or *Sichardus* (fl. 1073) may have been a relative, as also one *Sicardus*, dean of Notre-Dame of Saint-Omer (fl. 1076): Théodore Duchet and Arthur Giry, ed., *Cartulaires de l'église de Térouane* (Saint-Omer: Société des antiquaires de la Morinie, 1881), 3–4, nos. 3–4; Jean-Charles Bédague, "Grégoire VII contre les évêques de Thérouanne. Les chanoines séculiers de Saint-Omer

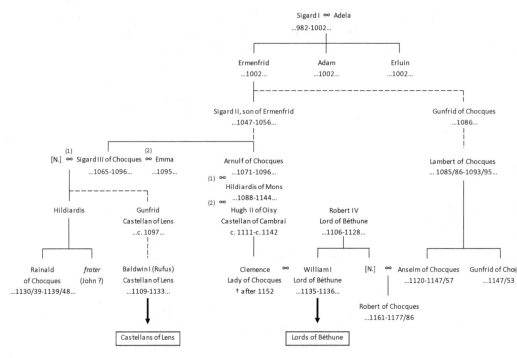

Fig. 6.2—Sigard I's descendants up to the twelfth century.

century comital charters—which may be regarded as significant, for a mere six authentic charter texts have been left from Count Baldwin V's government (1035–67).[21] Both documents were issued by Baldwin V for St Peter's Abbey, and both deal with the advocacy of St Peter's *villa* of Harnes in the region of Lens.[22] In the second charter,

au secours de la papauté," in *Schismes, dissidences, oppositions. La France et le Saint-Siège avant Boniface VIII. Actes de la 6ᵉ Table Ronde sur la Gallia Pontificia, 29 mai 2009*, ed. Bernard Barbiche and Rolf Grosse (Paris: École Nationale des Chartes/Deutsches Historisches Institut, 2012), 59–94.

21. Nieus and Vanderputten, "Diplôme princier," 20 n. 69.

22. Maurits Gysseling and Anton C.F. Koch (ed.), *Diplomata belgica ante annum millesimum centesimum scripta*, 2 vols. (Brussels: Belgisch Interuniversitair Centrum voor Neerlandistiek, 1950), 1: 201–2, no. 96 (1047: "signa … Segardi"); Auguste Van Lokeren, ed., *Chartes et documents de l'abbaye de Saint-Pierre, au Mont-Blandin, à Gand*, 2 vols. (Ghent: Hoste, 1868–71), 1: 95–96, no. 133 (1056: "Signum Segardi filii Ermenfridi"). The latter document has been reworked, but its witness list is reliable: Philip Grierson, "A visit of Earl Harold to Flanders in 1056," *English historical review* 51 (1936): 90–97; G. Declercq, "Van privaatoorkonde tot vorstelijke oorkonde. De oorkonden van de eerste graven van Vlaanderen, inzonderheid voor de Sint-Pietersabdij te Gent (10ᵈᵉ–11ᵈᵉ eeuw)," in *Chancelleries princières et scriptoria dans les anciens Pays-Bas, Xᵉ–XVᵉ siècles*, ed. Thérèse de Hemptinne and Jean-Marie Duvosquel (Brussels: Commission royale d'his-

Sigard (II) is reported as "the son of Ermenfrid," which makes him a probable grandson of Sigard (I) (Fig. 6.2). We know nothing about him, except that, in the footsteps of his grandfather, he attended the comital court and apparently had roots in southern Flanders. Later on, in the last third of the eleventh century, we have regular mention of a further Sigard, known as "Sigard of Chocques."[23] There is every reason to think that this Sigard (III) was a son of Sigard (II). He has gained some notoriety among historians thanks to his inclusion as a "tenant-in-chief" in the English *Domesday Book*.[24]

Things become interesting indeed with Sigard III, since there is an unusual amount of evidence available on him. First of all, he and his relatives were consistently associated in documents with the place-name Chocques (Table 6.1). This place, located between Lillers and Béthune in the Artois region (some twenty kilometres from Sigard I's *villa* of Boëseghem), has never been discussed by the historians of medieval Flanders.[25] Still, there are strong indications that Chocques played a significant role in the early shaping of regional powers in the southern part of Flanders. The Norman chronicler William of Jumièges reports that shortly before 1030 Count Baldwin IV (988–1035) was expelled from Flanders by his son, the future Baldwin V, and took refuge in Normandy. Duke Robert I (1027–35) then launched an attack on Flanders, aimed at restoring the old count. His campaign is described as a successful *Blitzkrieg*: he besieged and burned the castle of Chocques (*castrum quod Cioca vocabatur*) with its defenders, which immediately prompted other Flemish magnates (*reliqui proceres*) to ask for peace.[26] One can infer from William's nar-

toire, 2010— special issue of *Bulletin de la Commission royale d'histoire* 176 (2010)), 41–77, at 58. Harnes: Fr., dép. Pas-de-Calais, arr. Lens, cant. Harnes.

23. See below.

24. Katharine S.B. Keats-Rohan, *Domesday People: A Prosopography of Persons Occurring in English Documents, 1066–1166. I. Domesday Book* (Woodbridge: Boydell, 1999), 419–20.

25. Fr., dép. Pas-de-Calais, arr. and cant. Béthune. Extant literature is limited to a bare notice by Adolphe de Cardevacque in the *Dictionnaire historique et archéologique du département du Pas-de-Calais. Arrondissement de Béthune*, 2 vols. (Arras: Commission départementale des monuments historiques du Pas-de-Calais, 1875), 1: 175–83.

26. William of Jumièges, *Gesta Normannorum ducum*, 6.6, ed. Elisabeth Van Houts, vol. 2 of *The* Gesta Normannorum Ducum *of William of Jumièges, Orderic Vitalis, and Robert of Torigni*, Oxford Medieval Texts (Oxford: Clarendon Press, 1995), 52–53: "Cuius [= Baldwin IV] calamitatem dux miseratus contractis militum viribus, velut turbo horridus a patria egressus, Flandoniam est adorsus, illam exterminans flammis exitialibus. Progrediensque ad castrum quod Cioca vocabatur, confestim illud subvertit, combustis omnibus in eo consistentibus. Videntes autem reliqui proceres et similia pati formidantes, relicto filio,

rative that Chocques was by 1030 a key stronghold in southern Flan-
ders. Later records, from twelfth-century descriptions to as late as the
"Napoleonic" cadastre, confirm that Chocques was indeed the site of
a very significant fortification.[27] When registered on the map of early
Flemish castles tentatively sketched by Adriaan Verhulst in 1976,[28]
Chocques only looks like another link on a regular alignment of cas-
tles running from Saint-Omer to Douai, directly south of the "Neuf-
Fossé," a huge earthwork possibly dug in the mid-eleventh century for
Baldwin V.[29] However, this alignment is not as consistent as it might
seem at first sight. It is possible that by 1030 Chocques and Béthune
were the only existing fortifications between Saint-Omer and Lens.[30]
I would tentatively suggest that Chocques was built by the Counts of
Flanders at an early date, conceivably as part of a strategic response
to the formation of autonomous counties and lordships in the southern
region. Béthune, for instance, might have been one of the targeted
local lordships, as it is only four kilometres from Chocques.[31] This theory, as fragile as it may seem, is nevertheless backed by the fact that

---

ad patrem sunt reversi, obsides dirigentes duci." ("Full of compassion for the count's mis-
fortune the duke assembled all his warriors and like a fearsome whirlwind left the country
for Flanders, which he wasted with fire. Upon his arrival at the stronghold of Chocques,
he quickly seized it and burnt it down with everyone in it. Seeing this, the other magnates
were terrified that they might be treated in the same way. They abandoned the son and
returned to the father, handing over hostages to the duke.") For the historical context, see
Koch, "Het graafschap Vlaanderen," 376, and Jean-François Nieus, *Un pouvoir comtal
entre Flandre et France: Saint-Pol, 1000–1300* (Brussels: De Boeck Université, 2005), 54.

    27. Raoul Van Caenegem, "The Sources of Flemish History in the Liber Floridus," in
*Liber Floridus Colloquium. Papers Read at the International Meeting Held at the Univer-
sity Library Ghent, 1957* (Ghent: Story-Scientia, 1973), 71–85, at 84 (*Soccas* is cited in a
1120 list of major Flemish *castella*); André Duchesne, *Histoire généalogique de la maison de Béthune* (Paris: Cramoisy, 1639), *Preuves*: 25–26 (1147 x 1163); Arras, Archives
départementales du Pas-de-Calais, 3 P 224, nos. 18–23 ("Napoleonic" cadastre, available online: "Plan cadastraux," accessed 1 March 2018, http://www.archivespasdecalais.fr/
Archives-en-ligne/Plans-cadastraux). The 1837 cadastre still shows the lineaments of large
earthworks in the village centre, next to the parish church.

    28. Adriaan Verhulst, "Die gräfliche Burgenverfassung in Flandern im Hochmittelalter,"
in *Die Burgen im deutschen Sprachraum. Ihre rechts- und verfassungsgeschichtliche
Bedeutung*, ed. Hans Patze, 2 vols. (Sigmaringen: Thorbecke, 1976), 1: 267–82.

    29. Bernard Delmaire, *Le diocèse d'Arras de 1093 au milieu du XIVe siècle. Recherches
sur la vie religieuse dans le nord de la France au Moyen Âge*, 2 vols. (Arras: Commission
départementale d'histoire et d'archéologie du Pas-de-Calais, 1994), 1: 27.

    30. Aire and Lillers castles may not have existed before the mid-eleventh century: Bri-
gitte Meijns, *Aken of Jeruzalem? Het ontstaan en de hervorming van de kanonikale instel-
lingen in Vlaanderen tot circa 1155*, 2 vols. (Leuven: Universitaire Pers Leuven, 2000), 1:
483–86 and 496–99. Houdain could be even more recent: ibid., 506–8.

    31. The ill-documented, but definitely ancient, origins of Béthune are discussed by Mei-
jns, *Aken of Jeruzalem?*, 1: 502–4. Béthune: Fr., dép. Pas-de-Calais, arr. and cant. Béthune.

the Count of Flanders owned the church of Chocques until 1067.[32] It would imply that Sigard and his heirs were initially entrusted with the custody of a princely fortress—or, at the very least, that they settled in this place with full comital support.

However, what we can see in Chocques at a later stage strongly resembles what we see in every other castellan lordship in the Artois region. The castle of Chocques appears to be the heart of a coherent local barony,[33] whose lords apparently behaved just like other magnates in the area. The aforementioned *Gesta* of William of Jumièges inform us that it was held around 1030 by a *procer* who had joined Young Baldwin's rebellion. This *procer* was most certainly Ermenfrid or his son Sigard II. Indeed, what we can learn about the subsequent family history (notably thanks to the early charters of the abbey of St John Baptist in Chocques) reveals that Sigard II once held Chocques in shared lordship with a brother named Gunfrid (Fig. 6.2); this configuration necessarily implies that the whole barony had once been in the possession of their father Ermenfrid.[34] This situation of divided lordship, which would evolve by the 1060s into a further and long lasting division into three shares,[35] deserves a brief digression. Far from there being any strong impulse towards primogeniture at this time, division between multiple sons was a relatively common, though ill-studied, practice among Northern French aristocratic families in the eleventh century. It was by no means simply the sort of behaviour of lesser families indifferent to their lineage, for we can also observe it in the greatest of houses, where one would imagine that anxiety about

32. Alexandre Pruvost, ed., *Chronique et cartulaire de l'abbaye de Bergues-Saint-Winoc, de l'ordre de saint Benoît*, 2 vols. (Bruges: de Zuttere, 1875–78), 1: 57–63: Baldwin V gives away two-thirds of the local tithe, i.e. the *ecclesia*.

33. The components of this barony can be traced in the archive of St John Baptist, Chocques: Arras, Archives départementales du Pas-de-Calais, 25 H. I am currently completing a critical edition of this archive.

34. Of critical importance in St John Baptist's archive are three episcopal confirmations of all donations made to this religious house by the late eleventh-century co-lords of Chocques and their successors: Abbé Robert, *Histoire de l'abbaye de Chocques, ordre de Saint-Augustin, au diocèse de Saint-Omer* (Saint-Omer: Société des antiquaires de la Morinie, 1876), 532–44, nos. 4, 5 and 7 (1120, 1138 and 1147). A careful analysis of these documents has shown that the late eleventh-century co-lords were Sigard III, his brother Arnulf and their uncle Gunfrid's heir Lambert. It also appears that the assets possessed by Sigard III and his brother originated from a coherent set of lands and rights, in all likelihood their father's own share of inheritance. For more details, see Jean-François Nieus, "Stratégies seigneuriales anglo-flamandes après 1066. L'*honor* de Chocques et la famille de Béthune," *Revue belge de philologie et d'histoire* 95 (2017): 163–92, at 173–78.

35. See above, n. 34.

the dignity of a lineage would demand the concentration of resources on one son in every generation.[36] Partible inheritance between several heirs, and especially between brothers, was indeed the practice in significant castellan lordships such as Picquigny in 1066 (with two *domini castri*), Ardres in 1070 (three relatives *Ardam tenentibus*), Aubigny-en-Artois in 1093 (three *seniores castri*), and even the County of Saint-Pol in 1078 (two brothers jointly styled *comites de castro Sancti Pauli*).[37] What the eleventh-century partitions of Chocques might also suggest is that, around the year 1000, Ermenfrid had not inherited the widespread estates of his father Sigard I, but only the portion of lands where the family fortress was to be erected before 1030.

Sigard III and the Destiny of Chocques

Let us now turn to the defining character of this family saga, namely Sigard III, alias "Sigard of Chocques." A dozen of his attestations to princely charters, ranging from 1065 to the mid-1090s, have been collected (Table 6.1).[38] They give us a partial glimpse of the loyalties that

36. On this topic, see the fundamental study by Hélène Débax, *La seigneurie collective. Pairs, pariers, paratge: les coseigneurs du XIe au XIIIe siècle* (Rennes: Presses universitaires de Rennes, 2012), which focuses on southern French "pariages," but makes insightful comparisons with Northern France and the German Empire (especially at 80–87). I fully agree with Débax's statement (86) that "le morcellement successoral et les coseigneuries ont été très largement sous-estimés par les historiens des régions septentrionales, bien souvent engagés dans cette voie par des codifications juridiques du XIIIe siècle—ou postérieures— qui énonçaient clairement des principes inverses. La coseigneurie générée par des partages successoraux semble beaucoup plus répandue qu'il n'a longtemps été affirmé." For a comparable debate in English historiography, where the dominance of primogeniture in medieval society was an article of faith for most of the eighteenth and nineteenth centuries, see the challenging study by James C. Holt, "Politics and Property in Early Medieval England," *Past & Present* 57 (1972): 3–52, and for the historiographical background, David Crouch, *The Birth of Nobility: Constructing Aristocracy in England and France, 900–1300* (Harlow: Longman, 2005), 116–21. See also Sara McDougall, "The Chivalric Family" in this volume.

37. Picquigny (Fr., dép. Somme, arr. Amiens, cant. Ailly-sur-Somme): *Gallia christiana*, 16 vols. (Paris: Typographia Regia, 1716–65), 10 (1751): *Instrumenta*, cols. 290–91, no. 9.— Ardres (Fr., dép. Pas-de-Calais, arr. Calais, cant. Calais 2): Duchet and Giry, eds., *Cartulaires de l'église de Térouane*, 2, no. 2.—Aubigny-en-Artois (Fr., dép. Pas-de-Calais, arr. Arras, cant. Avesnes-le-Comte): Fernand Vercauteren, ed., *Actes des comtes de Flandre, 1071–1128* (Brussels: Commission royale d'histoire, 1938), 54–57, no. 17.—Saint-Pol-sur-Ternoise (Fr., dép. Pas-de-Calais, arr. Arras, cant. Saint-Pol-sur-Ternoise): Julius von Pflugk-Harttung, ed., *Acta pontificum Romanorum inedita. Vol. 2: Urkunden der Päpste vom Jahre c. 97 bis zum Jahre 1197* (Stuttgart: W. Kohlhammer, 1884), 134–35, no. 167.

38. 1065: Charles Duvivier, *Quelles étaient l'importance et les limites du* Pagus Hainoensis *jusqu'au XIe siècle ?*, 2 vols., Mémoires et publications, 2nd s. 9 (Mons: Société des sciences, des arts et des lettres du Hainaut, 1863–64), 2: 411–12, no. 50.—1069: Aubertus

shaped his rich life story. He first appears in the entourage of Baldwin V's son in Hainaut, in the period when the soon-to-be Baldwin VI of Flanders (1067–70) was indeed still Baldwin I, Count of Hainaut (thanks to his marriage with Countess Richilde in 1051). A few years later, in 1071, he is seen with Baldwin I/VI's son, Count Arnulf III (1070–71), and next with his widow, Countess Richilde (d. 1087). These occurrences are followed by an eight-year gap, which is actually a fourteen-year gap, if we consider that in 1080, when subscribing a Flemish charter, Sigard was not really attending Robert the Frisian's (1071–93) court: he was only escorting Count Eustace II of Boulogne and Lens (1047–87) there. Afterwards, from 1086 on, Sigard occurs repeatedly not in Flanders, but in Hainaut, in the entourage of Count Baldwin II (1071–98), the surviving son of Baldwin I/VI. His apparent withdrawal and later repositioning in Hainaut[39] are obviously linked to the political turmoil after the death of Baldwin I/VI, which resulted in Robert the Frisian's accession in Flanders.[40] We know from the genealogical writing called *Flandria Generosa* that a contingent of men from Chocques, presumably led by Sigard and his uncle Gunfrid, fought at the Battle of Cassel (February 1071) on the side of Arnulf III and his mother Richilde, together with other contingents raised by the counts and castellan lords from southern Flanders,

Miraeus and Johannes Franciscus Foppens, *Opera diplomatica et historica*, 4 vols. (Louvain: A. Denique, 1723–48), 1: 158.—1071: *Gallia christiana*, 3 (1725): *Instrumenta*, cols. 855–56.—1071: Karl Hanquet, ed., *La chronique de Saint-Hubert dite Cantatorium* (Brussels: Commission royale d'histoire, 1906), 68 (I am grateful to Nicolas Ruffini-Ronzani for this reference).—1080: Vercauteren, *Actes des comtes*, 11–16, no. 5 (a later edition by Jan Dhondt, "Bijdrage tot het cartularium van Meesen (1065–1334)," *Handelingen van de Koninklijke Commissie voor Geschiedenis* 106 (1941): 95–234, at 164–71, gives a corrupt version of Sigard's subscription).—1086: Jules Dewez, *Histoire de l'abbaye de Saint-Pierre d'Hasnon* (Lille: Imprimerie de l'Orphelinat de Don Bosco, 1890), 562–65, charter A.—1087: Miraeus and Foppens, *Opera diplomatica*, 1: 515.— 1088: Duvivier, *Quelles étaient l'importance*, 457–58, no. 72.—1089: ibid., 448–50, no. 68.—1091: Miraeus and Foppens, *Opera diplomatica*, 4: 186.—1086 x 1093: Duchet and Giry, eds., *Cartulaires de l'église de Térouane*, 5, no. 5.—1092 x 1096: Alphonse Wauters, "Exploration de chartes et de cartulaires belges existants à la Bibliothèque nationale à Paris," *Bulletin de la Commission royale d'histoire* 4ᵉ sér. 2 (1875): 78–198, at 182–84, no. 4.—1095 x 1096: Jean-Pierre Gerzaguet, *Les chartes de l'abbaye d'Anchin (1079–1201)* (Turnhout: Brepols, 2005), 104–5, no. 13.

39. This years-long "withdrawal" might partly result from a documentary bias, for we only have two charters issued by Countess Richilde and her son Baldwin for the period 1072–85: Duvivier, *Quelles étaient l'importance*, 440–43, nos. 64–65 (1081 and 1082).

40. Thérèse de Hemptinne, "Vlaanderen en Henegouwen onder de erfgenamen van de Boudewijns, 1070–1244," in *Algemene geschiedenis der Nederlanden*, 2 (1982): 372–98, at 372–77.

Table 6.1—Attestations to charters by Sigard III, Arnulf and Lambert of Chocques.

Date	Author	Beneficiary	Mention
1065	Hainaut (count)	St-Ghislain (abb.)	*Signum* […] *Segardi de Mochis* (sic)
1069	Thérouanne (bishop)	Ardres (chap.)	*S. Sichardi de Scoches*
1071	Flanders-Hainaut (count)	Hasnon (abb.)	*Signum Segardi et Arnulphi de Joches*
1071	Hainaut (countess)	St-Hubert (abb.)	*testibus* […] *Segardo, Arnulpho* (calend.)
1080	Flanders (count)	Messines (abb.)	*Signum Segardi*
1086	Hainaut (count)	Hasnon (abb.)	*Segardus, Arnulfus*
1087	Hainaut (count)	Hasnon (abb.)	*Signum Segardi de Joches* […], *signum Ernulphi de Joches*
1088	Hainaut (count)	Hautmont (abb.)	*Signum Sigardi, Signum Arnulfi*
1089	Hainaut (count)	St-Denis-en-Broqueroie (abb.)	*Signum Segardi de Ceocs*
1091	Hainaut (count)	Crespin (abb.)	*Signum Segardi de Crocs* (sic), *signum Ernulphi fratris eius*
1086 x 93	— (*notice*)	Thérouanne (bishop)	*Arnulfus et Segardus et Lambertus de Chochis*
1092 x 96	Hainaut (count)	Hasnon (abb.)	*Ernulfus de Crois* (sic)
1095 x 96	Flanders (count)	Hesdin (priory)	*S. Segardi et Arnulfi de Coches*

References: see footnote 38.

Artois and Hainaut.[41] For Sigard and his relatives Robert the Frisian's crushing victory generated a long-term estrangement from the Flemish branch of the comital dynasty. Likewise, many noble families from the southern part of Flanders rejected the new prince and searched for alternative patronage, especially in the contemporary Eldorado of the Anglo-Norman realms.

41. *Flandria generosa usque ad annum 1164*, chap. 19, ed. Ludwig C. Bethmann, Monumenta Germaniae Historica, Scriptores (in Folio) 9 (Hanover: Hahnsche Buchhandlung, 1851), 313–25, at 322. This text was mainly written in the 1130s: Jean-Marie Moeglin, "Une première histoire nationale flamande: l'Ancienne chronique de Flandre (XIIᵉ–XIIIᵉ siècles)," in *Liber Largitorius. Études d'histoire médiévale offertes à Pierre Toubert par ses élèves*, ed. Dominique Barthélemy and Jean-Marie Martin (Geneva: Droz, 2003), 455–76, at 456–57. It speaks of *Jochenses*, which is an intriguing spelling, but some charters also have the form *Joches* (see Table 6.1).

Eljas Oksanen, in his recent study on the relations between England and Flanders, has skilfully outlined the massive participation of aristocrats originating from southern Flanders and Artois in the Norman conquest and colonisation of England—not least the very influential Count of Boulogne, Eustace II.[42] Oksanen has also identified, within the Artesian group of Flemish participants, a nexus of people somehow linked to the former County of Lens (now in Eustace II's hands), perhaps brought together by Countess Judith, daughter of the last Count of Lens and one of the wealthiest Domesday tenants-in-chief.[43] Sigard III and his uncle Gunfrid were among those who crossed the Channel and chose to settle in England. Both are recorded in the *Domesday Book* as holding estates in Northamptonshire, the county where most Artesian immigrants were indeed granted land.[44] They were not major Domesday tenants, yet they did as well in terms of land grants as any other Flemish tenant-in-chief.[45] Since their activities in England are not further documented, we will pass by the question of why William the Conqueror favoured them. Their military skills were certainly to be employed as the Norman monarchy seized control of the English kingdom, but we should probably not forget that an ecclesiastic called Arnulf of Chocques (d. 1118) was at the time schoolmaster of the abbey of Holy Trinity in Caen and a tutor to William's daughter Cecilia.[46] Arnulf's parentage cannot be established, but he was most probably kin to the lords of Chocques—Sigard III had a brother named Arnulf.[47] Whatever the case, Sigard and Gunfrid's connections with

42. Oksanen, *Flanders*, esp. 178–208, and his chapter "Knights, Mercenaries and Paid Soldiers: Military Identities in the Anglo-Norman Regnum" in this volume. See also Johan Verberckmoes, "Flemish Tenants-in-Chief in Domesday England," *Revue belge de philologie et d'histoire* 66 (1988): 725–56.

43. Oksanen, *Flanders*, 203–4.

44. Keats-Rohan, *Domesday People*, 239–41 (Gunfrid) and 419–20 (Sigard).

45. Verberckmoes, "Flemish Tenants-in-Chief," 731 and 737–39; Oksanen, *Flanders*, 188–91.

46. He would later become Duke Robert Curthose's chaplain and Patriarch of Jerusalem: Raymonde Foreville, "Un chef de la première croisade: Arnoul Malcouronné," *Bulletin philologique et historique du comité des travaux historiques et scientifiques* (1953–4): 377–90; William M. Aird, *Robert Curthose, Duke of Normandy (c. 1050–1134)* (Woodbridge: Boydell, 2008), 165.

47. This brother was a layman and an assiduous follower of Sigard (see Table 6.1). He cannot therefore be identified with the cleric Arnulf of Chocques (*contra* David Douglas, "The Domesday Tenant of Hawling," *Transactions of the Bristol and Gloucestershire Archaeological Society* 84 (1965): 28–30, and Keats-Rohan, *Domesday people*, 420).

the immigrant community from Artois—and especially from Lens[48]—
certainly helped them find their fortune overseas.

Sigard and Gunfrid both left descendants in England, though it is not
clear whether they took wives there or on the Continent.[49] Sigard, however, did not end his life in England. Shortly before the Conqueror's
death in 1087, he was back on the Continent, engaged in a new, fully
Hainautian, phase in his career. He had taken with him his younger
brother Arnulf, and possibly other Artesian followers such as Walter
of Douai (the similarly-named Domesday tenant?) and one Manasses
of Béthune.[50] From 1086 on, Sigard was obviously a senior member
of the entourage of Count Baldwin II of Hainaut. He witnessed most
comital charters issued between 1086 and 1091, and this in a relatively
prominent position.[51] His full integration within the Hainautian political community is also reflected by his possession of substantial estates
in the central part of the county. In 1089, he participated in a grant
of local dependents to the newly-created monastery of Saint-Denis-
en-Broqueroie near Mons.[52] A later deed reminds us that he also held
lands in Frameries.[53] Another charter was issued by Sigard himself in
1095, to record the donation of a mill and some land in Angre to the

48. Sigard and Gunfrid's ties to Lens (Fr., dép. Pas-de-Calais, arr. and cant. Lens) can
only be inferred from their descent: Sigard's presumed son apparently married the heiress
to the castellany of Lens (see below, n. 60), while Gunfrid's probable son or grandson
Lambert bears a name which suggests kinship to the Counts of Lens. Countess Judith (d.
after 1086), daughter of Count Lambert II (d. 1054) and a niece of William the Conqueror,
married Waltheof, Earl of Northumbria (d. 1076), whose vast landholdings ultimately came
to her. She was the most prominent Domesday tenant-in-chief within the Artesian group
of tenants. Her manors were mixed with those held by several immigrants from the Lens
region—including Gunfrid— who she might have attracted in England to help her defending her interests. On her, see Oksanen, *Flanders*, 203–4.
49. See Keats-Rohan, *Domesday People*, 239–41 and 419–20; eadem, *Domesday
Descendants: A Prosopography of Persons Occurring in English Documents, 1066–1166.
II. Pipe Rolls to "Cartae Baronum"* (Woodbridge: Boydell, 2002), 396–97. The genealogical reconstructions proposed by Keats-Rohan are at times inaccurate, especially with
regard to the complex continental descent of Sigard and Gunfrid in the early twelfth century.
50. Both men repeatedly occur in Hainautian deeds along with Sigard, hence the sup-
position. On Walter, see (with caution, though) Keats-Rohan, *Domesday People*, 450–51.
51. Although his ranking appears unstable, perhaps due to the use of multiple columns
for the witness lists on lost originals.
52. Duvivier, *Quelles étaient l'importance*, 448–50, no. 68. Interestingly enough, there
is a group of *Normanni* involved in the donation.
53. Léopold Devillers, ed., *Chartes du chapitre Sainte-Waudru de Mons*, 4 vols. (Brussels: Commission royale d'histoire, 1899–1913), 1: 52–53, no. 29: 1196 confirmation of an
earlier deed, with mention of a *decimam terre Segardi de Czokes*. Frameries: Belg., prov.
Hainaut, arr. Mons.

Fig. 6.3—Charter of Sigard III and his wife Emma for Crespin Abbey (1095). Lille, Archives départementales du Nord, 4 H 25, no. 190 (Photo: Aurélie Stuckens).

abbey of Crespin (Fig. 6.3).[54] This elegant piece is important to the present study, not only because it illustrates quite well its issuer's elevation in Hainaut at the time, but, more crucially, because it specifies that Sigard was acting for the souls of King William the Conqueror, Count Baldwin II and a third man whose name was regrettably torn away on the preserved original: *proque horum salute anim[ar]um, scilicet Willelmi regis, Balduini co[mitis]* [lacuna of about twenty letters] *mei, avunculi Balduini.* However, one can still read that this man was both close kin to Sigard (possessive pronoun *mei*), and the uncle of Baldwin II. He was in all likelihood Sigard's father-in-law, the father of his wife Emma who solemnly co-authored the charter (*ego Segar-*

54. Original: Lille, Archives départementales du Nord, 4 H 25, nr. 190. Edited by Michelle Courtois, "Chartes originales antérieures à 1121 conservées dans le département du Nord" (mémoire de maîtrise, Université de Nancy 2, 1981), 149. See also Giraud, Renault, and Tock, eds., *Chartes originales*, no. 423. Angre: Belg., prov. Hainaut, arr. Mons, comm. Honnelles.

dus atque Emma <...>ere coniugii mihi conligata). Emma was presumably a niece of Countess Richilde, and therefore a high-ranking
woman, who had made Sigard a significant baron and landowner in
Hainaut.[55] Besides this, one can reasonably infer from later evidence
that Sigard's brother Arnulf also got married in Hainaut in the 1080s
to a daughter of the prominent baron Gossuin I of Mons (d. after 1088)
called Hildiardis (d. after 1144) who would later remarry Hugh II of
Oisy, castellan of Cambrai.[56] These distinguished alliances within the
Hainautian upper aristocracy were most probably arranged by Count
Baldwin II himself. They express the prince's determination to bind
the Flemish family of Chocques to the post-1071 Hainautian political
community.

Although the Crespin charter displays great reverence towards King
William and Count Baldwin, and consequently highlights the importance, in Sigard's own eyes, of his Norman and Lotharingian connections, one should not assume that he and his relatives had by then lost
contact with their fatherland. Sigard's last attestations to charters show
him attending assemblies presided over by Counts Robert the Frisian
and his son Robert of Jerusalem (1093–1111), with whom some sort
of reconciliation had necessarily occurred in the meantime. Around
1090, we can even see all three representatives of the Chocques family, the then co-lords, at a judicial court in Thérouanne. Next to Sigard
and his brother Arnulf stands one Lambert of Chocques, the presumed
heir of Gunfrid.[57] This Lambert is known to have contributed to the
foundation of a Benedictine priory at Labeuvrière, in the vicinity of

55. Richilde's parentage is unfortunately ill-documented. However, we do know that
she had a niece, called Ada, who married the castellan of Cambrai Hugh I of Oisy before
1071: Nicolas Ruffini-Ronzani, "Église et aristocratie en Cambrésis (fin IXe–milieu XIIe
siècle). Le pouvoir entre France et Empire au Moyen Âge central," 2 vols. (PhD diss.,
Université de Namur, 2014), 1: 170. The existence of another niece is therefore plausible.

56. Hugh II of Oisy was in 1120 one of the three co-lords of Chocques: Robert, *Histoire de l'abbaye de Chocques*, 532–35, no. 4. He certainly owed this position to his wife
Hildiardis, whose personal landholdings in Chocques are cited in the same 1120 charter,
and explicitly described as descending from Arnulf in a later deed: ibid., 535–39, no. 5 (for
a detailed discussion, see Nieus, "Stratégies seigneuriales," 175). Hildiardis was thus able
to transfer her first husband's patrimony to her new husband. For her origins and family,
see Lille, Archives départementales du Nord, 4 G 711, no. 7005, and 36 H 63, no. 674 (my
thanks to Nicolas Ruffini-Ronzani for both references); Ernest Matthieu, "Les premiers
châtelains de Mons et la famille des Gossuin de Mons," in *Mélanges d'histoire offerts à
Charles Moeller à l'occasion de son jubilé de 50 années de professorat à l'Université de
Louvain. Vol. 1: Antiquité et Moyen Âge* (Louvain-Paris: Université de Louvain-A. Picard
et Fils, 1914), 377–92.

57. Duchet and Giry, eds., *Cartulaires de l'église de Térouane*, 5, no. 5 (1086 x 1093).

Chocques, about the same time.[58] Furthermore, Sigard, Arnulf and Lambert jointly promoted the installation (or restoration) of a chapter of secular canons within the castle of Chocques in the late eleventh century. This initiative is poorly documented, but it certainly accompanied, in the religious and symbolic sphere, a revival of local lordship after a probable period of vacuum.[59] And finally, still around the same period, Sigard must have negotiated the marriage of his son Gunfrid to the heiress to the castellany of Lens.[60] The Chocques family was still very active in southern Flanders during the last decades of the eleventh century.

After Sigard III's death (*ca.* 1096), however, the persistence of the divided lordship in Chocques eventually led to the absorption of its three main portions into external patrimonies, and the "Sigardian" dynasty similarly left the scene after its various branches on the Continent and in England became extinct or became involved with other lineages. Interestingly enough, however, the prestige that surrounded the old fortress of Chocques and its past lords long survived the fading of the Sigards in the early twelfth century. Not only did the insular descendants of Sigard III and Gunfrid preserve the memory of their Flemish roots by maintaining the reference to Chocques in their top-

---

58. Vercauteren, *Actes des comtes de Flandre*, 70–74, no. 24 (1100). This charter has been reworked, but the names of the nobles responsible for the foundation, which took place between 1085 and 1095, are reliable: Adriaan Verhulst, "La fondation des dépendances de l'abbaye poitevine de Charroux dans le diocèse de Thérouanne: Andres, Ham et La Beuvrière," *Le Moyen Âge* 69 (1963): 169–89, at 184–85. Labeuvrière: Fr., dép. Pas-de-Calais, arr. and cant. Béthune.

59. Meijns, *Aken of Jeruzalem?*, 1: 570–2; 2: 795–97 and 830–31. This secular chapter would later evolve into an abbey of regular canons affiliated to the order of Arrouaise.

60. The evidence is indirect but congruent. In 1120, the third co-lord of Chocques was one "Baldwin Rufus" (Robert, *Histoire de l'abbaye de Chocques*, 532–35, no. 4), to be identified with Baldwin I, hereditary castellan of Lens (before 1109–after 1133), whose son Baldwin II will claim Sigard's English honour in 1160, and whose later descendants will still possess shares of lordship on Chocques (on all this, see Nieus, "Stratégies seigneuriales," 174–5). Baldwin I's predecessor in Lens during the 1090s was one *Gonfridus:* Claire Giordanengo, ed., *Le registre de Lambert, évêque d'Arras (1093–1115)* (Paris: CNRS Éditions, 2007), 380, no. E.39. (A list of early castellans compiled by Pierre Feuchère, "L'origine et la formation constitutionnelle de l'office de châtelain à Lens," *Bulletin de la Commission départementale d'histoire et d'archéologie du Pas-de-Calais* 7 (1948): 463–73, lacks any ground.) This Gunfrid must be Sigard's son and heir, and the "missing link" who transmitted Sigard's share of lordship in Chocques to Baldwin "Rufus" of Lens. This Chocques-Lens connection is all the more plausible as, during the second half of the eleventh century, the former County of Lens belonged to the Counts of Boulogne, with whom Sigard seems to have been somehow acquainted (see the 1080 charter discussed above, and cited on n. 38).

onymy[61] (a reference also preserved in the designation of their English
fiefs, known for long as the "honour of Chocques,"[62]) but several continental noble families made substantial efforts to recover parts of the
Chocques legacy well up to the thirteenth century. Hugh II of Oisy has
already been mentioned: he gained Arnulf of Chocques' inheritance by
marrying his widow Hildiardis of Mons around 1100. The castellans
of Lens, whom we have identified as Sigard III's descendants in the
male line, inherited his third of the lordship of Chocques. Much later,
in 1160, they also struggled to recover his English fiefs (initially conveyed to Sigard's "English" daughter Hildiardis), but eventually were
forced to abandon their claims in favour of the lords of Béthune.[63]
The Béthunes were one of the most prominent, if not the most prominent noble family in Flanders until the early thirteenth century.[64] They
deployed a fascinating long-term strategy aimed at taking over both
the castle of Chocques (which abutted their estates) and the English
honour of Chocques. Robert IV (d. *ca.* 1128) married his male heir
to a daughter of Hugh II of Oisy, who abandoned his co-lordship of
Chocques as her dowry. He also gave his daughter to one of Gunfrid's
"English" heirs (Fig. 6.2). Later on, Robert V (d. 1191) manoeuvred
to acquire both Sigard III's and Gunfrid's English lands. His holding
of the honour of Chocques indeed helped him to get a foothold in
England, and eventually to become a major Anglo-Flemish baron by
the end of his life.[65]

61. Keats-Rohan, *Domesday Descendants*, 396–97. Rainald of Chocques (fl. *ca.*
1130–50), son of Sigard III's daughter Hildiardis, consistently bears his maternal surname.
62. See William Farrer, *Honors and Knights' Fees*, 3 vols. (London: Spottiswoode, Bal-
lantyne & Co., 1923–25), 1: 20–53.
63. Lille, Archives départementales du Nord, B 1005, no. 79. Calendared by John
H. Round, *Calendar of Documents Preserved in France, Illustrative of the History of
Great Britain and Ireland. Vol. 1: A.D. 918–1206* (London: Eyre & Spottiswoode, 1899),
494, no. 1359. See also Benoît-Michel Tock (ed.), *Chartae Galliae* (Orléans: Institut de
recherche et d'histoire des textes, 2014), accessed 1 March 2018, http://www.cn-telma.fr/
chartae-galliae/charte212752/, no. F12115.
64. A comprehensive study of this family is still lacking, though. See Duchesne, *Histoire généalogique*; Warlop, *De Vlaamse adel*, 2/1: 65–78, no. 20; Alain Derville, "Seigneurs, bourgeois et paysans (900–1500)," in *Histoire de Béthune et de Beuvry*, ed. Alain
Derville (Arras: Westhoek Éditions, 1985), 29–78.
65. Nieus, "Stratégies seigneuriales," 179–86. For the Béthune family's growing influence in England, see also Oksanen, *Flanders*, 88–89 and 207–8.

Conclusion

Without doubt, the rich life story of Sigard III of Chocques is that of a man of high standing, and a leading magnate of his homeland. His attestations to princely charters after 1065 tell us that he was a peer of the most distinguished nobles in Flanders and Hainaut. Despite an initial setback in Flanders in 1071, he was very successful in attracting princely patronage and in building up a wide-ranging network of alliances. By the 1080s, his social and material resources were at once Flemish, Lotharingian and English—a true ubiquity, more widespread than the more usual duality of Anglo-Norman barons. What needs to be emphasised here is that this position did not come out of nowhere. Talented nobleman though he may have been, such a success within the aristocratic society of his time could only be achieved thanks to the inheritance of generations of distinguished forebears, their prestige and honours.

This observation brings us back to Sigard III's great-grandfather Sigard I and his evocative "belt of military duty." Reconstructing his line of descent can help us contextualise what he was in his own day. Clearly it was not just his genes he bequeathed to his descendants. His successes and standing in Flanders laid the ground work for his great-grandson's remarkable and wide-ranging career. So the story of the house of Chocques is definitely not one of upward social mobility by military service in a warband.[66] Seen through the lens of his own progeny, Sigard I does not match with Warlop's low-profile *miles,* nor with Le Jan's rich allodial landowner converted into a professional soldier. There is every reason to think that Sigard I belonged to the very top of the late tenth-century Flemish aristocracy, a social identity that self-evidently went along with the possession of large estates and with the performance of military activities. The refined Latin terms used by St Peter's monks were probably intended, as suggested in the introduction, to stress Sigard's commanding position within the army of Count Arnulf II. For all that, his descendants do not give the impression that they were particularly oriented towards military pursuits. The unnamed *procer* (Sigard I's son or grandson) besieged in Chocques by

---

66. It must be noted here that Ernest Warlop did not detect the presence of any "new men" among the eleventh-century Flemish nobles. He strongly believed that the entire Flemish aristocracy derived from the Carolingian or post-Carolingian nobility: Warlop, *De Vlaamse adel,* 1: 15–54.

the Normans around 1030 controlled a major castle in southern Flanders, but this only made him but one of the various castellan lords who prospered in Flanders at the time—among whom were the *castellani* officially appointed by the counts to keep their own castles, who had all been chosen within prominent noble families.[67] Nor does Sigard III appear to have been any kind of "*condotierre*." He and his ancestors were nobles as much as, or indeed more than, warriors.

67. Ibid., 1: 113–55.

— Part III —

MARTIAL IDEALS IN CRUSADING MEMORIES

John D. HOSLER

KNIGHTLY IDEALS AT THE SIEGE OF ACRE, 1189–1191

The place of medieval knights can be studied in a number of ways, including analysis of the concept of knighthood as expressed in chivalric literature or examination of the roles knights played in military operations and on the battlefield. An equally revealing method, however, is to look at knights through the eyes of those witnesses who recorded their deeds and ask whether or not these elite warriors lived up to the expectations put upon them. Using the siege of Acre during the Third Crusade (1189–92) as a setting, this essay examines knightly performance through the eyes of those primary sources commenting upon their military activities therein. The respective authors expected certain degrees of prowess, honour and piety from the knights: valorous deeds and martial successes were celebrated, while poor behaviour and perceived cowardice were harangued. Defeats in battle were pinned on the knights, regardless of other intervening factors, such as poor leadership, battlefield conditions or the quality of their adversaries. By linking military effectiveness to idealised conduct, they contrasted what happened in battle with what should *have happened. A recognition of such cognitive bias can help military historians better to scrutinise and evaluate the evidence for medieval campaigns.*

One of the major western sources for the Third Crusade, the *Itinerarium peregrinorum et gesta regis Ricardi*, contains an elegant depiction of some knights encamped outside the walls of the city of Acre:

> Although the study of arms flourishes throughout the whole country, Champagne is uniquely privileged in knightly pursuits, excelling and surpassing everywhere else. Martial youths from this area rode out powerfully and boldly deployed against the enemy the skills which they had practised in tournaments. They put off their imaginary practice-battles and turned their pugnacious minds to real war.[1]

---

1. *The Chronicle of the Third Crusade: The Itinerarium Peregrinorum et Gesta Regis Ricardi*, bk. 1, chap. 29, trans. Helen J. Nicholson, Crusade Texts in Translation (Aldershot: Ashgate, 1997). For the Latin original, see *Itinerarium peregrinorum et gesta regis Ricardi*, in *Chronicles and Memorials of the Reign of Richard I*, ed. William Stubbs, Rolls Series, 2 vols. (London: Longman 1865), 1: 67–68: "Est quaedam pars Franciae quae Campania dicitur, et cum regio tota studiis armorum floreat, haec quodam militiae privilegio singularius excellit et praecellit. Hinc Martia pubes, potenter egressa, vires quas in tiroci-

Youth, boldness, martial display, tournament: several of the customary
markers of high medieval knighthood. Arguably, as much ink has been
spilt on the social place and cultural aspects of this warrior class as on
its actual performance on actual fields of battle. For military historians,
the latter is of great interest because the role of knights (either historical or mythological) in combat has in many ways coloured the interpretation of the conduct of medieval war throughout the years. Older
views saw cavalry as the principal arm of western armies, populated as
it was by knights, who were typically people of rank and prestige who
expected key roles of position or command. Although some historians
still maintain such a view, the prevailing notion today is that few battles in the West were actually won by means of dashing knights in cavalry charges. On the other hand, the single most dominant feature of
crusading warfare in the East was indeed the cavalry charge, employed
not only in the course of a set battle but also while on the march.[2]

But the *Itinerarium*'s passage raises another sort of question: just
how well did the martial training of knights actually translate into real
war (*ad verum Martem*)? Most often, military historians answer it by
looking at tactics, combat, and results. Another method, however, is
to gauge knightly performance through the lenses of the authors who
wrote about it. This requires moving beyond how knightly behaviour
was idealised in texts—well-trodden ground, indeed—and asking if
that behaviour in battle matched those ideals. Authors, especially those
who actually participated in campaigns, held expectations about how
the knights should fight, but in the environment of war such notions
were validated or dashed once swords were drawn. Writing in hind-
sight, they then judged if martial displays had been chivalric, in their
own understanding, or not. The dissemination (written or oral) of their
works and the syntheses of chivalric ideals contained within could
potentially influence the expectations of others.

The siege of Acre, conducted in 1189–91, is a useful setting in which
to study the distance between the idealised and the real. The siege was
one of the longest of the entire medieval period, and it featured an
enormous number of land and naval engagements that are reported in

niis exercitaverat, in hostem audentius exserit: et imaginaria bellorum prolusione postpos-
ita, pugnaces animos ad verum Martem intendit."

2. See the exchange between Jan Frans Verbruggen, "The Role of the Cavalry in Medi-
eval Warfare," *Journal of Medieval Military History* 3 (2005): 46–71, and Bernard S.
Bachrach, "Verbruggen's 'Cavalry' and the Lyon-Thesis," *Journal of Medieval Military
History* 4 (2006): 137–63.

a balanced array of Christian and Muslim narrative sources. At different points, their authors explicitly state that the course and result of engagements were linked to the relative presence or absence of one aspect of chivalry, defined by Craig Taylor as "the martial values associated with knighthood and aristocracy."[3] Such statements include overt celebrations of combat deeds or depictions of knights doing their duties in relation to their fellows and the crusader camp, as well as stinging critiques of knights who acted contrary to accepted ideals or failed to behave appropriately in hostile situations. This essay examines what twelfth-century writers expected from knights during a crusade and argues that they often attributed positive or negative outcomes to the mere behaviour of warrior elites, even when tactics or other elements were really to blame.

The principal texts utilised in this study are four western accounts of the siege of Acre. The Anglo-Norman verse chronicle of the jongleur Ambroise is the most literary in tone and approach, and Ambroise himself was present towards the end of the siege. His poem is extremely useful in any study of knighthood in the twelfth century because knights and their retinues were his primary audience.[4] The *Itinerarium* is longer and in prose but borrows heavily from Ambroise; its purported author, Richard de Templo, was also a likely participant on the Third Crusade.[5] The different versions of *La continuation de Guillaume de Tyr*, in Old French, present a separate, cumulative account, which seems to have originated in commercial circles in Acre after the crusade. It has a complicated transmission, one not especially germane to the present inquiry. I have used the "Lyon *Eracles*" version, which, unlike the well-known *Chronique d'Ernoul*, is fuller for the years 1187–91.[6] Finally, there is an important letter from the chaplain

3. Craig Taylor, *Chivalry and the Ideals of Knighthood in France during the Hundred Years War* (Cambridge: Cambridge University Press, 2013), xi.

4. Ambroise, *The History of the Holy War: Ambroise's Estoire de la Guerre Sainte*, ed. and trans. Marianne Ailes and Malcolm Barber, 2 vols. (Woodbridge: Boydell, 2003), 2: 13.

5. Richard also borrowed from a similarly-titled work that ends in 1190, *Das Itinerarium peregrinorum: eine zeitgenössische englische Chronik zum dritten Kreuzzug in ursprünglicher Gestalt*, ed. Hans Eberhard Mayer, Schriften der Monumenta Germaniae Historica 18 (Stuttgart: Hiersemann, 1962). See *Chronicle of the Third Crusade*, 6–14, for questions of compilation and authorship.

6. John France, *Great Battles: Hattin* (Oxford: Oxford University Press, 2015), 135. On the Lyon manuscript see Peter W. Edbury, trans., *The Conquest of Jerusalem and the Third Crusade: Sources in Translation*, Crusade Texts in Translation (Aldershot: Ashgate, 1998), 3–6. For Ernoul, see *Chronique d'Ernoul et de Bernard le Trésorier*, Publications de la Société de l'histoire de France 157 (Paris: Renouard, 1871); and on his text after 1187, John

of Baldwin, archbishop of Canterbury, to the religious in that city, which records details of a catastrophic offensive in July 1190 against the sultan of Egypt and Syria, Ṣalāḥ al-Dīn (hereafter Saladin).[7]

I have grouped the source commentary into the three chivalric categories outlined by Richard Kaeuper as fundamental to the understanding of what chivalry was, in both history and literature. These are prowess and status, prowess and honour, and prowess and piety; Kaeuper dubs the common denominator of prowess—demonstrated effectiveness in fighting—"the key chivalric trait."[8] For the paired qualities, Maurice Keen defined them thus: status relates to social rank and the fear of losing esteem among one's peers; honour involves maintaining the social imperatives of one's rank; and piety renders military service that is pleasing to God.[9] The Acre sources comment on each of these aspects and make clear their expectations of proper behaviour of knights who operated within them.

Prowess and Status

One of the persistent questions involving knights has been their role on the battlefield. Knights are synonymous with horses, and horses denote status. In the Anglo-Norman period, it steadily became common for lords to be depicted as mounted warriors, and by 1200 knighthood could qualify a man for inclusion in the aristocracy.[10] Mounted combat was the ideal and preferred manner of fighting for men of such elevated status. During the Crusades, mounted knights charging *en masse* was the defining feature of western field tactics.[11] There

Gillingham, "Roger of Howden on Crusade," in *Richard Coeur de Lion: Kingship, Chivalry and War in the Twelfth Century* (London: Hambledon, 1994), 147–48 n. 33. This is not to say that the Lyon *Eracles* is always the most original of the Continuations, however; see Edbury, "The Lyon *Eracles* and the Old French Continuations of William of Tyre," in *Montjoie: Studies in Crusade History in Honour of Hans Eberhard Mayer*, ed. Benjamin Z. Kedar, Jonathan Riley-Smith, and Rudolf Hiestand (Aldershot: Ashgate, 1997), 139–53

7. Translated in *Conquest of Jerusalem*, chap. 6c; in Latin, see "Epistolae Cantuarienses," in *Chronicles and Memorials of the Reign of Richard I*, ed. Stubbs, 2: 328–29.

8. Richard W. Kaeuper, *Chivalry and Violence in Medieval Europe* (Oxford: Oxford University Press, 2001), 304–10 and 135.

9. Maurice Keen, "Chivalry: Overview," in *The Oxford Encyclopedia of Medieval Warfare and Military Technology*, ed. Clifford J. Rogers, 3 vols. (Oxford: Oxford University Press, 2010), 1: 375.

10. David Crouch, *William Marshal*, 3rd ed. (London: Routledge, 2016), 197.

11. Michael Prestwich, *Armies and Warfare in the Middle Ages: The English Experience* (New Haven: Yale University Press, 1996), 221–22.

was also an important tradition, particularly in the twelfth century, of knights dismounting to stand alongside infantry, even in the East.[12] Yet even off their horses, the status of knights remained superior to that of common men-at-arms; because knights were more prominent members of medieval society, their individual deeds in battle are commonly described in literary, narrative, and record sources. Moreover, these texts often celebrate knightly deeds whether performed astride or not: as elite warriors, knights were expected to fight well.

At the siege of Acre, one finds knights serving in a role that, at first glance, might seem below their station. This was the defence of the crusader camp outside the city walls, specifically, the defensive ditches and ramparts constructed to keep Saladin's relief army at bay. Saladin's strategy against the besiegers was three-fold. First, the city garrison defended the walls and launched sorties against the crusaders when possible. Second, the sultan's own forces attacked the enemy camp in different ways, including daily skirmishing at its edges and periodic concentrated assaults with larger components of his army. Third, he protected against crusader advances by coordinating his efforts with the garrison: when the crusaders addressed Acre's walls, his men rode at their camp as a distraction. These cooperative moves were planned and executed by means of flags, smoke signals, carrier birds, and messengers swimming across the city harbour. During the autumn and early winter of 1189, the crusader camp was essentially undefended, save for soldiers posted at its perimeter, and it was nearly overrun. But once finished, the defensive ditches and ramparts erected by the crusaders protected them on two sides and allowed them to remain outside Acre over the course of nearly two years.[13] John Pryor has recently argued that once the crusaders had finished the ditches and ramparts the city's capture was all but assured, for Saladin never figured out how to break through their defences and end the siege.[14]

12. For the West, see Stephen Morillo, *Warfare under the Anglo-Norman Kings, 1066–1135* (Woodbridge: Boydell, 1994), 150–60; for the East, John France, *Victory in the East: a Military History of the First Crusade* (Cambridge: Cambridge University Press, 1994), 125–27.

13. *Itinerarium peregrinorum*, bk. 1, chap. 31.

14. John H. Pryor, "A Medieval Siege of Troy: the Fight to the Death at Acre, 1189–1191 or the Tears of Ṣalāḥ al-Dīn," in *The Medieval Way of War: Studies in Medieval Military History in Honor of Bernard S. Bachrach*, ed. Gregory I. Halfond (Farnham: Ashgate, 2015), 115.

While unspectacular and mundane in comparison to field combat, the trenches were critical to the cause at Acre, and the labourers
needed protection as they dug. The digging commenced in late 1189
and the work was finished in rough form by the end of the year, with
later improvements and refinements, such as wooden ramparts and
gates, added in 1190. Ambroise insinuates that both regular archers
and more elite warriors contributed to the effort, for "the most comfortable [now] lived a life of sacrifice, in fear and watching, labouring
night and day."[15] That the knights dug with shovels is not explicitly
stated; if they did, it would represent a remarkable instance of deign-
ing to engage in work that many believed eroded their status.[16] The
work was done in shifts, with half of the available men making the
trench while others guarded them from attacking Muslims: "Our men
sought to dig it; they sought to destroy it."[17]

This practice of stationing the best warriors on the ramparts continued well into 1191. For example, following the arrival of Philip
Augustus at Acre in April, both the knights and the men-at-arms again
divided into two groups, the first to attack the city and the second to
defend against Saladin's relief effort.[18] Even on 3 July 1191, when the
capitulation of Acre seemed certain, a general assault on the city walls
was preceded by a precautionary stationing of guards along the outer
ditches in order to repel any possible charges from Saladin's army.
Thus we read in Ambroise's *Estoire*:

> There they were in the morning; there they mounted, the proud
> and worthy people. That day those who had no cowardice in
> them were set to guard the ditches. All around there were the
> best men in the world.[19]

15. Cf. 1 Thessalonians 2:9 and 2 Thessalonians 3:8.
16. As explained in Catharina Lis and Hugo Soly, *Worthy Efforts: Attitudes to Work and Workers in Pre-Industrial Europe* (Leiden: Brill, 2012), 167–68.
17. Ambroise, *Estoire*, lines 3128–37 and 3102–3: "Tut cist a cest passage vindrent, / Martyrs e confessors devindrent, / Car li plus aisiez—ço os dire—/ I fud assez en grant martire / E de petir e de veillier / E de jor e nuit travillier, / Car ne poeient reposer, / N'il ne s'osouent pas [p]oser / Devant ço qu[ë] il orent fait / Le fossé ou tant mal ot fait" ("They all came at this time and became martyrs and confessors of the faith, for the most comfortable [now] lived a life of sacrifice, in fear and watching, labouring night and day, for they had no respite and could take none until they had completed the trench over which there was such loss"); and "Li nostre le voleient faire, / E cil tendouent al desfaire." See also *Itinerarium peregrinorum*, bk. 1, chap. 31.
18. Ambroise, *Estoire*, lines 4621–36; *Itinerarium peregrinorum*, bk. 3, chap. 5.
19. Ambroise, *Estoire*, lines 4835–40: "Eht vos al matin monté / La fiere gent de grant bonté. / Cel jor fist as fossez la garde / Tel gent qui n'esteit pas coarde, / Car tot entor a la reonde / Aveit des meillor genz del monde."

And in the words of the author of the *Itinerarium*:

> So in the morning they all armed themselves. They placed
> preeminent and picked warriors of exceptional valour in the
> outer ditches as a precaution against any problems or unex-
> pected Saracen attack. ... The desperate Turks attacked, and
> the magnificent Christians threw them back...[20]

The personal and professional qualities of these guards are highly
lauded. Unlike wars in the West, where such defences were custom-
arily protected by infantry while knights patrolled the area in small
groups, the close proximity of the Acre camp to Saladin's position
required the strongest perimeter defence possible. Knights were
accustomed to service in garrisons or castle guards, so defending a
camp perimeter was not beneath their martial status.[21]

Guarding the completed ditches was a crucial job, and several individual warriors are celebrated and praised for their strong defence
thereof. These include William, earl of Derby, who killed a hundred
Muslims with his bow, as well as the knight Guy of Dampierre from
Champagne and Bishop Adelard of Verona, the papal legate.[22] Geoffrey of Lusignan is particularly singled out as an exceptional defender
of the earthworks. In September 1190, when the Acre garrison rushed
forward to fill in the ditches with wood, Geoffrey fought at the line
alongside men-at-arms. "Fresh in prowess," he killed ten Muslims
with an axe and captured an unspecified number as well. Ambroise
sings of the "sounds of [the] blows" of this worthy knight, the likes of
which had not been heard since the days of Roland and Oliver.[23] He

20. *Itinerarium peregrinorum*, bk. 3, chap. 9: "Mane itaque, cunctis armatis, disponun-
tur ad exteriora fossata custodes virtutis eximiae praecipui et praeelecti, propter contingen-
tes importunitates et Saracenorum repentinas incursiones. ... Ingruunt Turci improbissimi,
quos rejiciunt Christiani praestantissimi..."

21. Clifford J. Rogers, *Soldiers' Lives throughout History: The Middle Ages* (Westport:
Greenwood Press, 2007), 82–82; Richard Barber, *The Knight and Chivalry* (Reprint; New
York: Harper, 1974), 195.

22. Ambroise, *Estoire*, lines 3120–27. Adelard, notably, is called "a *prodome*" ("a most
worthy man") in the text; its Latin cognate, *probus homo*, was a man of admirable qualities
whose behaviour, mannerisms, and virtues would eventually be subsumed into "chivalry"
in the thirteenth century. See David Crouch, *The Birth of Nobility: Constructing Aristocracy in England and France, 900–1300* (London: Longman, 2005) 30–37; idem, "The
Violence of the Preudomme," in *Prowess, Piety, and Public Order in Medieval Society:
Studies in Honor of Richard W. Kaeuper*, ed. Craig M. Nakashian and Daniel P. Franke
(Leiden: Brill, 2017), 87–101.

23. Ambroise, *Estoire*, lines 4651–60: "Quant cil de Luizeignan, Jefreis, / Qui de
proesce iert toz jorz freis, / Vint a la barre ou il esteient, / Que sor noz genz ja pris aveient,

was accompanied in this defence by the Flemish knight Baldwin of Caron—called "an excellent knight, confident as a lion"— the knights Walter of Oiry and Baldwin of Dargus, Count Henry of Champagne, and a host of Knights Templar.[24]

On the other hand, there were times when the knights did not measure up to their status. At Acre, this generally manifested itself in a refusal to sally forth against Saladin's army. One interesting example is from the summer of 1190. Suffering from a lack of food and a general sense of boredom, the men-at-arms began to agitate against their betters; accusing the knights of cowardice, they decided to march against the Muslim camp on their own. According to the Lyon *Eracles*:

> Matters in the host got to the point where no knight would dare go into the field of combat unless taunted and shamed into going. The sergeants adopted such a haughty attitude toward the knights that they regarded themselves as being of greater worth than they were and imagined that they could easily fight against Saladin without their [the knights'] help. On many occasions the sergeants asked the king [Guy] and the barons to let them mount an attack. When they realised that they were not to be dissuaded, they told them that they could go at their own risk. If they did well there would be great joy, and if ill befell them they would find no one to help them.[25]

/ Sis reüsa a force ariere / E en mist plus de dis en biere / D'une hache qu[ë] il teneit. / A tanz cops tanz en reteneit / Que puis Rodland e Olivier / Ne fud tel los de chevalier" ("for Geoffrey of Lusignan, still fresh in prowess, came to the barrier where they were and which they had already taken from our men and repulsed them with force, sending more than ten of them to their graves using an axe that he carried. Everywhere resounded so to the sound of his blows that not since Roland and Oliver had there been such a praiseworthy knight"). See also the elaboration of his deeds in *Itinerarium peregrinorum*, bk. 3, chap. 5.

24. Roger of Howden, *Chronica magistri Rogeri de Houedene*, ed. William Stubbs, 4 vols., Rolls Series 51 (London: Longman, 1868–71), 3: 73. On Baldwin of Caron, see *Itinerarium peregrinorum*, bk. 4, chap. 19.

25. *Conquest of Jerusalem*, chap. 103; in French, see "L'Estoire de Éracles empereur et la conqueste de la Terre d'Outremer," in *Recueil des historiens des croisades: Historiens occidentaux*, 5 vols. (Paris, 1844–1879), 2: 150: "Il estoient si atornez en l'ost que chevalier n'osoit aler en lices, qui ne fust hues et maumenes de paroles. Li sergent avoient pris si grant orgueil encontre les chevaliers que il cuidoient plus valoir des chevaliers, et que il se cuidoient bien combatre a Salahadin sanz l'aide des chevaliers. Li sergent requistrent au roi Gui et as baronz, et par plusors fois de issit fors. Quant il virent que il ne les poeent retenir, si distrent que il alassent a lor aventure; se bien lor avenoit, il auroient joie; et se mau lor avenoit, il ne troveroient home qui les alast secorre."

In the *Itinerarium*, the soldiers then marched to battle:

> Madness overcame good advice, impulse overcame reason, and the multitude took command. Whenever an impulse seizes the common people, they think that rashness is a virtue, judge that what they want is best, do not stop to think about the outcome, flee correction and despise direction. On St James' Day, that mournful and inimical day, the ill-fated troop of common knights sallied forth from the camp.[26]

The importance here lies in the social distinction between the common soldiers (*vulgus*) who marched to fight and those who remained. The *Itinerarium* text identifies the former as *gregarii milites*, which has been translated as "common knights." This is a mistranslation. Although the temptation is to equate *miles/milites* with knights, recent scholarship has demonstrated the danger of doing so too readily. For example, mistranslation of the word in John of Salisbury's *Policraticus* has led historians erroneously to attribute to him a definition of chivalry; other studies have pointed out similar errors.[27] In the present case, the context suggests rather sergeants (who are explicitly identified in the Lyon *Eracles*) or perhaps constables, since the marching soldiers are also called *plebs* and *vulgus* in the *Itinerarium*. These so-described *gregarii milites*, then, were most likely common unit leaders of the foot-soldiers and missile troops.[28] In July 1190, they were "those that fought": they rejected the decision-making role afforded to the knights,

26. *Itinerarium peregrinorum*, bk. 1, chap. 40: "Nihil tamen vel illorum dissuasio, vel hujus interminatio proficit; vincit enim furor consilium, rationem impetus, imperium multitudo. Vulgus, quocunque impellitur, temeritatem virtutem putat, id optimum quod optat judicans, et rerum exitu non expenso, corrigentem refugit, et regentem contemnit. Die igitur Sancti Jacobi, die luctifica et infesta, infelix illa, gregariorum militum turba prorumpit."

27. John D. Hosler, *John of Salisbury: Military Authority of the Twelfth-Century Renaissance* (Leiden: Brill, 2013), 12–22 and 184–87; see also David S. Bachrach, "*Milites* and Warfare in Pre-Crusade Germany," *War in History* 22 (2015): 310. These stand contra to assumptions such as that in Maurice Keen, *Chivalry* (New Haven: Yale University Press, 1984), 27.

28. *Itinerarium peregrinorum*, bk. 1, chap. 40: "Plebs rerum novarum cupida, principum incusat ignaviam, et pari desiderio aestuans, se vicissim invitat ad pugnam" ("The common people, greedy for excitement, began to accuse the princes of being cowards and started agitating for a fight") and "Principes quidem, quantum possunt, ausus vulgi temerarios laborant comprimere" ("The princes tried to restrain the rash daring of the common crowd as far as they could"). On the translation of constable, see R.E. Latham, ed., "Greg/arius," *Revised Medieval Latin Word List from British and Irish Sources* (Reprint, Oxford: Oxford University Press, 1994), 216; on their rank and duties, see Clifford J. Rogers, "Constables," *Encyclopedia of Medieval Warfare*, 1: 423–24.

ignored their advice, and rashly moved into battle. Underlying all the passages, however, is the distinct image of the knights acting counter to their status and preferring to remain in camp.[29]

Unhappily for the soldiers, the end result was the ill-fated offensive on 25 July 1190, the feast of St James, in which they were enticed into the Muslim camp with a feigned retreat and massacred.[30] Who was to blame for such a disaster? Richard de Templo seems split on the matter: on the one hand, the soldiers had been rash and foolish; on the other, just some semblance of leadership might have enabled their success. He actually compliments the common soldiers on their bravery and impulse to action but sighs, "If only they had a chief."[31] The *Eracles* blames the sergeants, who had, after all, been warned by their betters in advance; however, it offers a pointed and stinging critique of the knights' cowardice and shame as well. As Keen would say, only the fear of loss of esteem prompted them to fight.[32] Archbishop Baldwin's chaplain assigns blame all around but is also most critical of the elites: "our knights lurk in their tents ... as if defeated, they let the insults of the enemy go unpunished."[33] Certainly, the knights' caution could have been justified: R.C. Smail pointed to the need for patience when engaged in the East, specifically, the notion of refraining from offensive actions unless victory was likely.[34] But whether it was for strategic reasons or not, both writers and crusaders interpreted the knights' unwillingness to engage with some suspicion.

The predicament was similar in November of that same year: once more, the common soldiers expressed a desire to march out towards

29. This was the reverse of the behaviour of knights outside Antioch during the First Crusade, when Raymond of Aguilers notes that the knights left camp to ambush Ridwan of Aleppo while the fearful foot soldiers guarded the camp. See Conor Kostick, "Courage and Cowardice on the First Crusade, 1096–1099," *War in History* 20 (2013): 47.

30. See John D. Hosler, *The Siege of Acre, 1189–1191: Saladin, Richard the Lionheart, and the Battle That Decided the Third Crusade* (London and New Haven: Yale University Press, 2018), 67–71.

31. *Itinerarium peregrinorum*, bk. 1, chap. 40: "si caput nacta."

32. The subject of medieval conceptions of cowardice in war has been studied in great detail in three grouped articles: Richard Abels, "'Cowardice' and Duty in Anglo-Saxon England;" Steven Isaac, "Cowardice and Fear Management: the 1173–74 Conflict as a Case Study;" and Stephen F. Morillo, "Expecting Cowardice: Medieval Battle Tactics Reconsidered," *Journal of Medieval Military History* 4 (2006): 29–49, 50–64, and 65–73.

33. "Epistolae Cantuarienses," 329: "Milites nostri infra tentoria sua delitescunt, et qui sibi festiname promittebant victoriam, ignavi et torpidi, et quasi convicti, contumelias sibi ab hostibus infra impune patiuntur."

34. R.C. Smail, *Crusading Warfare, 1097–1193*, 2nd ed. (Cambridge: Cambridge University Press, 1995), 139.

Saladin's lines, and they were frustrated by the knights' continuing delays. On this occasion other motivations are given in the western sources, such as the costliness of the siege operations and a dwindling food supply.[35] The Arabic account of Saladin's *qadī* Ibn Shaddād particularly corroborates the food issue, noting increasing wheat prices in Tyre; prices were higher at Acre, and the lack of food led some crusaders to surrender. He also claims that the crusaders had learned of Saladin's severe illness and believed the moment ripe for an assault.[36] Whatever the reason, the elites' response in November was the opposite of that of July: when the commoners expressed their displeasure at the delay in fighting, the knights and princes agreed to lead them. They therefore met the expectations of their status and promptly led their social inferiors out to engage the enemy.[37]

Prowess and Honour

The aforementioned St James offensive of July 1190 leads us into the second of Kaeuper's categories, that of prowess and honour. Beyond the question of status, which concerns the military and social position of knights as the leaders of the army, honour relates to expectations of behaviour as determined by a knight's peers in light of accepted (and ever-shifting) social norms. Honourable actions boosted or maintained a knight's reputation and helped him avoid shame.[38] As J.F. Verbruggen and Kaeuper have noted, knights did their martial duty for the sake of their honour: "the practice of one produces the other."[39] Honour is not the same as duty, which has a strict ethical or moral

35. *Itinerarium peregrinorum*, bk. 1, chap. 62; Ambroise, *Estoire*, line 3955. The November shortage is also mentioned in *Gesta regis Henrici secundi Benedicti abbatis*, ed. William Stubbs, Rolls Series, 2 vols. (London, 1867), 2: 34–35 and the poem "De expugnatione civitatis Acconensis," in Roger of Howden, *Chronica*, 3: cxxii, lines 485–86.

36. *The Rare and Excellent History of Saladin by Bahā' al-Dīn Ibn Shaddād*, trans. D.S. Richards, Crusade Texts in Translation (Farnham: Ashgate, 2002), 135. On wheat prices, see Satō Tsugitaka, *State & Rural Society in Medieval Islam: Sultans, Muqta's, and Fallahun* (Leiden: Brill, 1997), 70.

37. For a full analysis of the November campaign, see John D. Hosler, "Clausewitz's Wounded Lion: a Fighting Retreat at the Siege of Acre, November 1190," in *Acre and Its Falls: Studies in the History of a Crusader City*, ed. John France (Leiden: Brill, 2018), 30–48.

38. See the discussion in Taylor, *Chivalry*, 54–56.

39. Jan Frans Verbruggen, *The Art of Warfare in Western Europe during the Middle Ages, from the Eighth Century to 1340*, trans. S. Willard and Mrs. R.W. Southern, 2nd ed., Warfare in History (Woodbridge: Boydell, 1997), 55; Kaeuper, *Chivalry and Violence*, 129.

basis, but there are similarities in that both relate to the expectations of others. In war, a knight declining to engage the enemy might well be criticised for it, depending upon the situation. There are contrasting examples in the Acre sources of knights supporting their comrades with their own arms but also knights abandoning both their peers and their lessers when the fighting became too dangerous and their own lives were on the line.

The knights had refused to take part in the St James offensive, and this inaction damaged their honour amongst the army in general. It was a disaster. The mass of "leaderless" crusaders advanced towards the Muslim lines: Saladin promptly abandoned his camp, and when the crusaders discovered the empty tents they stopped to pillage and eat.[40] Distracted in this way, they were caught unawares by the sultan's predictable counter-attack. Saladin's herald cried, "See, the enemies of God are now in His power, now that they have been forward enough to descend on your tents."[41] A massacre of the crusaders then ensued. Baldwin's chaplain numbered the dead at some four thousand, the *Estoire* at seven thousand, and the *Eracles* at sixteen thousand.[42] Most of them were killed within the Muslim camp, but a sizable number escaped and fled back towards Acre.

As their defeated comrades fled and were chased down by the Muslim cavalry, the western knights refused to leave their defences to rescue them. Here we arrive at the point of the authors' disdain. The Christians were cut down as they fled, but the knights stayed behind their ditches:

> Our princes heard the roar and saw the carnage, but pretended not to notice. Hard, inhuman and pitiless!—they saw their brothers being cut to pieces in front of them yet made no attempt to rescue them from death … Some held back out of cowardice…[43]

40. *Itinerarium peregrinorum*, bk. 1, chap. 40.
41. *Rare and Excellent History of Saladin*, 118–19.
42. "Epistolae Cantuarienses," 329; "L'Estoire de Éracles," 2: 151.
43. *Itinerarium peregrinorum*, bk. 1, chap. 40: "Audito fremitu, et strage conspecta, principes nostri dissimulant: duri certe, inhumani et impii, qui fratres suos coram se trucidari conspiciunt, nec opem perituris impendunt, quibus hoc solum fuit pro crimine contra factam inhibitionem a castris exisse. Porro caeteris ex ignavia potius quam offensa haesitantibus…"

A few of the elite did leave the safety of their fortifications in order to aid the retreat, but the only one singled out for praise was Ralph d'Hauterive, archdeacon of Colchester, who helped many escape and was celebrated in knightly terms:

> He was a man of remarkable height and appearance, graced by a double laurel wreath, outstanding in both the ecclesiastical and secular militias, for he was renowned both for his learning and the feats of arms.[44]

However, the archdeacon had few helpers in his rescue attempt. Ambroise notes that the fleeing Christians "received no [other] help apart from some knights who hurried over, but there was not a large number of them, so the foot-soldiers died quickly."[45] Refusing to lend aid to a retreating comrade was clearly seen as dishonourable.

The most prominent victim of abandonment at Acre was Andrew of Brienne, the brother of Erard II, count of Brienne. He died in an earlier offensive against Saladin, on 4 October 1189, after being left on the field. Quite cruelly, it was his brother himself who abandoned him: Erard heard Andrew's cries and even saw him lying on the ground but in the end fled to safety.[46] The *Itinerarium* laments Andrew's death: "His valour had raised him so far above all the French that he was regarded as first among knights, while all the rest contended for second place;" not so Erard, for whom "cowardice declined the glory which chance had offered." For Ambroise, "never did another such knight die, nor any who came to the rescue of so many."[47]

On a more positive note, when knights were willing to engage at the proper times and for the proper reasons, western authors readily celebrated their deeds. The honour acquired in defending comrades is

44. Ibid., bk. 1, chap. 40: "archdiaconus Colecestriae Radulfus de Alta Ripa, laborantibus subvenit, lapsuris succurrit: vir statura spectabilis et forma: quem laurus gemina et utriusque militiae commendabat perfectio, scientia scilicet praecluem et armis insignem." See also Roger of Howden, *Chronica*, 3: 70.

45. Ambroise, *Estoire*, lines 3481–85: "As serjanz tant tost s'eleisserent, / Que plus de .vii. Mile en leisserent / Que onques succurru ne furent / Fors de chevalers qui corurent, / Mais n'en i curut pas grantment, / Ainz i mururent eralment."

46. *Itinerarium peregrinorum*, bk. 1, chap. 30.

47. Ibid., bk. 1, chap. 30: "quem adeo supra omnes Francos virtus extulerant, ut ei militiae primatu concesso, caeteri de laude secunda certarent," and "gloriam quam casus obtulerant, ignavia declinavit." Ambroise, *Estoire*, lines 3008–11: "La fud ocis Andreu de Braine / Qui ja s'alme ne seit en paine, / Car tels chevalers ne murut / Ne tantes genz ne socurut."

consistent across the sources, and different individuals are singled out for their behaviour in this regard. The aforementioned, albeit equally unsuccessful, foray against Saladin's camp on 4 October 1189 presents a series of comparisons. Geoffrey of Lusignan and his brother Guy, the titular king of Jerusalem, also dashed to assist those in flight, in the process saving from death Conrad, the despised marquis of Montferrat.[48] Despite the general rout of the crusaders, the Knights Templar fought well, and their grand master, Gerard of Ridefort, was praised. As the crusader host turned in retreat, Gerard refused to flee to safety, instead remaining to safeguard the reputation of his Order.[49] He purportedly exclaimed, "Never! It would be my shame and a scandal for the Templars. I would be said to have saved my life by running away and leaving my fellow-knights to be slaughtered."[50] Although Gerard's loyalty on this occasion cost him his life, he is Richard de Templo's exemplar of a knight full of both prowess and honour. He had remained in the fight for three reasons: to avoid tainting his Order's reputation, to avoid personal shame, and to rescue his peers. While the first reason could well highlight political concerns, such as the position and influence of the Templars in the Kingdom of Jerusalem, the latter two certainly relate to the need to behave honourably on the field of combat.

Other knights are singled out for exceptional praise. This same October battle also showcased the knightly deeds of the aforementioned Andrew of Brienne. Prior to his tragic death, Andrew led the vanguard and was thus in the perfect position to witness the crusaders' panicked flight. Andrew urged them to stand firm, but in the mad rush of warriors he was cut down.[51] Geoffrey of Lusignan is called "noble and daring" and "highly praised" by Ambroise.[52] In November 1190, he led a daring cavalry charge against a mass of Muslims at the Doc bridge, which lay over the River Belus. Accompanied by five knights, he charged and knocked more than thirty enemies into the

48. Ibid., lines 3012–15.
49. Ibid., lines 3016–29.
50. *Itinerarium peregrinorum*, bk. 1, chap. 29: "'Absit!,' inquit, 'ut vertatur in opprobrium et Templariis in scandalam, ut fugiendo dicar vitam servasse et commilitones meos caesos reliquisse'."
51. "L'Estoire de Éracles," 2: 130.
52. Ambroise, *Estoire*, lines 2830–33: "La ot Jiefrei de Leuzengnan / A l'ost defendre grant haan, / Qui pieça iert preuz e osez, / Mais or fud il mult alosiez"; ("Geoffrey of Lusignan endured great labour in the defence of the army; he was already [held to be] noble and daring; from then on he was highly praised").

water. The crossing was thus secured, thanks to the deeds of this honourable knight.[53] The Frenchman Aubrey Clément led a bold attack on
the Cursed Tower in Acre on 3 July 1191. Vowing to enter the city on
that day or to die trying, he scaled a ladder laid against the tower and
several Frenchmen followed him up. The ladder collapsed under their
combined weight, and Aubrey was left alone atop the wall. He was
soon killed, and the attack was subsequently called off. He was a well-
known figure: he was Philip Augustus' marshal, and his father, Robert
Clément, had been the king's former tutor, so his death was widely
mourned.[54] Finally, James of Avesnes, lord of Condé and Guise, was
saved when a nearby, but unnamed, knight dismounted and gave him
his horse. James himself is dubbed by Ambroise as a better knight than
Alexander, Hector, or Hercules.[55] We thus have several firm expressions of honourable conduct, in which the right course for knights was
to engage in combat or intercede to help a fellow warrior.

The ill-fated crusader offensive of 4 October showcases another element of apparent knightly dishonour: the taking of plunder. Plunder,
the stripping of goods and monies from fallen enemies and/or their
residence, should be differentiated from theft and rapine, which is generally a method of securing victuals while on campaign. Depending on
whom one asked in the period, rapine was either condemned as deleterious and sinful or applauded when employed strategically to ravage
an enemy's lands.[56] Plunder was treated similarly. By itself, it was not
considered dishonourable: indeed, there were different and sometimes
elaborate collection and distribution methods employed to ensure that
soldiers received fair shares of the booty.[57] What was dishonourable,
however, was plundering before the fighting had concluded. In Octo-

53. Ibid., lines 4073–80; *Itinerarium peregrinorum*, bk. 1, chap. 62.
54. Ambroise, *Estoire*, lines 4882–4902; *Itinerarium peregrinorum*, bk. 3, chap. 10;
Roger of Howden, *Chronica*, 3: 117; John W. Baldwin, *The Government of Philip Augustus: Foundations of French Royal Power in the Middle Ages* (Berkeley: University of California Press, 1986), 33–34.
55. Ambroise, *Estoire*, lines 2848–51.
56. On this, warriors differed from intellectuals. John of Salisbury was a harsh critic
of rapine, arguing that it also raised questions of soldierly discipline; see Hosler, *John of
Salisbury*, 80–81. On the other hand, in 1173 Count Philip of Flanders is depicted as advis-
ing King Louis VII of France, "This is the way to begin to fight, to my way of thinking:
first lay waste the land, then destroy one's enemies" ("Issi deit l'em cumencier / guerre—
ço m'est vis— / Primes guaster la terre / e puis ses enemis"): Jordan Fantosme, *Jordan
of Fantosme's Chronicle*, ed. and trans. R.C. Johnston (Oxford: Oxford University Press,
1981), 42.
57. Rogers, *Soldiers' Lives throughout History*, 218–22.

ber 1189 it was the knights who were again poor role models in this respect.

The action began well enough. The crusader infantry approached the Muslim ranks *en masse* and then suddenly split its ranks in two, which allowed the cavalry to charge through the middle.[58] The eruption of the knights makes a glamorous impression in the narrative:

> The main strength of the army followed, a brilliant sight with their horses and arms and their various insignia. Their faces and bearing declared the passion of their minds. They were the hope of the faithful and the terror of the enemy.[59]

The use of massed cavalry charges during the crusades is well known, and on this occasion the horse was typically effective. However, as the Muslims fled the cavalry lost its discipline, ceased its pursuit, and turned to plunder. The hastily-left sundries in the enemy camp were seized, and the vacant tents were turned out and emptied of their contents and food. Count Henry I of Bar-le-Duc—"no more courtly a man than he from here to the Far"—actually entered Saladin's tent and looted it.[60] Certainly, one can speculate that many of the foot-soldiers, arriving at the scene in the minutes following the cavalry charge, took part in the looting as well. But the specific attribution to the count and his cavalry suggests that many of these looters were knights; as prominent men, their deeds were at this moment worth denouncing. Again and again the authors complain of their greed.

In the midst of their looting, the crusaders were startled by two rumours. First, the Acre garrison had emerged from a city gate, which brought about an immediate danger. The garrison threatened to flank the army, which had now ranged far from the confines of the crusader camp; the two could potentially be cut off from each other. Second, there was apparently a bustle when one of the knight's horses bolted from the Muslim camp and began galloping back towards the city. As a result, soldiers panicked, either because they believed they were

58. For a full narrative of this battle, see Hosler, *Siege of Acre*, 27–38.

59. *Itinerarium peregrinorum*, bk. 1, chap. 29: "subsequitur belli robur praecipum equis, armis, et variis effulgens insignibus. Ignem vero animi facies et gestus indicant: fidelibus ad votum, hostibus ad terrorem." The battle is described in brief detail in Smail, *Crusading Warfare*, 187–88.

60. Ambroise, *Estoire*, lines 2928–29: "E si i vint li cuens de Bar, / N'ot plus corteis desi qu'al Far."

being flanked or because they suspected that a rout had begun. As one, they fled in a haphazard manner back towards their camp:

> Their ordered battalions were thrown into disorder, their units dispersed, no one paid attention to their standards. The leaders themselves rushed headlong into flight and scarcely anyone had the courage to remain.[61]

Probably disbelieving their good fortune, the Muslims called off their retreat and charged back into battle: as the crusaders fled, their enemies chased down and massacred them. Thus the dishonourable thirst for booty, succumbed to first by the knights, had arrested the army's momentum in mid-battle and ultimately cost many crusaders their lives.

Prowess and Piety

Finally, some of the writers' judgements were grounded in their desire for pious, virtuous warriors. Piety was a necessary virtue in a knight in the context of a crusade. The difficult conditions at Acre tested not only the stamina of the soldiers but also their faith. There were months of down time in the crusader camp, either during the winter or in the periods in which the men were stricken by disease or suffering from food shortages. These conditions, along with a string of defeats to Saladin's men, contributed to a burgeoning dissoluteness among the soldiers. Baldwin's chaplain lamented the general faithlessness of the crusading army at large: "The Lord is not in the camp," the chaplain complained; "there is no chastity, sobriety, faith, love or charity."[62]

That said, the proper measure of visible devotion was often credited as the reason for victory. Calling out to God for assistance was seen as efficacious, especially for knights. For example, the *Itinerarium* relates the story of a Norman knight, Ivo of Vieuxpont, whose faith saved him and his crew as their ship attempted a voyage from Acre north to Tyre. Ivo and ten sailors encountered a galley crewed by eighty Muslims,

---

61. *Itinerarium peregrinorum*, bk. 1, chap. 29: "Illic bellorum ordo condunitur: disperguntur cunei, nullus signorum respectus: ipsi duces ad fugam praecipites, et vix aliquis fiduciam concipit resistendi."

62. "Epistolae Cantuarienses," 328: "In castris non est castitas, sobrietas, fides, dilectio, caritas."

and as it approached the sailors became fearful. Ivo denounced their lack of faith, proceeded to leap aboard the galley, and once aboard he began beheading Muslims with an axe. His fellows took heart in his deeds and joined him, fighting until all the enemy had been captured or decapitated:

> Thus those who placed their hope in God were given a triumph, for He did not allow them to be conquered. It was their unfeigned faith which gave them strength, rather than a large number of fighters; because it is of no consequence to God whether there are few or many. He gives strength for the battle and total victory.[63]

Reliance upon God's grace was equally important in an anecdote told of an anonymous knight in camp. The poor fellow had answered the call of nature and was busy relieving himself in a defensive trench when a mounted Muslim charged him with a spear. The knight managed to pull his lower clothes up and somehow dodge the blow; falling backwards, he grabbed a stone and threw it with such force that it struck the Muslim on the temple and killed him. His aim was true because he "call[ed] on the help of God, who is always present with his people through grace."[64]

Knights were obligated to defend the name of God against blasphemy. In the summer of 1190, there were several instances of Acre's defenders desecrating crosses that had once stood atop the city's churches. One particular Muslim took some crosses to the city walls and thereupon, in sight of the besiegers, proceeded to beat them and spit and urinate upon them. At length, one crusader, who is identified only as a "courtly crossbowmen" (*arbalestiers corteis*), released a bolt that struck the Muslim in the groin and killed him: "thus as he died he perceived the futility of attempting anything against God."[65]

---

63. *Itinerarium peregrinorum*, bk. 1, chap. 53: "Sic his datur triumphare qui in Deo spem ponunt, qui vinci non novit, ad quod fides non ficta valet, non multitudo dimicantium: quia non refert apud Deum, sive in paucis sive in pluribus, belli consistat virtus et summa victoriae."

64. Ibid., bk. 1, chap. 49: "Invocato vero, Qui semper Suis per gratiam praesens est, Deo in auxilium." For Ambroise's version of the story, see *Estoire*, lines 3578–619.

65. *Itinerarium peregrinorum*, bk. 1, chap. 56: "sicque moriendo persensit quam nihil sit quidquid quispiam contra Deum agendum tentaverit." In Ambroise's telling, "listen what a just avenger God is" ("Oiez com Deus est dreit vengieres"), *Estoire*, line 3605.

Piety was also naturally to be found among those clergy who encamped alongside the other crusaders at Acre. The sources depict clergymen as secular soldiers (*corporalis militia*): some priests and bishops actually took part in physical combat.[66] But in the context of crusade, these men were more than mere soldiers—they were likened to knights. The most prominent is Hubert Walter, the bishop of Salisbury. Hubert is singled out during the aborted November 1190 campaign, which, although failing to reach its target of Haifa in the south, nonetheless managed to withstand intense Muslim attacks and conduct a fighting retreat back to the camp at Acre. On this campaign, "the clergy claimed no small share of military glory." Among those who fought were a number of unnamed abbots and bishops, but Hubert is specifically called heroic: "his virtues made him a knight in battle, a leader in the camp, and a pastor in ecclesiastical matters."[67] Noteworthy as well was Philip, the bishop of Beauvais, who is called "a man more devoted to battle than books, who revelled in knightly pursuits. He would have been the equal of Turpin if he could have found a Charlemagne."[68]

Those clergy who did not actually fight represented a different sort of warrior, the spiritual soldier (*spiritualis militia*). They wielded weapons of a different sort, namely, prayer, fasting, and almsgiving. Some of the attending prelates were connected to the pious virtue of charity. In the winter and early spring of 1191, the crusaders were suffering from a lack of food and persistent disease when Hubert Walter, along with Adelard of Verona and Monaldus of Fano, organised a general collection of money and food for the needy. Ambroise then names those elites who were especially responsive to the bishops' appeal: the Norman knights Walkelin of Ferrers and Robert Trussebot; Jocelyn of Montoire; and the counts Henry of Champagne and Ralph of Clermont. The collection came from the most noble of the army

66. For a recent analysis of this phenomenon, albeit with an emphasis on monks, see Katherine Allen Smith, *War and the Making of Medieval Monastic Culture* (Woodbridge: Boydell, 2011), 39–51.

67. *Itinerarium peregrinorum*, bk. 1, chap. 61: "Clerus autem non modicum militaris gloriae partem vendicat" and "hujus virtus in armis militem, in castris ducem, in ecclesiasticis implet pastorem." On Hubert Walter, see also Lawrence G. Duggan, *Armsbearing and the Clergy in the History and Canon Law of Western Christianity* (Woodbridge: Boydell, 2013), 26.

68. *Itinerarium peregrinorum*, bk. 1, chap.29: "vir armis potius deditus quam armariis, qui gloriatur in militia; et Turpino par esse contenderet se Carolum inveniret."

and was distributed to the ranks of lesser knights and men-at-arms.[69] Mirroring the generosity of the bishops, these knights waged spiritual combat through almsgiving: the collection saved the common soldiers from starvation and thus engendered the continuance of the siege, which, in the summer of 1191, finally succeeded in capturing Acre.[70]

Conclusion

What the preceding examples tell us is that when confronted with the multiple dangers, enticements, and opportunities of battle, knights responded in different ways. For some, real combat and the prospect of sudden death tempered martial enthusiasm. For others, it stirred their sense of honour and piety, developed from years of training and experience, and prompted them to engage with ferocity and skill. Those who did not live up to the ideals found in much of the chivalric literature were denigrated by writers, while those who did were celebrated. The former was a more uncomfortable subject; indeed, Verbruggen has argued that "literature which was often intended for knightly readers and was devoted to their praise cast a mantle of silence over these delicate and private matters."[71] Yet, as demonstrated here, the gap between the ideal and the real can sometimes be teased out from the commentaries of extant narrators. In their understanding, these knightly deeds or lack thereof helped to determine the course of the siege of Acre. Counterfactually, the authors may have even supposed that a victory during, say, the St James offensive, would have brought the siege to a speedier conclusion. As a speculation, perhaps the narrators hoped that their critiques would spur better, future behaviour from any knights who chanced to read or hear their stories.

Equally important, the linking of military effectiveness with socially-mandated behaviour invites us to consider the burgeoning effort today to approach combat from different perspectives. These medieval writers were interested in both *what* happened and what *should* have happened, and they thought it best to convey their syntheses of the two

69. Ambroise, *Estoire*, lines 4407–56.
70. On twelfth-century understandings of spiritual vs. secular warriors and spiritual weapons, see Hosler, *John of Salisbury*, 126–31; and for knights engaging in pious works, Richard Kaeuper, *Holy Warriors: the Religious Idea of Chivalry* (Philadelphia: University of Pennsylvania Press, 2009), 35.
71. Verbruggen, *Art of Warfare*, 109.

to a wider audience. Their attitudes may or may not have been shared by their audiences or even (and perhaps especially) the very warriors they described. Richard Abels puts the issue succinctly:

> What was honourable, unremarkable, or shameful was deter-
> mined both by the author who described the actions and by his
> audience, and we need not assume that author and audience
> always agreed.[72]

Indeed, participants in the Third Crusade who lived to tell the tale may well have disagreed with judgements of their behaviour. Moreover, not every writer chose to opine about knightly virtue. One example is the anonymous "Monachus" (perhaps Aimery, the archbishop of Cae-sarea), who wrote an eyewitness account of the siege of Acre in Latin verse. In his narrative of the St James offensive there is no critique of the knights' honour per se, only a note that their sally might have helped the fleeing soldiers survive. Monachus, however, was not a crusader: he was an eastern resident whose perspective differed from that of those writers who joined the grand expedition (Ambroise, Rich-ard de Templo, Baldwin's chaplain) and the next generation reflecting on it (the *Eracles* author).[73] Perspectives, tempered by proximity and expectations, naturally differed.

Still, the need for so many writers to offer moral lessons within the narrative of battle speaks to the socio-cultural influence of knighthood in the late twelfth century, which in turn helps us better understand its role in practised warfare. Close readings that seek to ferret out the expectations of writers can thereby aid and enrich modern interpreta-tion of crusade history. And in a broader sense, it befits military his-torians to add a consideration of martial biases to our repertoire of source criticism.

---

72. Richard Abels, "Cultural Representations and the Practice of War in the Middle Ages," *Journal of Medieval Military History* 6 (2008): 1–31, at 8.

73. "De expugnatione civitatis Acconensis," in Roger of Howden, *Chronica*, 3: cxix, 373–74.

Nicholas L. PAUL*

WRITING THE KNIGHT, STAGING THE CRUSADER: MANASSES OF HIERGES AND THE MONKS OF BROGNE

The 1177–1211 period saw the composition of a collection of texts commemorating the translation of a major relic of the True Cross from the eastern crusading frontier to the abbey of St Gerard of Brogne near Namur. Although the texts are notionally devoted to the relic, in fact they contain extended meditations on the qualities of knighthood as demonstrated by the local lord, Manasses of Hierges, who was responsible for the relic's acquisition and translation. Most striking in these texts is the use of the crusading frontier as a stage for the performance of Manasses's virtues and the accumulation of reputation and prowess, which returns home with him in material form as the cross relic given to him by the princess of Antioch. This use of the crusading frontier as a stage for knighthood allows us a new perspective on the relationship between chivalry and crusade. Often seen as in tension by historians who understand knighthood as essentially secular and crusading as a project of the church, the case of Manasses shows that while crusading itself could be fully understood within the context of devotional practice, the crusading frontier could function separately as a space for aristocratic performance.

At some point during his tour of the sacred sites of the Low Countries that was the basis for his wonderfully named 1627 book *Hierogazophylacium Belgicum*, the Douai canon Arnold de Raisse visited the Benedictine abbey of Brogne near Namur.[1] De Raisse noted that just before the entrance to the choir "one can see a rather deep well, from which water is drawn and which, when consumed by the sick, restores them to perfect health in consequence of the promise made to

---

* This project could never have been accomplished without the kind assistance of many colleagues in Belgium, including Steven Vanderputten, Xavier Hermand, Jean-François Nieus, and Nicolas Ruffini-Ronzani. Thanks especially to my colleague Wolfgang Mueller for his assistance with transcription of the Namur MSS and to the editors of this volume for their many helpful suggestions. All errors herein are my own.
1. Once located in the diocese of Liège, since 1559 Brogne fell within the diocese of Namur. For the abbey see Eugène del Marmol, "L'abbaye de Brogne ou de Saint Gérard," *Annales de la Société archéologique de Namur* 5:4 (1858): 225–86 and 375–450 and Alain Dierkens, *Abbayes et chapitres entre Sambre et Meuse, VIIe–XIe siècles* (Sigmaringen: Thorbecke, 1985).

the founder Gerard by the Apostles Peter and Paul."[2] An inscription at the well read: "Let the sick, the healthy, the thirsty, the contented come together. I will provide sweet refreshment to all."[3]

The well, which was described by both de Raisse and Gabriel Bucelin, and which elicited a lengthy response from the Bollandists in the *Acta sanctorum*, is certainly striking in its position at the physical heart of the sanctuary.[4] It is less surprising, however, to find that in the pre-modern period a well might lie at the imaginative heart of a community. Indeed, in the early thirteenth century, a writer at Brogne played with the symbolic significance of the well, invoking Brogne's *puteus* as the central stylistic conceit of the beginning of a major narrative work he was writing. Comparing himself to Isaac in the valley of Gerar in Genesis chapter 26, the writer likened the process of writing to wandering in a dry landscape, avoiding earlier wells that might have been filled in with earth by scornful readers, by enemies, mad preachers, heretical detractors, and false brothers. Like Isaac, the writer says he will seek to find water anew:

> By divine dispensation I undertake to draw up and draw out from this well some weighty matters regarding the church of Brogne, namely how in modern times the Cross of the Lord was translated from Antioch-on-the-Orontes, the first residence of [Saint] Peter, to this rather little place, humble but excelling in multiple relics of the saints.[5]

The work from which these words were drawn was only one of a group of texts composed at the abbey of Brogne in the late twelfth and early thirteenth centuries which celebrated the gift to the abbey of a major relic, a fragment of the True Cross encased in the cruciform reliquary

2. Arnold de Raisse, *Hierogazophylacium Belgicum* (Douai: Gerard Pinchon, 1627), 125. For the well see del Marmol, "L'abbaye de Brogne," 414; Dierkens, *Abbayes et chapitres,* 256 and n. 501.

3. "Concurrant aegri, sani, bibuli, sitibundi. Praestabo cunctis dulce refrigerium." del Marmol, "L'abbaye de Brogne," 414.

4. Corneille de Bye, "De S. Gerardo abbate Broniensi in comitatu Namurcensi in Belgio. Commentarius praevius," in *Acta Sanctorum*, Oct. II (Antwerp: Vander Plassche, 1768), 298–300.

5. Namur, Bibliothèque du Séminaire, MS 57 fol. 123v: "Ex hoc igitur puteo haurire conor et elicere, pensata dispensatione diuina circa Broniensas ecclesiam qualiter crux domini modernis temporibus ibidem translata et data extiterit ex antiochia prima petri sedi eidem quippe locello satis humili suppetentia sed multiplicibus sanctorum pignoribus excellenti."

which, for its provenance in the crusader capital of northern Syria, was known as the "Holy Cross of Antioch."

The corpus of texts from Brogne relating to this object is extensive, perhaps among the largest associated with any twelfth-century relic translation.[6] They include a longer work of *ca.* 25,000 words, a brief narrative fragment, and a set of liturgical materials intended to celebrate the anniversary of the abbey's acquisition of the relic each 22 February (the Feast of St Peter's Chair). The rubrics and prologues in all of these works loudly announce the cross relic and its translation, classifying them as texts of a purely devotional nature and interest, and this is doubtless one of the reasons why, outside a small circle of Belgian scholars and erudits, they have been almost completely forgotten. To understand the Brogne Holy Cross tradition as exclusively or even principally devoted to the relic itself, however, is to commit a serious error. A sacred object may have been the ostensible focus of these works, but in fact the narrative *materia* that the monastic authors drew up from their well of collective memory was dedicated at least as much to the life and reputation of the local lord Manasses of Hierges. It was Manasses who was responsible for the cross's translation from Antioch and who had promised the relic to the monks on his deathbed in 1177.

In addition to being an impressive collection of writings consecrated to a relic, the Brogne narrative corpus represents one of the largest programmes of writing dedicated to a lay nobleman primarily in his capacity as a knight and nobleman. While there is nothing extraordinary about a religious community writing in praise of the lay aristocrats who were their founders and benefactors, the manifestation of this impulse at Brogne differs substantially from other prominent cases. The life of Gilbert, sheriff of Surrey (d. 1125), composed at the Augustinian priory he founded at Merton, for instance, offers a description of the sheriff's noble qualities in its account of his petitioning on the abbey's behalf at the court of the English King Henry I.[7]

---

6. For a catalogue of True Cross relic translations in this period, see Anatole Frolow, *Les reliquaires de la Vraie Croix*, Archives de l'Orient Chrétien 8 (Paris: Institut français d'études byzantines, 1965). For discussion of the translation of passion relics in the Central Middle Ages see Nicholas Vincent, *The Holy Blood. King Henry III and the Westminster Blood Relic* (Cambridge: Cambridge University Press, 2001), 31–81.

7. See Marvin L. Colker, "Latin Texts Concerning Gilbert, Founder of Merton Priory," *Studia Monastica* 12 (1970): 241–72. For the Merton texts as evidence of noble ideals, see David Crouch *The Birth of Nobility: Constructing Aristocracy in England and France* (New York: Routledge, 2005), 42–43.

In Germany, the monks of Pegau and Arnstein similarly composed short biographies of their respective founders, Margrave Wiprecht of Groitzsch (d. 1124) and Count Ludwig of Arnstein (d. 1185).[8] More akin to the Brogne texts in scope and in its focus on a sacred object, the *Chronicle* written after 1177 at the abbey of Waltham in Essex privileges the figures of King Harold Godwinson and the Anglo-Danish thegn Tovi, the community's chief benefactor and the discoverer of their major True Cross relic, respectively.[9] As we shall see, however, the Brogne tradition is distinct from works like these both in its stylistic conceits but perhaps most importantly in its general orientation not towards the origins and history of the religious institution but instead towards the life, death, and legacy of the knight.

The recovery and recognition of these works is important to the study of chivalry for several reasons. The Brogne texts represent a contribution to our understanding of life-writing that took a knight as its subject (so-called "chivalric biography"), a genre most often associated with the later Middle Ages but prefigured in the comparatively early *History of William Marshal (ca.* 1224–26).[10] Dating to the decades before the appearance of the *History*, the Brogne texts fall within the period between roughly 1180 and 1220 identified by some historians of chivalry as the critical time for the codification of aristocratic behaviour.[11] Most important, then, is what these works can tell us about the negotiation and articulation of chivalric ideals. Here, strategies are deployed for the construction of status and prowess that are distinct from other texts from the same period and which reveal how chivalric identity could occupy a central place in local discourses of privilege, sacrality, and power. Particularly striking among the Brogne strategies is the adoption of the eastern Mediterranean crusading frontier as a stage for the demonstration of Manasses's qualities. An intro-

8. *Noble Society: Five Lives from Twelfth-Century Germany*, trans. Jonathan R. Lyon (Manchester: Manchester University Press, 2017), 22–91 and 220–248.

9. *The Waltham Chronicle: An Account of the Discovery of our Holy Cross at Montacute and its Conveyance to Waltham*, ed. and trans. Leslie Watkiss and Marjorie Chibnall, Oxford Medieval Texts (Oxford: Clarendon Press, 1994).

10. Sumner Ferris, "Chronicle, Chivalric Biography, and Family Traditions in Fourteenth-Century England," in *Chivalric Literature: Essays on Relations between Literature and Life in the Later Middle Ages*, ed. Larry D. Benson and John Leyerle (Kalamazoo, MI: Medieval Institute Publications, 1980), 25–38.

11. See Crouch, *Birth of Nobility*, 80–86 and idem, "Chivalry and Courtliness: Colliding Constructs," *Soldiers, Nobles, and Gentlemen: Essays in Honour of Maurice Keen*, ed. Peter Coss and Christopher Tyerman (Woodbridge: Boydell & Brewer, 2009), 32–48, esp. 33–37.

duction to this important narrative tradition and an exploration of its contribution to the study of chivalry cannot proceed until we have established the context for its creation: the life of Manasses of Hierges.

Who Was Manasses of Hierges?

The broad outlines of the life and crusading career of Manasses of Hierges have been previously established in two biographical essays, the first published by Charles Gustave Roland in 1907, and the second by Hans Eberhard Mayer in 1988. Both historians worked primarily from the appearances of Manasses in documentary evidence and in the chronicle of the Frankish East written in around 1184 by the chancellor of the Latin Kingdom of Jerusalem, Archbishop William of Tyre.[12] Thanks to these efforts, it can be established that Manasses was born in the year 1112, the son of a man named Heribrand, a castle functionary at Bouillon, and a noble lady, Hodierna, daughter of Count Hugh of Rethel. As Georges Despy has shown, the family's status seems to have risen in the first decades of the twelfth century, when they appear for the first time as lords of the modest fortified settlement of Hierges.

At the same time, Manasses's family found themselves connected in two ways to the ruling house of the crusader kingdom of Jerusalem, ruled first by his father's lord Godfrey of Bouillon and later by his uncle Baldwin of Le Bourcq, who ruled as King Baldwin II from 1118–31.[13] The last year of his uncle's reign in Jerusalem was also the year that Manasses seems to have succeeded in the lordship of Hierges, witnessing a charter in the company of the count of Namur as *Manasses adolescens*.[14] Nine years later he decided to travel East to the crusading

12. Charles-Gustave Roland, "Un croisé ardennais: Manassès de Hierges," *Revue historique ardennaise* 14 (1907): 197–212; Hans Eberhard Mayer, "Manasses of Hierges in East and West," *Revue Belge de philologie et d'histoire* 66 (1988): 757–66; Georges Despy, "La formation de la 'Terre de Hierges' du XIᵉ au XVᵉ siècle," in *La seigneurie rurale en Lotharingie. Actes des 3ᵉ journées lotharingiennes, 26–27 octobre 1984*, Publications de la Section historique de l'Institut grand-ducal de Luxembourg 102 (Luxembourg: Linden, 1986), 11–30.

13. For the best prosopographical study of the early rulers of Jerusalem see Alan V. Murray, *The Crusader Kingdom of Jerusalem: a Dynastic History 1099–1125*, Prosopographica et Genealogia 4 (Oxford: Unit for Prosopographical Research, Linacre College, 2000), esp. 124.

14. Namur, Archives de l'État, Archives ecclésiastiques 2585. The most recent edition is that of Leopold Genicot, *L'économie rurale namuroise au Bas Moyen Âge, III: Les hommes—le commun*, Recueil de Travaux d'Histoire et de Philologie, 6e série 25 (Lou-

frontier.[15] A garrulous charter of the bishop of Liège finds Manasses, *vir nobilis*, agreeing on 25 February 1140 to place two allodial properties into the hands of the monks of Brogne in return for 80 marks of silver.[16] For Despy, this represented a crucial moment in the development of the lordship of Hierges itself, both in terms of the patterns of landholding reflected but also in the way the document seems to construct Manasses as a member of the landholding aristocracy. Michel Lauwers points to the adoption of the title *nobilis* and to an additional gift which supported perpetual prayer for Manasses's parents as further evidence that by 1140 Manasses was aspiring to a higher social status.[17]

On 10 March the transaction was completed as Manasses placed branches and earth from each property upon the high altar of Brogne.[18] He was, on that occasion, "Manasses, preparing to go to Jerusalem for the love of God and for the remission of his sins."[19] If he departed as a pious penitent, career and family seem to have come quickly to the forefront in the Crusader States where, shortly after the death of King Fulk of Jerusalem in 1143, Manasses was elevated by his cousin Melisende, Fulk's widow, to the position of constable of Jerusalem. It was in this capacity that he appears in six charters of Melisende and her son Baldwin III.[20] By 1151, he was well enough established to

vain-la-Neuve: Bureau du Recueil, 1982), 370–73. See also *Diplomata Belgica. The Diplomatic Sources from the Medieval Southern Low Countries*, ed. Thérèse de Hemptinne, Jeroen Deploige, Jean-Louis Kupper, and Walter Prevenier (Brussels: Royal Historical Commission, since 2015), accessed 1 March 2018, http://www.diplomata-belgica.be, DiBe ID 5577. Jean-Louis Kupper noted inconsistencies in the seal of the bishop Alexander I of Liège affixed to this charter, but the authenticity of the charter's text has not been directly challenged: Jean-Louis Kupper, "La charte du comte Henri de Namur pour l'église de Brogne (1154): Étude critique," *Revue Benedictine* 95 (1985): 293–310.

15. No source provides a satisfactory explanation for the timing of this journey, but since there is no evidence that Manasses had any siblings, it may have taken him some time to devise a plan to secure his lordship in his absence.

16. *Cartulaire de l'église Saint-Lambert de Liège*, ed. Stanislas Bormans, Émile School-meesters, and Édouard Poncelet, 6 vols., Publications de la Commission royale d'Histoire—Chroniques belges inédites 25 (Brussels: Hayez, 1893–1933), 1: 63–66, no. 39; *Diplomata Belgica*, DiBe ID 1145.

17. Michel Lauwers, *La mémoire des ancêtres, le souci des morts. Morts, rites, et société au Moyen Âge* (Paris: Beauchesne, 1997), 295.

18. *Cartulaire de l'église Saint-Lambert*, 1: 64–65; *Diplomata Belgica*, DiBe ID 7539.

19. "Manasses ob amorem dei et remissionem peccatorum suorum dissoluisset ire Iherusalem." Ibid., 1: 63.

20. *Die Urkunden der Lateinischen Könige von Jerusalem*, ed. Hans Eberhard Mayer, 4 vols, Monumenta Germaniae Historica (Hanover: Hahn, 2010), 1: 355–57 at 357 (no. 177), 358–60 at 359 (no. 178), 360–62 at 362 (no. 179), 399–401 at 401 (no. 215), 402–4 at 403 (no. 2016), 550–53 at 552 (no. 316).

marry Helvisa, the widowed heiress of the lordship of Ramla. Ramla was an exceptionally important lordship: later in the twelfth century it would serve as the rock on which the great house of Ibelin was built and, had matters gone differently, it might have been the Hierges, and not the Ibelins, who guided the kingdom's fortunes through the thirteenth century.

According to the Latin Kingdom's chronicler William of Tyre, Manasses's marriage to Helvisa was his undoing. Hated in some quarters for his haughtiness and the arrogance with which he wore the queen's favour, Manasses was heavily implicated in the fighting that broke out between Melisende and her barons in 1151–52.[21] The queen's faction was the losing side, and so Manasses was exiled not just from the kingdom, but as Mayer points out from *la terre d'Outremer* altogether. He returned home and appears in charters again in 1158 and 1170 as "Manasses of Hierges"—meaning that he had regained his lordship from the monks at Brogne. He was remarried (Mayer kindly assumes after the death of Helvisa of Ramla) to Alice, daughter of the count of Chiny. At some point near his death in 1176–77, he became a monk of Saint Gerard of Brogne.

The Brogne Tradition

The above account of Manasses's life, as reconstructed by Roland and Mayer, is hardly a flattering one. This is largely due to the doubt cast over his motives by William of Tyre, who rehearses a vengeful, almost certainly pro-Ibelin version of his fall from grace in the East. Both Roland and Mayer knew, however, that there was another tradition, emanating from Brogne, which was concerned with Manasses's role in the translation of a fragment of the True Cross from the Levant to the abbey.[22] A series of annals probably once kept in the abbey's Easter tables but now surviving only in a fifteenth-century copy give the basic story in outline:

> Died [in this year] the noble man Manasses of Hierges, who carried the Holy Cross from the city of Antioch into these parts and promised it as a gift to the church of Brogne. After his

21. William of Tyre, *Chronicon*, ed. Robert B.C. Huygens, 2 vols., Corpus Christianorum. Continuatio Mediaevalis 63–63A (Turnhout: Brepols, 1986), 1: 777–80.

22. Roland, "Un croisé ardennais," 206–10; Mayer, "Manasses of Hierges," 765–66.

death his son Heribrand refused to give it and he died forty days after his father. In the same year the cross was brought to Brogne back by his brother Henry, accompanied by many miracles and portents.[23]

Evidence of the relic's importance to the community can be found across the abbey's surviving manuscripts. An obituary notice written in the margins of the abbey's later thirteenth-century Martyrology for 8 January makes reference to Manasses, *conversus et monachus,* who gave to this church the Holy Cross."[24] His wife Alice is similarly recalled (at 9 August) as "Alice, lady of Hierges, wife of lord Manasses who gave to us the Holy Cross."[25] These entries are absolutely unique in the Martyrology: no other sacred relic or gift other than in land or coin is mentioned. Gifts are in fact very rarely mentioned, and although emperors, counts, and dukes pop up here and there, the only name to be accorded more prestige than Manasses's is that of Count Philip of Namur, who gave Brogne the church at Flavion in 1212.[26] Similarly, although this would be understood in many cases where gifts had been made *pro anima*, no other gift is explicitly said to extend benevolence to both husband and wife in the same way as the Holy Cross. Other individuals with relationships to Manasses are also listed in the obituaries, including his son Heribrand, whose death is listed as occurring on 16 February (40 days after his father's) and whose memory is said to have been rehabilitated by a gift from his wife of 10 *sous* in support of a *refectio* for the monks.[27]

23. Namur, Archives de l'État, Archives écclésiastiques MS 2586, fol. 7r = "Notae Bronienses," ed. Georg Waitz, Monumenta Germaniae Historica, Scriptores (in Folio) 24 (Hanover: Hahn, 1879), 27. For the *notae* as annals see Xavier Hermand, "La bibliothéque médiévale de l'abbaye de Brogne," *Annales de la Société archéologique de Namur* 85 (2011): 115–169, at 130. The *notae* can be profitably compared with the Easter table annals kept in the Bible of the nearby abbey of Floreffe (London, British Library, MS Add. 17737, fol. 18r). The date given in the *notae* for Manasses's death is 1175, but nearly all other texts agree that it occurred later in 1176 or 1177.
24. "Manasses de Hirgia conversus et monachus huius loci qui donauit huic ecclesie sanctam crucem; cuius anniversarium tenemur facere." Namur, Bibliothèque du Séminaire, MS 48, fol. 3r = Joseph Barbier, "Obituaire de Brogne ou de Saint-Gérard, de l'ordre de Saint-Benoît," *Analectes pour servir à l'histoire ecclésiastique de la Belgique* 18 (1882): 289–336, at 293–94.
25. "Obiit Alaidis domina Hierge uxor domini Manassis qui nobis contulit sanctam crucem." Namur, Bibliothèque du Séminaire, MS 48, fol. 88r = Barbier, "Obituaire de Brogne," 334.
26. Barbier, "Obituaire de Brogne," 346 and n. 2.
27. Namur, Bibliothèque du Séminaire, MS 48, fol. 14r.

A series of confraternity agreements from the period of Brogne's abbot Robert (r. 1192–1221) confirms that by this time the relic's presence led to a fundamental re-evaluation of the community's identity. In the agreements, the monks claim anachronistically that, in addition to St Peter, their abbey had been *founded* in honour of "the most victorious" (*victoriosissime*) cross.[28] In the same period an abbot of Brogne described his house, in an agreement for mutual prayer (*societas*) between Brogne and the canonesses of La Thure, as "the church of Brogne, filled up with the life-giving wood."[29]

What was important to the monks about the relic was not simply that it acted as a sacred reminder of the Passion itself, nor the miracles that it could work, but its association with Manasses, an individual whom the monks of Brogne deliberately figured as an ideal chivalric hero. At least two narratives were composed at Brogne which purportedly set out to tell the story of the Cross's translation but in fact focused on the deeds and character of the man who acquired it. The first of these can be found in a twelfth-century manuscript (Namur, Bibliothèque du Séminaire, MS 80) containing a collection of works on the common theme of wonders and miracles.[30] A text beginning on fol. 34v is entitled *Prologus in miraculis sancti crucis*, but this prologue is then followed on fol. 35r by a text rubricated *Qualiter lignum domini delatum ab Antiochia locatum fuerit per Manasse de Hirge in Broniensi ecclesia* (hereafter, I will refer to this text as *Qualiter*). What follows is only a fragment of the original *Qualiter* text: four quires were hereafter cut out of the manuscript and only the first folio of *Qualiter* was restored at a much later date. *Qualiter* begins in 1141 with the arrival in the region of repeated messages from the queen of Jerusalem, inviting her cousin Manasses to come to the East. The text moves immediately to the East, and by the end of fol. 34v Manasses is still fighting in the principality of Antioch. We have as yet no reference to the cross or the abbey, so the entirety of this part of the *Qualiter* text is about Manasses and his virtues.

28. Ibid., fol. 142v.
29. Ibid.: "ecclesiam Broniense salutari lignum refertam."
30. The manuscript is described, although its context is poorly characterised, as a compilation of miracles of the Virgin in *Catalogue des manuscrits conservés à Namur*, ed. Paul Faider, Catalogue général des manuscrits des bibliothèques de Belgique 1 (Gembloux: J. Duculot, 1934), 512–13. Xavier Hermand, "La bibliothèque médiévale," 131–32 n. 42, cites Carine Billiard, "Présentation et description du manuscrit 80 [Grand Séminaire, Salzinnes Namur]" (Mémoire de licence, Université Catholique de Louvain-la-Neuve, 1984). I thank Xavier Hermand for his appraisal and summary of Billiard's work, which I have not personally consulted.

The loss of an unknown amount of further writing in the *Qualiter* manuscript leaves a major lacuna, but we are fortunate that in 1211 a writer at Brogne created a new version of this text; not copying it, but completely rewriting it and massively amplifying it to a work of roughly 30,000 words entitled *Quomodo sancta crucis ab Antiochia allata sit in Broniense coenobium* (to be known hereafter as *Quomodo*).[31] The precise impetus for this rewriting is not known. It may have been linked to the abbey's need to compete with other religious communities in the region who had recently been showered with major Passion relics thanks to the conquest of Constantinople by the Fourth Crusade.[32] The conquering crusaders were led by the count of Flanders, whose dynasty had conclusively supplanted the old comital house of Namur in 1195: the monks had many reasons to draw the attention of their new masters.

In 1211 the task of rewriting was assigned to an author of considerable knowledge and talent as a storyteller. His voice interrupts the narrative on a handful of occasions, announcing the year that he is writing,[33] that he has only recently become a monk,[34] having fled the

31. The earliest surviving copy of *Quomodo* was made in 1590 (Namur, Bibliothèque du Séminaire, MS 57, fols. 122r–174v). A colophon informs us that the MS was copied by Lambert Derhet de Flavion at Easter that year. For the MS see Faider, *Catalogue*, 497–99. Extracts from the first two books were transcribed in Antoine-François Le Paige, *Histoire de l'Ordre héréditaire du Cigne dit l'Ordre Souverain du Clèves ou du Cordon d'Or* (Basel: Hoffman, 1780) and a smaller section reprinted in Frédérick-Auguste de Reiffenberg, *Le chevalier au cygne et Godefroid de Bouillon*, 4 vols. (Brussels: Hayez, 1846–59), 1: 147–49. Extracts from the third book were edited in François Baix, "Les miracles de la sainte croix à Brogne," *Annales de la Société archéologique de Namur* 45 (1950): 253–61. Books 1–3 (without the prologue) were transcribed in Xavier Sottiaux, "Manassès de Hierges et la sainte Croix de Brogne. Étude critique d'un manuscrit du XIIIe siècle" (Mémoire de maîtrise, Université Libre de Bruxelles, 2010). Due to restrictions on access to *mémoires de maîtrise*, I have been able only to consult Sottiaux's introduction and transcription. All transcriptions and translations from the text below are my own unless otherwise indicated.

32. Before 1204, Brogne was one of only two communities in the region with a passion relic (the other was Florennes). After 1204 it was one of the only houses not to receive the treasures of Constantinople. For the Florennes relic, see Ursmer Belière, "Frédéric de Laroche, évêque d'Acre et archevêque de Tyr. Envoi de reliques à l'abbaye de Florennes (1153–1161)," *Annales de l'Institut archéologique de Luxembourg* 43 (1908): 67–79.

33. Namur, Bibliothèque du Séminaire, MS 57, fol. 170v: "*Venite et videte opera Domini, qua posuit prodigia super terram* [Ps. 45:9] et ut credatis procedentium operationi quae vera est et cuius multis testes usque in hunc annum gratiae millesimum ducentissimum undecimum supersunt: qui viderunt ea qua facta sunt." ("*Come and see the works of the Lord, what wonders He has placed upon the earth* and you should trust in the foregoing work which is true and for which there are many witnesses still alive up until this year of Grace 1211: they saw what happened.")

34. Ibid., fol. 142v: "Ergo quidem quare nuper monachus effectus sum, et disciplinabiliter ordini et religioni servire teneor…" ("I have only recently become a monk, and I am obligated to rigorously serve the order and religion…")

world,[35] and that he has consulted eyewitnesses to confirm the veracity of events in his story.[36] This "new" monk had read widely; he moves easily between Scriptural exegesis and quoting authorities such as Ovid, Augustine, and Juvenal's *Satires,* the *chansons de geste* tradition and the crusade chronicle of Robert the Monk. His high style combined with his obvious familiarity with the world beyond the cloister suggest a refugee from the schools, an idea that is perhaps supported by Brogne's proximity to the sophisticated schools of Liège.

Virtutes Militiae

I have already stated that the central concern of the surviving fragment of the *Qualiter* is Manasses and his deeds. The same concern was adopted by the *Quomodo* author, a master storyteller, who constructed in the first and second books of his work nothing less than a complete biography of Manassses, from his youth and his decision to take the cross and travel to Jerusalem (I.4–5) through the exceptionally long and detailed account of his time in the Crusader States (I.7–16), his return journey to the West (I.18–26), his adventures upon his return to Namur (II.1–6) his illness, death, and burial (II.7–10). But it would seem to have been the objective of both authors to shape Manasses, who had started out from relatively modest origins, into a true nobleman and even a model of nobility. The monks effected this transformation through a combination of approaches, some of which are familiar but which nonetheless manifest themselves in ways that are unique to this tradition.

Both texts begin by establishing Manasses's inborn but still inchoate nobility through reference to his status as a lord, his lineage, and his virtues. The brief and fragmentary *Qualiter* narrative first offers a sequence of intitulature divided by elevated *punctus*: Manasses * *adolescens nobilis * miles insignis * princeps castelli Hirgiensis.* The text then sets out his relationship with the royal house of Jerusalem. The writer of *Quomodo* expands the treatment of lineage and identity very dramatically, devoting an entire chapter of the first book (I.4) to introducing "Manasses the Noble Youth." As florid as the prose is here, we

35. Ibid., fol. 122v: "Quia nuper cum Israel exivi de Egypto, de seculo nequam et *in baculo meo transivi Iordanem istum* [Gen. 32:10]." ("Because recently like Israel I came out of Egypt, out of the worthless world, and *with only my staff I crossed this Jordan*.")
36. Ibid., fols. 122v–123r.

must admire the writer's efficiency in managing to treat divine grace, descent of virtues through blood, and two different mythic lineages (one Arthurian and the other the Swan Knight) into only just the first few lines.

> In the latter days of the aging world, the flawless flower of Mary who brings forth the flower of virtue that never wilts plucked from the end of the world Manasses. Of free and respectable origin, he was born into the lineage of King Mark. He was not inferior to his ancestors in strength nor in virtues, but only in the wealth of his possessions. He had the noble and golden spark of a long line of ancestors and lived as the direct descendant of one who had been drawn by a swan, attached to a small boat, as he voyaged on the Rhine River to the port of Mainz. His eloquence, valour in arms, and prowess had helped reunite the noble matron of the people of Lorraine with her only daughter.[37]

Here we are in the presence of discourse explicitly focused on nobility. Themes emerge that are familiar from the world of chivalric romance: while not quite Perceval or the Bel Inconnu, the *Quomodo* notes the disjuncture between the nobility of his lineage (which is somewhat obscured by the far-off Jerusalem dynasty and equally distant mythical ancestors) and the modesty of his holdings, reinforced later in the same chapter with a reference to his lordship as Hierges as composed of *villas et redditus satis tenues*.

Although it was not as common as claims to Carolingian origins, the invocation of mythic ancestry was not uncommon among writers praising aristocratic families in the later twelfth and early thirteenth centuries.[38] While the *Quomodo*'s mention of King Mark is unique and intriguing, the association with the Swan Knight can be found in

---

37. Ibid., fol. 129r: "In fine mundi senescentis inmarcessibilem virtutis florem germinans flos Mariae indeficiens a finibus mundi Manassen elegit. Qui natalibus ingenuis et spectabilibus oriundus de stirpe Marci regis [n]atus animis et virtutibus etsi rerum copia non degenerabat. In ipso nobilis et rutilans atavorum felix antiquitas subradians inconuulsis radicibus vivebat precipue illius preclarissimi cui cignus in Reno nauclerus. extitit applicans ad portum Maguntie, cuius eloquentia, armis et industria nobilis Lotharingiorum matrona cum unica filia sua restituta est." My thanks to Wolfgang Müller for his assistance with the transcription and translation of this passage.

38. For the phenomenon of dynastic origin stories among the nobility see Nicholas Paul, "*Origo consulum:* Rumours of Murder, a Crisis of Lordship, and the Legendary Origins of the Counts of Anjou," *French History* 29 (2015): 139–60,

a wide range of texts from the same period as the *Quomodo*, including the chronicle of William of Tyre, the letters of Guy of Bazoches, the dynastic history of Lambert of Ardres and the *Red Book of the Exchequer*.[39] What sets the *Quomodo* apart is the author's decision not just to mention the Swan Knight but to rehearse the basic narrative of the first part of his legend as it is known from the *Chevalier au Cygne*, which survives as part of the Old French Crusade Cycle.[40] The part of the *Chevalier au Cygne* which is emphasised is the story of the arrival of the Swan Knight (later revealed to be named Helyas) and his duel with a Saxon giant in order to rescue a Lotharingian princess. Read together with what the author otherwise suggests about Manasses in the chapter—that he is the literal embodiment of the virtues of his mythical ancestors—this is a clever narrative device. Later in the *Quomodo*, when we read that Manasses fights to defend the honour of Melisende of Jerusalem and Constance of Antioch, he can be seen to be performing essentially the same chivalric defence of an endangered noblewoman. Like Helyas, moreover, Manasses arrived from over the water.

A main concern of both the Brogne narratives is to show how Manasses embodied the ideals of knighthood. Even the brief *Qualiter* fragment makes a powerful gesture in this direction:

> And because we have intended to serve brevity by all means [and also] to restrict within the narrow confines of the refuge of this book into how much fame the aforesaid man was propelled through constant effort, by facing dangers most frequently, and by protecting the fatherland through knightly virtues (*virtute militari*) far and wide.[41]

39. The literature on the Swan Knight is very extensive, but for the appearances cited here see now Simon John, "Godfrey of Bouillon and the Swan Knight," in *Crusading and Warfare in the Middle Ages: Studies in Honour of John France*, ed. Simon John and Nicholas Morton (Abingdon, Oxon.: Ashgate, 2014), 129–42.

40. *"Le Chevalier au Cygne" and "La Fin d'Elias"*, ed. Jan Nelson, Old French Crusade Cycle 2 (Tuscaloosa, AL: University of Alabama Press, 1985). The *Quomodo* version of the story is also much more extensive than the one found in a thirteenth-century genealogy of the counts of Boulogne, cf. de Reiffenberg, *Le chevalier au cygne*, 1: viii.

41. Namur, Bibliothèque du Séminaire, MS 80, fol. 35v: "et quoniam brevitati modis omnibus servire intendimus, opusculi presentis angustia coartare refugo in quantam claritudinem strenue agendo. Sepissime periculis obviam eundo, virtute militari longe lateque patriam protegendo vir praedictus provectus sit." My thanks to Wolfgang Müller for his assistance with the transcription and translation of this passage.

The *Quomodo* narrative is interested not only in establishing how Manasses embodies his ancestral virtues, but in enumerating and discussing them. The narrative's forward momentum periodically stops so that the author can pause and consider Manasses's qualities. In 1141, the year he took the cross, for example, Manasses is described as "youthful in his years, ardent of spirit, reliable with weapons, wary in his counsel, generous in his support, eloquent in his speech, skilful in his answers, moderate in his speech: by his actions beyond reproof in all that becomes a young man."[42]

Staging Knighthood

References to the potentially virtuous knightly life in *Qualiter* and *Quomodo* may suggest that the monks of Brogne saw a didactic value in the example of Manasses of Hierges with regard to the behaviour of local knights and noblemen. The basic narrative frame that they provided of the knight's lineage, the establishment of his status and reputation through deeds, his marriage and begetting of children, and his ultimate deathbed reconciliation with his God is familiar. We find it in vernacular texts, such as the *chansons* of the cycle of William of Orange, and in the stories other monasteries told about their founders and benefactors.[43] In its broad outlines it is also not unlike the canonical chivalric biography of this period, *The History of William Marshal.* Where the Brogne narratives about Manasses differ, however, is in their emphasis on the knight's participation in a crusade, and especially in his performances of ideal aristocratic behaviour in the Eastern Mediterranean crusading theatre.[44]

---

42. Namur, Bibliothèque du Séminaire, MS 57, fols. 129v–130r: "dictus Manasses annis tener, animis acer, armis industrius, consilio circumspectus, suffragio munificus, eloquio disertus, responsione peritus, sermone temperatus opere quantum condecet tyronem irreprehensibilis."

43. For conversion to religious life in old age see Jonathan Lyon, "The Withdrawal of Aged Noblemen into Monastic Communities: Interpreting the Sources from Twelfth-Century Germany," in *Old Age in the Middle Ages and the Renaissance*, ed. Albrecht Classen (Berlin and New York: De Gruyter, 2007), 143–69.

44. For the problem of the missing crusading episode in the *History of William Marshal* see David Crouch, *William Marshal: Knighthood, War and Chivalry, 1147–1219*, 3rd edition (Oxford: Routledge, 2017), 67–68; Nicholas Paul, "In Search of the Marshal's Lost Crusade: The Persistence of Memory, the Problems of History, and the Painful Birth of Crusading Romance," *Journal of Medieval History* 40 (2014): 292–310; Thomas Abridge,

Crusading appears in the *Quomodo* as a much more prominent theme than in other contemporary accounts of the lives of knights. Few texts from the Middle Ages offer insight into the reasoning behind a knight's decision to take the cross as a crusader or to stay at home. Exceptions to this from the late thirteenth century include the trouvère Rutebeuf in his *Débat du croisé et du décroisé*, and John of Joinville who, in his *Vie de Saint Louis*, explained his reasons for refusing to join Louis IX's second crusade after having participated in the king's first campaign.[45] By contrast, in the *Quomodo* one chapter is dedicated to tracing Manasses's dual motivations, which are said to be *imitatio Christi* on the one hand and support for his kin in Jerusalem on the other.[46] *Quomodo* considers how, in taking the cross, he was transformed in terms that could have come directly from the mouth of Bernard of Clairvaux. He was "cleansed, consecrated more to divine than secular knighthood … entirely lifted up by his piety and by his waging of double warfare [that is spiritual and secular]."[47]

A central part of crusading was the unique opportunity it provided to demonstrate prowess against a dangerous other whose death meant no dishonour to the Christian knight. The *Qualiter* narrative imagines an epic scenario, emphasising the enemy's overwhelming strength and the knight's enjoyment of holy triumph: "Incredible to relate how with only a small force and the support of divine assistance he vanquished so many companies of the enemy. With such efficacy of virtue he turned back the tide of the army of the Turks from the region of

---

The Greatest Knight: The Remarkable Life of William Marshal, the Power Behind Five English Thrones (New York: Simon & Schuster, 2015), 160–68.

45. While remaining reticent about his own motivations for taking the cross in 1248, John of Joinville offers some explanation of his decision not to join the 1270 campaign against Tunis. See Joinville, *Vie de Saint Louis*, ed. Jacques Monfrin (Paris: Dunod, 1995), paragraphs 106–22 and 730–37; translated in *Chronicles of the Crusades*, trans. Caroline Smith (London and New York: Penguin Classics, 2008), 173–76, 328–29. For Rutebeuf's song, see Rutebeuf, "Débat du croisé et du décroisé," in *Œuvres complètes*, ed. Michel Zink (Paris: Bordas, 1989–90), 355–73. Commentary on both texts and what they reveal about crusader motivation is offered by Caroline Smith, *Crusading in the Age of Joinville* (Aldershot and Burlington: Ashgate, 2006), 170–79.

46. Namur, Bibliothèque du Séminaire, MS 57, fols. 129v–130r: "De quare ivit Hierosolimam. cap. 5"

47. Ibid., fols. 130r–v "ita quod putabatur plus divinae quam terrenae militiae consecratus … qui totius pietate ferebatur et duplici militia comitante cum eo semper angelo Domini." The motivations attributed to Manasses resonate with the core elements of twelfth-century "crusading spirituality" identified in William Purkis, *Crusading Spirituality in the Holy Land and Iberia, c. 1095–c. 1187* (Woodbridge: Boydell & Brewer, 2008), 30–119.

Antioch."[48] "Frequently," *Qualiter* continues, "with swords bared he displayed the banner before the Damascenes and Egyptians and carried it back, happily stained with the enemy's blood."[49]

In both the *Qualiter* and *Quomodo*, however, crusading means much more than just military confrontation or even penitential activity. Rather, both works emphasise the opportunities provided by the crusading frontier for the performance of noble virtue. The *terre d'Outremer* provides Manasses with crucial opportunities to demonstrate not just prowess but also courtesy before an audience of the military orders and a royal court. The *Qualiter* explains that Manasses's deeds in the east were witnessed by observers of high rank from both the East and (because of the coming of the Second Crusade) the West. What had they seen? The text explains that they were "frequently received at his banquets, pleased by his witticisms, served by his magnanimity, enriched by his manifold gifts."[50] Vanquishing companies of the enemy and driving back the tide of the army of the Turks was part of the story, but it was not the only or even the most noteworthy aspect of his conduct in the East.

Quomodo of course goes much further, this time explicitly framing Manasses's time in the East in theatrical terms. This learned author alludes to performance in the very first chapter, quoting from Juvenal's seventh satire: "*Quod non dant proceres dabit histrio.*"[51] He meant, in effect, that a new young actor like Manasses must now be relied upon to do what the old wealthy aristocrats will not. To the *Quomodo* author, the kingdom of Jerusalem provided a unique setting for what the "actor" must do. Because "truly that city is situated upon a mountain," it was impossible for Manasses to hide his virtues once there, and so word quickly spread of the "flower of knighthood, the

48. Namur, Bibliothèque du Séminaire, MS 80, fol. 35v: "incredibile memoratu est divino fretus praesidio quantas hostium catervas parva manu fuderit. Quanta virtutis efficati[a] Turcorum exercitus Antiochenis partibus influentium reflexerit."

49. Namur, Bibliothèque du Séminaire, MS 57, fol. 131v: "Frequenter Babiloniis et Damascenis vexilla deplicans gladios nudabat, et iocundam ex inimici sanguine maculam reportabat."

50. Namur, Bibliothèque du Séminaire, MS 80, fol. 35v: "principibus regni popularibus universis quam carus in breui vel celebris extiterit. Nobis autem hec omnia tacentibus inperator Romanorum F[ridericus] Francorum rex l[udovicus] innumera multitudo ducum vel consulum nobilium quoque infinitus exercitus scire volentibus fidei praebent argumentum, qui conviviis eius frequenter asciti, facetiis iocundati, liberalitate usi, dat[is] amplissimis locupletati sunt."

51. Namur, Bibliothèque du Séminaire, MS 57, fol. 126r.

shield of David, the spear of Jonathan, the second Judas Maccabeus, the new Gideon."[52]

The East is then the greatest stage, and the drama that unfolds makes the most of set-piece dramatic scenes full of dialogue. Manasses's arrival, for instance, is described in highly emotive detail, including his tears at the Holy Sepulchre, the public rejoicing of the *vox populi* and even the conversation, reported as direct discourse, between him and the queen: "O long hoped for one! You must be tired from such a journey," she says, "tired by such a distance and such tempestuous seas."[53] This is not the only warm reception he receives. Having fought to secure the kingdom's borders, he is received by another grateful princess at Antioch with excessive feasting and drinking.[54] The following chapters describe the evil envy stirred up against Manasses in the heart of the queen's son, the young king of Jerusalem, and the ensuing civil war, ending with Manasses's defence of the tower of David. The final set-piece of the struggle sees the Templars and the Hospitallers plead with the young king to reconsider, again in an extended directly reported speech extolling the virtues of Manasses.[55]

The Matter of Nobility

Whether it was the *Qualiter*, written soon after Manasses's death, or the *Quomodo*, composed thirty years later, the Brogne texts were written in a context occupied by more than just people and their stories. At the abbey of Brogne, the powerful object with which Manasses had returned from the East occupied the attention of the monks and their wider community. Neither writer leaves us in doubt as to his conviction that the object was understood to be the wood of the cross on which Christ was crucified. Both engage with generic discourses about sacred matter in general and the wood of the cross in particular. In the prologue to both texts and in the third book of *Quomodo* these discourses take centre stage. But in much of the rest of the writing the

52. Ibid., fol. 130v: "Verum quia supra montem civitas collocata latere non potuit, apparens in montibus Israel, mons ille novus virtutum, flos militaris, clipeus David, sagitta Jonathae, secundus Machabaeus, novus Gedeon."
53. Ibid., fols. 130v–131r: "O diu desiderate per tot itinerum fatigationes, et discrimina, per procellosa Maria…"
54. Ibid., fols. 131v–132r.
55. Ibid., fol. 135v.

object can be seen to operate as a different type of material, commemorating acts and embodying virtues other than, or in addition to, those associated with the Passion.

First and foremost it is essential to understand that the relic in question was not seen as just any fragment of the True Cross, but as *the* "Holy Cross of Antioch." Late in the second book of *Quomodo*, Bishop Henry of Liège is heard to say to Manasses "Great is the thing that you have obtained, this Holy Cross that, as I have been well informed, Raymond of Antioch prince and martyr had always carried before him."[56] The claim would appear to be that the cross at Brogne is identical to the cross that was carried by the Antiochene army at the Battle of the Field of Blood in 1119 and that this relic had continued to act as the battle standard of the principality of Antioch through the time of Count Raymond of Poitiers, who ruled Antioch from 1136 until his death in 1149.[57] The cross itself, which is preserved to this day in the cathedral treasury of Namur embedded in a sixteenth-century silver altar reliquary, does indeed appear to have some type of fastening allowing it to be mounted as a processional cross (Fig. 8.1). According to *Quomodo*, the cross came to Manasses via the princess of Antioch, Raymond's widow Constance, whom Manasses is said to have defended during his sojourn in the East.[58]

Prior to the third book's collection of quite generic miracles, the cross is not a particularly miraculous object. Rather it is Manasses who uses the cross to symbolise and harness the elevated status he had gained in the East and to bring it home. So we hear of Manasses "protected by the Holy Cross" defeating his rival Gilles of Chimay in battle. As in the East, he fights like Judas Maccabeus. "Where is your courage (*virtus*)?" he shouts, trying to rouse his men to action. "Why

56. Ibid., fol. 143r: "Magnum est quod obtinuisti: hanc vero sanctam crucem, sic mihi bene relatum est, Raymundus Antiochiae princeps et martyr in bellis preambulam semper habebat."

57. Thomas Asbridge, *The Creation of the Principality of Antioch, 1098–1130* (Woodbridge: Boydell, 2000), 212. For a brief description of the reliquary see *Trésors classés de la Cathédrale de Namur* (Brussels: Fondation Roi Baudouin, 2013), 21. It is worth noting that a cross brought to Bromholm in England in the wake of the Fourth Crusade seems to have had a similar fixture, and that the monks of Bromholm similarly described it as a military cross. For the Bromholm cross see Francis Wormald, "The Rood of Bromholm," *Journal of the Warburg Institute* 1 (1937): 31–45, at 32.

58. For Constance see Alan Murray, "Constance, Princess of Antioch (1130–1164): Ancestry, Marriages, and Family," in *Proceedings of the Battle Conference 2015*, ed. Elisabeth M.C. van Houts, Anglo-Norman Studies 38 (Woodbridge: Boydell & Brewer, 2016), 81–96.

Fig. 8.1—Sixteenth-century silver "Cross of Brogne" reliquary of Abbot Guillaume de Beez of Brogne (d. 1507). Reverse, showing the earlier (twelfth-century?) Holy Cross of Antioch embedded within. Namur, Musée Diocésain et Trésor de la Cathédrale Saint Aubain. © KIK-IRPA, Brussels.

do you fear your fellow Christians, you who shattered the Saracens?"[59] The cross is also his banner as he restores justice to the lawless territories around the castle of Bouillon.[60]

In the same way as many other relics obtained in the context of the crusades in the twelfth and thirteenth centuries, the Holy Cross of Antioch played a central role in shaping and transmitting memories associated with a crusader.[61] Once again, the Brogne tradition, and in particular the *Quomodo* narrative, allow us a unique vantage point. According to *Quomodo* the cross was a physical reminder of the prowess and nobility that Mansasses and other, earlier Christian knights such as the prince of Antioch had demonstrated in the East. The cross enabled Manasses to maintain the standing of a holy warrior even after his return home, and the *Quomodo* text implies that he was able to truly elevate his status: now he does not differ from counts in appearance."[62] This elevated status translated into an advantageous marriage to Alice, daughter of count Albert of Chiny.

The monks of Brogne clearly thought it legitimate that Manasses had kept the cross, often secretly, as his own private possession in his castle of Hierges. According to their version of events, after Manasses had promised them the relic, his sons unjustly attempted to retain control over it and refused to yield it to the community. Perhaps ironically, the entire Brogne tradition makes their case easy to understand: the object, as a symbol of the family's rise in status during Manasses's lifetime, would have been of the greatest importance to his sons Henry and Heribrand. Following Georges Despy's analysis, Manasses's agreements with Brogne at the time of his departure for the East (and evidently his unknown dealings with them when he returned) were fundamental to the establishment of the lordship of Hierges itself. If, as the text argues vociferously, the cross was linked inextricably to

59. Namur, Bibliothèque du Séminaire, MS 57, fol. 144v: "Ubi virtus tuas? Ubi animus? ... quid times conchristianos qui concussisti Sarazinos?"
60. Namur, Bibliothèque du Séminaire, MS 57, fol. 145r.
61. Nicholas Paul, *To Follow in Their Footsteps: The Crusades and Family Memory in the High Middle Ages* (Ithaca: Cornell University Press, 2012), 90–133; Anne E. Lester, "What Remains: Women, Relics, and Remembrance in the Aftermath of the Fourth Crusade," *Journal of Medieval History* 40 (2014): 311–28 and eadem, "Remembrance of Things Past: Memory and Material Objects in the Time of the Crusades, 1095–1291," in *Remembering the Crusades and Crusading*, ed. Megan Cassidy-Welch (Abingdon: Routledge, 2017), 73–94.
62. Namur, Bibliothèque du Séminaire, MS 57, fol. 145v: "iam non differt a comitibus specie."

his crusade, then it may have symbolised both his children's claims to their noble seigneury and their inherited chivalric honour.

An Avatar in Action

In fostering the traditions of Manasses and the Holy Cross of Antioch, the monks of Brogne undoubtedly intended to bolster the reputation of their house as a site of Christian devotion in the diocese of Liège. They may also have intended to showcase how their skill at storytelling and ritual performance empowered them to grant approbation and legitimacy to members of the lay aristocracy. By doing so, however, they also reveal how and in what circumstances an image of knightly excellence was constructed in the later twelfth and early thirteenth centuries.

If the period *ca.* 1180–*ca.* 1220 was a crucial time for the codification of the ideals of knighthood and nobility that would be associated with chivalry for the balance of the Middle Ages, then the Brogne materials act as an important reminder that these ideals were worked out not just by knights themselves or by clerics seeking to Christianise knighthood. They should rather be seen to emerge from the dialogue between various communities within a locality. By the end of the *Quomodo* text, the dispute over ownership of Manasses's sacred relic has come to involve his heirs, the abbey, the count of Namur, other members of the local aristocracy, and the people of the lordship of Hierges. The monks of Brogne represented Manasses in a way that they felt would appeal to his heirs, to devotees of the relic, and to other potential benefactors. To do this, they needed to demonstrate that they, too, fully understood the importance of what he had accomplished on crusade and upon his return home. The Brogne model of writing a knight's life was apparently successful, if only locally: the basic outline of the career of Manasses, and in particular his time in the East, seems to have served as the model for the romance *Gilles de Chin*, which appeared within a decade or two of *Quomodo* and which was composed in honour of a dynasty ascendant in Namur in the first quarter of the thirteenth century.[63] Later in the thirteenth century, something very close to the approach of the *Quomodo* author was

63. Gautier de Tournai, *L'histoire de Gilles de Chyn*, ed. Edwin B. Place (Evanston, IL: Northwestern University Press, 1941).

adopted by monks of the nearby Cistercian abbey of Villers. A mere 35 kilometres north-west of Brogne in Brabant, Villers had among its brethren a former knight named Gobert of Apremont (d. 1263). When they came to record a *Vita Goberti*, the monks of Villers, like the monks of Brogne, lingered upon his career in secular knighthood, emphasising in particular his time on crusade with Frederick II.[64]

As the ideals of aristocratic behaviour came to be encoded in courtly and chivalric practices and ultimately in texts such as the *Ordene de chevalerie*, there can be no doubt that exemplary figures or "avatars" such as Manasses remained crucially important.[65] We may even detect the influence of the story of Manasses, as shaped in the Brogne texts, around the region. The thirty-eighth chapter of the second book of *Quomodo* contains a list of prominent individuals from the wider community who demonstrated their devotion to the cross.[66] First on this list of lay devotees is James of Avesnes (*vir inclitus*), whose lord-ships encompassed the castles of Leuze, Condé, Avesnes, Landrecies, Bohain, and Treslon.[67] James made a provision of light before the cross at Brogne, and, according to *Quomodo*, his gift inspired many others who showered the abbey with similar donations.

What *Quomodo* does not explain but is evident from another surviv-ing document is that James's gift was made in the immediate context of another act. It was in the winter or early spring of 1189, as he was departing for the Third Crusade (*in mocione mea ad succurrendum terre Iherusalem*), that he arranged for 100 *sous* to be collected annu-ally by the monks from his hall in Avesnes to light two candles before the Holy Cross.[68] As the writer of *Quomodo* doubtless knew, James had distinguished himself as one of the most outstanding knights on the Third Crusade. After his death two years later at the battle of Arsuf

64. "Vita Goberti Asperimontis," ed. Petrus Dolmans, in *Acta Sanctorum*, Aug. IV (Antwerp: Vander Plassche, 1739), 377–94. Dutch translation, with comments: Stefan Meysman, "De vita van Gobert van Aspremont (ca. 1187–1263)," *Novi Monasterii: jaar-boek abdijmuseum Ten Duinen 1138* 12 (2013): 83–133.

65. For the importance of avatars in the period before the codification of chivalry, see Crouch, *The Birth of Nobility*, 29–86, esp. 30–37. For an application of the concept to the crusades see Paul, *To Follow in Their Footsteps*, 21–53.

66. Namur, Bibliothèque du Séminaire, MS 57, fol. 166r–v.

67. Charles-Albert Duvivier, "Jacques d'Avesnes," *Revue trimestrielle* 10 (1856): 99–150, at 107.

68. Namur, Archives de l'État, 2586, 108r. Edited in Barbier, "Obituaire de l'abbaye de Brogne," 367–68, no. 7. See also *Diplomata Belgica*, DiBe ID 4131. For the larger phenomenon of departure charters see Corliss K. Slack, *Crusade Charters, 1138–1270* (Tempe, AZ: Arizona Center for Medieval & Renaissance Studies, 2001).

in 1191, writers in both East and West lionised him as a model of prowess, piety, and knightly virtue. Gilbert of Mons called him "very virtuous in arms, vigorous in all things, outstanding and very powerful."[69] He was compared with Hector, Achilles, and the Maccabees, and Richard I described him as "a great man whose merits had recommended him to the whole army."[70] A quarter of a century later preachers in England were advised to invoke stories about James in their sermons in their attempts to recruit knights for the Fifth Crusade.[71]

James was an exemplary knight, but whence or from whom did he take *his* example? The fact that he thought of Brogne and the cross at the moment of his own departure on crusade would suggest that perhaps he had Manasses in mind as he undertook his own trial in the East. If he knew the Manasses represented in the Brogne texts, he would have known that the East was the most important stage for his noble conduct, one on which it was essential he should acquit himself well.

Conclusions

Within the textual tradition of the monastery of Brogne, and in the local traditions of *Gilles de Chin* and Gobert of Apremont perhaps also influenced by Brogne, the eastern crusading frontier is deployed within narrative as an ideal stage for chivalric performance. Existing outside the hero's (and the audience's) politically charged local geography, in a distant land of exotic (although also recognisably European) courts ruled by powerful women and before an audience that included the highly renowned warriors of the Military Orders and other esteemed

69. Gilbert of Mons, *La chronique de Gislebert de Mons*, ed. Léon Vanderkindere (Brussels: Kiessling, 1904), 78: "valde probus et vividus in cunctis ac discretus plurimumque potens." English translation: *The Chronicle of Hainaut by Gilbert of Mons*, trans. Laura Napran (Woodbridge: Boydell, 2005), 45.

70. An overview of his life, based mainly on narrative and some post-medieval sources is Duvivier, "Jacques d'Avesnes," 99–150; for the key references to his reputation see Paul Riant, *Expéditions et pèlerinages des Scandinaves en Terre Sainte au temps des croisades* (Paris: Lainé and Havard, 1865). For the letter of Richard I, see Roger of Howden, *Chronica magistri Rogeri de Houedene*, ed. William Stubbs, 4 vols., Rolls Series 51 (London: Longman, 1868–71), 3: 129–30. English translation in Malcolm Barber and Keith Bate, trans., *Letters from the East: Crusaders, Pilgrims, and Settlers in the 12th–13th Centuries*, Crusade Texts in Translation (Abingdon, Oxon: Ashgate, 2013), no. 51.

71. "Ordinacio de predicacione s. crucis in Anglia," ed. Reinhold Röhricht, in *Quinti Belli Sacri Scriptores Minores* (Geneva: Fick, 1879), 20.

knights, the Latin East was a particularly useful narrative *mise-en-scène*. The implications, however, of this presentation of crusading go far beyond this group of texts, providing an important corrective to the scholarship of crusade and knighthood more generally.

As Jay Rubenstein has remarked, "[c]rusade and chivalry, despite their obvious historical and cultural resonances, have not always sat easily with one another."[72] Indeed, within the long twin traditions of historical research on chivalry and the crusades, we still lack a satisfactory explanation for the relationship between these phenomena, both of which had their origins in the eleventh century but came of age only in the later twelfth or thirteenth centuries. Where Léon Gautier, writing in 1884, saw crusading as absolutely central to the whole conception of knightly life ("war against the infidel" being one of his ten commandments of chivalry), in more recent scholarship crusading is often relegated to the periphery of the history of chivalry.[73] Maurice Keen, while noting that the crusading frontier was often an important backdrop for knightly deeds such as those remembered in the Scrope and Grosvenor case brought before the English Court of Chivalry in 1389, nonetheless saw the origins of chivalry as resolutely secular, not emerging from clerical discourses of pious violence.[74] To contemporary historians of the aristocracy, crusading might be nothing more than "the church's answer" to the problem of allowing "the nobility to fight regularly without doing something actually so sinful as to kill other Christians."[75] According to Richard Kaeuper, the fusion of violence and penitential suffering was something that knights were eager to co-opt for themselves, and so the later medieval knight gained many of the attributes of the crusader, rendering crusading in many ways redundant to self-conscious Christian knighthood.[76]

---

72. Jay Rubenstein, "Poetry and History: Baudry of Bourgeuil, the Architecture of Chivalry, and the First Crusade," *Haskins Society Journal* 23 (2014): 87.

73. Léon Gautier, *La chevalerie*, 3rd ed. (Paris: Librairie Universitaire, 1895), 70–72.

74. Maurice Keen, "Chaucer's Knight, the English Aristocracy, and the Crusades," in *English Court and Culture in the Later Middle Ages*, ed. Vincent J. Scattergood and James W. Sherborne (New York: St Martin's Press, 1983), 45–61, repr. in idem, *Nobles, Knights, and Men-at-Arms* (London: Hambledon Press, 1996), 101–20 at 106–10; idem, *Chivalry* (New Haven: Yale University Press, 1984), 18–63.

75. Constance Brittain Bouchard, *Strong of Body, Brave, and Noble: Chivalry and Society in Medieval France* (Ithaca: Cornell University Press, 2008), 122–23.

76. Richard Kaeuper, *Holy Warriors: The Religious Ideology of Chivalry* (Philadelphia: University of Pennsylvania Press, 2009), 104.

In all of this, crusading is understood primarily as a devotional exercise, its importance with regard to chivalry determined in large part by attitudes among historians to what Adolf Waas called "knighly piety" (*Ritterfrommigkeit*).[77] While the devotional character of crusading is beyond question, realising that the crusading frontier was also a critical zone for the cultivation of reputations and prowess, a place for the fulfilment of dynastic obligations and the collection of important trophies helps us to understand that crusading and chivalry were related in other ways.[78] An abiding concern for the preservation of the Latin states in the East that made up the frontier would always be linked to the desire among knights to walk in Christ's footsteps and safeguard the places of his suffering. But for knights who followed the example of Manasses of Hierges, what needed to be protected or restored was as much an arena for chivalric performance as a stage for Holy War.

77. Adolf Waas, *Geschichte des Kreuzzüge*, 2 vols. (Freiburg: Herder, 1956), 2: 57–70.
78. Cf. Paul, *To Follow in Their Footsteps*.

— Part IV —

WOMEN IN CHIVALRIC
REPRESENTATIONS

Louise J. WILKINSON*

THE CHIVALRIC WOMAN

In view of chivalry's strong connection with the masculine cult of knighthood, it is perhaps unsurprising that relatively little has been written about its appeal for women. Yet, as this chapter argues, aristocratic ladies in the Middle Ages readily became immersed in the chivalric culture of their husbands and male kin. So intimately, in fact, was chivalry entwined with ideals of noble conduct and lifestyle that it offered women potent ideals of feminine appearance, behaviour and virtue, so that a lady might be regarded as chivalrous if she embraced moral superiority. The social and moral values assumed by the landed elite of the twelfth and thirteenth centuries were closely aligned with the obligations that aristocratic women shared with their fathers, brothers or husbands in managing great households, in preserving family lineages, in exercising lordship and in shaping dynastic identities. Ladies readily adopted heraldry, with its martial associations, and actively employed it on their seals and in architectural schemes, to promote their noble status and connections. They also espoused chivalrous qualities by battling, figuratively, in the spiritual realm for their own souls and those of their kin, through their personal religious observances, benefactions and charitable giving.

As a code of conduct linked to knightly values, chivalry arguably had little to offer women. Royal and aristocratic women often figured in vernacular literature in which chivalric qualities were championed either as ladies or lovers, for whom knightly men performed various feats of arms.[1] A good case in point is Ulrich von Liechtenstein's autobiographically framed poem *Frauendienst*, completed in 1255, where the narrative is dominated by Ulrich's personal devotion to a beautiful, older and initially unattainable noble lady, who is already joined in marriage to another. First through service to her as a page and later through feats of arms in tournaments as a knight, Ulrich attempts to earn his lady love's devotion, sometimes at considerable personal cost.[2] In works addressed to the moral formation of knights,

* The author is grateful to David Crouch and Jeroen Deploige for their helpful advice in preparing this chapter.

1. For discussion, see Nigel Saul, "Chivalry and Women," in idem, *For Honour and Fame: Chivalry in England, 1066–1500* (London: Pimlico, 2012), 262–70.

2. Ulrich von Liechtenstein, *Frauendienst*, ed. Reinhold Bechstein, 2 vols. (Leipzig: F. A. Brockhaus, 1888); Ulrich von Liechtenstein, *The Service of Ladies*, trans. John Wesley

however, certain groups of women were viewed instead as weak and vulnerable objects of masculine pity, deserving of male protection. In Ramon Llull's *Libre del orde de cavalleria*, a treatise written between 1274 and 1276, this author impressed upon his readers the idea that it was a knight's duty "to support widows, orphans and the helpless," since it was "customary and right that the mighty help to defend the weak, and the weak take refuge with the mighty."[3]

Yet chivalry as a way of life permeated, shaped and informed female aristocratic culture more fully than might at first appear. Even if women were, by virtue of their inability to assume knighthood, excluded from the militaristic ethos and martial practices associated with chivalry, there was, for example, a shared expectation of appropriate forms of "noble" conduct and lifestyle for elite men and women among the ruling houses and aristocracies of Western Europe in the Central Middle Ages. Certain forms of behaviour and personal qualities or virtues therefore assumed particular significance for elite women in fiction and reality, especially in connection with the core rituals and responsibilities of aristocratic life, such as exercising hospitality, dispensing patronage, and engaging in pious works. The countesses and other ladies who headed great estates in widowhood, or who aided their husbands during marriage, shared similar values and moral or social obligations to earls, counts and barons. Like their fathers, husbands and sons, they were expected to profess and maintain their personal loyalty to the lords from whom they held their lands. Inheritance customs which allowed women in England to succeed to estates held by military service as heiresses or co-heiresses if there were no male heirs in the same generation, created situations where women performed homage to their lords.[4] In a similar fashion, although notions of hon-

Thomas, intr. Kelly Devries (Woodbridge: Boydell Press, 2004); Marion E. Gibbs and Sidney M. Johnson, *Medieval German Literature* (London: Routledge, 2000), 311–13.

3. "Offici de cavayler és mantenir vilves, òrfens, hòmens despoderats; cor, enaxí con és custuma e rahó que los majors ajuden a deffendre los menors, e los menors ajen refuge als majors." Rámon Llull, *Llibre de l'orde de cavalleria*, 2.19, ed. Albert Soler Llopart, Els Nostres Clàssics 127 (Barcelona: Barcino, 1988), 181; Ramon Llull, *The Book of the Order of Chivalry*, trans. Noel Fallows (Woodbridge: Boydell Press, 2013), 50. For a brief commentary on Ramon's views on women, see Richard W. Kaeuper, *Medieval Chivalry* (Cambridge: Cambridge University Press, 2016), 324. For discussion on protecting women and the weak in the context of the "Davidic ethic," see David Crouch, *The Birth of Nobility: Constructing Aristocracy in England and France, 900–1300* (Harlow: Pearson/Longman, 2005), 71–79.

4. J.C. Holt, "Feudal Society and the Family in Early Medieval England, IV: The Heiress and the Alien," in idem, *Colonial England, 1066–1216* (London: The Hambledon

our among elite women were tied more firmly to their sexual reputations than those of men, these ladies, and those who wrote about them, set great store by their lineages and celebrated their own nobility of birth and bloodlines.[5] This chapter explores the connections between chivalry, female nobility and aristocratic life.

Noble Ideals of Feminine Appearance, Behaviour and Conduct

As Maurice Keen observed, the "aristocratic" or "noble" aspect of chivalry in the Middle Ages was "a matter of worth as much as ... of lineage."[6] Since antiquity, writers such as Cicero had argued that true nobility was based on virtue (*virtus vera nobilitas est*); high birth and worldly riches were not a sufficient basis for true nobility on their own.[7] These ideas pervaded medieval literature. In his *Communiloquium*, the thirteenth-century friar, John of Wales, instructed his readers on how true nobility stemmed from a virtuous life, so that those who were not of aristocratic birth might become noble through their conduct,[8] sentiments that were echoed in the works of William Peraldus (d. *ca.* 1275), a French Dominican scholar.[9] Similar themes appeared in *Le Livre des manières* of Stephen de Fougères (d. 1178), a work dedicated to Cecilia, countess of Hereford, which emphasised

Press, 1997), 247–49 (originally published in *Transactions of the Royal Historical Society* 35 (1985): 1–28). If an heiress was married, her husband was expected to perform homage on behalf of his wife in England. A person who performed homage to a single woman who later married was expected to perform it again for the same tenement to the woman's new husband: *The Treatise on the Laws and Customs of the Realm of England commonly called Glanvill*, ed. and trans. G. D. G. Hall, Oxford Medieval Texts (London: Nelson, 1965; repr., Oxford: Clarendon Press, 2002), 106, 108. For damsels and widows performing homage in Champagne, see *Feudal Society in Medieval France: Documents from the County of Champagne*, ed. and trans. Theodore Evergates (Philadelphia: University of Pennsylvania Press, 1993), nos. 37 and 38.

5. Dominique Barthélemy, "Kinship," in *A History of Private Life: Revelations of the Medieval World*, ed. Georges Duby and trans. Arthur Goldhammer (Cambridge, MA: The Belknap Press of Harvard University Press, 1988), 119–24 and 145–46.

6. Keen argued that the "three essential facets" of chivalry were "the military, the noble and the religious:" Maurice Keen, *Chivalry* (New Haven: Yale University Press, 1984), 16–17.

7. Ibid., 158.

8. Jenny Swanson, *John of Wales: A Study of the Works and Ideas of a Thirteenth-Century Friar* (Cambridge: Cambridge University Press, 1989), 130–32.

9. William Peraldus, *De eruditione principum*, I.4, ed. Roberto Busa, in vol. 7 of *S. Thomae Aquinatis Opera omnia* (Stuttgart and Bad Canstatt: Frommann and Holzboog, 1980); István P. Bejczy, *The Cardinal Virtues in the Middle Ages: A Study in Moral Thought from the Fourth to the Fourteenth Century* (Leiden: Brill, 2011), 271.

the moral elements of knighthood.[10] It therefore followed that women might be regarded as chivalrous if they embraced moral superiority, just as knights were supposed to do. External beauty might be taken as a symptom, or reflection, of a woman's inner qualities of moral superiority.[11] Agnes of Harcourt, the author of a French prose *Life* of King Louis IX of France's sister, Isabel, observed how this princess was "graceful and of great beauty, and even though she was so noble in lineage, she was even higher and more noble in morals."[12] In *Equitan*, one of the twelve *lais* composed by Marie de France in or around 1170, the wife of Equitan's seneschal was portrayed as "a lady of fine breeding and extremely beautiful with a noble body and good bearing. Nature had spared no pains when fashioning her."[13] In Chrétien de Troyes' tale of *Erec and Enide*, written in the second half of the twelfth century, the young couple were "very well and evenly matched in courtliness, in beauty, and in graciousness."[14]

Natural attractiveness, in particular, was regarded by contemporary writers as a marker of a woman's inner worth, and was evoked in literature by comparisons of elite women with flowers, most notably the lily and the rose, both of which had strong Marian associations; the lily, in particular, was associated with purity.[15] The noble maiden to whom Lanval, the hero of another *lai*, was escorted by two finely

10. Stephen de Fougères, *Le Livre des Manières*, ed. and trans. Jacques T.E. Thomas, Ktemata 20 (Louvain: Peeters, 2013), 9–10, stanzas 148–58. For discussion, see Anthony Lodge, "The Literary Interest of the *Livre des Manières* of Etienne de Fougères," *Romania* 93 (1972): 479–97, at 490.

11. Olga V. Trokhimenko, *Constructing Virtue and Vice: Femininity and Laughter in Courtly Society (ca. 1150–1300)* (Göttingen: V. & R. Unipress, 2014), 34.

12. "elle estoit moult gracieuse et de grant beauté, et ja soit ce qu'elle fust si noble de lignage, encore fu elle plus haute et plus noble de mœurs." Agnes of Harcourt, "Vie d'Isabelle de France," ed. and trans. Sean L. Field, in *The Writings of Agnes of Harcourt: The Life of Isabelle of France and the Letter on Louis IX and Longchamp* (Notre Dame, IN: The University of Notre Dame Press, 2003), 52–53, lines 14–16.

13. "La dame ert bele durement / E de mut bon affeitement, / Gent cors out e bele faiture; / En li former uvrat nature." Marie de France, "Equitan," in *Marie de France Lais*, ed. Alfred Ewert, intr. Glyn Burgess (London: Bristol Classical Press, 1995), 26, lines 31–34; Marie de France, "Equitan," in *The Lais of Marie de France*, trans. Glyn S. Burgess and Keith Busby (London: Penguin Classics, 1986), 56.

14. "mout estoient igal et per / de corteisie et de biauté / et de grant deboneretё." Chrétien de Troyes, *Erec et Enide*, ed. Pierre Kunstmann (Ottawa: Université d'Ottawa, 2009), 32, lines 1484–86. See also Chrétien de Troyes, "Erec and Enide," in *Chrétien de Troyes, Arthurian Romances*, trans. William W. Kibler (Harmondworth: Penguin, 1991), 56. I have modified Kibler's translation to reflect better the meaning of the word "deboneretё."

15. Teresa McLean, *Medieval English Gardens* (Mineola, NY: Dover Publications, 2014), 129–31.

Fig. 9.1—Seal of Alice, countess of Eu (*ca.* 1234-40). Plate reproduced from Weston S. Walford and Albert Way, "Examples of Medieval Seals," *The Archaeological Journal* 11 (1854): 369.

attired damsels "surpassed in beauty the lily and the new rose when it appears in summer."[16] "Her body was well-formed and handsome," and her skin "whiter than the hawthorn blossom."[17] In *Anticlaudianus,* a poetic allegory written by Alan of Lille in 1181–83, the personification of the Virtue Prudence was a noblewoman with "radiant eyes," a "lily-like" forehead, teeth to rival "ivory" and "her mouth, the rose"; her complexion was also devoid of all shameful cosmetics in keeping with the Christian condemnation of vanity.[18] After all, beauty achieved by cosmetics was a mark of inner deceit and falsity, a point made by Stephen de Fougères.[19] Among the qualities given human form by the male narrator of the *Roman de la Rose,* a text first composed in France between 1225 and 1230, was Beauty, a young noblewoman, who pos-

16. "Fleur de lis [e] rose nuvele, / Quant ele pert al tens d'esté, / Trespassot ele de beauté." Marie de France, "Lanval," ed. Ewert, 60, lines 94–96 (trans. Burgess and Busby, 74).

17. "Mut ot le cors bien fait e gent ... / Plus ert blanche que flur d'espine." Marie de France, "Lanval," ed. Ewert, 60, lines 100, 106 (trans. Burgess and Busby, 74).

18. "Luminis astra jubar, frons lilia, ... / Dens ebur, os que rosam ... / ... nec candor adulter / Turpiter effingit tanti phantasma decoris." Alan of Lille, *Anticlaudianus,* 1, ed. Robert Bossuat, *Anticlaudianus: texte critique,* Textes philosophiques du Moyen Âge 1 (Paris: Vrin, 1955), 65, lines 277–80; Alan of Lille, *Anticlaudianus: Or The Good and Perfect Man,* trans. James J. Sheridan (Toronto: Pontifical Institute of Medieval Studies, 1973), 57.

19. Stephen de Fougères, *Livre,* stanzas 254–58.

sessed soft, lily-coloured skin, long fair hair, shapely limbs, and a slender body.[20] Aristocratic women's engagement with these ideals in life was reflected by the adoption of lilies and roses on the portrait seals with which they authenticated documents. It also found expression in this artistic medium through their almost stereotypical depiction as tall, slim and elegantly proportioned figures.[21] The seal employed by Alice, countess of Eu, in the 1230s, for instance, portrayed this lady as a slender, standing figure in profile, with a fleur-de-lys in her right hand (Fig. 9.1).[22]

"Outer" beauty was also associated with particular modes of conduct that were desirable for noblewomen. The overall effect of Beauty's physical appearance in the *Roman de la Rose* was enhanced by her "pleasant and agreeable, courteous and elegant ... and charming and lively manners."[23] Contemporary perceptions of beauty were commonly linked to proper feminine deportment and socially pleasing behaviour for young noblewomen from maidenhood through into adult life—in literature and reality.[24] In Marie de France's *lai* of *Le Fresne*, the well-born heroine of the same name grew into a model of young womanhood in both looks and demeanour: "there was no fairer, no more courtly girl in Brittany, for she was noble and cultivated, both in appearance and in speech."[25] When Gurun, a local lord from Dol, first met Le Fresne, her beauty, her courtliness, her upbringing and

20. Guillaume de Lorris and Jean de Meun, *Le Roman de la Rose*, ed. Félix Lecoy, 3 vols., Les classiques français du Moyen Âge 92, 95 and 98 (Paris: Champion, 1965–70), 1: 31–32; English translation: *The Romance of the Rose*, trans. Frances Horgan (Oxford: Oxford University Press, 1999), 16–17.

21. Brigitte Bedos-Rezak, "Women, Seals, and Power in Medieval France, 1150–1350," in *Women and Power in the Middle Ages*, ed. Mary Erler and Maryanne Kowaleski (Athens: University of Georgia Press, 1988), 75–76; Susan M. Johns, *Noblewomen, Aristocracy and Power in the Twelfth-Century Anglo-Norman Realm* (Manchester: Manchester University Press, 2003), 127–30.

22. Canterbury Cathedral Archives, DCc/ChAnt/E/203 (attached to a document recording the settlement of a dispute over the patronage of Elham church in Kent, in *ca*. 1234–40).

23. "Briement el fu jonete et blonde, / sade, plesant, cortoise et cointe, / grasse, graillete, gente et jointe." Guillaume de Lorris and Jean de Meun, *Le Roman de la Rose*, 1: 32, lines 114–16 (trans. Horgan, 17).

24. For a discussion of the social status of women described as maidens or dames in the *lais* of Marie de France, see Glyn S. Burgess, *The Lais of Marie de France: Text and Context* (Manchester: Manchester University Press, 1987), chap. 6 ("Women in Love").

25. "En Bretaine ne fu si bele / Ne tant curteise dameisele: / Franche esteit e de bone escole / [E] en semblant e en parole; / Nul ne la vist que ne l'amast / E a merveille la preisast." Marie de France, "Le Fresne," ed. Ewert, 41, lines 237–42 (trans. Burgess and Busby, 64).

her wisdom all impressed him.[26] In the *lai* of *Guigemar*, the lady of
the "ancient city, capital of its realm" visited by the story's eponymous hero was, similarly, characterised as "noble, courtly, beautiful
and wise."[27] It is not therefore altogether surprising that similar connections between "inner" and "outer" qualities were made in the *Lives*
of female saints or well-born holy women. Clemence of Barking's
twelfth-century *Life* of St Catherine of Alexandria[28] described Catherine, the daughter of a king, as a beautiful, wise maiden, who preferred
God to an earthly bridegroom.[29]

Although St Catherine eschewed an earthly bridegroom, her beauty
and virtuous behaviour were recognisable in the portrayal of other
young royal and aristocratic women in chronicles. Similarly flattering
language was used to describe the appearance and conduct of Isabel,
the sister of King Henry III of England, on the eve of her marriage to
the Holy Roman Emperor Frederick II of Hohenstaufen in 1235. In
recounting Isabel's "viewing" by the imperial ambassadors, the author
of the *Flores Historiarum* portrayed her as a lady "in her twenty-first
year, beautiful to look upon, adorned with virgin modesty, and distinguished by her royal dress and manners," qualities that rendered her
worthy in every way for marriage to Emperor Frederick II.[30] When
Isabel entered the German city of Cologne on her journey to meet her
bridegroom, she greatly pleased the noble ladies of that city by raising
her cap and her hood, so that they might see her face, whereupon she
received "great commendations for her beauty as well as her humility"
and decorum.[31]

---

26. Marie de France, "Le Fresne," ed. Ewert, 41, lines 253–56 (trans. Burgess and
Busby, 64).

27. "une antive cité, / Ki esteit chief de cel regné" and "Franche, curteise, bele et sage."
Marie de France, "Guigemar," ed. Ewert, 8, lines 207–8, 212 (trans. Burgess and Busby,
46). "Altogether, no fewer than eight of the thirteen beautiful royal or noblewomen courted
by the heroes of the *Lais* were described as "wise" (*sage*):" Burgess, *Marie de France: Text
and Context*, 114.

28. On the similarities between this text and the *Lais* of Marie de France, see "Introduction," in *Virgin Lives and Holy Deaths: Two Exemplary Biographies for Anglo-Norman
Women*, trans. Jocelyn Wogan-Browne and Glyn S. Burgess (London: Everyman, 1996), xxix.

29. Clemence of Barking, "The Life of St Catherine," in *Virgin Lives and Holy Deaths*, 5.

30. "vicesimum primum aetatis agentem annum, speciosam, flore virginitatis insigni-
tam, indumentis et moribus regiis decenter ornatam." Roger of Wendover, *Rogeri de Wendover Liber qui dicitur Flores Historiarum*, ed. Henry G. Hewlett, 3 vols., Rolls Series 84
(London: Eyre and Spottiswoode, 1886–89), 3: 108.

31. "pulchritudinem illius pariter et humilitatem plurimum commendantes." Roger of
Wendover, *Flores Historiarum*, 3: 111.

Fig. 9.2—Crowned female Virtues. Miniature from Frère Laurent, *Somme le Roi* (1294). Paris, Bibliothèque nationale de France, fr. 938, fol. 147r. Reproduced with permission.

The representation of the Virtues as women was a longstanding and enduring literary motif by the late twelfth and thirteenth centuries, and one that was also relevant to the chivalric woman. As early as the fifth century, Prudentius' *Psychomachia* (or "Battle for Man's Soul") had depicted the Virtues as women who battled the Vices.[32] The association between female nobility and virtuous qualities was a central theme of *Anticlaudianus*, where each of the Virtues called upon to assist Nature in creating the perfect man was personified as a noblewoman. Nature herself was depicted as a great, courtly lady who summoned her "sisters" (*sorores*)—Concord, Plenty, Favour, Youth, Laughter, Temperance, Moderation, Reason, Decorum, Prudence, Piety, Sincerity and Nobility—to her council, just as a queen or countess might summon her advisers to attend her.[33] Similar depictions of the Virtues as elite women infused medieval art, providing moral edification and instruction for those who saw them.[34] Among the cycle of pictures included in the *Somme le roi*, a treatise on the Virtues and Vices composed in 1279 by the Dominican Frère Laurent for King Philip III of France, are a series of miniatures that depict the Virtues (the four "cardinal" virtues of Prudence, Temperance, Fortitude and Justice, alongside Humility, Friendship and Mercy) as crowned, regal female figures (Fig. 9.2).[35] At around the same time, the Virtues were personified in sculpture at Strasbourg cathedral as contemporary noblewomen, while the Vices, whom they trampled underfoot, were portrayed as crude burghers' wives—the distinction conveying strong elements of feminine social snobbery (Fig. 9.3).[36] Ladies were apparently better able to control their temperaments as heiresses of Eve than their social inferiors were.

If true nobility was virtue and virtue was the central tenet of chivalry then a woman could by that measure be as chivalrous as a man. The author of the *History of William Marshal*, a biography of the earl of Pembroke that was compiled in the 1220s in a Francien dialect of the Touraine, singled out the Marshal's eldest daughter, Matilda, for

---

32. Veronica Sekules, "Women and Art in England in the Thirteenth and Fourteenth Centuries," in *Age of Chivalry: Art in Plantagenet England, 1200–1400*, ed. Jonathan Alexander and Paul Binski (London: Royal Academy of Arts, 1987), 46.

33. Alan of Lille, *Anticlaudianus*, 1, 57–58, lines 12–52 (trans. Sheridan, 45–46).

34. Veronica Sekules, *Medieval Art* (Oxford: Oxford University Press, 2001), 132.

35. *The Parisian Miniaturist, Honoré*, intr. Eric G. Millar (London: Faber and Faber, 1959), plates 5–8.

36. Marina Warner, *Monuments and Maidens: The Allegory of the Female Form* (Berkley, LA: University of California Press, 2000), 152 and plate 51.

Fig. 9.3—The Virtues, who are personified as noblewomen, trample the Vices, who are personified as burghers' wives, in the northern portal of the west façade of Strasbourg Cathedral (copies of the late thirteenth-century originals). © Fondation de l'Œuvre Notre-Dame, Strasbourg.

particular praise, since she was endowed with "the gifts of wisdom, generosity, / beauty, nobility of heart, graciousness, / and, I can tell you in truth, all the good qualities / which a noble lady should possess."[37]

Another mode of conduct that was closely linked to superior morality for noblewomen was restraint.[38] In the moral treatise *Des .IIII. tenz d'aage d'ome* ("The Four Ages of Man"), which he wrote in or around 1265, the elderly Cypriot crusader Philip of Novara stressed the importance of young elite women behaving in an appropriate fash-

37. The full passage describing Matilda's qualities is: "Maheut out non la premereine, / A qui Dex fist si bele estreine / Qu'il mist en lui sens e largesse, / Bealté, franchice et gentillece / E tot li bien, gel di por veir, / Qu'en gentil feme deit aveir." *History of William Marshal*, ed. Anthony J. Holden and David Crouch, trans. Stewart Gregory, 3 vols. (London: Anglo-Norman Text Society, 2002–6), 2: lines 14917–22.

38. Restraint was also desirable for knights, who were expected to behave with humility and moderation: William H. Jackson, *Chivalry in Twelfth-Century Germany: The Works of Hartmann von Aue*, Arthurian Studies 34 (Cambridge: D. S. Brewer, 1994), 96.

ion, namely in an obedient, calm, modest, poised and chaste manner.[39] In keeping with these ideals of restraint, Robert de Blois, Philip's contemporary, strongly advised women to avoid loud, unseemly laughter in *Le Chastoiement des Dames* ("The Chastisement of Ladies").[40] Female virtue in noblewomen was associated with "perfect bodily control" and "self-possession"—modes of conduct that, in Christian thought, were modelled on those of the Virgin Mary, and removed from the transgressions and untamed desires of Eve—and which also found expression in contemporary sculptures depicting the Five Wise Virgins in cathedral settings, such as those at Magdeburg.[41] Noblewomen were therefore expected to observe chastity before marriage and to be sexually faithful to their husbands during marriage; the Church did not tolerate adultery in life.[42] This was an important area where romance literature sometimes differed from life.

Set against the permissible and desired types of behaviour were more deleterious qualities that women of the nobility ought to avoid. Guillaume de Lorris, the first author of the *Roman de la Rose* personified a number of emotions and negative character traits as female and stressed their ignoble nature. At the beginning of the narrator's dream sequence in this text, he encountered paintings on a high, crenelated wall of female figures, such as Hate, who was angry, argumentative and of unpleasant countenance, and Cruelty, Baseness, Covetousness, Avarice, Envy, Sorrow, Old Age, Religious Hypocrisy and Poverty.[43] These were all personal traits or conditions that Christian teaching roundly condemned in women, as well as men. Hence the Franciscan friar Adam Marsh's stern reminder to Henry III's youngest sister, Eleanor, countess of Leicester, "that a wife is most strictly bound to her husband by her strength and constancy, her prudence and her meekness and kindness," while counselling her against disturbing the

39. Philip of Novara, *Les quatre âges de l'homme: traité moral de Philippe de Navarre*, ed. Marcel de Fréville (Paris: Didot, 1888), 14–15 (chap. 21), 17–18 (chap. 27), 19 (chap. 29).
40. Discussed in Trokhimenko, *Constructing Virtue and Vice*, 117.
41. Ibid., 188.
42. For discussion of the terms applied to bastards, including those born to noblewomen who slept with men other than their husbands, see Sara McDougall, *Royal Bastards: The Birth of Illegitimacy* (Oxford: Oxford University Press, 2017), 44–49 (esp. 48).
43. Guillaume de Lorris and Jean de Meun, *Le Roman de la Rose*, 1: 5–15, lines 139–460 (trans. Horgan, 4–9).

"peace" (*pacem*) of marriage "by demonic fits of anger."[44] "Anger" (*ira*), for Marsh, was "the source of quarrels, mental disturbance, insults, shouting, indignation, faint-heartedness and blasphemy" that led to hatred.[45] Such behaviour was deeply damaging to a lady's reputation and her soul. A woman who was angry, cunning and deceitful, who slandered others, who employed spiteful words, who spoke foolishly and who displayed arrogance rather than humility went against the moderation and mores of courtly society, earning opprobrium and gaining notoriety.[46]

Other personal circumstances or modes of feminine conduct were presented as unbecoming in a noblewoman. For ladies, as for knights and lords, worldliness and luxury, "riches without high qualities" were worth "nothing."[47] In the *Roman de la Rose*, Idleness was personified by a beautiful, "rich and powerful lady."[48] She was finely dressed in "a tunic of rich Ghent green," who passed her time in enjoying and amusing herself.[49] Wealth, similarly, was gendered female and depicted as "a lady of great dignity, worth, and rank."[50] She was a noblewoman, who, quite consciously, adopted rich and ostentatious attire; who inspired envious and insincere flattery at her court; and who commanded great power over those who were enthralled by her riches.

Yet costly attire in the form of luxurious fabrics, furs and jewels was an important aspect of the noble style of living and one that might, indeed, serve as "markers of noble status" by projecting the "nobility of the wearer."[51] It was with this in mind that the mother of Le Fresne,

44. "quia uxor viro districtissime tenetur et per vigoris constantiam, et per discretionis prudentiam, et per benignitatis clementiam … per demoniales irarum furores." *The Letters of Adam Marsh*, ed. C. H. Lawrence, Oxford Medieval Texts (Oxford: Clarendon Press, 2006–10), 2: no. 157.

45. "De ira rixe, tumor mentis, contumelie, clamor, indignatio, pusillanimitas, blasphemie proferuntur." ibid.

46. See, for example, the knight's wife and mother of Le Fresne: Marie de France, "Le Fresne," ed. Ewert, 35, lines 25–28 (trans. Burgess and Busby, 61); the wife of Sir Amiloun in "Amis and Amiloun," in *Middle English Romances*, ed. and trans. Kenneth Eckert (Leiden: Sidestone Press, 2015), 59, lines 1562–70.

47. Keen, *Chivalry*, 153.

48. "Rice fame sui et poissanz." Guillaume de Lorris and Jean de Meun, *Le Roman de la Rose*, 1: 19, line 582 (trans. Horgan, 11).

49. "Cote ot d'un riche vert de Ganz." Guillaume de Lorris and Jean de Meun, *Le Roman de la Rose*, 1: 18, line 562 (trans. Horgan, 10).

50. "une dame de grant hautece, / de grant pris et de grant afaire." Guillaume de Lorris and Jean de Meun, *Le Roman de la Rose*, 1: 32, lines 1018–19 (trans. Horgan, 17).

51. James A. Schultz, *Courtly Love, the Love of Courtliness, and the History of Sexuality* (Chicago: The University of Chicago Press, 2006), xx, 169.

aided by her maid "of very noble birth," abandoned her daughter in a church, having first wrapped the baby in "fine linen" and "the finest piece of striped brocade which her husband had brought from Constantinople, where he had been."[52] A gold ring set with a ruby was attached to the child's arm with a ribbon, so that "Wherever she was found, people would then truly know that she was of noble birth."[53] In a similar fashion, the clothing and jewellery adopted by comital and baronial ladies reflected their noble status. As the sister of a king and the wife of an earl, Eleanor, countess of Leicester, was conscious of the importance of personal display. Her purchases from London and other places in 1265 for herself and her daughter included a cloth of "sanguine" scarlet from the Italian merchant, Luke de Lucca,[54] a hood of black muslin,[55] a fur of miniver,[56] and 25 gilded stars with which to decorate the younger woman's hood.[57]

Even largesse, in the sense of "lavish generosity," which in contemporary literature encapsulated the ability to reward a lord or lady's followers, might inspire gendered criticism, especially if it was exercised without discrimination.[58] In the *Roman de la Rose*, Largesse was personified as a lady "who was well trained and instructed in the art of doing honour and spending money."[59] With a characteristically satirical eye, the author noted how, through Largesse's gift-giving, both "the wise and the foolish" held her in high esteem, as did the rich and the poor.[60] Similar concerns were expressed in conduct literature. Philip of Novara, for example, warned his readers against married women in particular being allowed to engage in gift-giving; if a wife was more

52. "une meschine, / Que mut esteit de franche orine;" "un chief de mut bon chesil;" "E desus un paile roé— / Ses sires l'i ot aporté / De Costentinoble, u il fui." Marie de France, "Le Fresne," ed. Ewert, 37–38, lines 99–100, 121, 123–25 (trans. Burgess and Busby, 62).
53. "La u la meschine ert trovee, / Bien sachent tuit vereiement / Que ele est nee de bone gent." Marie de France, "Le Fresne," ed. Ewert, 38, lines 132–34 (trans. Burgess and Busby, 62).
54. *Manners and Household Expenses of England in the Thirteenth and Fifteenth Centuries*, ed. H. T. Turner (London: Roxburghe Club, 1841), 25.
55. Ibid. 18.
56. Ibid.
57. Ibid., 65.
58. Sidney Painter, *French Chivalry: Chivalric Ideas and Practices in Medieval France* (Cornell, Ithaca: Cornell University Press, 1964), 30–32; Richard W. Kaeuper, *Chivalry and Violence in Medieval Europe* (Oxford: Oxford University Press, 1999), 198.
59. "qui bien fu duite et bien aprise / de fere honor et de despendre." Guillaume de Lorris and Jean de Meun, *Le Roman de la Rose*, 1: 35, lines 1126–27 (trans. Horgan, 18).
60. "les sages et les fox." Guillaume de Lorris and Jean de Meun, *Le Roman de la Rose*, 1: 36, line 1138 (trans. Horgan, 18).

generous than her lord and husband, she might well bring dishonour on him.[61] A courtly lady, it seems, walked a fine line between social acceptance and social condemnation.

Noble Lifestyle, Upbringing and Marriage

The social and moral values that "chivalric" women were encouraged to exhibit were closely aligned to the obligations they shared in the wider world with their fathers, brothers or husbands. Noblewomen were expected, like their male kin, to reside in castles or manor houses, participate in the affairs of a great household, assist in managing a family's estates, and engage in religious observances and charitable giving. Formularies used to teach letter writing preserve models of correspondence between lords and their wives touching matters such as the supply of goods, the management of estate business in a husband's absence, and wifely supervision of officials and building projects on their properties.[62]

With her responsibility for welcoming and entertaining visitors, both clerical and lay, it is easy to understand how a lady's courteous behaviour, in particular, was seen as essential for the smooth functioning, reputation and renown of any aristocratic establishment. The narrator of the *Roman de la Rose* personified Courtesy as "a worthy and gracious lady," who was a pretty, amiable, polite, level-headed, judicious and considerate hostess, a woman mindful of the needs and comforts of her guests.[63] It was Courtesy who invited the narrator as a newcomer to join the "noble people" dancing in a fine garden.[64] Politely receiving, welcoming, entertaining, housing and, indeed, feeding guests was closely linked in life to the expectation that lords and ladies (whether married or widowed) would exercise hospitality, a key component of

61. Almsgiving was, in this author's eyes, the only acceptable form of giving for a wife, provided that she had secured her husband's approval: Philip of Novara, *Les quatre âges*, chap. 23, 15–16; Margaret Wade Labarge, *A Baronial Household of the Thirteenth Century* (London: Eyre and Spottiswoode, 1965), 42.

62. See, for example, *Lost Letters of Medieval Life: English Society, 1200–1250*, ed. and trans. Martha Carlin and David Crouch (Pennsylvania: University of Pennsylvania Press, 2013), nos. 75–77, 100.

63. "la vaillant et la debonaire." Guillaume de Lorris and Jean de Meun, *Le Roman de la Rose*, 1: 25, line 779 (trans. Horgan, 13, 20).

64. "Franches genz et bien enseignies." Guillaume de Lorris and Jean de Meun, *Le Roman de la Rose*, 1: 40, line 1280 (trans. Horgan, 20).

noble living. The *Rules* that Robert Grosseteste compiled in 1245–53 to advise Margaret de Lacy, the widowed countess of Lincoln, on the good governance of her household and estates impressed upon their reader the importance of supervising the reception of visitors, both clerical and lay, to ensure that they were treated with consideration during their sojourn.[65] In order to achieve this, both lords and ladies were expected to follow a certain lifestyle, which was by its very nature expensive and required prudent financial management, but which was another marker of nobility.[66] Ladies, like lords, for example, were expected to maintain domestic establishments where fine food was served, especially on feast days or when entertaining highborn guests; where their servants looked after their own and their visitors' needs; and where their officials and other followers were clothed in ways that befitted their status within the household hierarchy. In the *Rules*, the countess of Lincoln was advised to ensure that members of her retinue were smartly and cleanly attired in appropriate livery (*robes*), so that they did not disgrace her good name with scruffy or dirty clothing.[67] The household roll of Eleanor, countess of Leicester, regularly records the purchase of new clothes and shoes for members of this comital establishment. Twenty-four and a half ells of perse, a dark-blue wool-len cloth were among the items purchased in the countess's name for servants, such as Wileqin, the groom of Richard de Montfort, Guillot, the clerk of the chapel, and Roger and Peter, grooms of the chamber.[68] Such smart, conspicuous consumption, which echoed the fine apparel of the lady herself and the fine furnishings of her residences, served as another visual expression of the privileged position associated with nobility.

Elite women were educated in the appropriate forms of conduct, the later responsibilities expected of them and the demands of noble living from childhood. Goldeboro's guardian in the Middle English romance *Havelok the Dane* promised to look after her "Until she was twelve years old [the age of canonical consent for marriage for

65. "The Rules of Robert Grosseteste," in *Walter of Henley and Other Treatises on Estate Management and Accounting*, ed. Dorothea Oschinsky (Oxford: Clarendon Press, 1971), 388–407 (400–3, no. xx). On the date of this work, see Louise J. Wilkinson, *Women in Thirteenth-Century Lincolnshire* (Woodbridge: Boydell for the Royal Historical Society, 2007), 58–61.
66. Keen, *Chivalry*, 153–54.
67. "The Rules," 402–3, no. xxi.
68. *Manners*, 85; Labarge, *A Baronial Household*, 132.

a woman] / And she was confident in speech / And could understand courtesy."[69] Arrangements for the education of fictional maidens in noble manners and lifestyle mirrored reality, and resonated with the experiences of daughters in royal, comital and baronial families. At the court of King Henry III, well-born women were appointed as mistresses and instructresses of younger women. Cecilia of Sandford is a good case in point. She served as *magistra* to Henry III's sister Eleanor, and then to Joan de Munchensy, the wife of his half-brother William de Valence, earning the praise of Matthew Paris for being "of noble blood but nobler manners" (*sanguine nobilis, sed moribus nobilior*) as well as "learned" (*docta*) and "eloquent" (*eloquens*).[70]

As part of their upbringing noblewomen were often taught to dance, perform on musical instruments, sing, embroider, read, perhaps write, hunt with hawks and hounds, and play chess or other games, pastimes that were considered suitable for ladies of rank.[71] Isabel of France learned to embroider with silk and sewed stoles for clergymen.[72] Her choice of thread was appropriate for a woman of her status; the author of *Piers Plowman*, a fourteenth-century work, carefully distinguished between noblewomen who used their "longe fyngres" to make "Chesibles for chapeleyns chirches to honoure" with "silk and sandel," and peasant women who sewed sacks "for shedyng of the wheat."[73] Isabel also studied the Scriptures and was instructed in letters.[74] St Catherine of Alexandria, as a virgin martyr of noble birth and character, offered a role model for aristocratic girls, since she had received instruction in letters and in appropriate speech.[75]

For most noble girls preparations for marriage were particularly important aspects of their upbringing. Ideally, noble brides were given

69. "Til þat she were twelf winter hold / And of speche were bold / And þat she couþe of curteysye." "Havelok the Dane," in *Middle English Romances*, 145, lines 192–94. I have amended Eckhart's translation of "curteysye."

70. Matthew Paris, *Matthaei Parisiensis Monachi Sancti Albani Chronica Majora*, ed. Henry Richards Luard, 7 vols., Rolls Series 57 (London: Longman, 1872–83), 5: 235.

71. Eileen Power, *Medieval Women*, ed. Michael M. Postan (Cambridge: Cambridge University Press, 1975), 69–70. Hawks were also a popular motif on women's seals as markers of elite status: Bedos-Rezak, "Women, Seals, and Power in Medieval France," 76.

72. Agnes of Harcourt, "Vie d'Isabelle de France," 54–55, lines 34–35.

73. William Langland, *The Vision of Piers Plowman. A Complete Edition of the B-Text*, ed. Aubrey V.C. Schmidt (London and New York: Dent and Dutton, 1978), 66, passus 6, lines 9–12.

74. Agnes of Harcourt, "Vie d'Isabelle de France," 54–55, lines 31–33.

75. Clemence of Barking, "The Life of St Catherine," 5, 6.

in marriage by their parents, guardians or lords to suitors of comparable status, wealth and good character. In the *Frauendienst*, Ulrich von Liechtenstein, for instance, recalled how "Prince Leopold of Austria gave / his lovely daughter to a brave / and noble Saxon who desired / her for his wife whom all admired," whereupon great festivities took place.[76] The social realities of courtship and the value that was placed upon marriage by landed families as a means of forging alliances and/or acquiring property ensured that arranged marriages, rather than love matches, predominated. The author of the *History of William Marshal* described how the Marshal and Roger Bigod, earl of Norfolk, negotiated a mutually advantageous union between the Marshal's eldest daughter, Matilda, "a very young thing and both noble and beautiful," and Roger's son Hugh, a "worthy, mild-mannered and noble-hearted" boy.[77] Similar unions were subsequently arranged for the Marshal's other daughters, Isabel, Sybil, Eve and, finally, Joan, who as the youngest was married off by her male kin after her father's death in 1219.[78] In England daughters or sisters, who inherited lands as sole heiresses or as co-heiresses when there were no male heirs in the same generation, were particularly prized as potential brides, since their persons and lands passed legally into the hands and control of their husbands when they married.[79] Something of the value attached to heiress-marriage is conveyed in the *lai* of *Eliduc*, where "a very old and powerful man" who lived near Exeter provoked a war and was besieged in his own castle when he refused to allow one of his "peers" to marry his only daughter and heiress.[80]

Even if few families could afford to marry off their children without giving some consideration to the material benefits that a match might bring, the value attached to noble birth and lineage as components of nobility sometimes outweighed other considerations behind the selec-

76. "Der fürst Liupolt ûz Œsterîch / gap dâ sîn tohter minneclîch / von Sahsen einem fürsten wert: / der het ihr ze eine konen begert." Ulrich von Liechtenstein, *Frauendienst*, 15, line 40 (trans. Thomas, 7).
77. "Giene chose e gentil e bele;" "proz e doz e gentiz:" *History of William Marshal*, 2: lines 13336–48 (esp. lines 13344, 13346).
78. Ibid., lines 14929–56.
79. See, for example, *Glanvill*, 75, 77, 80.
80. "un hum mut poëstis, / Vieuz hum." Marie de France, "Eliduc," ed. Ewert, 129, lines 92–93 (trans. Burgess and Busby, 112). Although there was more regional variation in inheritance customs in medieval France, heiresses were especially valued there too, hence the anxiety shown by the French crown in 1284 to establish Jeanne, the heiress of Champagne, in possession of her county prior to her marriage to the heir Philip: *Feudal Society in Medieval France*, no. 38.

tion of a spouse. In Chrétien's *Erec and Enide*, Erec readily acknowledged the poverty of his chosen bride, but boldly stated that her beauty
and lineage—she was the daughter of a poor vavasour and the niece
of a count—rendered her a suitable spouse.[81] In fact, such weight was
given to nobility of birth and lineage in both romance literature and
aristocratic culture that marriages between socially disparate people
were widely regarded as mésalliances.[82] Hence the *History of William
Marshal*'s concern to emphasise that Joan, in particular, was married
off to a man, Warin de Munchensy, who was "of such high birth / that
she did not marry beneath her."[83] Other heiresses found themselves
exposed to less desirable suitors. In 1225, Raymond de Burgh, the
nephew of Henry III's justiciar Hubert de Burgh, attempted to secure
the hand in marriage of Ela Longespée, *suo jure* countess of Salisbury,
when false reports of her husband's death reached the English court.
With the king's support, Raymond, who came from a family of minor
landholders in Norfolk and Suffolk, dressed "in knightly attire" (*in
nobili apparatu militari*) and visited Ela to press his suit. Ela, however, was left singularly unimpressed by his "soft speeches and great
promises" (*blandis sermonibus et promissionibus magnis*); rebuffing
his advances "with the greatest indignation" (*cum indignatione max-
ima*), she furiously explained not only that she had received letters
informing her that her husband was alive, but that, even had Earl William been dead, "the superiority of her descent" (*generis ejus nobilitas*) prevented a marriage with him.[84]

In refusing or attempting to refuse a suitor of inferior birth, Countess
Ela demonstrated a strong sense of pride in how her birth and rank
set her apart from those below her in society. The value placed by
individual families on their dignity as nobles was sometimes hinted at
in royal government records. In 1185, for instance, the compilers of
the *Rotuli de dominabus et pueris et puellis,* which recorded the findings of a nationwide inquiry in England into the widows and underage

---

81. Chrétien de Troyes, *Erec et Enide*, 33, lines 1534–47 (trans. Kibler, 56–57).

82. Fear of disparagement was such a grave matter for concern among English landed
elites in life that clause 6 of the 1215 Magna Carta attempted to protect the interests of the
landed aristocracy by stating that "Heirs are to be given in marriage without disparagement" (*Heredes maritentur absque disparagacione*): James C. Holt, *Magna Carta*, 3rd ed.
(Cambridge: Cambridge University Press, 2015), 380–81.

83. "Si hautement fu enpleiee / Qu'el ne fu pas deparagiee." *History of William Marshal*, 2: lines 14947–56 (esp. lines 14951–52).

84. Raymond was left to seek another wife: Roger of Wendover, *Flores Historiarum*,
2: 294–95.

heirs who were in the king's gift, referred to the children of the minor landholder Beatrice de Saiton as "born of knights" (*sunt nati de militibus*).[85] The phrasing apparently reflected the hereditary capacity of Beatrice's children to qualify for and, in the case of girls, transmit claims to knighthood.

The association between female nobility, ancestry and high birth was reinforced, satirically, in Alan of Lille's *Anticlaudianus,* where Nobility was personified as the daughter of Fortune and "the last and least beautiful of the virtues."[86] Lacking obvious gifts with which to endow the perfect man, Nobility endowed him instead with "impressive nobility, illustrious lineage, free-born parents, unrestricted liberty, [and] noble birth."[87] Nobility was therefore also a condition that was perpetuated and transmitted to the next generation by noblewomen themselves, since one of their primary functions as wives was to bear heirs, especially male heirs. The Middle English romance *Amis and Amiloun,* for example, begins with a description of how "two noble barons lived" in Lombardy "And had two ladies of proven nobility, / Who were elegant in appearance. / From those two courteous ladies / They had two boys, / Who were valiant in deeds, / And were true in all things."[88] Goldeboro, Havelok's wife and eventual queen, bore her husband no fewer than fifteen children altogether, sons, as well as daughters.[89] The author of the *History of William Marshal* similarly described each of the ten surviving children, five boys and five girls, who were fathered by the Marshal "and born of a worthy mother."[90]

85. Beatrice held half a knight's fee in Norfolk as an under-tenant of Walter Giffard, whose barony had escheated to the crown on his death: *Rotuli de dominabus et pueris et puellis de xii comitatibus,* ed. J. H. Round, Pipe Roll Society 35 (London: St Catherine Press, 1913), xxvi–xxvii, 53.

86. James Simpson, *Sciences and Self in Medieval Poetry: Alan of Lille's* Anticlaudianus *and John Gower's* Confessio Amantis (Cambridge: Cambridge University Press, 2005), 290. Cf. Alan of Lille, *Anticlaudianus,* 1, 58, lines 33–36 (trans. Sheridan, 46).

87. "Nobilitas augusta, genus presigne, parentes / Ingenui, libertas libera, nobilis ortus." Alan of Lille, *Anticlaudianus,* 8, 176, lines 129–30 (trans. Sheridan, 193); Simpson, *Sciences and Self,* 290.

88. "Two barouns hend wonyd in lond / And had two ladyes free to fond / Þat worþy were in wede. / Uppon her hend ladyes two / Twoo knave childre gat þey þoo / Þat douȝty were of dede / And trew weren in al þing." "Amis and Amiloun," 23, lines 28–34.

89. "Havelok the Dane," 208, lines 2843–44.

90. "E nasquirent de bone mere." *History of William Marshal,* 2: lines 14861–62.

Female Noble Agency, Identity and Piety

Ladies could be more than mere ornaments in both the fictional world
of romance literature and in the events recorded in chronicles and
contemporary biographies; they could also be actors and agents who
worked sometimes for the good and sometimes for the ill of their husbands and other male protagonists. As Judith Weiss aptly observed
in her study of women in Anglo-Norman romance, "in portraying
women who were energetic, able, even formidable ... some of these
poets had before them in their daily lives just such women, who were
educated, interested in learning, [and] relatively independent."[91]
Within marriage, the lady fulfilled a variety of roles in supporting her
husband. Lords and their wives were, after all, expected to display
personal loyalty to each other. The *lai* of *Eliduc*, for example, opens
with the description of how the hero and his wife "lived together for a
long time and loved each other with great loyalty," reminiscent of the
loyalty of a knight to his lord.[92] Noblewomen were expected to stand
by and actively support their husbands in schemes that protected and
advanced couples' mutual interests. In *Havelok the Dane,* it was Goldeboro who counselled her husband Havelok, after his recovery of his
own throne, "To journey back to England / To conquer her heritage,
/ For which her guardian had exiled / And very unjustly disinherited
her," whereupon Havelok amassed a fleet and took his queen with
him.[93]

In life, lords evidently valued the territorial rights and connections
that their wives brought with them, and saw their spouses as capable
agents of lordship in their lands. The breadth of responsibility that
these roles gave aristocratic women is conveyed, extremely effectively, by Gerald of Wales's characterisation of Matilda de St Valery,
the wife of the marcher lord, William de Braose, as "a prudent and
chaste woman, a woman well equipped to command her household,
a woman as highly skilled in preserving her property inside as in

91. Judith Weiss, "The Power and the Weakness of Women in Anglo-Norman Romance,"
in *Women and Literature in Britain, 1150–1500,* ed. Carol M. Meale (Cambridge: Cambridge University Press, 1996), 19.

92. "Ensemble furent lungement, / Mut s'entr'amerent lëaument." Marie de France,
"Eliduc," ed. Ewert, 127, lines 11–12 (trans. Burgess and Busby, 111).

93. "Que il passast en Engleterre / Pur son héritage conquerre / Dont son oncle l'out
engettée / Et à grant tort désheritée." "Havelok the Dane," 197, lines 2368–78 (esp. lines
2369–72).

enlarging it outside."[94] The *History of William Marshal* describes how the Marshal left his pregnant wife, the great heiress Countess Isabel, behind in Ireland to govern their estates there in the early 1200s.[95] Before his departure, the author has Marshal parading Isabel before their Irish tenants, reminding them that "She is your lady by birth, / the daughter of the earl who graciously, / in his generosity, enfieffed you all," and urging them "all to give her unreservedly / the protection she deserves by birthright, / for she is your lady."[96] The Marshal clearly hoped that his wife's presence would inspire loyalty in their Irish followers.

Although Countess Isabel's efforts in Ireland met with mixed success, resourcefulness and the ability to negotiate potentially complex political and social encounters were important facets of female nobility. A lord's wife needed to be able to dissolve tensions, diffuse difficult situations and restore harmony within her husband's household and estates, especially when he was away on business elsewhere. She might also be expected, like the women in romance literature, to attend and play a role in court celebrations, feasts and ceremonies. In *Erec and Enide*, knights, "rich ladies and maidens, noble and beautiful daughters of kings" attended the mythical King Arthur's court at Cardigan castle.[97] In twelfth- and thirteenth-century chronicles, noblewomen attended royal women at their marriages, their coronations and their churchings after childbirth.[98] Ladies and damsels of noble birth, who helped to maintain the affairs of their mistresses within

94. "mulier inquam, prudens et pudica, mulier domui suae bene praeposita, mulier non tantum intus conservando, verum etiam extra multiplicando providentissima." Gerald of Wales, "Itinerarium Kambriae et Descriptio Kambriae," ed. James F. Dimock, vol. 6 of *Giraldi Cambrensis Opera*, Rolls Series 21 (London: Longman, 1868), 23.

95. She was probably there on her own between 1200 and 1203, as well as in 1207–8: David Crouch, *William Marshal*, 3rd ed. (London: Routledge, 2016), 102–4.

96. "Vostre dame naturalment, / Fille al conte qui bonement / Vos fefa tuz par sa franchise, … Vos pri a toz que bonement / La gardez e naturalment, / Que vostre dame est, ce savon." *History of William Marshal*, 2: 13535–43.

97. "riches dames et puceles, / filles de rois, gentes et beles." Chrétien de Troyes, *Erec et Enide*, 2, lines 33–34 (trans. Kibler, 37).

98. For examples, see Matthew Paris's account of Eleanor of Provence's churching, attended by "noble ladies" (*nobiles dominae*), in 1239: Matthew Paris, *Chronica Majora*, 3: 566. Noblewomen had also been present when Eleanor's son, Edward, was baptised: ibid., 3: 540. See also later descriptions of ladies in attendance at the nuptials of Edward I's daughter Margaret and John of Brabant in July 1290: *Bartholomaei de Cotton, Monachi Norwicensis, Historia Anglicana*, ed. Henry Richards Luard, Rolls Series 16 (London: Longman, 1859), 176–77.

Fig. 9.4—A lady assisting a knight as he prepares to participate in a tourney. Heidelberg Universitätsbibliothek, *Große Heidelberger Liederhandschrift* ("Codex Manesse"), Cod. Pal. Germ. 848, fol. 397v. (*ca.* 1300). Reproduced with permission.

their households, attended queens and royal daughters on a daily basis and were privy to the politics of court life.[99]

Noblewomen might also be present—as spectators and patrons—at tournaments. The description of one such tournament in *Erec and Enide* describes how the lances used by knights on the tournament field were decorated with wimples and sleeves given by ladies as tokens to men whom they favoured.[100] Earlier, in the same tale, Enide is described as arming Erec "from head to foot" (*de chief an chief*) in preparation for another tournament—lacing the "iron greaves" (*les chauces de fer*) and securing them, dressing him in his "hauberk of good chain mail" (*hauberc li vest de boene maille*), placing his helm on his head, girding his sword, and handing him his shield and, finally, his lance.[101] Although such actions served to emphasise Erec and Enide's devotion to one another, Enide's actions were not, necessarily, unconventional. In a scene from the Codex Manesse, produced in Zurich between 1300 and 1340, a well-dressed lady is portrayed assisting a knight with his helm and holding his lance, as he prepares to participate in a tourney (Fig. 9.4). In a similar fashion, an illustration at the end of Psalm 108 in the Luttrell Psalter, an English manuscript of similar date, depicts this text's patron, Sir Geoffrey Luttrell of Irnham, mounted on his warhorse in full armour and preparing for a tournament (Fig. 9.5); Sir Geoffrey receives his helm from his wife Agnes Sutton, while his daughter-in-law stands patiently behind her, waiting to pass Sir Geoffrey his shield. More striking still are the deeds of men preserved in chronicles, such as Sir William Marmion mentioned in the *Scalacronica*, who were equipped with arms by ladies or who had vowed to take part in specific campaigns or ventures for them.[102]

Although knighthood was closed to ladies as an occupation, its association with heraldry offered women another way of participating in aristocratic, martial culture. Nonetheless the medieval imagination amused itself with the idea of women in the lists. Intriguingly, two jousting women in long flowing gowns and carrying shields with a heraldic device grace a folio of the Queen Mary Psalter, a work that was

---

99. Such women—ladies and damsels—are, for example, mentioned in the royal wardrobe accounts of King Henry III's reign, in attendance upon the queen, Eleanor of Provence: *The Wardrobe Accounts of Henry III*, ed. Benjamin Linley Wild, Publications of the Pipe Roll Society 96, n.s. 58 (London: Pipe Roll Society, 2012), 8, 24–26, 35, 39, 136–37.
100. Chrétien de Troyes, *Erec et Enide*, 44, lines 2081–87 (trans. Kibler, 63).
101. Chrétien de Troyes, *Erec et Enide*, 16, lines 709–26 (trans. Kibler, 46).
102. Saul, "Chivalry and Women," 269.

Fig. 9.5—Sir Geoffrey Luttrell preparing for a tournament with the assistance of his wife and daughter-in-law. London, British Library, Add. MS 42130 ("The Luttrell Psalter"), fol. 202v (1325–35). © The British Library Board.

perhaps made for Isabel of France, Edward II's queen in *ca.* 1310–20; their lack of other protective armour or equipment suggests that their combat here is figurative rather than real (Fig. 9.6).[103] Heraldry, which had first served as a means of identifying individual knights on the battlefield and at tournaments, had by the Central Middle Ages come to offer a visual reminder and celebration of a noble family's descent from a long, illustrious line of ancestors. This situation helped to ensure that the transmission of arms, in the sense of "family insignia," from one generation to another became important marks of nobility not only among knights but also ladies too in the twelfth and thirteenth centuries.[104] Ladies often adopted the heraldic devices of their husbands and natal kin on the embroideries and tapestries that decorated their clothing and the furnishings of their homes, respectively. A colourful impression of how such dresses may well have appeared is again conveyed by the Luttrell Psalter, where Sir Geoffrey's shield, his

---

103. For more on this, see Nicolas Ruffini-Ronzani, "The Knight, the Lady, and the Poet: Understanding Hugh III of Oisy's *Tournoiement des Dames* (*ca.* 1185)" in this volume.

104. Keen, *Chivalry*, 143.

Fig. 9.6—Jousting women in a figurative combat. London, British Library, MS Royal 2 B VII ("The Queen Mary Psalter"), fol. 197v (1310–20). © The British Library Board.

surcoat, his ailettes, his pennon and his horse's equipment (a fan crest, trapper and saddle) all proudly bear the Luttrell family's arms, while the two women wear dresses decorated with heraldic designs that likewise advertise their natal and marital family connections (Fig. 9.5).[105]

Heraldry was also, quite self-consciously, adopted on women's seals. So, although women were unable to bear arms in battle, they were proudly able to share and display in their own way the heraldic insignia that decorated the shields and other equipment that their husbands, fathers and sons used to identify themselves in battle and in tourney. As early as *ca.* 1156, Rohese, the widow of Gilbert de Gant, earl of Lincoln, and wife of Robert *dapifer*, a man of lesser social status than his bride, made the decision to move from using a vessica-shaped portrait seal to using another vessica-shaped seal that depicted in its field the eight heraldic chevrons of the Clares, her natal kin.[106] Significantly, a similar seal design that recalled Rohese's Clare connections was

105. For discussion, see Ann Payne, "Medieval Heraldry," in *Age of Chivalry*, ed. Alexander and Binski, 58.

106. Adrian Ailes, "Armorial Portrait Seals of Medieval Noblewomen: Examples in the Public Record Office," in *Tribute to an Armorist*, ed. John Campbell-Kease (London: The Heraldry Society, 2000), 219.

adopted by her daughter, Alice, countess of Northampton, the wife of
Simon de St Liz, just a few years later, suggesting a desire on the part
of this woman to celebrate her female ancestral connections.[107] By the
thirteenth century, other ladies of rank—the female kin of earls and
barons in particular—also adopted heraldic designs on their portrait
seals—on their dresses (as in life) and in the scenery that surrounded
them.[108] Margaret (d. 1235), the widow of Saher de Quincy, earl of
Winchester, is shown wearing a dress on her seal that is decorated with
the mascles of her husband; her eyes gaze towards a shield, suspended
from the branches of a tree, that is decorated with the Quincy arms
(seven mascles), while another shield, decorated with a fess between
two chevrons, hangs from a lower branch. These were the arms of
Saher, Margaret's husband, before he became earl of Winchester.[109]

Architectural schemes in churches, castles and manor houses offered
other mediums through which ladies advertised their noble status and
connections. A sculpture in Worcester cathedral shows a well-dressed
noblewoman of *ca.* 1230 giving personal instructions to a stone mason
working on the building.[110] The same was true of funerary monuments. Since many aristocratic widows served as their husbands'
executors, they were often among those responsible for overseeing
their husbands' funerary arrangements and the construction of their
monuments.[111] In 1312, for example, Matilda, countess of Artois,
arranged for a contract to be drawn up with Jean Pépin de Huy, who
was to carve her dead husband's tomb from stone and white alabaster.

107. Ibid. For examples of this seal, see *Sir Christopher Hatton's Book of Seals*, ed. Lewis
C. Lloyd and Doris Mary Stenton (Oxford: Clarendon Press, 1950), nos. 88, 425. For a discussion of seals used by aristocratic women in the Anglo-Norman realm, see Johns, *Noblewomen, Aristocracy and Power*, 122–51. See also Loveday Lewes Gee, *Women, Art and
Patronage From Henry III to Edward III, 1216–1377* (Woodbridge: Boydell, 2002), 67–72.
108. This practice can be traced as early as 1188 in France: Ailes, "Armorial Portrait
Seals," 221.
109. The couple's associate and kinsman, Robert fitzWalter, a leading baronial rebel during the civil war of 1215–17, also used them: ibid., 221–22; Gee, *Women, Art and Patronage*, 70. For further discussion of women's heraldic seals, see Peter Coss, *The Lady in Medieval England, 1000–1500* (Stroud: Sutton, 1998), 38–47, which has an excellent analysis
of the range of arms displayed of the seals on non-inheriting and inheriting noblewomen.
See also Elizabeth Danbury, "Queens and Powerful Women: Image and Authority," in *Good
Impressions: Image and Authority in Medieval Seals*, ed. Noël Adams, James Cherry, and
James Robinson (London: British Museum Research Publication 168, 2008), 19–20.
110. Veronica Sekules, "Women's Piety and Patronage," in *Age of Chivalry: Art and
Society in Late Medieval England*, ed. Nigel Saul (London: Brockhampton Press, 1992),
128 (plate).
111. Sekules, "Women's Piety and Patronage," 126–27.

Fig. 9.7—Female figure, armed with a "shield of faith," assailed by the Devil. London, Lambeth Palace Library, MS 209 ("The Lambeth Apocalypse"), fol. 53r (late thirteenth century). Reproduced with permission.

The contract specified that Mahaut's husband was to be portrayed as a knight with a shield, sword and armour on his effigy, and laid down that Mahaut would determine the tomb's precise, final location.[112] In the later Middle Ages, women's own tombs were often decorated with a woman's marital and/or natal family arms, while her rich, ornate style of dress again reminded those who saw it of her social rank.[113] Strikingly, the family networks celebrated on women's funerary monuments in France, like that of Mary de Bourbon (d. 1274), countess of Dreux, sometimes reflected a wider range of kinship connections than those of their husbands, which tended, instead, to focus on a narrow group of patrilineal associations.[114]

Awareness of lineage and of the identities of well-born ancestors was also fostered through religious observances and patronage intended to safeguard or assist the souls of the living and the dead. In life noblewomen were not usually expected to fight in armed combat in person, except, perhaps, in the spiritual realm in the eternal battle with the Devil for their souls. Hence the appearance of a female figure, armed with a "shield of faith," who is quite literally assailed by the Devil himself in the Lambeth Apocalypse, a book that belonged to Eleanor de Quincy, countess of Winchester, in the 1260s (Fig. 9.7).[115] In the original manuscript of the *Concordantiae Caritatis* of Ulrich, abbot of Lilienfeld, written in the 1350s, *Anima* is even personified as a female knight, who rides side-saddle, attended by fourteen Virtues who equip both *Anima* and her horse (Fig. 9.8).[116]

112. Teresa G. Frisch, ed. and trans., *Gothic Art, 1140–c. 1450: Sources and Documents* (Toronto: University of Toronto Press, 1987), 113–14. Matilda also commissioned tombs for her children: Stephen Perkinson, *The Likeness of the King: A Prehistory of Portraiture in Late Medieval France* (Chicago: University of Chicago Press, 2009), 102.

113. Gee, *Women, Art and Patronage*, 119–20; Nigel Saul, *English Church Monuments in the Middle Ages: History and Representation* (Oxford: Oxford University Press, 2009), 299–302, 309.

114. Anne McGee Morganstern, *Gothic Tombs of Kinship in France, the Low Countries, and England* (Pennsylvania: Pennsylvania State University Press, 2000), 51, 161–63 (appendix II). The same was also true of their seals. On kinship connections of noblewomen, see also Sara McDougall, "The Chivalric Family" in this volume.

115. For discussion, see Sekules, "Women's Piety," 129.

116. This text drew inspiration from Alan of Lille's description of the arming of the perfect man in his *Anticlaudianus*: Michael Evans, "An Illustrated Fragment of Peraldus's *Summa* of Vice: Harleian MS 3244," *Journal of the Warburg and Courtauld Institutes* 45 (1982): 34–35 and plate 7c; Flora Lewis, "The Wound in Christ's Side and the Instruments of Christ's Passion: Gendered Experience and Response," in *Women and the Book: Assessing the Visual Evidence*, ed. Jane H. M. Taylor and Lesley Smith (London: The British Library, 1996), 228 n. 73.

Fig. 9.8—Female personification of *Anima* as a horseback warrior, surrounded by fourteen Virtues arming her. The Virtues, all of whom are depicted as long-haired young women, include Sight, Faith, Abstinence and Prudence. Miniature from Ulrich of Lilienfeld, *Concordantiae Caritatis* (*ca.* 1355). Lilienfeld, Zisterzienserstift, MS 151, fol. 253r. Reproduced with permission (Photo: Harald Schmid).

Fig. 9.9—Eleanor de Quincy, original owner of the Lambeth Apocalypse, praying to the Virgin Mary. London, Lambeth Palace Library, MS 209 ("The Lambeth Apocalypse"), fol. 48r (late thirteenth century). Reproduced with permission.

Fig. 9.10—A noblewoman at prayer in the Grandisson Psalter. London, British Library, Additional MS 21926, fol. 135r (1270–80). © The British Library Board.

Spirituality offered an acceptable arena for female noble activity. The heroines in romances attended chapel, said their prayers and expressed their pious dedication to the saints, like royal and aristocratic women in everyday life. In *Erec and Enide*, Enide is described attending church with Erec; while Erec prayed at the altar of the Holy Cross, Enide was led to pray at the altar of Our Lady and perform her devotions.[117] Deluxe manuscripts commissioned or owned by female patrons allowed noblewomen to express their personal piety, whilst also demonstrating their privileged status and connections. One image in the Lambeth Apocalypse shows Eleanor de Quincy herself praying to the Virgin Mary in a dress decorated with heraldic motifs (Fig. 9.9),[118] while a decorated initial in the Grandisson Psalter of *ca.* 1270–80 depicts another finely attired lady, who is kneeling in prayer before an altar, as a recipient of God's blessing (Fig. 9.10).

Religious benefactions and charitable giving were also important aspects of noble life for women, as they were, indeed, for men. When Gilbert Foliot, bishop of London, confirmed an earlier grant by Hawise de Redvers, countess Roumare, to the hospital of St Giles in Holborn in the 1180s, he recited the contents of the "charter of the noble woman Hawise, formerly countess Roumare."[119] Noble wives and widows who lived nobly were expected to demonstrate their piety through material support for religious foundations and, in doing so, commemorate, celebrate and safeguard their own souls and the souls of their families, past and present, in the afterlife. When Amice de Redvers, countess of Devon, chose the nunnery of Lacock in Wiltshire between 1245 and 1265 as the final resting place for her heart in death, she carefully specified that her gift was made for her own soul, and the souls of her father Gilbert de Clare, earl of Gloucester, her mother Countess Isabel, her husband Earl Baldwin, her eldest son, her other sons, her siblings, and all persons, alive and dead, connected to her by kinship for whom she ought to pray.[120] The testament of Lady Agnes

117. Chrétien de Troyes, *Erec et Enide*, 49–50, lines 2318–52 (trans. Kibler, 66).

118. For discussion, see Sekules, "Women's Piety," 129.

119. "cartam nobilis femine Hadewise quondam comitisse de Rumare." *Charters of the Redvers Family and the Earldom of Devon, 1090–1217*, ed. Robert Bearman, The Devon and Cornwall Record Society n.s. 37 (Exeter: Devon & Cornwall Record Society, 1994), appendix I, no. 36.

120. *Lacock Abbey Charters*, ed. Kenneth H. Rogers, The Wiltshire Record Society 34 (Devizes: Wiltshire Record Society, 1979), no. 449. See also nos. 450–53. Amice's daughter, Margery, became a nun at Lacock: *Lacock Abbey Charters*, no. 455.

de Condet, which was drawn up before the death of her husband Walter de Clifford (d. *ca.* 1223), is one of the few extant English wills for a thirteenth-century lady and offers a fascinating insight into this woman's posthumous gift-giving. The testament itemises a whole series of bequests for the salvation of Agnes' soul to Christ Church cathedral priory, her chosen place of burial, St Augustine's abbey, St Gregory's priory and St Sepulchre's priory, all in Canterbury. In addition to this, she also remembered the five hospitals there, the local anchorites, the city's parish churches, the church of St Andrew in Wickhambreaux, and left gifts for the fabric of other religious houses in Kent, Lincolnshire, Shropshire and Herefordshire.[121] The variety and geographical spread of the religious communities mentioned in this document presumably reflected Alice's own diverse religious interests in the English counties in which she and her husband held their lands, many of which she had conveyed to him as an heiress through marriage.

Conclusion

Noble ladies occupied a central, if subordinate, place in aristocratic society, but a place that none the less conventionally allowed them to engage with chivalric culture. The ideals of chivalry connected with nobility shaped expectations of women's appearance, their modes of conduct and their virtues. Yet these ideals also drew on and lent authority to the social realities of aristocratic life. Aristocratic women were intimately bound up in the operation of lordship—in both ceremonial and practical terms. These women possessed keen senses of their own ancestry, of their place within their families, and of the dignity that birth, rank, marriage and wealth brought them. They partook fully in the noble lifestyle, in its lavish display, its conspicuous consumption and its inherently chivalric qualities.

---

121. Agnes also bequeathed goods to the hospital of St Wulfstan outside Worcester, and remembered her daughters, her sons, servants, local craftsmen, close acquaintances and members of her household: *The Registrum Antiquissimum of the Cathedral Church of Lincoln: Volume I*, ed. C. W. Foster, The Publications of the Lincoln Record Society 27 (Lincoln: The Lincoln Record Society, 1931), 293–95.

Nicolas RUFFINI-RONZANI*

THE KNIGHT, THE LADY, AND THE POET: UNDERSTANDING HUON OF OISY'S *TOURNOIEMENT DES DAMES (CA.* 1185–1189)

The Tournoiement des dames *is a fragmentary lyrical lay of 216 verses composed at the dawn of the 1180s by Hugh III, lord of Oisy, castellan of Cambrai and viscount of Meaux. The* Tournoiement *is a satirical and humorous work written shortly before Hugh's departure for the Third Crusade. It tells of an imagined tournament in which the competitors are not the prominent knights of northern France but their wives. This chapter reads the poem from a political perspective. The analysis of the origins of the ladies in the* Tournoiement *reveals that Hugh's intended audience was mainly the French elites that surrounded King Philip II Augustus, and not Hugh's traditional allies from Flanders and Lower Lotharingia. The article therefore puts forward the hypothesis that Hugh was using his poetry as a political tool to charm potential new allies belonging to the French upper aristocracy in the context of the continuing rise in power of Philip II Augustus.*

Between the end of the eleventh and the beginning of the thirteenth century, a new knightly culture gradually emerged in northern France and Lotharingia—a culture the values and behaviours of which were widely shared within their warring elites. Although our views on medieval knighthood have profoundly evolved since the beginning of the 1990s, the main features of this twelfth-century aristocratic culture have been well known for a long time, thanks to the works of some prominent English and French historians, such as Maurice Keen, Georges Duby, and Jean Flori.[1] For several decades, it has been generally acknowledged that from the end of the eleventh century the high aristocracy, followed by the second- and third-rank nobles and then

---

* I am grateful to Harmony Dewez, Giovanni Palumbo, and Jean-François Nieus, my colleagues in Namur, for their comments and advice on a first draft of this article. My thanks also go to Jeroen Deploige and David Crouch for their patience and their help.

1. Georges Duby, *The Chivalrous Society*, trans. Cynthia Postan (Berkeley: University of California Press, 1977); idem, *The Knight, the Lady, and the Priest. The Making of Modern Marriage in Medieval France*, trans. Barbara Bray (Chicago: The University of Chicago Press, 1983); Jean Flori, *L'idéologie du glaive. Préhistoire de la chevalerie* (Geneva: Droz, 1983); Maurice Keen, *Chivalry*, 4th ed. (New Haven and London: Yale University Press, 1990).

the elite warriors, gradually acquired coats of arms on their military equipment and seals which identified them, took part in the ritualised competitions of tournaments, sometimes developed a kind of cultural patronage around their courts and castles, and progressively defined a code of chivalry which was formally established during the first quarter of the thirteenth century.[2] These times were also, and more importantly, characterised by the emergence of a secular literature composed and performed in the vernacular by the lay elites.

Recently, historians have taken a renewed interest in the vernacular poetry written by the trouvères during the High Middle Ages. As Florian Mazel has shown in a brief but excellent overview of recent research in medieval poetical art,[3] French and Italian scholarship demonstrate a growing interest in studying the diffusion of songs and in reconstructing the authors' individual career paths, sometimes with the intention of building up a sociological background of the poets' world.[4] In such a context, their attention is mainly, but not exclusively, focused on the most important figures of twelfth- and early thirteenth-century literature, whose works are well preserved and whose talent has been celebrated since the Middle Ages. In this paper, I intend to investigate the literary path of Hugh III of Oisy, a twelfth-century trouvère whose poems are probably less widely known than the works of his more famous contemporaries such as Cono of Bethune, Gace Brulé, and

2. On these aspects, see David Crouch, *Tournament* (London and New York: Hambledon and London, 2005); idem, "When was Chivalry: Evolution of a Code" in the present volume; Dominique Barthélemy, "Les origines du tournoi chevaleresque," in *Agôn. La compétition, V^e–XIIe siècle,* ed. François Bougard, Régine Le Jan, and Thomas Lienhard, Haut Moyen Âge 17 (Turnhout: Brepols, 2012), 111–29; Jean-François Nieus, "Early Aristocratic Seals: An Anglo-Norman Success Story," *Anglo-Norman Studies* 28 (2016): 97–123; idem, "L'invention des armoiries en contexte. Haute aristocratie, identités familiales et culture chevaleresque entre France et Angleterre, 1100–1160," *Journal des savants* (2017): 93–155.

3. Florian Mazel, "De l'usage des troubadours en histoire médiévale," *Ménestrel* (13 November 2013), accessed 1 March 2018, http://www.menestrel.fr/spip.php?rubrique2026.

4. The American historian John F. Benton was among the first to develop such a prosopographical approach in "The Court of Champagne as a Literary Center," *Speculum* 36 (1961): 551–91. This approach has been since pursued by Martin Aurell, *La vielle et l'épée. Troubadours et politique en Provence au XIIIe siècle* (Paris: Aubier, 1989), 101–29; idem, *Le chevalier lettré. Savoir et conduite de l'aristocratie aux XIIe et XIIIe siècles* (Paris: Fayard, 2011), 138–208; Saverio Guida and Gerardo Larghi, *Dizionario biografico dei trovatori* (Modena: Mucchi, 2014); Laurent Macé, *Les comtes de Toulouse et leur entourage, XIIe–XIIIe siècles. Rivalités, alliances et jeux de pouvoir* (Toulouse: Privat, 2000), 138–46; Silvère Menegaldo, *Le dernier ménestrel ? Jean de Le Mote, une poétique en transition (autour de 1340)* (Geneva: Droz, 2015).

Blondel of Nesle. Hugh was lord of Oisy, castellan of Cambrai, and viscount of Meaux. He is best known as *Huon* of Oisy by medieval philologists. His poetical oeuvre was once probably more extensive, but only two of his poems are preserved today: the *Tournoiement des dames*, composed between 1185 and 1189, and the concise *Maugré tous sainz*, written after Hugh's departure to the Latin East in 1189. Of these two works, the *Tournoiement* is probably the more interesting, because it is a unique source of information about Hugh's networks, the performance of poetry, and the competitive spirit of the twelfth-century aristocracy. The analysis of the *Tournoiement* will be at the centre of this article.

In order to investigate this fragmentary lyric *lai* of 216 verses, my argument proceeds along two lines of enquiry. By examining Hugh's little-known biography through charter evidence,[5] I will first demonstrate how he became a prominent figure in Flanders, Champagne, and the Latin East during the second half of the twelfth century. Then I will turn to the *Tournoiement* and explain its significance for the study of the high medieval courtly society the values of which are uniquely highlighted in the poem. By examining the origins of the ladies mentioned in the text, I will argue that Hugh used his poetical talents as a means of identifying with the French lay elites that surrounded King Philip II Augustus.

Between Flanders and Champagne: Hugh's Political Horizons

Since so little has been written on the twelfth-century lords of Oisy, it is necessary first to establish the roots of their power and to provide an overview of their activities in the border-county of Cambrai and in Champagne.[6] Hugh's ancestors included the castellan Walter II of Cam-

5. On the notion of an *"itinéraire biographique,"* cf. Isabelle Rosé, *Construire une société seigneuriale. Itinéraire et ecclésiologie de l'abbé Odon de Cluny (fin du IXᵉ–milieu du Xᵉ siècle)* (Turnhout: Brepols, 2008), 22.

6. The survey by Adolphe de Cardevacque, "Oisy et ses seigneurs depuis l'origine de ce bourg jusqu'à l'époque de sa réunion à l'Artois," *Mémoires de la Société d'émulation de Cambrai* 37 (1881): 53–212, is entirely outdated. Two recent works about the Oisys remain unpublished: Nicolas Charles, "Formation et déclin d'une seigneurie chatelaine en Cambrésis: les sires d'Oisy (973–1189)" (Mémoire de maîtrise, Université de Lille 3, 2003), and my own "Église et aristocratie en Cambrésis. Le pouvoir entre France et Empire au Moyen Âge central (fin IXᵉ–mil. XIIᵉ siècle)" (PhD diss., Université de Namur, 2014). See also Stefan Meysman, "Degrading the Male Body: Manhood and Conflict in the High-medieval Low Countries," *Gender & History* 28 (2016): 367–86, at 374–75. Hugh's

brai, who gained some notoriety amongst historians for his quarrels
with Bishop Gerard I of Arras-Cambrai, a prelate celebrated by Georges
Duby in his *Three Orders: Feudal Society Imagined.*[7] Hugh himself
was the second son of Simon of Oisy and Ada of Meaux (Fig. 10.1).
His name appears in several charters from 1156 onwards. Towards
1165, he married Gertrude, the daughter of Thierry of Alsace, count
of Flanders.[8] Twenty years later, that union was followed by a second
marriage to Margaret, daughter of Count Theobald V of Blois.[9] Hugh
married women from powerful families, as in their days had also his
great-grandfather (who espoused a niece of Countess Richilde of Hainaut), his grandfather (who married a daughter of the lords of Mons), and
his father (who wed the heir of Viscount Godfrey of Meaux).[10] Hugh
was related to the lords of Béthune and to the lords of Saint-Aubert, two
of the most important noble families in the borderland regions of Artois
and Cambrésis, by the marriage of his paternal aunts.[11] These marriages
reveal a certain talent among the Oisys for matrimonial strategies.

activity as poet has been evoked by Andrea Pulega, *Ludi e spettacoli nel Medioevo: I
Tornei di dame* (Milan: Istituto editoriale cisalpino and La Goliardica, 1970), and Guy
Muraille and Françoise Fery-Hue, "Huon d'Oisy," in *Dictionnaire des Lettres françaises.
Le Moyen Âge,* ed. Geneviève Hasenohr and Michel Zink (Paris: Fayard, 1994), 708.

7. Georges Duby, *The Three Orders: Feudal Society Imagined,* trans. Arthur Goldhammer (Chicago and London: The University of Chicago Press, 1980). On the conflicts
between Gerard I and his vassals, see, in particular, Steffen Patzold, "*Inter pagensium nos-
trorum gladios vivimus.* Zu den Spielregeln der Konfliktführung in Niederlothringen zur
Zeit der Ottonen und frühen Salier," *Zeitschrift der Savigny-Stiftung für Rechtsgeschichte.
Germanistische Abteilung* 118 (2001): 66–82. On conflicts in the border county of Cambrai, see also Karen S. Nicholas, "When Feudal Ideals Failed: Conflicts between Lords and
Vassals in the Low Countries, 1127–1196," in *The Rusted Hauberk: Feudal Ideals of Order
and Their Decline,* ed. Liam O. Purdon and Cindy L. Vitto (Gainesville: University Press
of Florida, 1994), 206–8.

8. Benoît-Michel Tock and Ludo Milis, ed., *Monumenta Arroaensia,* Corpus Christianorum. Continuatio Mediaeualis 175 (Turnhout: Brepols, 2000), 230.

9. Benoît-Michel Tock, ed., *Les chartes de l'abbaye cistercienne de Vaucelles au
XIIe siècle* (Turnhout: Brepols, 2010), 177–78. Gertrude took the veil at the Benedictine
abbey of Messines in 1181.

10. On each of these marriages, see "*Gesta Lietberti episcopi,*" ed. Ludwig Bethmann,
Monumenta Germaniae Historica, Scriptores (in Folio) 7 (Hanover: Hahn, 1846), 495–96;
Jean-François Nieus, "Sigard's Belt: The Family of Chocques and the Borders of Knighthood (*ca.* 980–1100)," in the present volume; Michel Bur, *La formation du comté de Champagne, v. 950–v. 1150* (Nancy: Université de Nancy-II, 1977), 249. The marriage between
Hugh III of Oisy and Agatha of Pierrefonds inferred by the chronicler Gilbert of Mons
did not leave any trace in Hugh's charters and seems doubtful to me (Gilbert of Mons, *La
chronique de Gislebert de Mons,* ed. Léon Vanderkindere (Brussels: Kiessling, 1904), 136.

11. Ernst Warlop, *The Flemish Nobility before 1300,* 4 vols. (Kortrijk: Desmet-Huysman, 1976), 2: 659; Sébastien Ziegler, "Les origines de la ville de Bohain-en-Vermandois
dans l'Aisne," *Revue archéologique de Picardie* 3 (2006): 91–104, at 95.

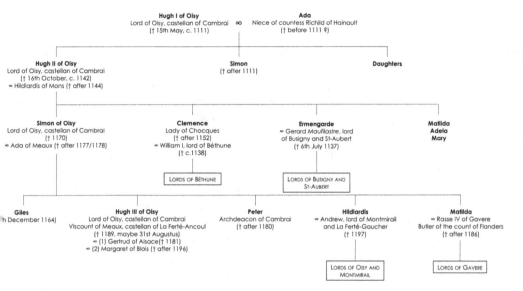

Fig. 10.1—The lords of Oisy, castellans of Cambrai (twelfth century).

Hugh was the only male heir to his father's lands in 1170 after the death of his elder brother Giles in a battle in 1164. His younger brother, Peter, was a canon of St Mary's cathedral church in Cambrai.[12] From the middle of the eleventh century, the Oisys' core estates were located in the tiny Lotharingian county of Cambrai, at the crossroads between the Kingdom of France, the German Empire, and the county of Flanders. Hugh held rights and estates in the north-western part of the principality, among which were his castles of Oisy and Inchy, and his castellanry in the episcopal city of Cambrai. There were other estates some fifteen kilometres to the south of the city, in the area in which his grandfather, Hugh II, had founded the Cistercian abbey of Vaucelles.[13] Hugh III was therefore, as his ancestors had been, one of the most prominent lay lords on the borders of France and the Empire. A large part of the nobility in Cambrésis seems to have been subor-

12. Lambert of Wattrelos, *"Annales Cameracenses,"* ed. Georg Heinrich Pertz, Monumenta Germaniae Historica, Scriptores (in Folio) 16 (Hanover: Hahn, 1859), 536; Tock, *Vaucelles*, 137–38.

13. On the foundation of Vaucelles, see Stéphane Lebecq, "Autour de la foundation de l'abbaye de Vaucelles. La charte de confirmation de l'évêque Liétard de Cambrai (1133)," *Revue belge de philologie et d'histoire* 89 (2011): 439–53 and Fulk of Cambrai, *La fondation de l'abbaye de Vaucelles*, ed. and trans. Benoît-Michel Tock, Les classiques de l'histoire de France au Moyen Âge 56 (Paris: Les Belles Lettres, 2016).

dinated to him, particularly in its western end. Charters reveal that he was surrounded by a group of knights who were drawn from the vicinity of Oisy. Furthermore, he had privileged relationships with several abbeys and secular chapters in Artois and in Cambrésis, like the Cistercians of Vaucelles, the Premonstratensians of Mont-Saint-Martin, the Benedictines of Anchin, and the regular canons of Cantimpré in Cambrai, an Augustinian abbey that he founded towards 1179.[14]

Because of his father's marriage with Viscountess Ada in 1147 at the latest, Hugh sometime towards 1180 inherited the viscounty of Meaux and the fortress of La Ferté-Ancoul (Fig. 10.4).[15] Thereafter, his estates were spread between the Cambrésis and Champagne. We can detect that the presence of the Oisy family in Champagne dates back to the middle of the twelfth century, as lord Simon of Oisy appears in the witness lists of Henry the Liberal's charters from 1152.[16] Hugh now became a comital fiefholder there.[17] Thanks to a few charters and the *Feoda Campanie* (1178), the count of Champagne's inventory of dependent landholders, we have an accurate view of the Oisys' properties in Champagne, which were mainly located near Meaux and La Ferté-Ancoul.[18] Moreover, these documents reveal that Hugh had to perform a full-time castle-guard (*annum custodie*) in Châtillon

---

14. Lille, Archives départementales du Nord, 37 H 1/1 and 37 H 131/114 and 116.

15. Ada's father, Viscount Godfrey of Meaux, died around 1152, but Hugh inherited the viscounty only after his mother's death, shortly before 1180 (Bur, *Formation*, 248). By the mid-1180s, Hugh's third seal matrix mentioned his title of viscount of Meaux on the counterseal (Nicolas Ruffini-Ronzani, "L'aristocratie cambrésienne et ses sceaux. Appropriation et diffusion de la pratique sigillaire entre France et Empire (mil. XIIᵉ–début XIIIᵉ siècle)," in *Le sceau dans les Pays-Bas méridionaux, Xᵉ–XVIᵉ siècles. Entre contrainte sociale et affirmation de soi*, ed. Marc Libert and Jean-François Nieus (Brussels: Archives et bibliothèques de Belgique, 2017), 157–183. The mention of a counterseal referring to Hugh's title of viscount in 1173 by Jean-Pierre Gerzaguet, *Les chartes de l'abbaye d'Anchin (1079–1201)* (Turnhout: Brepols, 2005), 266, is an error). On medieval Meaux, see Mickaël Wilmart, *Meaux au Moyen Âge. Une ville et ses hommes du XIIᵉ au XVᵉ siècle* (Montceaux-lès-Meaux: Éditions Fiacre, 2013).

16. John Benton and Michel Bur, ed., *Recueil des actes d'Henri le Libéral, comte de Champagne (1152–1181)*, 2 vols. (Paris: De Boccard, 2009–2013), 1: 31–32 and 260–61.

17. Theodore Evergates, *Henry the Liberal: Count of Champagne, 1127–1181* (Philadelphia: University of Pennsylvania Press, 2016), 34–35.

18. Benton and Bur, ed., *Recueil*, 19–20, 154–55, 572–73; Auguste Longnon, ed., *Documents relatifs au comté de Champagne et de Brie, 1172–1361*, 3 vols. (Paris: Imprimerie nationale, 1901–14), 1: 45 and 92. For an analysis of the *Feoda Campaniae*, see Theodore Evergates, *The Aristocracy in the County of Champagne, 1100–1300* (Philadelphia: University of Pennsylvania Press, 2007), 17–21.

and Fismes.[19] The Oisys promptly took advantage of their presence in Champagne to enlarge their networks. In such a context, they built up good relationships with some of the region's ecclesiastical institutions, like the priory of Collinances.[20] Hugh also arranged a marriage for his sister Hildiardis with the lords of Montmirail and La Ferté-Gaucher, one of the most powerful families in Champagne. She married Andrew of Montmirail sometime in the 1160s, and their son, John I, was eventually to be Hugh's sole heir after the Third Crusade.

Hugh appears as a more conciliatory and pacific lord in comparison with his ancestors. The Cambresian chronicles written in the second half of the twelfth century never present him as a warrior, but it must be admitted that these texts, mostly produced in the episcopal entourage, are less accurate and less critical than they were in the late eleventh and early twelfth centuries. Hugh's apparent military apathy could be explained by the political context. From the end of the 1150s until 1189 the Cambresian borderland was totally under the counts of Flanders' control. The marriage between Gertrude of Alsace and Hugh III sealed an alliance between the rulers of Flanders and the Oisys, not to mention the union between Matilda, Hugh's sister, and Rasse IV of Gavere, cupbearer to the count of Flanders. In 1167 and 1173, Thierry and Philip of Alsace were able to impose Peter, Thierry's youngest son, and Robert, provost of Aire and close adviser of Philip, on the episcopal see of Cambrai.[21] The counts of Flanders were in consequence the unquestionable masters of the Cambrésis during Hugh's lifetime. In such circumstances, the Flemish prince constituted a kind of model for the Oisys and, beyond them, all the Cambresian aristocracy. It appears, for instance, in the shared iconography of their seals from the mid-1180s.[22]

Owing to his relationship with Philip of Alsace, Hugh took part in the Third Crusade with the count in 1189, as well as so many Flemish and Artesian lords, such as Cono of Béthune, Baldwin II of Aire, and Hellin I of Wavrin.[23] As appears from a charter for the Benedictine abbey

19. Longnon, ed., *Documents*, 1: 22. It must be said, however, that Hugh's name does not appear in Henri I's charters.

20. Paris, Bibliothèque nationale de France, lat. 5528, fol. 10r–v; Benton and Bur, *Recueil*, 19–20 and 572–73.

21. The influence of Robert of Aire upon Count Philip of Alsace has been underlined by Adriaan Verhulst, "Un exemple de la politique économique de Philippe d'Alsace: la fondation de Gravelines (1163)," *Cahiers de civilisation médiévale* 10 (1967): 15–28, at 26–28.

22. Ruffini-Ronzani, "L'aristocratie cambrésienne," 162–63 and 166.

23. Hans Van Werveke, "La contribution de la Flandre et du Hainaut à la troisième croisade," *Le Moyen Âge* 78 (1972): 55–90.

of Anchin, Hugh made careful preparations for his military campaign in the Latin East.[24] As it turned out the expedition was nothing but a disaster for the Oisys. During the crusade some obscure tensions arose between Hugh and his former pupil and relative Cono of Béthune. In a brief and satirical *serventois* known as the *Maugré tous sainz et maugré Diu ausi* ("Despite all the saints and despite God himself")—written between 1189 and the departure of the king of France to the Latin East during the summer of 1190—Hugh appears particularly critical of Cono, whom he reproaches for his cowardice on the battlefield.[25] It is likely, nevertheless, that Cono and Hugh became reconciled before the latter's death, since Cono made a donation in memory of Hugh to the chapter of St Gaugericus in Cambrai in 1203.[26] Any other details of Hugh's military campaign are unfortunately lacking, but it is beyond any doubt that he died in the Orient towards 1190, and along with him his relative and companion Philip of Alsace (d. June 1191). As his two marriages were infertile, Hugh's estates and dignities fell to his nephew John I of Montmirail, the son of his sister Hildiardis.[27]

The *Tournoiement des dames*: Staging the French Aristocracy

Hugh's governance of Oisy and his other lands was marked by a growing use of the written word. Charter production increased continuously under his administration, as he created a kind of "chancery" during his lifetime.[28] His seal matrices were also more frequently updated than they were under his predecessors' regimes.[29] Moreover, as some of his northern-French contemporaries, such as Blondel of Nesle and

24. Gerzaguet, ed., *Chartes d'Anchin*, 346–47.

25. Joseph Bédier and Pierre Aubry, ed., *Les chansons de croisade* (Paris: Honoré Champion, 1909), 51–64. On this satirical poem, see Philipp August Becker, "Die Kreuzzuglieder von Conon de Béthune und Huon d'Oisi," *Zeitschrift für französische Sprache und Literatur*, 64 (1942): 305–12, at 308–12.

26. Lille, Archives départementales du Nord, 7 G 70/983 and 983bis.

27. The most recent survey on John I of Montmirail, his sanctity, and his burial at Longpont is Anne E. Lester, "The Coffret of John of Montmirail. The Sacred Politics of Reuse in Thirteenth-Century Northern France," *Peregrinations: Journal of Medieval Art and Architecture* 4 (2014): 50–86.

28. On the use of the written word by lay lords in the twelfth and thirteenth centuries, see Jean-François Nieus, "Des seigneurs sans chancellerie ? Pratiques de l'écrit documentaire chez les comtes et les barons du nord de la France aux XIIᵉ–XIIIᵉ siècles," *Bulletin de la Commission royale d'histoire* 176 (2010): 285–311.

29. Ruffini-Ronzani, "L'aristocratie cambrésienne," 162–63.

the anonymous *Chastelain de Couci*, Hugh was both a powerful lay lord and an acclaimed poet singing for courtly audiences. In his *Bien me deüsse targier de chançon faire* ("I really ought to give up making songs"), for instance, the notorious trouvère Cono of Béthune, a major figure in the twelfth-century poetic world, described Hugh, his relative, as his "master of Oisy who has taught me to sing since my childhood."[30] As some of his estates were in Champagne, and maybe because of his good reputation as a poet, Hugh probably performed his works far from his native Cambrésis. Even if his presence at the court of Champagne is never attested in the sources, it is more than likely that Hugh sang some of his poems there. As a vassal of the counts of Champagne, he was probably in a good position to perform his works at their court, which was one of the most important literary centres in the twelfth century.[31] In such circumstances, Hugh's presence in Meaux and La Ferté-Ancoul could explain why the northern French aristocracy plays a such an important role in his poetry, as we shall see.

The surviving works of the lord of Oisy—the *Tournoiement des dames* and the *Maugré tous sainz*—are to be found in two luxurious song-books in the Bibliothèque nationale de France. The first manuscript is known as the *Manuscrit du Roi* and was probably produced in Picardy during the second half of the thirteenth century, whereas the *Chansonnier de Noailles*, the second song-book, originates in Artois and dates from the last quarter of the thirteenth century. It leaves no doubt, however, that the two manuscripts were copied from the same exemplar, as they have several errors in common.[32] Of the two poems

30. Cono of Béthune, "Bien me Deüsse Targier de Chançon Faire," ed. Axel Wallen-sköld, in *Les chansons de Conon de Béthune* (Paris: Honoré Champion, 1921), 9: "a mon mastre d'Oissi, qui m'at apris a chanter tres m'anfance." English translations of some poems written by Cono of Béthune and Huon of Oisy are provided by Linda Patterson and Ruth Harvey, "Troubadours, Trouvères and the Crusades" (University of Warwick), accessed 1 March, 2018, http://www2.warwick.ac.uk/fac/arts/modernlanguages/research/french/crusades/. I make use of their translations in the present publication. Cono was the son of Robert V of Béthune, and the grandson of William I of Béthune and Clemence of Oisy (Warlop, *Flemish Nobility*, 659–60).

31. Several famous authors such as Simon Aurea Capra, Gace Brulé, and probably Chrétien of Troyes were present in Champagne under the government of Henry and his wife Mary, as it has been shown by Benton, "Court of Champagne," 561–63, 566–67, and 570. For a less enthusiastic view of the literary role of the court of Champagne, see Ever-gates, *Henry the Liberal*, 86–99, 119–23, and 145–47.

32. Paris, Bibliothèque nationale de France, fr. 844, *Manuscrit du Roi*, fols. 50r–51r; Ibid., fr. 12615, *Chansonnier de Noailles*, fols. 53r–54. On these manuscripts, see: Jean Beck and Louise Beck, *Le Manuscrit du Roi, fonds français 844 de la Bibliothèque nation-ale. Analyse et description raisonnée du manuscrit restauré*, 2 vols. (London: Milford,

written by Hugh, the *Tournoiement* is probably the more interesting as well as the more original, as it is the oldest text pertaining to the poetical genre of the *Tournoi aus Dames*.[33]

In the *Tournoiement des dames*, Hugh provides a detailed account of an imagined tournament that would have happened at Lagny-sur-Marne, some fifteen kilometres to the south-west of the viscounty of Meaux, at a crossroads between Champagne and the royal demesne.[34] In this satirical and humorous work, the competitors are not the prominent knights of northern France (the poet says that "in that year ... the knights were away")[35], but their wives. Each stanza of the *Tournoiement* narrates the brave deeds of these great ladies, who were largely drawn from the French aristocracy. By describing convincingly the tactics used by the "female knights," by reproducing their war cries, and by identifying, in one case, their coats of arms, Hugh pictures the fictional meeting of Lagny in a vivid and realistic way, as has been underlined by David Crouch.[36] Hugh's background could explain the realistic nature of the poem. In his accurate depictions of the practical aspects of the fight, the lord of Oisy is probably speaking from of his own experience as a tourneyer. It is likely that the *Tournoiement* echoes the realities which Hugh had experienced in his youth. Even if the twelfth-century sources never describe him in such a way, it seems

1938), 2: 37–38; Maria Carla Battelli, "Il codice Parigi, Bibl. nat. F. fr. 844: un canzonere disordinato ?," in *La filologia romanza e i codici. Atti del convegno, Messina, Università degli Studi, Facoltà di Lettere e filosofia, 19–22 dicembre 1991*, ed. Saverio Guida and Fortunata Latella, 2 vols. (Messina: Sicania, 1993), 1: 273–308; Daniel E. O'Sullivan, "Thibaut de Champagne and Lyric *Auctoritas* in Paris, BNF fr. 12615," *Textual Cultures* 8 (2013): 31–49. Eduard Schwan, *Die Altfranzösischen Liederhandschriften, ihr Verhältniss, ihre Entstehung und ihre Bestimmung. Eine litterarhistorische Untersuchung* (Berlin: Weidmann, 1886), gives a dry and detailed analysis of the different families of French song-books. I am grateful to Giovanni Palumbo for his help in the analysis of the manuscript tradition of the *Tournoiement des dames*.

33. Pulega, *Ludi e spettacoli*, ix–xi. A brief and incomplete *Tournoiement* written by Richard of Semilly is probably contemporary with Hugh's poem (Guy Muraille and Françoise Fery-Hue, "*Tournoiement des dames*," in *Dictionnaire des Lettres françaises*, 1443–44).

34. Alfred Jeanroy, ed., "Note sur le *Tournoiement des dames*," *Romania* 28 (1899): 240–44 (the French edition to which I refer in this paper); Pulega, *Ludi e spettacoli*, 3–9. For an English translation, see Crouch, *Tournament*, 167–71.

35. Jeanroy, ed., "Note," 240, lines 1–6: "En l'an que chevalier sont adaubi, ke d'armes noient ne font li hardi, lez dames tournoier vont a Laigni." Translation in Crouch, *Tournament*, 167. The poem specifies further down that the ladies "mustered in front of Torcy." Lagny and Torcy are neighboring localities.

36. Crouch, *Tournament*, 92 and 158.

beyond reasonable doubt that he took his pleasure at tournaments during his lifetime, as did so many other knights living in the Cambrésis.[37]

The *Tournoiement des dames* is above all a poem that represents the flourishing twelfth-century courtly society and its values, in the context of what Dominique Barthélemy provocatively calls a *"mutation ludique."*[38] It is striking, indeed, that the *Tournoiement* does not present any features which may be regarded as religious, other than the references to God and St Denis in the war cries *"Dex Aïe"* and *"Saint Denise"* shouted by two of the ladies.[39] Rather, it celebrates secular values by praising the merits of some of the most honourable French ladies. Just like the "real" knights on the tournament field, the "fictional" noble ladies demonstrate a competitive spirit, which is not surprising, as this was a key concern in knightly identity. Hugh clearly puts emphasis on the pursuit of prowess. Women are not held up to ridicule in the *Tournoiement*, in which they appear as skilful as their husbands. Despite the brevity of the poem, the passages highlighting the bravery of the "women knights" are numerous. For instance, the text describes Emily of L'Isle-Adam as "hardy," Mary of Champagne as a woman who "rides directly into the fight," and countess Isabel of Saint-Pol as a tourneyer who "attacks like a mad thing, crying over and over her war cry, 'Let's get them, Châtillon!'"[40] Using a humor-

37. Hugh's interest in tournaments was widely shared within the Cambresian nobility since the beginning of the twelfth century. Towards 1138, the anonymous author of the *Gesta Nicholai episcopi* evoked the death of Giles of Chin at a tournament. See *"Gesta Nicholai episcopi,"* ed. Georg Heinrich Pertz, Monumenta Germaniae Historica, Scriptores (in Folio) 14 (Hanover: Hahn, 1883), 236–37). Thirty years later, Walter of Honnecourt died also in a tournament in Maastricht, according to Gilbert of Mons, *Chronique*, 95. The case of Matthew of Walincourt is probably more famous and more interesting, as his name appears in the *History of William Marshal*, in which he is humiliated by the Marshal. See *History of William Marshal*, ed. Anthony J. Holden and David Crouch, trans. Stewart Gregory, 3 vols. (London: Anglo-Norman Text Society, 2002–6), 1: 164 and 170. Hugh of Hamelincourt is described as a companion of William Marshal in the same narrative. See Ibid., 2: 233, 339, 347, and 367. John I of Montmirail, Hugh's successor, is also described as a noble man who spent large amounts of money in tournaments before his monastic conversion. See *Vita Johannis de Monte Mirabili*, ed. Constantin Suysken, in *Acta Sanctorum*, Sept. VIII (Antwerp: Vander Plassche, 1762), 219.

38. Dominique Barthélemy, *La chevalerie. De la Germanie antique à la France du XIIe siècle* (Paris: Perrin, 2007), 329. For a more balanced opinion, see François Bougard, "Des jeux du cirque aux tournois: que reste-t-il de la compétition antique au haut Moyen Âge ?," in *Agôn*, ed. idem et al., 40–41.

39. Jeanroy, ed., "Note," 243, lines 135 and 162.

40. Ibid., 241–42, lines 26 ("Amisse au corz hardi"), 88 ("Touz lez encontre et atent"), 106–8 ("Ez lour fiert a bandon / Sovent crie s'ensaigne : 'Alom lour, Chastillon'"); Crouch, *Tournament*, 167–69.

Fig. 10.2—Counterseal of Gerard II of Saint-Aubert. Lille, Archives Départementales du Nord, 28 H 46/1204 (1194).

Fig. 10.3—Seal of Cono of Béthune. Lille, Archives Départementales du Nord, 7 G 70/983 (1203).

ous distorting prism in order to amuse his audience, Hugh depicts the so-called "weaker sex" in a transgressive position. In a similar way as the thirteenth-century *Frauenturnier* analysed by Albrecht Classen, the *Tournoiement* suggests "that men do not have a guaranteed position of dominance in society."[41]

Therefore, by describing this fantastic and eccentric tournament, Hugh emphasises the role of women in courtly milieus, in which the relationships between the sexes were an important topic. Moreover, he demonstrates that the martial meetings were not an entirely male affair.[42] Some women probably had a real passion for tournaments, which they attended with their husbands and friends. Flirtation played a major role in such events, as appears in the very first lines of the *Tournoiement*, where it is said that the fictional ladies "wanted to experience the sort of strokes that their lovers gave out for their

41. Albrecht Classen, "Masculine Women and Female Men: The Gender Debate in Medieval Courtly Literature. With an Emphasis on the Middle High German Verse Narrative *Frauenturnier*," *Mittellateinisches Jahrbuch* 43 (2008): 205–22, at 222. For a feminist analysis of the *Tournoiement*, see Helen Solterer, "Figures of Female Militancy in Medieval France," *Signs* 16 (1990): 522–49. On the German *Frauenturnier*, see also Ute Von Bloh, "Heimliche Kämpfe. Frauenturniere in mittelalterlichen Märe," *Beiträge zur Geschichte der deutschen Sprache und Literatur* 121 (1999): 214–38.

42. Crouch, *Tournament*, 156–59.

sake."[43] There is no doubt that Hugh's values and ideals were widely shared by the aristocracy at the borders of France and the Empire, as appears, for instance, through the seals of Cono of Béthune and Gerard of Saint-Aubert, on which these two of Hugh's relatives chose to be depicted as noble poets trying to seduce a lady (Figs. 10.2 and 10.3).

The *Tournoiement* is undated, but it is likely that the lord of Oisy wrote it after his marriage with Margaret of Blois (*ca.* 1185), and before the disastrous expedition to the Latin East in 1189, perhaps during the wars between Philip II of France and Henry II Plantagenet in 1187–89, as suggested by David Crouch.[44] More specifically, we can reasonably hypothesise that the text was composed only shortly before Hugh's departure for the Third Crusade, or even on his way to Palestine,[45] as the presence of Ida of Boulogne in the poem could be explained by her marriage with Renaud of Dammartin towards 1188.[46] The table below demonstrates that the thirty-four ladies mentioned in the *Tournoiement* were all real women belonging to the French aristocracy during the last years of Hugh's lifetime (Table 10.1).[47] The map

43. Jeanroy, ed., "Note," 241, lines 10–13: "Dient que savoir voudront quel li colp sont que pour eles font lour ami." Crouch, *Tournament*, 167.

44. Ibid., 167.

45. It is interesting to note that, towards 1200, a tournament was organized "somewhere between Bray and Encre" just before the departure for the Latin East of the tourneyers. Count Baldwin IX of Flanders, the Flemish nobility, and some French barons such as the count of Blois took part in that competition, according to the *Chronique d'Ernoul et de Bernard le Trésorier*, ed. Louis de Mas Latrie (Paris: Société de l'histoire de France, 1871), 337. Therefore, crusade and tournament may have been closely linked at the end of the twelfth century. I am grateful to Jean-François Nieus for his remarks on the chronicle of Ernoul and Bernard the Treasurer.

46. The marriage between Ida of Boulogne and Renaud of Dammartin is undated by Lambert of Ardres, *Historia comitum Ghisnensium*, ed. Johannes Heller, Monumenta Germaniae Historica, Scriptores (in Folio) 24 (Hanover: Hahn, 1879), 605, but Georges Poull situated it towards 1188–89 in *La Maison souveraine et ducale de Bar* (Nancy: Presses universitaires de Nancy, 1994), 132. Renaud was a close ally to King Philip II Augustus at the end of the 1180s. See Nicolas Civel, *La fleur de France. Les seigneurs d'Île-de-France au XIIe siècle* (Turnhout: Brepols, 2006), 126. My thanks to Jean-François Nieus for his remarks on Lambert of Ardres and Ida's marriage.

47. The case of Countess Isabel / Elisabeth of Saint-Pol, who is described as Isabel of Châtillon in the poem, is nevertheless problematical, as her marriage with Walcher of Châtillon happened towards 1196, that is to say seven years after Hugh's death (Jeanroy, ed., "Note," 242, lines 104–8). In 1189, Isabel was only ten years at the most; see Jean-François Nieus, "Élisabeth Candavène, comtesse de Saint-Pol († 1240/47): une héritière face à la Couronne," in *Femmes de pouvoir, femmes politiques durant les derniers siècles du Moyen Âge et au cours de la première Renaissance*, ed. Éric Bousmar et al. (Brussels: De Boeck, 2012), 187–88. In such circumstances, how could we explain her presence in the poem? Neither André Duchesne nor Theodore Evergates make mention of another "Isabel" in the Châtillon family at the end of twelfth century. See André Duchesne, *His-*

below—on which the dots represent the geographical origins of the ladies' husbands, when they are known, or, otherwise, their own birth-places—reveals that most of the "dames" evoked by Hugh came from Île-de-France and southern Picardy, that is to say from Philip Augustus's royal demesne. Another group among the lady tourneyers came from Champagne or the northern borders of the county of Blois, from where Hugh's wife originated. It is as if Hugh's aim was to enhance the image of the Capetian French upper aristocracy, a group that probably constituted the audience for whom Hugh wrote his song.

The question of the audience of the *Tournoiement* is necessarily linked to the problem of its performance. There has been speculation about the way Hugh's lyrical poem was sung in the twelfth century. In 1970, the Italian philologist Andrea Pulega developed the idea that the text was performed as a play by the greatest ladies mentioned in the text.[48] I do not share Pulega's opinion. In my view, it is more likely that the *Tournoiement* was sung in public by its author, maybe when there was a banquet after a "real" tournament—possibly in Lagny. The reference to Lagny in the *Tournament* is probably not coincidental, as a great tournament was held there in 1179.[49] As David Crouch has suggested, Hugh's work "may even be such a song composed for the evening after the tournament, written to amuse both the male participants and the female onlookers with a topsy-turvy mirror version of what they had just been experiencing in the field."[50] It is tempting, therefore, to conjecture that Hugh may have performed his song at the court of Champagne, or elsewhere in the French realm, in the presence of the "real" ladies of the poem, and also in front of their husbands.[51]

toire de la Maison de Chastillon sur Marne (Paris: Cramoisy, 1621), 23–44; Evergates, *Aristocracy*, 254. Furthermore, it is unlikely that the thirteenth-century manuscript copies of the *Tournoiement* have been interpolated or changed, given the extremely complex metrical structure of the poem (Jeanroy, ed., "Note," 238–40). In such a context, I think that Isabel's presence in the poem could be explained by a possible betrothal between her and Walcher of Châtillon before 1189. My hypothesis is that the union between the powerful families of St-Pol and Châtillon had been prepared since Isabel's childhood. As a *custos* at the Châtillon castle in the 1180s, Hugh might have been well informed of the situation. See Longnon, *Documents*, 1: 22.

48. Pulega, *Ludi e spettacoli*, xxiv–xxviii.

49. See, for instance, Matthew Strickland, *Henry the Young King, 1155–1183* (New Haven and London: Yale University Press, 2016), 242–44 and *William Marshal*, ed. Holden, 3: 84–85.

50. Crouch, *Tournament*, 109 and 158.

51. In northern France, as in southern, twelfth-century poets wrote for the aristocracy, see Aurell, *Chevalier lettré*, 116–38.

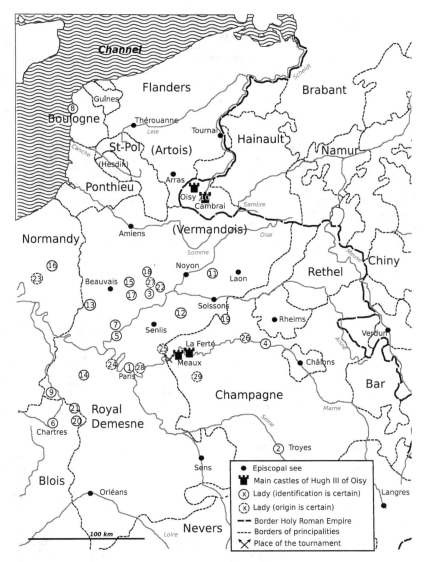

Fig. 10.4—The ladies in Hugh of Oisy's *Tournoiement des dames* (1185–89).

Consequently, we can suggest further that Hugh was using his poetry as a political tool to charm potential new allies belonging to the French upper aristocracy as much as to establish his own reputation as a poet and arbiter of culture.

Table 10.1—The ladies in Hugh of *Oisy's Tournoiement des dames* (1185–89).

Ladies whose identification is certain		
1. *Ysabel, ki ferir* [...] *La roïne sour Ferrant* (l. 51 and 64) Isabel of Hainaut, wife of Philip II Augustus, king of France	2. *La contesse de Canpaigne* (l. 82) Mary of France, wife of Henri I the Liberal, count of Champagne	3. *La contesse de Clermont* (l. 117) Adele of Breteuil, wife of Raoul I, count of Clermont
4. *Ysabiauz, che savon* [...] *sovent crie s'ensaigne "Alom lour, Chastillon"* (l. 104 and 107–8) Isabel of St-Pol, wife of Walcher, lord of Châtillon	5. *La contesse de Crespi* (l. 8) Elanor of Vermandois, wife of Matthew III, lord of Beaumont	6. *Katherine au viz cler* [...] *Et "Passe avant" a crier* (l. 34–35) Katherine of Clermont, wife of Louis, count of Blois and Chartres
7. *Ade de Parcais les voit, "Biaumont" crioit* (l. 180–81) Ada, wife of Hugh II, lord of Persan, viscount of Beaumont	8. *Quant "Bouloigne" escria Yde au cors honoré* (l. 130–31) Ida of Boulogne, widow of Berthold V of Zähringen, and wife of Renaud, count of Dammartin	9. *De le prohece Yolent vous diré* (l. 194–95) Yolanda of Coucy, wife of Robert II, count of Dreux
10. *Margerite d'Oysi* (l. 24) Margaret of Blois, wife of Hugh III, lord of Oisy, castellan of Cambrai	11. *Et ma dame de Couci* (l. 9) Alice of Dreux, wife of Raoul I, lord of Coucy	12. *Adeline ki "Nantuel" vait criant* (l. 57–58) Adeline of Nanteuil, wife of Philip I, lord of Crépy
13. *Aeliz en vait devant de Trie, "Aguillon" criant* (l. 61–62) Alice of Dammartin, wife of John I, lord of Trie	14. *Aeliz "Monfort" criant* (l. 95) Alice of Montmorency, wife of Simon V, lord of Montfort	15. *Amice* [...] *"Lille" crie* (l. 110–15) Amilie of Milly, wife of Manasses of l'Isle-Adam and Rémérangles
16. *Climense* [...] *"Biausart" cria* (l. 122–25) Clemence of Breteuil, wife of Simon, lord of Beaussault	17. *Gertrus qui "Merlou" cria* (l. 143) Gertrude of Nesle, wife of Renaud, lord of Mello	18. *Agnes de Triecoc* (l. 145) Agnès, wife of Peter II, lord of Tricot
19. *Et Joie point d'Arsi* (l. 157) Joie of Arcy, wife of Guy, knight of Arcy-Sainte-Restitue	20. *Et fier Ysabel d'Ausnai* (l. 171) Isabel of Auneau, wife of Guy, lord of Aunay-sous-Auneau	21. *Belle Aelis qui "Garlandon" escrioit* (l. 175–76) Alice of Châteaudun, wife of Hervé III, lord of Gallardon
22. *Agnes i vi venir tost de Cressonessart* (l. 184–85) Agnes of Cressonsacq, wife of Dreux II, lord of Cressonsacq		

Ladies whose origins are certain		
23. *Yolenz de Cailli* (l. 22) Cailly: reg. Normandy, dep. Seine-Maritime	24. *Beatris « Poissi » cria* (l. 153) Poissy: reg. Île-de-France, dep. Yvelines	25. *Mariien de Juilli* (l. 159) Juilly: reg. Île-de-France, dep. Seine-et-Marne
26. *Aelis de Rolleïz* (l. 165) Reuilly-Sauvigny: reg. Hauts-de-France, dep. Aisne	27. *Sezile vint tout a droit de Conpeigne* (l. 169–70) Compiègne: reg. Hauts-de-France, dep. Oise	28. *Agnes venoit criant « Paris »* (l. 178–79) Paris: reg. Île-de-France
29. *Ysabiauz point aussi qui 'st de Villegaignart* (l. 186–87) Villegagnon: reg. Île-de-France, dep. Seine-et-Marne		
Unidentified ladies		
Jehane la gaaignant (l. 72)	*Aeliz [...] de Monciauz* (l. 76–77)	*Ysabiaus point de Marli* (l. 138)
Climence [...] de Bruai (l. 168)		

Bibliography: mainly Holger Petersen Dyggve, "Les dames du *Tournoiement* d'Huon d'Oisi," *Neuphilologische Mitteilungen* 36 (1935): 65–84, and Pulega, *Ludi e spettacoli*, 90–97, whose works should be complemented with Dominique Barthélemy, *Les deux âges de la seigneurie banale. Pouvoir et société dans la terre des sires de Coucy (milieu XIe – milieu XIIIe siècle)* (Paris: Publications de la Sorbonne, 1984), 56–57 and 111 (Coucy, Dreux); Civel, *Fleur de France*, 424–25, 430–31, 439, and 450–51 (Auneau, Beaumont, Dammartin, L'Isle-Adam, Monfort); Penny Eley, *Partonopeus de Blois: Romance in the Making* (Cambridge: D.S. Brewer, 2011), 192, n. 23 (Blois); Evergates, *Aristocracy*, 248 and 254 (Champagne, Châtillon); Lambert of Ardres, "*Historia*," 605 (Boulogne); William Mendel Newman, *Les seigneurs de Nesle en Picardie (XIIe – XIIIe siècle). Leurs chartes et leur histoire* (Paris: Picard, 1971), 81–88, 178–79, and 273–74 (Mello, Arcy, L'Isle-Adam); Nieus, "Élisabeth Candavène," 187–88 (Châtillon); Holger Petersen Dyggve, "L'Yolent à l'écu déchiqueté du *Tournoiemenet* de Huon d'Oisi," *Neuphilologische Mitteilungen* 37 (1936): 257–61 (Dreux); idem, "Deux dames du *Tournoiement* d'Huon d'Oisi," *Neuphilologische Mitteilungen* 41 (1940): 157–80 (Tricot, Beausart); Poull, *Maison souveraine et ducale*, 132 (Boulogne, Dammartin); Detlev Schwennicke, ed., *Das feudale Frankreich und sein Einfluss auf die Welt des Mittelalters. Stammtafeln zur Geschichte der Europäischen Staaten*, vol. 3/4 of *Europäische Stammtafeln* (Marburg: Stargradt, 1989), table 690 (Gallardon).

The *Tournoiement des dames* is, in my view, more than just the humorous description of an imagined competition for love and fame. In Hugh's work politics and poetry were closely linked. According to Florian Mazel, twelfth-century princes were keen on increasing the cultural influence of their court, and therefore their own authority, by attracting the most famous poets of their times.[52] The text can be regarded as a means Hugh used to win renown in the competitive courtly society of his day. It seems unlikely that Hugh was in search of a patron, as he was one of the most prominent lords at the borders of France and Empire. But we can assume that, by writing his lyric poem for a noble French audience, the objective of the lord of Oisy was to enlarge, or to reinforce, his networks in an area in which his family had not been established for all that long.

Given the geographical origins of the ladies in the *Tournoiement* (Fig. 10.4 and Table 10.1), it appears that Hugh's intended audience was mainly the French elites that surrounded the young Philip II Augustus in the second half of the 1180s, and not Hugh's traditional allies from Flanders and Lower Lotharingia. Lyric poetry, and humour, may have been used here as a mechanism for integrating himself into a lay aristocracy with which Hugh had only a few ties. Even if his efforts ultimately came to nothing because of his untimely death in the Orient, we cannot exclude the possibility that Hugh made use of his poetical talents in the hope of integrating into the entourage of the French king, whose authority was inexorably growing at the end of the twelfth century. Thanks to the works of Michel Bur, we know that Philip Augustus was developing a policy of friendship with the Champagne during the second half of the 1180s, in the political context of the wars against his Plantagenet rivals.[53] His relationship with the count of Flanders was more complicated. With the Peace of Boves (July 1185), a few years after the death of the Flemish Countess Elisabeth of Vermandois, the king humiliated his rival Philip of Alsace by depriving him of all his influence within the greater part of the Vermandois.[54] In such a context, it is therefore all but impossible that Hugh—who probably had a clear view of the situation, as his patri-

52. Florian Mazel, "La compétition chevaleresque dans la poésie de langue d'oc (XIIᵉ–XIIIᵉ siècles)," in *Agôn*, ed. Bougard et al., 177–78.

53. It seems, indeed, that Mary of Champagne and her relatives remained faithful to the king during the war against the Plantagenets and after Philip's departure for the Latin East in 1190. According to Michel Bur, Champagne fell into Philip's power only after the death of Theobald III in 1201: Michel Bur, "Rôle et place de la Champagne dans le royaume de France au temps de Philippe Auguste," in *La France de Philippe Auguste: le temps des mutations. Actes du colloque international organisé par le CNRS (Paris, 19 septembre–4 octobre 1980)*, ed. Robert-Henri Bautier (Paris: Éditions du CNRS, 1982), 248–51.

54. Thérèse de Hemptinne, "Aspects des relations de Philippe Auguste avec la Flandre au temps de Philippe d'Alsace," in ibid., 258–61; John W. Baldwin, *Philippe Auguste et son gouvernement. Les fondations du pouvoir royal en France au Moyen Âge* (Paris: Fayard, 1991), 50.

mony was shared between Champagne, Artois, and Cambrésis—could not have felt that a change was coming in France during the rule of Philip Augustus. As a talented political animal, Hugh must have been ambitious to insinuate himself into the Capetian court. Poetry would have helped him to achieve his goals.[55] According to his somewhat laudatory *Vita*, John I of Montmirail, Hugh's heir apparent in 1189, was also close to Philip Augustus towards the end of the 1180s and the beginning of the 1190s.[56] However, soon after his departure for the Latin East he suffered a setback in this regard. In 1189, Hugh's last poem reveals that he felt some bitterness towards Philip, whom he accused of being a "failed king" who must be "counted among the cowards" because he did not take part in the Third Crusade.[57]

Conclusion

Written by a castellan of Cambrai at the beginning of the 1180s, the *Tournoiement des dames* is an example of the blossoming of lay and vernacular culture in the second half of the twelfth century. More-

55. My interpretation of Hugh's main work differs from the explanations of Sophie Cassagne-Brouquet, *Chevaleresses: une chevalerie au féminin* (Paris: Perrin, 2013), who reads the poem as a plea for tournaments at a time when their *raison d'être* would have been questioned.

56. *Vita Johannis*, 224–25: "Est etiam memoriae commendandum, quod Johannes, cum sub glorioso Francorum rege Philippo militaret, a quo non sicut a caeteris de Montemirabili sed Johannes "Probitas" vocabatur, justissimarum ratione causarum ab ipso rege plurimum diligebatur. Nec immerito, quippe qui toties ei utilis et necessarius erat. Fuit autem in praelio Normanniae, quod commisit rex Francorum adversus regem Angliae apud castrum cui nomen est Gisortium…" ("We shall also commit to memory that John, while he was waging war under Philip, the glorious king of the French – by whom he was called John 'Probity', and not John of Montmirail like he was called by the others –, was highly esteemed by this king for very good reasons. This was deserved, because John was serviceable and indispensable to him so many times. He was present during a battle in Normandy which the king of the French led against the king of England near a castle which name is Gisors…"). These statements seem doubtful to me, but they are accepted by Civel, *Fleur de France*, 400–1.

57. Bédier and Aubry, ed., *Chansons de croisade*, 62–63: "Ne chantez mais, Quenes, je vouz en pri, / Car voz chançons ne sont mès avenanz. / Or menrez vous honteuse vie ci; / Ne vousistez por Diu morir joianz. / Or vous conte on avoec les recreanz, / Si remaindroiz avoec vo roi failli. / Ja Damediex, qui seur touz est puissanz, / Du roi avant et de vouz n'ait merci!" (trans. Patterson and Harvey, "Troubadours": "Sing no more, Cono, I pray you, for your songs are no more pleasing. Now you will live a shameful life here; you did not choose to die joyfully for God, and now you are counted among the cowards, so you will stay here with your failed king. May Our Lord, who has power over all people, have no pity, first on the king and [then] on you!" However, this sarcastic poem could be no more than the part of a literary game between Hugh and his relative.

over, it offers us new light on the biographical itinerary of Hugh III
of Oisy. Contrary to charter evidence, poetry does not picture him as
a pious and powerful lord exerting authority between Flanders and
Lower Lotharingia, giving to the religious communities, and moving
in Flemish circles. On the contrary, the analysis of his works indicates
that at the end of the 1180s, only a few months before his final departure for the Latin East, Hugh was keen to integrate into the Capetian
upper aristocracy, in the context of the continuing rise in power of
King Philip II Augustus. By celebrating bravery and physical strength
in a humorous way, the lord of Oisy may have been trying to charm
and curry favour with potential new allies, at a time when his traditional ally and relative, Count Philip of Alsace, was facing some
difficulties in Flanders. The *Tournoiement* illustrates therefore how
the knightly identity was growing more and more complex at the end
of the twelfth century, to such an extent that poetical art and politics
became closely linked.

— Part V —

DIDACTICS OF CHIVALRY

Claudia WITTIG

TEACHING CHIVALRY IN THE EMPIRE (*CA*. 1150–1250)

Chivalry as a code of conduct was adopted by the medieval secular elites from the mid-twelfth century onwards. Due to the specific social stratification within the Empire the chivalric ideal became particularly attractive for the lower nobility. This chapter argues that the norms and values associated with chivalry were consciously promoted to an audience of lower ranking secular elites, including former ministeriales. *Vernacular didactic literature bears witness to the teaching of chivalry in the thirteenth century. In these texts we can trace the development of a chivalric vocabulary, and comprehend which image of knighthood and chivalry didactic authors aimed to promote. Texts such as* Der Welsche Gast *offer guidelines to chivalry, while others such as* Der Winsbecke *address the benefits of a chivalric lifestyle, both for one's reputation in society and for one's eternal soul. The chapter shows that identification with chivalric ideals provided lower ranking elites with means of improving their social standing, legitimising their position between service and lordship and associating themselves with the great ones of the Empire.*

The phenomenon we call chivalry becomes visible in the sources from the mid-twelfth century onwards, when the elites in Western Europe found themselves faced with a variety of changes—political, social, intellectual, and economical—that forced them to redefine their status and function in the world.[1] European elites were increasingly concerned with good conduct, morality, and self-representation. It is in this historical moment of shifting boundaries and stratifying elite groups that the notion of a *militia Christi* comes to be increasingly adopted among those who have the prerogative to carry arms. While the ideal of the fighter in the service of Christ was already being promoted during the time of the First and Second Crusades, it really becomes part of the elite warrior's self-representation in the later twelfth century, precisely when the changes in the social composition of the nobility created the need to define the status and identity of a large and powerful group of people.[2] This is the time when chivalry begins to develop as a code of

---

1. Cf. Thomas N. Bisson, *The Crisis of the Twelfth Century. Power, Lordship, and the Origins of European Government* (Princeton and Oxford: Princeton University Press, 2009).
2. Richard W. Kaeuper, *Holy Warriors. The Religious Ideology of Chivalry* (Philadelphia: University of Pennsylvania Press, 2009), 94–115.

conduct and a social ideal tailored for an elitist but functional group that combined, with different focus, Christian ideals with warrior ethics, and an urge for self-perfection with modes of representation taken from the fashionable courts of England and France.

As a concept, chivalry is deeply rooted in its historical context. In the Holy Roman Empire, as this chapter will argue, it responded to the issues, insecurities and conflicting requirements of the lower ranks of the secular elites to which adoption of chivalric ideals offered opportunities to increase their reputation and elevate their social prestige. Because of its rootedness in specific historical conditions, chivalry is often presented in academic literature as if it simply emerged organically from previous notions of ethical behaviour.[3] However, it was also consciously constructed, promoted and disseminated by a variety of means, not least by a group of prescriptive texts which aimed to regulate the behaviour and to influence the value system of their specific audiences.

From the eleventh century onwards, German aristocrats began to rely on a group of specially trained servants for administration and military service. This *ministerium* exempted the latter from their usual duties and allowed them to use a fief for their services.[4] The term *milites,* which in the eleventh century could refer to the role of fighters and vassals of any rank, came to refer to a group of warriors positioned between the free (*liberi*) and the servants (*servientes*). This led to a convergence of *miles* and *ministerialis* in sources from the Empire, and by the twelfth century both terms were often used synonymously.[5] Due to their military and administrative responsibilities, these *ministeriales* gained privileges and sometimes significant influence at the courts, accumulated some wealth and eventually became all but indistinguishable from the lower nobility of the Empire.[6]

3. For example in the influential works by Maurice Keen, *Chivalry* (New Haven: Yale University Press, 1984) and more recently by Richard W. Kaeuper, *Medieval Chivalry* (Cambridge: Cambridge University Press, 2016) who both analyse the phenomenon in profound ways but without acknowledging the conscious efforts made towards chivalry's promotion and dissemination.

4. An excellent analysis of the development of German *ministeriales* and their role in the administration of the Empire is offered by Jan Keupp, *Dienst und Verdienst. Die Ministerialen Friedrich Barbarossa und Heinrichs VI.* (Stuttgart: Hiersemann, 2002); see also Benjamin Arnold, *German Knighthood, 1050–1300* (Oxford: Clarendon Press, 1985). Specifically on knighthood, see Jörg Peltzer, "Knigthood in the Empire" in this volume.

5. Keupp, *Dienst und Verdienst,* 53.

6. Josef Fleckenstein, "Die Entstehung des niederen Adels und das Rittertum," in *Herrschaft und Stand. Untersuchungen zur Sozialgeschichte im 13. Jahrhundert,* ed.

Part of the self-representation of the secular elites consisted of cultural patronage, visible not only in works of religious art and architecture, but also in an increasing number of literary works commissioned at the courts, often in the vernacular languages.[7] The degree to which knights participated in cultural patronage and even became authors of vernacular texts is debated, but we clearly find that knighthood is very present in vernacular secular literature.[8] David Crouch, in the next and last chapter of this volume, emphasises the role of vernacular conduct literature in promoting superior conduct to lay audiences in Occitan- and French-speaking areas. But early German literature likewise produced a group of texts that consciously promoted superior conduct and presented chivalry as a model. It is in these didactic texts that we can trace the appeal of a chivalric identity for an elite group that was nonetheless defined by its service to and dependency on its lords. For *ministeriales* and lower nobles, this literature provided a model which allowed them to understand their service as part of an ennobling ideal. This ideal integrated aspects of service but also of lordship, courtly conduct, military prowess and a glamorous lifestyle. Chivalry became part of a larger noble value system that treasured good conduct and refined manners, but it also presented noblemen as protectors of the weak, and hence it became adopted by the highest ranking members of the secular elites as well.[9] Men from all ranks of the secular elite, from the *ministerialis* to the king, could subscribe to the chivalric ideal and use it for their own self-representation.

This chapter explores the construction and dissemination of the ideal of chivalry in didactic texts written in the German vernacular between

Josef Fleckenstein (Göttingen: Vandenhoeck und Ruprecht, 1977), 17–39. Fundamental for the development of the German nobility are the works by Werner Hechberger, *Adel im fränkisch-deutschen Mittelalter. Zur Anatomie eines Forschungsproblems* (Ostfildern: Thorbecke, 2005).

7. Joachim Bumke, *Mäzene im Mittelalter. Die Gönner und Auftraggeber der höfischen Literatur in Deutschland 1150–1300* (Munich: Beck, 1979).

8. The term *Ritterdichtung* ("knightly poetry") became widely used in the early scholarship on medieval German literature as knights (the term used equivalent to *ministeriales*) were assumed to be its major carriers—authors as well as audience. Paul Kluckhohn, "Ministerialität und Ritterdichtung," *Zeitschrift für deutsches Altertum und Literatur* 52 (1910): 135–68. Since the comprehensive studies by Joachim Bumke this image has become much more nuanced, granting higher and lower nobility as well as clerics each their spheres of influence in the high medieval vernacular literature. Bumke, *Mäzene*. In particular on the role of clerics, see Timo Reuvekamp-Felber, *Volkssprache zwischen Stift und Hof: Hofgeistliche in Literatur und Gesellschaft des 12. und 13. Jahrhunderts* (Köln: Böhlau, 2003).

9. Cf. Peltzer, "Knighthood in the Empire," in this volume.

ca. 1150 and 1250, with a particular focus on a couple of early thirteenth-century poems. These texts, composed by clerical authors for lay audiences, aimed to construct and teach a particular image of chivalry that integrated the chivalrous knight into the divine order of the world. We will examine here why this clerical perspective might have appealed to the lower ranks of the secular elites in the Empire and how it positioned them in the courtly society.

In the first part of this chapter, I will introduce the Middle High German terminology used in the context of chivalry and some important vernacular texts that actively promoted the ideal in the twelfth and early thirteenth centuries. Next, I will analyse how knighthood and chivalry are represented in *Der Welsche Gast*, the most comprehensive and widely-transmitted didactic text, and which roles its author ascribed to the knights. In the last part, I will examine what appeal chivalry as a model could have to lay audiences and for the positioning of knights in the divine order of the world. By this I wish to show that chivalry provided a model that especially allowed the lower strata of the aristocracy to fashion an identity that accommodated their social function and associated them with the highest ideals of noble society.

Texts and terminology

The complications scholars face when attempting to define terms such as "knights", "knighthood" and "chivalry" is that they not only mean different things in different languages—or have no clear equivalent in another language at all— but also that the concepts behind the words could differ even within one linguistic area and period, from author to author. As the editors of this volume explain in the Introduction, the dominant modern sense of chivalry as a moral-ethical code was not established in European scholarship until the 1740s. Middle High German for its part does not distinguish between knighthood and chivalry, as modern English does. In Middle High German texts, the words *rîter* and *ritter* occur during the twelfth century, apparently without any semantic differentiation.[10] *Ritter* appears as a gloss for the Latin word *miles* and less frequently for *eques*. Apparently, a term for a warrior

---

10. Recorded spellings are *riter, ritter, rittar* or *ritir*, though by the mid-twelfth century *ritter* has become the most frequently used form. Throughout this chapter, I will use the spelling *ritter* unless recorded otherwise in the manuscripts.

was needed that was more neutral and prosaic than the older, poetic words *recke, wîgant, degen* or *helt* that had a glorifying overtone.[11] The first texts to transmit the term were, accordingly, not the heroic epics, but religious texts from the late eleventh and early twelfth centuries.[12] However, the term *ritter* soon developed the flavour of a cultural and educational ideal. While it is most often used for *ministeriales* and lower nobles, especially in the early Middle High German texts, from the end of the twelfth century it can encompass magnates and kings if the qualities associated with the chivalric ideal are meant to be highlighted.[13]

When writing about knighthood, high medieval authors often take for granted that their audiences already have an understanding of what is meant by the terminology they deploy. If they give an explanation nonetheless, it is to emphasise one particular aspect of the concept or to offer a particular interpretation of the pre-existing image their audiences might have. Therefore it is worthwhile not just to see what authors say knighthood (*ritterschaft*) is, but also to pay attention to the specific vocabulary they are using. The texts discussed in this chapter are the earliest didactic texts in the German vernacular that address the question of moral conduct specifically amongst mounted warriors and therefore offer insights into the establishment of a vocabulary of knighthood and chivalry in a didactic context.

The earliest secular didactic text that seems particularly to instruct a warrior of some status is commonly called the *Rittersitte* ("The Manners of a Knight"). It is a short poem composed probably around or shortly after 1150 and transmitted only fragmentarily.[14] The instruc-

11. Joachim Bumke, *Studien zum Ritterbegriff im 12. und 13. Jahrhundert*, 2nd ed. (Heidelberg: Winter, 1977), 20–21; English translation *The Concept of Knighthood in the Middle Ages*, trans. W.T.H. Jackson and E. Jackson (New York: Ams Press, 1982), 28.

12. Bumke, *Studien*, 29 lists the *Wiener Genesis* from *ca.* 1060 as the earliest record of the word *ritter*. The first epic text that uses the term is the Middle High German *Rolandslied* from 1145.

13. Bumke, *Studien*, 88–89.

14. The poem contains 82 lines and can be found in Vienna, Österreichische Nationalbibliothek, MS 2871 Adligat, fol. 5v. The edition of the text by Hermann Menhardt, "Rittersitte. Ein rheinfränkisches Lehrgedicht des 12. Jahrhunderts," *Zeitschrift für deutsches Altertum* 68 (1931): 153–63 (poem at 160–62), is still most widely used, despite its many flaws. Menhardt's reading of the manuscript is in parts erroneous. More significantly, his conjectures as well as those provided by his supervisor, Konrad Zwierzina, who never consulted the actual manuscript, are strongly coloured by a romanticised image of knighthood. For a new transcription of the text and a discussion of its contexts, see now Claudia Wittig, "Fragments of Didacticism: The Early Middle High German poems 'Rittersitte' and 'Der heimliche Bote,'" in *Prodesse et delectare. Fallstudien zur didaktischen Literatur des*

tion begins with a religious theme, connects lineage (*gislahti*) to the quality of honour (*ere*), and discusses women, warfare, friendship and hospitality. It mentions repentance and fidelity—*riuwe* and *triuwe*—two central aspects of secular and religious life in the German aristocratic society of the twelfth century, and closes by emphasising the pursuit of victories—all topics we find in later texts for the instruction of knights.[15] The word *ritter*, however, does not actually appear in the poem—the modern title is therefore misleading. Instead we find the word *tegen*, an older German term designating a warrior or hero. Do we have a witness here for the instruction in chivalry *avant la lettre*?[16] It seems that this poem testifies to the existence of a code of conduct for aristocratic mounted warriors independently of the use of the word *ritter*.

In the *Tugendspiegel*, composed around 1170–80 by the chaplain Wernher von Elmendorf in the collegiate church of Heiligenstadt in Thuringia, we can read for the first time in German vernacular literature explicitly about the moral obligations of warriors.[17] Wernher, who is adapting a pre-existing Latin moral compilation,[18] advises his audience of lords (*herre*) to ensure the good conduct and moral behaviour of their warriors: "Admonish your fighters immediately that they

europäischen Mittalalters / Case Studies on Didactic Literature in the European Middle Ages, ed. Norbert Kössinger and Claudia Wittig (Berlin: De Gruyter, 2019), 177–209.

15. Long before the age of chivalry, some of these themes are already prominent in the so-called Davidic ethic, which promotes the righteous behaviour of any Christian ruler and which begins to be ascribed to knights at the end of the eleventh century. See Jean Flori, *L'idéologie du glaive* (Genève: Droz, 1983), 68–72 and Crouch, *The Birth of Nobility. Constructing Aristocracy in England and France, 900–1300* (Harlow: Pearson, 2005), 71–79.

16. As a gloss for *miles*, *ritter* is attested only in the twelfth century, when it suddenly appears in a great number of cases. *Degan* (or *tegen*) is recorded since the ninth century, see Bumke, *Studien*, 20–21.

17. Joachim Bumke, "Tugendspiegel," in *Verfasserlexikon*, 2nd ed., 14 vols. (Berlin and New York: De Gruyter, 1978–2008), 10 (1999): 925–27. The standard edition is published by Joachim Bumke et al., *Wernher von Elmendorf*, Altdeutsche Textbibliothek 77 (Tübingen: Max Niemeyer, 1974). The text is transmitted in two manuscripts: Berlin, Staatsbibliothek, MS germ. oct. 226 (twelfth century) and Klosterneuburg, Stiftsbibliothek, MS 1056 (fourteenth century).

18. John Holmberg, *Das* Moralium dogma philosophorum *des Guillaume de Conches. Lateinisch, Afltfranzösisch, Mittelniederfränkisch*, Arbeten utgivna med understöd vf Vilhelm Ekmans Universitatsfond 37 (Uppsala: Almqvist and Wiksells, 1929) records 50 manuscripts and fragments; meanwhile more than 90 are known, see Frank Bezner, "Moralium dogma philosophorum," in *Verfasserlexikon*, 11 (2004): 1012–16. Its authorship has been ascribed to William of Conches or Walter of Châtillon, but could never be established beyond doubt, see John R. Williams, "The Quest for the Author of the *Moralium Dogma Philosophorum*, 1931–1956," *Speculum* 32 (1957): 736–47.

keep away from shameful behaviour ... admonish them to retain their honour."[19] Since the warriors' good conduct is presented as their lord's responsibility ethics and warfare are not yet connected in the *Tugendspiegel* to form a chivalric ideal. Wernher uses *riter* twice, yet not in the lines about moral conduct.[20] The term appears alongside *recken* and *helden* in the context of warfare, while *knecht* is used with regard to the aspect of dependent service that the term *riter/ritter* originally encompassed.[21]

The first didactic text that directly addresses *ritter* as part of its audience and includes a detailed discussion of a knightly ideal that we would, from a modern perspective, identify as chivalry is *Der Welsche Gast*. It was written in 1215/16 by the Italian canon Thomasin von Zerclaere who worked at the court of the patriarch of Aquileia, Wolfger von Erla, and is transmitted in 26 manuscripts.[22] Thomasin's own mother tongue was Friulian and this is why he presents his work as composed by a *welschen gast*, or a "stranger from Romance lands." The book collects, translates, and reorganises knowledge from a variety of Latin sources—classical, biblical, and patristic—but also adds substantial passages that are Thomasin's original contributions.[23] The Italian cleric organised the 14,752 lines of instruction into ten books, each on a certain aspect of morality and good conduct. In most manuscripts the text is accompanied by an elaborate cycle of images that

19. Bumke, *Wernher von Elmendorf*, 36, lines 785–88: "so mane dine helde zu den handen / daz si sich houwen uz den schanden ... mane si, daz si ir ere behalden."

20. Ibid., 11, line 189 and 34, line 718.

21. Ibid., 35, line 760; 36, line 785; 45, line 1014.

22. Thomasin von Zerclaere, *Der Welsche Gast des Thomasin von Zirclaria*, ed. Heinrich Rückert, introd. and register Friedrich Neumann (1852; repr. Berlin: De Gruyter, 1965). All manuscripts are fully digitised and accessible on the website *Welscher Gast digital* (Universität Heidelberg), accessed 1 September 2020, http://digi.ub.uni-heidelberg.de/ wgd/. Apart from the 24 medieval manuscripts listed on this website, ten manuscripts from the eighteenth and nineteenth century testify to the great interest the book could spark over several centuries. For a modern English translation: *Der Welsche Gast (The Italian Guest)*, trans. Marion Gibbs and Winder McConnell (Kalamazoo: Medieval Institute Publications, 2009). A new comprehensive study on the education in ethics and general knowledge provided by the text was recently published by Christoph Schanze, *Tugendlehre und Wissensvermittlung. Studien zum "Welschen Gast" Thomasins von Zerklaere*, Wissensliteratur im Mittelalter 53 (Wiesbaden: Reichert Verlag, 2018).

23. Thomasin von Zerclaere used the *Moralium dogma philosophorum*, the *Anticlaudianus* and the *De rerum natura* of Alan of Lille, the *Metalogicon* of John of Salisbury, and the *Moralia in Iob* by Gregory the Great, the only source he mentions by name. See Albrecht Classen, "Thomasîn von Zerclaere," in *Key Figures in Medieval Europe. An Encyclopedia*, ed. Richard K. Emmerson and Sandra Clayton-Emmerson (New York: Routledge, 2006), 625–26.

support the text and enhance the reception and memory of the instruction by the reader.[24] Thomasin offered his book to "brave knights,
good ladies and wise priests" (*vroume ritr, guote vrouwen unde wîse
pfaffen*).[25] Despite this varied audience, *Der Welsche Gast* offers a
comprehensive discussion of the duties and virtues of the chivalrous
knight while, at the same time, allowing us to get a glimpse of the
social reality of knighthood in the first quarter of the thirteenth century. The term *ritterschaft* (corresponding to the French term *chevalerie*) is always used in an idealistic sense: it refers to a moral code
of conduct and a set of associated (moral) duties and entirely neglects
the functional aspect of armed combat. To Thomasin, knighthood is an
office (*ritters ambet*) that is connected to a moral stance.[26] In one case,
Thomasin uses the French term *chevalier* (spelled as *schewalier*) to
refer ironically to the glamorous aspects of chivalric life.[27]

The fourth and last text to be dealt with in this chapter is the mid-thirteenth century father-son dialogue *Der Winsbecke*. In this anonymous
text, the father figure describes knighthood as an office that entails
chivalric duties.[28] In 80 stanzas each of 10 lines the father gives advice

24. On the images, see Claudia Brinker-von der Heyde, "Der 'Welsche Gast' des Thomasin von Zerclaere: Eine (vor-) Bildgeschichte," in *Beweglichkeit der Bilder. Text und
Imagination in den illustrierten Handschriften des "Welschen Gastes" von Thomasin von
Zerclaere*, ed. Horst Wenzel and Christine Lechtermann (Cologne, Weimar and Vienna:
Böhlau, 2002), 9–33. Christian Schneider has recently proposed similarities between the
macrostructure of the text and that of the cycle of images: "Textstruktur und Illustrations-
prinzipien im 'Welschen Gast' des Thomasin von Zerklaere," *Beiträge zur Geschichte der
deutschen Sprache und Literatur* 139 (2017): 191–220.
25. Thomasin von Zerclaere, *Der Welsche Gast*, 400, lines 14695–96.
26. Ibid., 212, line 7785.
27. Ibid., 99, lines 3649–50; Matthias Lexer, "schevalier," in *Mittelhochdeutsches
Handwörterbuch*, 3 vols. (Leipzig: Hirzel, 1872–78; repr. Stuttgart: Hirzel, 1979), 2: 715.
For the semantics of the French term, see Glyn S. Burgess, "The Term 'Chevalerie' in
Twelfth-Century French," in *Medieval Codicology, Iconography, Literature and Translation: Studies for Keith Val Sinclair*, ed. Peter Rolfe Monks and D.D.R. Owen (Leiden:
Brill, 1994), 343–58.
28. *Winsbeckische Gedichte nebst Tirol und Fridebrant*, ed. Albert Leitzmann, 3rd ed.
rev. Ingo Reiffenstein, Altdeutsche Textbibliothek 9 (Tübingen: Max Niemeyer, 1962),
26–46. An English translation of the poem and its female counterpart was published as
"Winsbecke, Winsbeckin, and Winsbecke-Parodies," transl. Ann Marie Rasmussen and
Olga Trokhimenko, in *Medieval Courtly Literature: An Anthology of Vernacular Guides to
Behaviour for Youths, with English Translations*, ed. Mark D. Johnston (Toronto, Buffalo,
and London: University of Toronto Press, 2009), 105–21. For a discussion of the pedagogic
effect of the debate/dialogue structure, see Bernd Bastert, "*den wolt er leren rehte tuon*.
Der Winsbecke zwischen Didaxe und Diskussion," in *Text und Normativität im deutschen
Mittelalter: XX. Anglo-German Colloquium*, ed. Elke Brüggen, Franz-Joseph Holznagel,
Sebastian Coxon, and Almut Suerbaum (Berlin: De Gruyter, 2012), 303–20.

on a courtly and chivalric life style, at one point defining a canon of associated duties and virtues of knighthood, which he calls *der schilt* (the shield), *schildes reht* (the order of the shield), or, indeed, *ritterschaft* (knighthood).[29] His use of the last term clearly encompasses both knighthood, the function, and chivalry, the code of conduct. After the father's instruction, the son admonishes him to turn away from a life in the world, and in the end both enter a monastery. This peculiar connection of secular advice and religious admonition indicates the complex interplay of values at work in the construction of the chivalric ideal.

Guidelines to Knighthood in *Der Welsche Gast*

Der Welsche Gast is particularly rich in its depiction of knighthood and its associated values in the early thirteenth century. Its author, Thomasin, describes the *ritter* in various situations. A number of passages deals with the knight on horseback, for example when Thomasin presents rules for proper behaviour of the horseman in the vicinity of ladies.[30] He links the privilege of riding with the moral superiority of the knight.[31]

On occasion Thomasin's picture of the knight is less that of a virtuous horseman and rather more of a courtier, participating in the pastimes and vainglory of noble society. The images of the "knight at court" or "courtly knight" by far outnumber those of the mounted warrior. At court, the virtuous knight may be a model to the noble offspring (*edele kint*), as imitation is, for Thomasin, a major principle of chivalric education.[32] But apparently being a model of virtues to the young was not how most knights defined their role at the courts. Instead, Thomasin indicates, it was by "good food and good wine" (*guote spîse and guote[r] wîn*), "garments and beautiful jewellery" (*durch kleider und durch schœne gesmît*) as well as pleasant social interaction with ladies, with peers, at a dance... that knights represented their social position.[33] And as much as Thomasin criticises the

29. Leitzmann, *Winsbeckische Gedichte*, 6, stanza 17/1; 7, stanzas 19/1 and 20/9. Rasmussen and Trokhimenko (77) translate *schildes reht* as "the nature of the shield," however in comparison with other contemporary texts, e.g. *Der Welsche Gast*, it becomes apparent that *schildes reht* refers to knighthood as an order.

30. Thomasin von Zerclaere, *Der Welsche Gast*, 12, lines 420–25.

31. Ibid., 176, lines 6453–56.

32. Ibid., 10, lines 344–48.

33. Ibid., 212, lines 7776 and 7779; 12, lines 434, 413, and 425; 333, line 12241.

vainglory of this merely representative side of chivalry he is aware that it is part of the social dimension of knighthood. He indicates also that the lower nobles could hope to benefit from contributing to the general atmosphere of high spirits and joyousness that courtly society so highly valued. The great number of precepts concerning dress, pleasant manners and refined speech support this impression.

The fashionable French term for the knight, *chevalier*, is used only once in the body of German moral-didactic texts from the twelfth and early thirteenth centuries. As noted above, it occurs only in *Der Welsche Gast* where it demonstrates once more Thomasin's suspicion of worldly fame. He encourages his reader to estimate critically whether the high regard in which he may be held due to his knightly status is actually justified, and not simply the deception of flatterers. It is in the mouth of these flatterers (exemplified by "heralds") that the French term is voiced: "When the heralds call out at the tops of their voices before the knights: 'Hurrah, knights! Good chevaliers! Noble and high-spirited!'"[34] Such words might please the knight and give him the false impression of being an esteemed warrior (a lion, in Thomasin's words), while actually he is a disgrace to "decent people" (*vrumen schar*).[35] The French term illustrates the fashionable association of knighthood and court culture, as the associated adjectives *edel* and *hôh gemuot* indicate—terms which are well known from imaginative literature as the supposed courtly ideal of *joie de la cour*.[36] This *joie de la cour* is a courtly life style, associated with dress, pleasant conversation, splendour and refined manners, but not with the hardiness, virtue and the fulfilment of social duties to which Thomasin wishes to lead his audience. In a different passage Thomasin intro-

34. Thomasin von Zerclaere, *Der Welsche Gast*, 99, lines 3647–50: "swenn die croiræere / vor den rîtern schrîent sêre / 'zâh schewaliers, rîter guot, / edel und ouch hôh gemuot'." (trans. Gibbs and McConnell, 99).

35. Thomasin von Zerclaere, *Der Welsche Gast*, 100, lines 3651–52: "sô dunkt sich der ein lewe gar, / der ein schande ist der vrumen schar." (trans. Gibbs and McConnell, 99).

36. In the so-called *Joie de la cour*-episode in the courtly romance *Erec* (both in the version of Chrétien de Troyes and the German adaptation by Hartmann von Aue) the hero re-establishes the right balance between inner harmony and relations to the outer world, proving himself worthy to be the rightful ruler of his land and an Arthurian knight. The term has become synonymous with the joyous courtly community and the individual's contribution to its maintenance, see Philipot Emmanuel, "Un épisode d'Érec et Énide: *La Joie de la Cour.* Mabon l'enchanteur," *Romania* 25 (1896): 258–94; comparing French and German Arthurian literature, see Walter Haug, "Chretien de Troyes und Hartmann von Aue: Erec und des hoves vreude," in *Die Wahrheit der Fiktion. Studien zur weltlichen und geistlichen Literatur des Mittelalters und der frühen Neuzeit*, ed. Walter Haug (Tübingen: Niemeyer, 2003), 205–22.

duces a man—not explicitly presented as a *ritter*—who wishes to acquire fame and esteem:

> So in his mind he arranges a tournament to which many a good knight will travel, and he wishes to perform very well there. Thus the spear of his foolish fantasies empties many a saddle. No one can compare with him: they must all give way before him. Just look, how his courage is bruited abroad in the world! And everyone says that he has such fine, courtly livery. His hauberk is very splendid, and no one can compare to him in this respect. His steed has an excellent gait. His armour fits him to perfection. His greaves are neither too big nor too small around his legs. My! How that man uses his legs! No one there rides as he does. He has a wealth of attributes at his disposal.[37]

The man's daydream describes knighthood in precisely the manner it is presented to a noble readership in courtly romances of the time. Authors swoon for page after page about the elegant manners, luxurious dress, and handsome bodies of their protagonists who not only gain personal reputation, land and the hand of a lady in marriage by their accomplishments in tournaments, but re-establish order in courtly society when they slay an opponent who has previously offended another member of the court.[38]

While Thomasin encourages the reading of courtly romances in a younger, less learned audience of lay nobles so that they can learn by imitation, he does so only in that part of his instruction which is mainly concerned with manners and social interaction at court (Book I). The actual ideal of knighthood he wishes to propagate is explicitly *not* the one drawn from fictional literature. He merely uses this literary model

---

37. Thomasin von Zerclaere, *Der Welsche Gast*, 104–105, lines 3831–52: "Sô leit er ûf in sînem muot / einn turnei dâ manec guot / rîter zuo bekomen sol, / dâ wil erz tuon harte wol. / sô machet manegen satel lær/sîner tœrschen gedanke sper. / niemen mac sich zim gelîchen: / si müezen im alle entwîchen. / wartâ, wie sîn vrümekeit / ist in der werlde umbe geseit!/ si redent ouch gemeinlîche / daz sîn zimier stê hüfschlîche. / sîn wâfenroc ist harte rîche: / im ist niemen dâ gelîche. / sîn ors daz vert harte wol: / sîn harnasch stêt im als er sol. / sîn îsenhosen umb diu bein. / die sint ze grôz noch ze klein. / hei wie der selbe man / sîniu bein vüeren kan! / niemen rît im dâ gelîche: / er ist aller vrümkeit rîche." (trans. Gibbs and McConnell, 101).

38. Both *Erec* and *Iwein* testify to the knight's function to restore order at the ideal court. The narrative pattern was so deeply ingrained into these romances that they hardly underwent any changes in the course of translation from Chrétien de Troyes's French version to Hartmann von Aue's German adaptation. Patrick Del Luca, "Chevalerie, amitié et noblesse de sang chez Hartmann von Aue: une étude comparée avec l'œuvre de Chrétien de Troyes," *Cahiers de civilisation médiévale* 55 (2012): 113–45.

to ease his audience into the more demanding elements of his instruction. The ideal of the "knight in shining armour" that the romances put forward was perceived by Thomasin's contemporaries as a glamorous way of raising a person's individual status. It particularly associated the lower nobility with the popular heroes of the time and thus raised esteem for the entire social group. While this ideal was used by many other authors, such as the writer of *Der Winsbecke*, to instruct about the merits of knighthood, Thomasin considered it as mere vanity, as empty praise rather than actual virtue.

Thomasin's condemnation of the limited vision that saw knighthood as only a mode of self-representation and a vehicle to gain status is well exemplified by his opinion on the most typical knightly pastime, the tournament. The tournament is mentioned in *Der Welsche Gast* only as a means of gaining what Thomasin condemns as empty praise, not true honour.[39] The image in the manuscripts associated with this passage shows two knights on horseback engaged in single combat, decorated with coats of arms, with plumes on their helmets, and fighting with either swords or lances (Fig. 11.1). However, this recognisable image of knighthood is not part of the chivalric ideal that Thomasin aims to promote.

Interestingly, the idea of a knight in actual battle does not occur at all in Thomasin's book. In fact, combat against a human enemy is explicitly discouraged. The only fight Thomasin sanctions is that against sinfulness or indeed against the devil. Book VI of *Der Welsche Gast* praises the pursuit of the virtues as reinforcing the divine order of the world. Knighthood, previously described as an office, is now fully developed as an ideal. The tone in which the Italian canon discusses this topic also changes. In this book, Thomasin addresses his audience several times directly, twice as "noble and virtuous knight" (*edel rîter guot*).[40] Knighthood is called an order (*orden*) or an office (*ambet*) and its duties and associated virtues are spelled out in the vocabulary of armed combat.[41] The virtuous knight "must advance bravely with the banner of virtue towards the enemy's host of vices, and in attacking he must destroy them all."[42]

39. Thomasin von Zerclaere, *Der Welsche Gast*, 104, line 3833.
40. Ibid., 201, lines 7385 and 7395.
41. Ibid., 211, lines 7769 and 7785.
42. Ibid., 201, lines 7381–84: "er sol mit der tugende van / punieren vrümeclîchen an / des vîndes untugende schar: / er sol si hurtent brechen gar." (trans. Gibbs and McConnell, 142).

Fig. 11.1—Knights on horseback engaged in single combat. Miniature from Thomasin von Zerclaere's *Der Welsche Gast* (1215/16). Gotha, Forschungsbibliothek, MS Memb. I 120, fol. 25r (*ca.* 1340). Reproduced with permission.

With *punieren* and *hurten* Thomasin employs technical terms from medieval warfare to encourage an interpretation of chivalry that embeds it much more in the moral sphere. Fighting cannot of course be separated from knighthood and it is not Thomasin's intention to do so. In fact, he specifies: "Whoever is a knight or is called one, must now prepare himself very carefully to defend himself. Every decent man must arm himself against vice."[43] This fight against wickedness is, to him, the epitome of knighthood:

> Anyone who vanquishes vice fights like a knight. To be sure,
> I am not calling it chivalry just because a man breaks a lance.
> That is proper chivalry when someone scatters a host of vices
> over the earth and does not allow them to come up again.[44]

43. Thomasin von Zerclaere, *Der Welsche Gast*, 202, lines 7419–24: "Swer rîter heizet ode ist, / der sol sich ze dirre vrist / ze wer bereiten harte wol / [and] sich wâfen gegen der untugent." (trans. Gibbs and McConnell, 142–43).
44. Thomasin von Zerclaere, *Der Welsche Gast*, 203, lines 7443–50: "swer untugenden an gesît, /der strît einn rîterlîchen strît. / jâ heize ich daz niht rîterschaft / daz ein man bricht

Fig. 11.2—A knight in combat against the vices. Miniature from Thomasin von Zerclaere's *Der Welsche Gast* (1215/16). Gotha, Forschungsbibliothek, MS Memb. I 120, fol. 56r (*ca.* 1340). Reproduced with permission.

The passage is emphasised to the reader graphically by an image of the knight in combat against the vices (Fig. 11.2). The composition of this image is reminiscent of the one of the knight in tournament—in most manuscripts it is even placed in the same position on the parchment—with the difference that the opponents, the vices, depicted in similar armour as the knight himself, are not on horseback. The image of the mounted warrior is reserved for the virtuous knight.

These vices are sins the knight must fight in himself as much as in the world. The armour in this allegorical war is provided by his own virtues: Wisdom offers him her banner, Justice grants him a sword, Prudence gives him her shield and Security her hauberk, while Faith is associated with the helmet. The knight's horse is offered by Hope, Courage adds the spurs and Chastity the bridle, Constancy gives the saddle, while

einen schaft. / daz ist rîterschaft gar, / swenn man der untugende schar / ûf die erde bestriu-wet nider / und lât sî niht ûf komen wider." (trans. Gibbs and McConnell, 143).

finally it is the spear of Humility that has to pierce the enemy.[45] Thus clad and armed by the virtues the knight goes to war against sin and evil, in all the various forms it can occur in, mostly, however, in the knight himself. Chivalry means in the first instance moral perfection and a turn away from the sort of sinful behaviour associated with the military elite.[46] Throughout, "knighthood" (*ritterschaft*), or "knightly service" (*schildes ampt*)[47] is used in a positive sense, but the "wicked knight" (*boese ritter*) too frequently appears in prescriptive texts from the twelfth and thirteenth centuries. This indicates that in fact, in the eyes of the clerical authors, one could be a knight and hold a social position without subscribing to knighthood, the ideal.

Thomasin, however, not only adds moral warfare to the list of chivalric duties, but actively discourages fighting against any other enemy while the knight is engaged with inner moral strife:

> I have read and taken to heart that anyone who wishes to defeat the devil must live well alongside other people, as he should live. He should not weaken his strength by engaging in any other enmity. I counsel every noble knight that as long as the devil's battle lasts he should do nothing else, for that way he can fight well.[48]

Thomasin's intention entirely to redirect the violence associated with the knight's function becomes clear. The ideal he promotes goes beyond the *miles Christianus*, who limits the use of violence to just causes identified by higher (clerical) authorities.[49] Instead of fighting

---

45. Thomasin von Zerclaere, *Der Welsche Gast*, 203–4, lines 7470–500. This allegorical image of a knight, armed in virtues, fighting evil was frequently employed not just in literature but also in visual arts. Kaeuper, *Holy Warriors*, 1–5 interprets a particularly striking example found in a bestiary manuscript, London, British Library, MS Harley 3244, fol. 27v–28r.

46. Thomasin himself, in book VI, chapter 4, names *hôhvart* (*superbia*), *unkiusche* (*luxuria*), *erge* (*malitia* or *avaritia*) and *trâkeit* (*acedia*) as the knight's characteristic sins. Thomasin von Zerclaere, *Der Welsche Gast*, 203, lines 7459–64.

47. *Ampt* can mean service, even in the sense of the holy mass, but is also used for office: Lexer, "ambahte," in *Mittelhochdeutsches Handwörterbuch*, 48.

48. Thomasin von Zerclaere, *Der Welsche Gast*, 211, lines 7745–56: "ich hân gelesen und vernomen, / swer den vâlant wil überkomen, / der sol mit allen liuten wol / leben, als er leben sol. / er sol niht krenken sîne kraft / mit deheiner andern vîentschaft. / swer im einem hât an gesît, / der hât verendet allen strît. / ich rât eim ieglîchn rîter wert, / die wîl des tiuvels strît wert, / daz er niht anders tuon sol, / wan sô mag er gestrîten wol." (trans. Gibbs and McConnell, 146).

49. Richard W. Kaeuper, *Chivalry and Violence in Medieval Europe* (Oxford: Oxford University Press, 1999), 64–73.

the enemies of the Church, Thomasin encourages the knight to fight
vices—in the world and in himself. In order to do so, he employs the
terminology of warfare to model a new heroic ideal that allows his
knightly audience to identify with the image he has constructed.

While the life of the knight at court is often criticised for its excess
and comfort, knighthood had at the same time long been associated
with physical exhaustion, discomfort and pain. Hardship is, however,
not a drawback in the chivalric ideal, but rather it contributes to its
quasi-sacral character. It is in this context that Thomasin refers to
knighthood as an order or office: "Knights, contemplate your order:
How did you become a knight?"[50] The Italian cleric spells out in this
passage that knighthood is supposed to be hard work, not comfort,
luxury and public appearance:

> Anyone who wishes to practise the office of a knight must cer-
> tainly pay more attention to his whole way of living than to
> eating. He shall have more to do than wear fine clothes and go
> along gesticulating with his hands. The man who only wishes
> to live in comfort cannot fulfil the office of knighthood.[51]

Instead of the easy or splendid life that, according to Thomasin, many
knights lived, they should earn their status in fulfilling the duties that
came to be associated with knighthood as the ideal developed in the
twelfth century: "If a knight intends to practise what he should by
rights be practising, he should work day and night with all his might
for the sake of the Church and for the sake of poor people."[52] The protection of churches, of religious people and of the weak (widows and
orphans) is probably the most frequently and anciently cited specific
moral obligation on the lay aristocracy, and its failure to carry it out is
a regular complaint made by clerics.[53] The aspect of knighthood that

50. Thomasin von Zerclaere, *Der Welsche Gast*, 211, line 7769: "gedenket, rîtr, an
iuwern orden: / zwiu sît ir ze rîter worden?" (trans. Gibbs and McConnell, 146).
51. Thomasin von Zerclaere, *Der Welsche Gast*, 212, lines 7785–92: "Swer wil rîters
ambet phlegen, / der muoz mêre arbeit legen / an sîne vuor dan ezzen wol: / mêr ze tuon er
haben sol / danne tragen schœne gewant / und varen swingent sîne hant. / der mac niht rîters
ambet phlegen, / der niht enwil wan samfte leben." (trans. Gibbs and McConnell, 147).
52. Thomasin von Zerclaere, *Der Welsche Gast*, 212, lines 7801–5: "Wil ein rîter phlegen wol / des er von rehte phlegen sol, / sô sol er tac unde naht / arbeiten nâch sîner maht /
durch kirchen und durch arme liute." (trans. Gibbs and McConnell, 147).
53. Flori, *L'idéologie du glaive*, 68–72; Crouch, *Birth of Nobility*, 71–79. The oath a
knight swore at his dubbing included the defence of the church as well as the protection of
widows and orphans; Keen, *Chivalry*, 57.

emphasised suffering and hardship might actually have increased the esteem of the chivalric ideal both in clerics and laymen, as suffering in the pursuit of the office could well be interpreted as an *imitatio Christi*, thus strengthening the connection of the chivalrous knight to the notion of a *militia Christi*.[54]

The Appeal of an Ideal

Did chivalry offer a model of sublimated moral warfare for knights who no longer actively participated in armed combat? Did it give a new function to the lower nobility who could not earn esteem by fighting but instead served their lords at the courts as advisors and administrators, or simply hung on in the hope that they would gain favour and, ultimately, a fief? Or is the representation of the knight fighting immorality in the world, rather than his secular rivals, the ideal that Thomasin and his fellow clerical writers wished to see established? I would argue that the medieval reality sat somewhere between these two possibilities, namely that the ideal of the knight fighting for virtue promoted by clerical authors was received more readily by precisely those lower nobles who spent their days at court rather than on the battlefield.

The audience addressed in instructional texts on knighthood could be broad and diverse, given that the Middle High German term *ritter* did not necessarily include only *ministeriales* but could also be used by members of the nobility in their own self-representation, even by a person as exalted as the Emperor himself. The authors often gave advice about both aspects of a knight's social relations, as a subordinate to a lord as well as a person superior over others. Thus, the chivalric ideal included aspects of service as well as aspects of good governance. However, the knight, even as a superior person, remains in a relatively low position. *Ritter* and *herre* are discussed separately in the didactic texts, though they subscribe to a shared canon of values. The term *herre* is as ambiguous as *ritter* in Middle High German. It can designate any kind of superior male person, the lord over a land, or a nobleman, and, of course, the highest authority in the medieval world order, God.[55] *Der Welsche Gast* emphasises this social division but

---

54. Kaeuper, *Holy Warriors*, 57–65 and 96–104.
55. Lexer, "herre," in *Mittelhochdeutsches Handwörterbuch*, 1259.

also common values: "Something that is not worthy of a knight does not well befit a lord, and anything that is supposed to adorn a lord must also be adornment for a knight."[56] In *Der Welsche Gast* the term *herre* generally refers to a nobleman and indicates a social status superior to that of the knight. Precepts concerning behaviour in social interaction (such as gestures, speech, courtly protocol, as well as anything related to combat) are directed at knights. The *herre*, in Thomasin's work, is presented principally through a catalogue of vices and virtues, based on the assumption that those who exert a great deal of power and dispose of much wealth are particularly prone to certain sins, such as greed and pride.[57]

Thomasin also explicitly regulates the relationship between *herre* and *ritter*. The knight owes his lord "help and advice" (*helfe unde rât*)[58] and must always be glad to fulfil his orders: "If one has a lord, one must always happily do what he orders."[59] The lord, in return, must not ask any unusual services of him. The relationship of a knight to his *herre* and his duties towards his own subordinates are discussed in the same passage, as they are identical. They can be summarised in the brief formula: "Therefore, never order anything that you would not want your lord to order you to do."[60] While Thomasin clearly wants his knightly audience to behave justly and mercifully towards its serv-

---

56. Thomasin von Zerclaere, *Der Welsche Gast*, 55, lines 2006–11: "swaz den rîter lastert gar, / dâ wirt der herre niht von gêrt, / wan swaz des rîters ist unwert, / daz kumt niht dem herren wol, / und swaz den herren zieren sol, / daz muoz gezierde dem rîter sîn." (trans. Gibbs and McConnell, 80).

57. See Miriam Sénécheau, "'Nu wil ich raten den herren allen ...': Herrscherbild und Herrscherkritik im 'Welschen Gast' des Thomasin von Zerklaere," in *In frumento et vino opima: Festschrift für Thomas Zotz zu seinem 60. Geburtstag*, ed. Heinz Krieg and Alfons Zettler (Ostfildern: Thorbecke, 2004), 247–66. A synopsis of the ten parts and the prologue are provided in English by Kathryn Starkey, *A Courtier's Mirror: Cultivating Elite Identity in Thomasin von Zerclaere's Welscher Gast* (Notre Dame, IN: University of Notre Dame Press, 2013), 153–95, based on Gotha, Forschungsbibliothek, MS Memb. I 120.

58. Thomasin von Zerclaere, *Der Welsche Gast*, 213, line 7814. The formula *consilium et auxilium* was part of the vassalic oath of allegiance, often captured by the term *fidelitas*. See Knut Görich, "*Fides* und *fidelitas* im Kontext staufischer Herrschaftspraxis (12. Jahrhundert)," *Das Mittelalter* 20 (2015): 294–310.

59. Thomasin von Zerclaere, *Der Welsche Gast*, 213, lines 7840–42: "swelch man einen herren hât / daz er gerne tuo swaz er gebiutet." (trans. Gibbs and McConnell, 147)

60. Thomasin von Zerclaere, *Der Welsche Gast*, 214, lines 7881–83: "dâ von sô gebiut nimêre / dan du wellest daz dîn herre / gebiete dir." (trans. Gibbs and McConnell, 148). Variations of this rule of thumb occur three times in the passage about the relationship between knight and lord. Thomasin von Zerclaere, *Der Welsche Gast*, 213–15, lines 7831–7918, and esp. lines 7836–38: "swie du wil daz dîn herr mit dir lebe, / alsô lebe du und der man / der ouch dir ist undertân."

ants, his focus is on the knight's service to his lord.[61] He is well aware that this is not always an easy relationship but advises his audience to accept the state of affairs gladly: "His good intention gives him the power that diminishes his hardship if he does it happily at all times."[62] *Der Welsche Gast* encourages its audience to accept and fulfil its role in the world, whether it likes it or not. A major function of its instruction is the creation of "stability" (*staetekeit*), a central social value only assured if everyone knows and accepts their position: "If you wish to trample underfoot the man who will perhaps be sitting above you in the kingdom of our Lord, that is not in keeping with chivalry."[63]

Thomasin ties knighthood to an acceptance of one's position in the world. The rank of each member of society has been defined by God; any attempt to deviate from it disqualifies the offender from his chivalric standing. For him, social mobility is not welcome, but a threat to a functioning society and even to the divine order of the world. This standpoint appears to be a direct reaction to the shifts and reorganisation taking place in the lower ranks of the imperial nobility. Some *ministeriales* acquired considerable possessions, prestigious offices and political influence; sometimes surpassing that of old noble families whose property had been diminished by shared inheritance. Chivalry could, as seen above, be used to elevate an individual's position in society, but it was not meant to change the established order. Medieval elite society was not stable, and loss of status was real enough for Thomasin to use it as a threat against those who aimed too high:

> You are probably saying: "I have no lord." Bear in mind that it could well happen that you acquire one. Thereupon you say: "I am a lord in my own land" but then I can say for a fact that you can never climb up there unless some feckless man is afterwards able to make you his subordinate.[64]

61. Thomasin explicitly refers to the *mannes reht* (rightful order of man) that ensures that he is not treated by his master as *vihe* (livestock); Thomasin von Zerclaere, *Der Welsche Gast*, 214, lines 7866 and 7863.

62. Thomasin von Zerclaere, *Der Welsche Gast*, 213, lines 7844–46: "sîn guoter wille gît im kraft /daz sînes kumbers minner ist, /tuot erz gerne zaller vrist." (trans. Gibbs and McConnell, 147)

63. Thomasin von Zerclaere, *Der Welsche Gast*, 214, lines 7870–74: "wil du vertreten mit dem vuoz / den der lîht hôher sitzen muoz / denne du in unsers herren rîche, / daz enstêt niht rîterlîche." (trans. Gibbs and McConnell, 148).

64. Thomasin von Zerclaere, *Der Welsche Gast*, 214, lines 7887–94: "Du sprichest lîht 'ich hân herren niht': / sô wizze daz ez vil lîhte geschiht / daz dun gewinnst.du sprichst zehant / 'ich bin ein herre in mînem lant': / sô mag ich sprechen wol vür wâr, / dune

All men, no matter their status, answer to a superior authority: "No one great or small is without a lord. We all have one lord in common, and that is our Lord God."[65] Submission to a lord is what knighthood eventually means to Thomasin. Knowing their place in the world and accepting the duties associated with their role, knights are integrated in a world order as interpreted from the perspective of the Church.[66]

On the individual level, chivalric values were thought to benefit the knight in this world as well as the next. This is exemplified very well by Wernher von Elmendorf in his *Tugendspiegel*, when he introduces his rendering of the chapter *De religione* in the *Moralium dogma philosophorum* with the formula: "I shall teach you another virtue that will enhance your reputation and also nourishes your soul."[67] The discussion of chivalric virtues in Book VI of *Der Welsche Gast* is introduced by a similar remark, which grants eternal bliss to those who strive for moral perfection.[68] Honour in this life and salvation thereafter are presented as the immediate consequences of the struggle for a virtuous life.

The mid-thirteenth-century dialogue *Der Winsbecke*, presents an interesting attempt to reconcile both sorts of aspiration. In the first part of the poem a father instructs his son in all the important things a young man of lower noble status needs to know to win esteem and reputation by means of "knightliness" (*schildes ambet*). The majority of his precepts are secular and in line with a representation of knighthood as we know it from romances, though his approach is much more pragmatic, much less idealistic and exaggerated, to the point of emphasising a domestic and comfortable lifestyle. The father speaks from his experience; he asserts several times that he is passing on what he found to work best during his time at court and as head of a household.

---

gestîgest nimmer dar, / dich enmüge ein lîhter man / dar nâch haben undertân." (trans. Gibbs and McConnell, 148).

65. Thomasin von Zerclaere, *Der Welsche Gast*, 215, lines 7896–98: "ân herren ist weder grôz noch kleine; / einen herrn hab wir gemeine, / daz ist unser herre got." (trans. Gibbs and McConnell, 148).

66. Kaeuper, *Holy Warriors*, 94–118 has shown in detail how chivalry was employed by nobles across Western Europe to justify warfare and to stage their own self-representation. Specifically for the situation in the Empire, see Arno Borst, "Das Rittertum im Hochmittelalter. Idee und Wirklichkeit," in *Das Rittertum im Mittelalter*, ed. Arno Borst (Darmstadt: Wissenschaftliche Buchgesellschaft, 1976), 212–46, esp. 240–46 (first published in *Saeculum* 10 (1999): 213–31).

67. Bumke, *Wernher von Elmendorf*, 27, lines 555–57: "Noch sal ich dich ein tugent lerin, di dir gut iz czu dinen erin vnd ouch di armin sele labit."

68. Thomasin von Zerclaere, *Der Welsche Gast*, 185, lines 6809–16.

The father figure in *Der Winsbecke* promises "high praise" (*hôhen prîs*) to his son if he pursues knighthood.[69] He evokes Gahmuret, the father of the Middle High German Parzival, to whom *aventiure*, the errant life in the pursuit of chivalric encounters, was the highest aim in life. This indicates what kind of benefit is meant by him: Gahmuret, says the father, wins the heart of a woman, land, and possessions and the son can expect no less.[70] The pursuit of (chivalric) virtues, explains *Der Winsbecke*, "makes you worthy of the most honourable company" (*machet dich den werden wert*).[71] The father also encourages the son to associate with these *werden* at court.[72] They are the members of courtly society who are held in the highest esteem, whether because of their social standing, their rank, their elegant manners or, as Thomasin likes to see them, because of their virtues. In French didactic texts, they appear as *preudome*.[73] Their appreciation of the boy can lead to offices, favours, a good reputation and other individual advantages in a society that defined rank relative to other people.[74] Thus, the recognition by a certain group of people could have results in practical and material benefits. Despite some clerics' attempts to connect chivalry with predominantly spiritual rewards, *Der Winsbecke* promises very immediate benefits.

Moreover, the father continues, the pursuit of virtue might also entail another kind of "bliss" (*saelde*), which is, again, "the favour of good women" (*guoter wîbe segen*).[75] The attention of courtly ladies is in fact frequently cited as an argument in favour of knighthood (vice versa, instruction for ladies also promises not just the high regard of

---

69. Leitzmann, *Winsbeckische Gedichte*, 7, stanza 18/9, (transl. Rasmussen and Trokhimenko, 77).

70. Leitzmann, *Winsbeckische Gedichte*, 7, stanza 18/7–8.

71. Ibid., 8, stanza 22/6, (transl. Rasmussen and Trokhimenko, 79).

72. Leitzmann, *Winsbeckische Gedichte*, 8, stanza 23/1–2.

73. The similarity of the Middle High German *werden* and the Old French *preudome* is discussed in Claudia Wittig, "Zur Konstruktion des Ritters in der deutschen und französischen Moraldidaxe des Hochmittelalters", *Francia* 46 (2019): 469–84. For a detailed discussion of the *preudome* in the chivalric ideal see the chapter by David Crouch in this volume.

74. Keupp, *Dienst und Verdienst*, 424–43. The *werden* are also used in *Diu Winsbeckin* as a measure for reputation and social standing: *Winsbeckische Gedichte*, 60, stanza 29, line 7: "sô dienestû der werden gruoz" ("you will earn the greeting of noble people," translation Rasmussen and Trokhimenko, 117).

75. Leitzmann, *Winsbeckische Gedichte*, 8, stanza 22/7–8 (transl. Rasmussen and Trokhimenko, 79).

courtly society but in particular the attention of young men).[76] Perhaps
it helps us better to understand the emphasis on this aspect if we bear
in mind that the instruction is directed at young nobles. We would
certainly not stray too far from the truth if we assumed that in young
men the care for one's eternal soul would often take second place to
the search for female attention.

Also Wernher von Elmendorf adapts a passage on love from the
Moralium dogma philosophorum in his *Tugendspiegel* and advice on
romantic relationships makes up a large part of the father's advice in
Der Winsbecke.[77] While there is no trace of the elaborate *minne*-con-
ception between knight and socially superior lady we find in the
romances of the time, love surely has its place in the multifaceted
chivalric ideal promoted by instructional texts in the courtly tradition.[78]

When the father in *Der Winsbecke* has finished his argument, his
son politely thanks him for his insights only to turn on him harshly
for the vanity of his advice, which he rejects in its entirety. In his
turn he advises his father to leave all worldly pleasure behind, give
all his possessions to a monastery and try his best to prepare his soul
for death. The father embraces the advice in tears, founds a religious
house (*spitâl*) and withdraws from the world together with his son.[79]
This turn of events has puzzled scholars for some time and has led
to the rejection of the son's stanzas in the edition as "pious continuations" which rendered the father's advice invalid.[80] However, nothing

76. Ann Marie Rasmussen, "'If Men Desire You, then You are Worthy': The Didactic Mother-Daughter Poem 'Die Winsbeckin'," in *Mothers and Daughters in Medieval
German Literature*, ed. Ann Marie Rasmussen (Syracuse, NY: Syracuse University Press,
1997), 136–57, at 140.

77. Bumke, *Wernher von Elmendorf*, 23–24, lines 439–70; Leitzmann, *Winsbeckische
Gedichte*, 4–6, stanzas 11–16.

78. C. Stephen Jaeger, *Ennobling Love: In Search of a Lost Sensibility*, The Middle
Ages Series (Philadelphia: University of Pennsylvania Press, 1999) discusses the relevance
of a new form of gender relationship for the moral edification of the high medieval nobility
and the role of romantic love in the representation of their own reputation and worthi-
ness, in particular in chap. 11: "Virtue and Ennobling Love (2): Value, Worth, Reputation"
(145–54).

79. Leitzmann, *Winsbeckische Gedichte*, 30, stanza 80/7.

80. Leitzmann, following Moritz Haupt, in *Winsbeckische Gedichte*, 8, separates the
son's stanzas in his edition and lists them as continuations (40) since, according to him,
they render the father's advice invalid. He is convinced that *Der Winsbecke* was an actual
knight writing for his son; the "continuations" must therefore have been added by a cleric
to give the chivalrous instruction a religious twist. Ann Marie Rasmussen has analysed
this editorial practice in the light of nineteenth-century patriarchal scholarship and found

in the transmission of the text supports the idea of the stanzas advo-
cating *contemptus mundi* as being a later addition.[81] It seems rather
that the poem contains two models which an audience might want to
consider in their own lives. One can withdraw from the world early
in life, like the son, who is presented in the manner of a *puer senex*.
The other option is to live in the world as honourably as possible and
prepare for death at the end of one's life. The chivalric and secular
model is not presented as invalid or inherently wrong, but preference
is clearly given to a life withdrawn from the world.

While the care of the soul is a vital element in all didactic texts, most
authors also describe at length the benefits of moral conduct for a life
in the world. We can safely assume that the fear for one's soul was
very real for most people in the Middle Ages, not least because of the
efforts of priests and monks to instil it in their audiences. However,
the more immediate benefits of a virtuous life seemed to have had
a greater appeal to the knights, judging from the preponderance in
which salvation and success in this life are used by authors to propagate their message.

Conclusion: Negotiating Chivalric Identity

Chivalry, in the Empire, was not just a profession, but a pattern from
which *ministeriales* and noblemen alike could model their lives in
order to live well and in accordance with Christian values. It was not
by any means an undisputed model. *Contemptus mundi* was still prev-
alent in society as a religious ideal and the number of lay converts
associated with monastic houses speaks of a lay piety that was more
than just affectation. While Christian elements were strong in medieval chivalry and while nobles across Western Europe founded monasteries for the salvation of themselves and their families, the realities

no evidence that would justify the separation of the poem in two parts. See Ann Marie
Rasmussen, "Fathers to Think Back Through. The Middle German Mother-Daughter and
Father-Son Poems Known as *Die Winsbeckin* and *Der Winsbecke*," in *Medieval Conduct*,
ed. Kathleen Ashley and Robert L. A. Clarke (Minneapolis: University of Minnesota Press,
2001), 106–34.

81. The earliest manuscripts all transmit the son's reply; those manuscripts which do not
transmit it omit several of the father's stanzas, too. The form in which Leitzmann publishes
the text is not transmitted in a single manuscript. A list of the manuscripts is on the website
Handschriftencensus, lemma "'Winsbecke' und 'Winsbeckin'," accessed 1 March 2018,
http://www.handschriftencensus.de/werke/431.

of knighthood were firmly rooted in a materialistic court culture and the necessities of armed combat. The texts studied in this chapter have shown us how clerics adapted their teachings to meet their audiences where they stood in life, but we have also seen how, all concessions aside, they allocated knights a place in a hierarchical structure that subdivided the elites according to an ecclesiastical interpretation of the world. The chronological perspective on chivalric instruction has shown that the texts did not develop from a clerical perspective in the earlier witnesses to a more secular tone in later examples, but that the weight could shift between Christian morals and secular values and that clerical and lay perspectives coexisted throughout the period.

As Richard Kaeuper has shown for France and England, members of the secular elites used the established model of knighthood for their own purposes, picking those aspects that legitimated their lifestyles, ignoring others that did not suit them.[82] The interpretation of the role of certain groups in the social order was no longer just the province of clergymen. A new vernacular literature represented the secular elites according to their own priorities, not as brutal warriors but as refined, elegant and honourable men, at least in their own minds. If such a new vision of knighthood was to be integrated into the divine world order, it was necessary to create a status for knights that reflected their needs. Between service and lordship, *ministeriales* and lesser aristocracy could adopt the ideal of the chivalrous knight. It elevated their individual position at court and in the service of a lord and offered them material benefits. But a chivalric identity also provided them with a model that could accommodate their social function and yet also portray them as servants of God. As Kaeuper sums it up:

> Chivalry in fact provided an *esprit de corps* for the laity in this world; it framed not only war and peace, the elevated and elevating nature of love, and ideal gender relationships, among much else. Its ideals and practices, in short, performed crucial societal work that was far from fanciful or merely silly, but rather was fundamental.[83]

82. Kaeuper, *Holy Warriors*, 104–15.
83. Richard Kaeuper, *Medieval Chivalry* (Cambridge: Cambridge University Press, 2016), 5.

Chivalry gave knighthood a place in a greater plan that was sanctioned by God and promised salvation as well as the status knights craved. It is no wonder—given the opportunities the model provided—that knights themselves began actively to promote the chivalric ideal.[84] If knighthood was to match up to the chivalry it embraced, it obliged all its devotees to comply with its duties and values so as to guarantee its esteem in society and thus advance the individual knight's status.

The promotion of this ideal was so successful that, by the end of the twelfth century, it was readily adopted by the highest ranking members of the secular elites. As a social ideal, chivalry was the answer to a number of issues important in earlier medieval society. But when the likes of Emperor Maximilian I (1459–1519) posed as a knight, the time of chivalry as an answer to social issues and an integrative ideal for the secular elite was already past. The "Last Knight," as scholars have called Maximilian, used chivalry to refer back nostalgically to a time when noble manners and splendid tournaments were the key to status and esteem.[85] But at the same time Maximilian participated fully in a Renaissance culture that embraced quite different ideals of superior living and which created quite different social categories.[86]

---

84. Fleckenstein, "Miles und clericus," 319–23.

85. Sabine Haag, Alfried Wieczorek, Matthias Pfaffenbichler, and Hans-Jürgen Buderer, eds., *Kaiser Maximilian I.: der letzte Ritter und das höfische Turnier* (Regensburg: Schnell & Steiner, 2014).

86. Karl-Heinz Spieß, "Idealisiertes Rittertum. Herzog Karl der Kühne von Burgund und Kaiser Maximilian I," in *Die Inszenierung der heroischen Monarchie. Frühneuzeitliches Königtum zwischen ritterlichem Erbe und militärischer Herausforderung*, ed. Martin Wrede (Munich: De Gruyter Oldenbourg, 2014), 57–75. On the performativity of Renaissance identities, see Stephen Greenblatt, *Renaissance Self-Fashioning. From More to Shakespeare* (Chicago: University of Chicago Press, 1980).

David CROUCH

WHEN WAS CHIVALRY? EVOLUTION OF A CODE

The study of chivalry as a code of conduct cannot be divorced from the study of conduct literature, but until very recently chivalry has been studied more or less in isolation from the copious literature of conduct that survives from the twelfth century. If "conduct literature" has been appealed to by students of chivalry it has been works like John of Salisbury's Entheticus *and* Policraticus *which, in terms of genre, barely fit the criteria. This chapter observes three associated sub-genres within the earlier literature which influenced and produced the hybrid chivalric tract, which appears at the end of the twelfth century. These are categorised here as firstly "Catonian," that is, hyper-moral conduct literature deriving from schoolroom exercises. The second is "Salomonic" literature associated with the critiques of the laity from the pulpit. The most significant is the third: the vernacular "Instructional" literature we find in twelfth-century manuals or* enseignements *intended to define for the youth the courtly conduct of the* preudomme. *It was when this last genre began exhibiting the hyper moral and theological expectations of the other two, which it did in the first decade of the thirteenth century, that we can be sure chivalry had come into being.*

Maurice Keen's classic study *Chivalry*, published in 1984, remains a remarkably influential work, and rightly so. It was in its day the first work for a century to attempt a comprehensive analysis of a social ideal which Keen believed was first to be found articulated in the western Europe of the first half of the thirteenth century. His twentieth-century social and literary analysis far surpassed what had been accomplished in an earlier high water mark of chivalric studies, Léon Gautier's ultramontane and chauvinistic *La Chevalerie* (1884), which in its eccentric way too had marked a turning point. Gautier's work had in fact brought to its fullest expression the previous eighteenth-century literary approach to chivalric culture, pioneered by Jean-Baptiste de la Curne de Sainte-Palaye, where the principal source was the study of medieval epics and romances: La Curne's "golden age" of chivalry. His approach made chivalry a province in which the literary, not the social, historian long ruled. Indeed the study of what we call chivalry is unusual until the later twentieth century in being a historical field where the basic ground rules of analysis have been largely constructed by literary scholars out of imaginative literature, rather than through historical, ethical or conduct texts.[1]

Maurice Keen changed this emphasis. For the purpose of this chapter one major change he accomplished was in his willingness to historicise chivalry, for he had the historian's fascination with origins. The appearance of the tract known as the *Ordene de Chevalerie* was for him a defining point in the appearance of the self-conscious code of Chivalry; he regarded it in fact as chivalry's ur-text.[2] La Curne for his part had done something similar, but he had taken as his chivalric ur-text the *Roman des Eles* of Raoul de Houdenc. However both texts, as it happens, belong to the same generation.

This of course begs more than one large question. Are we right in assuming with Keen, and indeed Gautier, that early thirteenth-century aristocrats actually conceived of their new manner of superior conduct as being a fully-articulated code unique to their generation? Did they indeed reify it as "chivalry?" This depends of course on how you define your terms. As an Anglophone, Keen had and employed the linguistic advantage denied the Francophone, which allows a distinction to be made between "knightliness" and "knighthood" (the skills and lifestyle of a knight down the centuries) and "chivalry" (the ideal of conduct expected of an elite male, a member of the knightly milieu). In French *chevalerie* has to suffice for both ideas, which has a capacity to mislead the English speaker.[3]

1. This introduction is drawn from the historiographical survey in David Crouch, *The Birth of Nobility: Constructing Aristocracy in England and France, 900–1300* (Harlow: Longman, 2005), 7–21. See also Mark Girouard, *The Return to Camelot: Chivalry and the English Gentleman* (New Haven: Yale University Press, 1981), esp. chap. 5, and the bibliographical essay in, F.J.C. Hearnshaw, "Chivalry: its Place in History," in *Chivalry: A Series of Studies to Illustrate its Historical Significance and Civilizing Influence*, ed. Edgar Prestage (London: Kegan Paul & Co., 1928), 29–33. The comment about the unusual nature of the source material for chivalric reconstruction is in Maurice Keen, *Chivalry* (New Haven: Yale University Press, 1984), 2–3. This chapter was written in the course of a major research fellowship offered by the Leverhulme Trust, a scheme whose remarkable generosity I am very happy to acknowledge. Keith Busby and Stephen Jaeger were kind enough to offer advice and read the text. Remaining errors are entirely my own.

2. Keen, *Chivalry*, 6–8, where he dated it vaguely "before 1250." The work of Keith Busby (published only just before Keen's) dates it more closely to the second decade of the thirteenth century, Raoul de Houdenc, *Le Roman des Eles. The Anonymous Ordene de Chevalerie*, ed. and trans. Keith Busby, Utrecht Publications in General and Comparative Literature 17 (Amsterdam and Philadelphia: Benjamins, 1983), and see also Keith Busby, "Three Anglo-Norman Redactions of *L'Ordene de Chevalerie*," *Mediaeval Studies* 46 (1984): 31–77.

3. A point made by François-Louis Ganshof, "Qu'est-ce que la chevalerie," *Revue Générale Belge* 25 (Nov. 1947), 78, though almost inevitably he misinterpreted English

To the Anglophone, "chivalry" can be distinguished from "knightliness". This allows a more clearly drawn division between the twelfth-and thirteenth-century ideas of the knight which we find on either side of the cultural turn which we characterise as Chivalry. Chivalry was understood by Keen to be a new thing in the thirteenth century: "an ethos in which martial, aristocratic and Christian elements were fused together." To his mind it was a coalescing of three earlier influences: masculine and knightly ideals were there, and so too were pre-existing ideals of superior conduct, those associated with the *preudomme*, and of course the religious gloss acquired from the ethical teaching of the Church (which Keen regarded as being the least weighty of the three).[4]

Imposing Chivalry on the Middle Ages

It was not until the very end of the eighteenth century that "chivalry" began to assume in French, German and British minds its now dominant sense of a behavioural code, as has been demonstrated in the Introduction to this book. The *Ordene de Chevalerie* takes its title not from any perceived behavioural code but from the act of inducting an aspirant into the condition of *chevaler*, even though knightly behaviour is the work's chief theme. *Chevalerie* here is "knighthood," a condition about which Saladin, king of Damascus, is supposed by the author to be curious. Though Maurice Keen called his book *Chivalry* he pointed (as had Claude-François Menestrier three centuries before) to the multiplicity of the word's meanings in the Middle Ages, of which a "code of values" certainly became one, but one among several.[5] Keen was prefigured in this conclusion by Jean Flori who in 1975 analysed four principal senses of the word in a survey of its uses in twelfth-century epic literature, but did at least find that towards the end of the century to be a knight had sometimes come to evoke "nuances morales, éthiques et religieuses."[6]

A study by Glyn Burgess, which used much the same methods as Flori's, is rather less equivocal in its conclusions, and finds *chevalerie*

---

usage. French does have possibilities, however. Jean Flori can use the word *cavalier* (from Late Latin *caballarius*) to construct a distinction in modern French between the "horseman" and the "knight," cf. *Chevaliers et chevalerie au Moyen Âge* (Paris: Hachette, 1998), 44.

4. Keen, *Chivalry*, 16–17.

5. Ibid., 2.

6. Jean Flori, "La notion de chevalerie dans les chansons de geste du XIIᵉ siècle: étude historique de vocabulaire," *Le Moyen Âge* 81 (1975): 211–44, 407–45, esp. 437.

almost always has a sense of military life and martial excellence. But nonetheless Burgess finds in the work of Gautier d'Arras *chevalerie* to have an abstract sense associated with positive moral qualities, in much the same way as Chrétien de Troyes's Gornemant—Perceval's mentor in the *Conte de Graal*—taught. *Chevalerie* can be characterised in Gautier's work as modest reticence and the defence of the powerless.[7] I would myself agree with Flori's position that in the last decades of the twelfth century the fact that moral excellence was being expected of the knight who took his order seriously coloured for some writers the meaning of the *chevalerie* he possessed, but it is only to that limited extent that the contemporary mind reified conduct on the word "chivalry."[8]

The word *chevalerie* was not therefore understood as a code of conduct by the knights of the year 1200. Early thirteenth-century aristocrats may have conceived of their manner of superior conduct as a fully-articulated code unique to their generation and class, but they did not reify it on the word "chivalry." Jean Flori discovered it undeniably in only one comment by Chrétien de Troyes, while Glyn Burgess found it only in some passing reflections by Chrétien's contemporary, Gautier d'Arras. If *chevalerie* had any dominant sense around the year 1200 it was as what English would translate as "knightliness" or "knighthood," meaning the condition, skills or deeds of the horseback warrior. This is in fact the sense in which it is used in the title of Keen's chivalric ur-text: the *Ordene de Chevalerie*, whose title (as given it by its author) is meant to be taken as "the Ordinal into the Degree of Knight."

However, though it is wise to be cautious when applying unhistorical labels to historical phenomena, I would argue that there is no getting away from it in the case of Chivalry. Menestrier, La Curne, Charles Mills, and many others down to Keen's own day were analysing what I would call a socio-cultural shift in medieval society. Keen identified the code the aristocracy began to expect of itself in the early thirteenth century as a new thing, as a social turn, and its unique character lay in its hyper-morality; it was, he said, "too idealistic."[9] This for him could

---

7. Glyn S. Burgess, "The Term 'Chevalerie' in Twelfth-Century French," in *Medieval Codicology, Iconography, Literature, and Translation: Studies for Keith Val Sinclair*, ed. Peter Rolfe Monks and D.D.R. Owen (Leiden: Brill, 1994), 343–58, esp. 356–57.

8. Jean Flori, "La notion de chevalerie dans les romans de Chrétien de Troyes," *Romania* 114 (1996): 289–315, returns to the subject and underlines the moral implications of the word in Chrétien's work, notably the episode of Gornemant's knighting of Perceval dealt with above.

9. Keen, *Chivalry*, 5.

be called Chivalry. The further question follows that if this new morality did not come from the *chevaler*, where did it come from?

The Seedbed of Chivalry

One pragmatic foundation on which the chivalric turn was built is
easily identified. The chivalrous thirteenth century had inherited an
ideal of a superior public man from previous generations. It had been
encapsulated since at least the eleventh century in romance societies
as the pragmatic *preudomme*, who was a creature of its habitus. The
preudomme was *homo habilis* to chivalry's *homo sapiens*; related
but operating on different principles in a different environment. The
preudomme was the sort of ideal male type we encounter in proverbs,
ensenhamens, the *sirventes* of Bertran de Born, and most profoundly
and polemically in the vernacular biography of William Marshal,
written as the new chivalrous male was emerging into consciousness.
The *preudomme* is presented also in a fictional form in the *chanson
de geste*, where his more admirable qualities were summed up in
the portrayal of Oliver in the *Song of Roland*, or Count William in
the Orange cycle. The *preudomme* was however an ideal male, not
an ideal warrior. Male clerics, townsfolk and even peasants could be
preudomme. Women had the consolation prize of being *preudefemme*.
This is what pinpoints Keen's cultural shift in the early thirteenth century. Clerics, peasants and women could obviously not embrace a new
mode of superior conduct devised exclusively for an aristocrat who
shared the distinctive culture and rituals of the *chevaler*, as Dominique
Barthélemy has explored them at the beginning of this volume.

The purpose of the rest of this chapter is to follow up Keen's idea of
a coalescence of earlier influences that produced the social and moral
stances of the *Ordene*. He did not himself spend much time survey-
ing this seedbed of chivalry, though it is by no means an impossible
study. As Claudia Wittig has already demonstrated for the German
vernacular in the previous chapter, there was in fact a literary field
concerned with the moral conduct of the laity long preceding the time
of the *Ordene*, and not just in the French cultural area.[10] It was out of

10. The primary catalogue of medieval conduct literature is, Alice A. Hentsch, *De la
littérature didactique du moyen âge s'adressant spécialement aux femmes* (Cahors: Con-
selant, 1903), though it is not analytic in its approach. For that see Jonathan Nicholls, *The
Matter of Courtesy: Medieval Courtesy Books and the Gawain-Poet* (Woodbridge: Brewer,

this field that older ideals of superior conduct grew and were transformed into the austere expectation of the chivalric male social elite.
Twelfth-century people indeed wrote quite a lot about such conduct,
and not just in Latin, but in the several principal vernaculars—Francien, Occitan and German.

Chivalric teaching crystallised out of a twelfth-century social discourse that became obsessive about what was moral, right and superior conduct, and for a reason we will go on to identify and examine. The debate spread much wider than archbishops, scholastics and
well-meaning abbots to the lay aristocracy itself, which was by no
means illiterate and not averse to picking up a pen and contributing
its own views. Even as basic a task as constructing a taxonomy of the
available literature produces some unexpected insights into the society
that preceded and generated the chivalric code.

When we deconstruct and trace back the ideas we find in early thirteenth-century, hyper-moral vernacular tracts intended to educate the lay
male elite, such as the *Ordene de Chevalerie*, the *Roman des Eles*, Guillaume de Lorris's *Roman de la Rose*, the *Prose Lancelot* and others such,
we find that the epistemology settles into three strands or traditions.

The Schoolroom or Catonian Tradition

A Latin "Catonian" tradition stands behind the vernacular tracts of
the 1210s— in some ways the most important in giving them their
tint of hyper-morality. It has a distinct lineage, continually referencing
itself and absolutely fixated on discussing moral conduct. It belongs
essentially to the schoolroom but it makes the crossover into the vernacular quite early. Its importance is not just that it fixates on moral
conduct; it is in its very pervasiveness. It touched everyone in society
who aspired to literacy. Its ultimate inspiration was that compendium
of commonplace moral reflections called the *Disticha Catonis*, an
anonymous work actually of the late third century, but Christianised
and revised in a standard form known as the *Cato Novus* by around

---

1985), App. B; Claude Roussel, "Le Legs de la Rose: Modèles et préceptes de la sociabilité
médiévale," in *Pour une histoire des traités de savoir-vivre en Europe*, ed. Alain Montan-
don (Clermont-Ferrand: Association des publications de la Faculté des lettres et sciences
humaines de Clermont-Ferrand, 1994), 1–90; and see also Roberta L. Krueger, "Introduction," in *Medieval Conduct Literature: An Anthology of Vernacular Guides to Behaviour
for Youths with English Translations,* ed. Mark D. Johnston, Medieval Academy Books 111
(Toronto: University of Toronto Press, 2009), ix–xxxiii.

1000.[11] The attribution to Marcus Porcius Cato is of course entirely gratuitous. Its importance was not so much in the depth of its moral reflections (for instance, "still waters run deep" (4:31) and "another's life is a teacher" (3:13)). It is in its universal use in the schools of western Europe as a primary reader for the instruction of younger children in Latin grammar and vocabulary.[12] Cato's distichs feature already as one of the four standard texts for Latin beginners by 1000, so we can be sure that most youths schooled in their letters—whether intended for the clergy or not—came into contact with them. They would carry the words of Cato with them for the rest of their lives, for good or ill.

You can see this pervasiveness best when the distichs spread out across genres and cross linguistic boundaries out of the schoolroom and into the vernacular. They were circulating by 1200 in at least three Anglo-Norman versions known collectively as the *Livre Catun*, which are not simply translation aids but pose as moral literature for general meditation.[13] Cato can be proved to have penetrated wider culture in the twelfth century and by two routes. Firstly, some of the distichs were absorbed into popular collections of vernacular proverbs, themselves a form of conduct literature. But the distichs also became cultural commonplaces. In the romance of *Tristan*, its author puts the (translated) words of Cato into the mouths of King Mark's barons when they implored their lord not to go unescorted into solitary places. Cato turns up too in the didactic passages of the *Conte de Graal*.[14]

11. Richard Hazelton, "The Christianisation of 'Cato': the *Disticha Catonis* in the light of late medieval commentaries," *Mediaeval Studies* 19 (1957): 157–73; Tony Hunt, "The *Auctores* and the 'Liber Catonianus,'" in *Teaching and Learning Latin in Thirteenth-Century England*, 3 vols. (Cambridge: Brewer, 1991), 1: 59–79; Roussel, "Les legs de la Rose," 3–4; Élisabeth Schulze-Busacker, *La didactique profane au Moyen Âge* (Paris: Garnier, 2012), 103–4.

12. As a twelfth-century author of a list of required reading for the young puts it: "Postquam alphabetum didicerit et ceteris puerilibus rudimentis imbutus fuerit, Donatum et illud utile moralitas compendium quod Catonis esse vulgus opinatur addiscat" ("After the child has learned his alphabet and is instructed in other basic grammar suitable for his age, he should be given and should learn from that useful little moral compendium which is generally called Cato's.") Latin text in Hunt, "The *Auctores* and the "Liber Catonianus,'" 79, from Cambridge, Gonville & Caius, MS 385, as discussed in Charles Homer Haskins, "A List of Text-Books from the close of the Twelfth Century," in *Studies in the History of Medieval Science* (Cambridge, Mass.: Harvard University Press, 1924), 356–76.

13. For the vernacular diffusion of the *Disticha*, Krueger, "Introduction," xiii; Schulze-Busacker, *La didactique profane*, 104–6.

14. *Disticha Catonis*, 4:23 in Chrétien de Troyes, *Le Conte du Graal (Perceval)*, ed. Félix Lecoy, 2 vols., Les classiques français du Moyen Âge 100, 103—Les romans de Chrétien de Troyes édités d'après la copie de Guiot (Bibl. nat. fr. 794) 5, 6 (Paris: Cham-

And before the end of the twelfth century, as the idea of chivalry was crystallising, an English master called Robert of Ho constructed a large moral compendium in the Anglo-Norman dialect framed largely around Catonian schoolroom themes, discoursing on and developing at length many of his moral maxims for—one assumes—more general edification than the schoolroom, though precisely what audience he had in mind is uncertain. But Robert of Ho does seem to have believed that the wisdom of Cato would be to the benefit of any reader, clerical or lay, once he had glossed it.

If that were not enough to make the Catonian tradition pervasive, the distichs spawned a number of twelfth-century imitators, some immensely successful in their own right. Writers who wanted to create supplementary teaching texts for more advanced pupils naturally wrote within the same area Cato had staked out: idealised conduct. The anonymous mid-twelfth-century poems known as *Facetus*, were its first later medieval fruits. Though written to be supplements to existing Latin readers for more adolescent youths, the inspiration of the *Disticha Catonis* required that these efforts be framed as tracts on conduct. There are two principal twelfth-century examples, *Cum nihil utilius* and *Moribus et Vita*, and they both set out their agenda of augmenting Cato in their first verses. *Cum nihil utilius* was the most successful and widely circulated. It aspires, as it says, to "augment what the teachings of wise Cato did not describe."[15] There follow over 300 lines in rhymed hexameters reflecting on human relations, personal hygiene, and table manners, most of them framed as two-line distichons in imitation of Cato, though there are more expansive passages on certain subjects. True to his word, the author does not repeat any Catonian material and makes a point of adding the overtly Christian verses which are so lacking in Cato.

Cum nihil utilius fulfilled its author's intention. In the thirteenth century it was established alongside the distichs themselves in the standard Latin primer known as the "*Auctores Octo*." It can be found in numerous manuscript readers of French, English, German and Bohemian prove-

---

pion, 1984), 1: 21, lines 527–28 on the benefits of knowledge. Cf. also Roussel, "Les legs de la Rose," 4.

15. "Quod minus exsequitur morosum dogma Catonis / supplebo..." Leopold Zatočil, *Cato a Facetus. Pojednání a texty. Zu den deutschen Cato- und Facetusbearbeitungen. Untersuchungen und Texte*, Spisy Masarykovy University v Brně, Filosofická Fakulta—Opera Universitatis Masarykianae Brunensis, Facultas Philosophica 48 (Brno: Masarykova Universita 1952), 287.

nance, so it can be fairly assumed that a large proportion of the literate population of northern and western Europe was exposed to its moral views when they were in the elementary schoolroom. This may have made it one of the most influential conduct texts of the Middle Ages, using the category loosely. It forms the basic inspiration and necessary grammatical foundation for a rather more rarified *cultus virtutum* which Stephen Jaeger finds characteristic of the teaching of the eleventh- and twelfth-century masters; teaching which (as he pointed out) spilled over into the education of the lay aristocracy, as Marbod of Rennes tells us.[16] It should be emphasised at this point that pervasive though Catonian influence was as an impulse towards engaging the lay mind in moral discourse and the formation of the vernacular chivalric tract, it was indeed basic. The higher sentiments in the expression of ethics which eventually made their way into the vernacular would owe more to Cicero and Seneca and the teaching of rhetoric than to the teaching of grammar.

If this was true of the elementary school, the Catonian tradition was equally dominant in the *magna schola* where adolescents learned advanced grammar, obscure vocabulary, and the finer points of versification. This is nowhere more evident than in the work called the *Liber Urbani*, neatly translated by Robert Bartlett as the "Book of the Civilised Man." Of its author we know nothing but his name, Daniel of Beccles, though it is easy to work out that he was a schoolmaster.[17] Its production is likely to have been between the years 1177 and 1183 though there are indications that it was not originally a unified work, but brought together from several existing teaching tracts. Although of English provenance, copies appear in French libraries already in the early thirteenth century. It evidently circulated widely by 1200 and by 1250 was a fixture in the libraries of Augustinian houses, including those of the order's provincial chapter abbeys.[18] The *Liber Urbani* is a large and miscellaneous work of 2,840 hexameters which actually makes it one of the more substantial conduct works of the Middle Ages. It has many things to say

16. C. Stephen Jaeger, *The Envy of Angels: Cathedral Schools and Social Ideals in Medieval Europe, 950–1200* (Philadelphia: University of Pennsylvania Press, 1994), 76–117.

17. Frédérique Lachaud, "L'enseignement des bonnes manières en milieu de cour en Angleterre d'après l'*Urbanus magnus* attribué à Daniel de Beccles," in *Erziehung und Bildung bei Hofe*, ed. Werner Paravicini and Jörg Wettlaufer (Stuttgart: Thorbecke, 2002), 53.

18. For a consideration of authorship and compilation, Fiona Whelan, *The Making of Manners and Morals in Twelfth-century England: the Book of the Civilised Man* (London: Routledge, 2017), esp. 1–24.

about proper conduct, some of them quite surprising if you took it to
be straightforward conduct literature, for it veers towards the scurrilous
and scatological in its bid to engage the mind of the male adolescent.
Its miscellaneous nature is because it is a book of Latin exercises: it is
not a unified work and its moral stances on occasion contradict each
other. It is intended as an advanced supplement to school grammatical
teaching texts, not least in its complimentary allusion to Cato by name
and its flattering imitation of its distichs.[19] So, like Cato, it saturated in
quasi-moralistic discourse the minds of the young who came into contact with it. Since the youths who used it were given earnest advice on
how to be a seneschal, a civil lawyer, a garrison commander and a lord
of men, its author clearly expected those youngsters who used his exercises to be intended for lay occupations, not just the Church.

Daniel did not write to form real life conduct, only to provide Latin
exercises. But it says something of his day and age that readers might
very well take such a work as more than a pedagogic text and use
it indeed as a conduct book. There exists in the Bodleian Library a
later thirteenth-century florilegium which abstracts 445 lines from the
first two books of the *Liber Urbani*.[20] The florilegist rubricated his
abstracted selection as "*Proverbia Urbani*," choosing each distichon
for its moral content and deliberately omitting those many he found
less than moral. In effect he edited and improved the *Liber* so as to
convert it from a Latin exercise book into a meditation on conduct
appropriate for the chivalric age. The medieval florilegist knew his
source better than we do. The sort of hyper-moral discourse that could
be distilled from the *Liber Urbani* was in demand in the thirteenth
century because by then it had escaped the grammarian and the classroom and had become a social posture, the one we find in the *Roman
des Eles* and the *Ordene de Chevalerie*.[21]

The Biblical or Salomonic Tradition
A moral posture was subliminally inculcated in the teaching of any
educated youth from the moment he began his schooling in Latin. But
it was not the only influence on the young twelfth-century mind. A
second tradition identified here is more explicitly theological and far

19. *Urbanus Magnus Danielis Becclesiensis*, ed. J. Gilbart Smyly (Dublin: Hodges Fig-
gis, 1939), lines 1862–75, 2014–24, 2218–31.
    20. Oxford, Bodleian Library, MS Rawlinson C 552, esp. fol. 19v.
    21. This is a development I deal with in *The Chivalric Turn: Conduct and Hegemony in
Europe before 1300* (Oxford: Oxford University Press, 2019)

and away the best explored so far by historians interested in chivalry. I call it the "Salomonic," because if Cato loomed over the schoolroom, Solomon ruled from the pulpitum.[22] Cato's distichs were so embarrassingly humanistic that their tenth-century editor and twelfth-century imitators had to add overt Christian sentiments and offer Christian supplements. The Biblical Books of Proverbs, Wisdom and Ecclesiastes provided an attractive alternative model for conduct literature. Like Cato's their contents were frequently composed of paremiological sayings, not unlike distichs, which can be by turn worldly-wise, polemical or despairing, with (especially in Ecclesiastes) a distinctly jaded view of the human condition, which theologians since Alan of Lille have categorised as *contemptus mundi* (rejection of the world's vanity).[23] But these books of Wisdom had a biblical authority and a theological edge that Cato did not, and it is to King Solomon (their supposed author) that the mid twelfth-century cleric and Angevin courtier Master Stephen de Fougères appealed as his inspiration when he produced a remarkable compendium of somewhat pessimistic social studies which he called the *Livre des Manières*. He addresses by turn all conditions of humankind, from the pope to the peasant. Women get a long and depressing chapter all to themselves. With each category he sketches out firstly what the ideal of that condition should be, and then discourses on how its practitioners have fallen from it, not least the knight.

Stephen's *Livre* was probably composed in the late 1150s or early 1160s, when he was a chaplain in the household of King Henry II in England.[24] In terms of genre it defies categorisation, but one possible explanation is that it was a compendium of moral reflections condensed from his sermons, of which a popular genre since the beginning of the

22. For the movement of the person of Solomon out of theological commentary and into vernacular literary genres, Mishtooni Bose, "From Exegesis to Appropriation: The Medieval Solomon," *Medium Aevum* 65 (1996): 187–210.

23. Alan of Lille, *Summa de Arte Praedicatoria*, ed. Jacques-Paul Migne, in *Patrologiae cursus completus: series Latina*, 221 vols. (Paris, 1847–67), 210 (1855): cols 114–16 (*de mundi contemptu*). Alan classified the posture (col. 114) as including the emptiness (*vanitas*) of daily life, the inherent vileness of men and the transitory nature of all things.

24. The latest of several editions dates the work to Stephen's tenure of the see of Rennes (1168–78), see *Le Livre des Manières*, ed. and trans. Jacques T.E. Thomas, Ktemata 20 (Leuven: Peeters, 2013), 9–10. This fails to note the significance of its colophon where the author refers to himself *Mestre Esteinve de Fougieres*, which he would not have done after he was promoted. Its dedication to Countess Cecilia of Hereford in her widowhood also indicates an earlier date, and that it was written after 1155 probably in England where the Angevin court was for long periods until 1163.

twelfth century was those called *ad status*, that is, sermons addressed to specific types and conditions of people, which naturally discourse— as does Stephen—on the vices and virtues of each.[25] In which case it might be compared with the collection of early twelfth-century sermon digests by Honorius Augustodunensis, though what survives of them is in Latin and not the vernacular. Nonetheless the abstracts also reflect at various occasions on the conditions of different sorts of men in terms not dissimilar from Stephen's.[26] By this reasoning, what we read in his *Livre* are likely to be Stephen's notes for what he might well have preached before the aristocracy and clergy in French at the Angevin royal court.

Stephen de Fougères, like the authors of the *Ordene de Chevalerie* and *Prose Lancelot* two generations later, believed that knights formed an order or degree in society, though he believed that they were sadly fallen from what they ought to be. Instead of fighting for and supporting the Church, living honestly and decently, knights were caught up in loose living, gallivanting around Europe from tournament to tournament and abusing their power, which was represented by the sword they carried. It is implicit in what he says that power without moral constraint is sinful and obnoxious to God. Stephen had in fact many predecessors in these views, going back to the Church Fathers, who played with the image of the Roman legionary to produce the metaphorical *miles Christi*; the disciplined, dauntless and prayerful believer. In due course it came to describe the elite of believers, the regular monks. In the tenth century the phrase was turned back on lay society as a rebuke. Archbishops, abbots and scholars preached against the disruptive violence of lords and their military households whose conscienceless and immoral *militia* was no more than *malitia*.[27]

25. Mark Zier, "Sermons of the Twelfth-Century Schoolmasters and Canons," in *The Sermon*, ed. Beverly Mayne Kienzle, Typologie des sources du Moyen Âge occidental, 81–83 (Turnhout: Brepols, 2000), 325–51.

26. Honorius Augustodunensis, *Speculum Ecclesie*, ed. Migne, in *Patrologia Latina*, 172 (1854): cols. 815–1108. A case has been made for the *Livre* as being part of a genre of early "estate satires" looking back from a thirteenth-century Salomonic *Deyputeysun*, which has some resemblances in subject matter though not in organisation, Tony Hunt, "Solomon and Marcolf," in *"Por le soie amisté". Essays in Honor of Norris J. Lacy*, ed. Keith Busby and Catherine M. Jones (Amsterdam and Atlanta: Rodopi, 2000), 205, citing also Jill Mann, *Chaucer and Medieval Estates Satire* (Cambridge: Cambridge University Press, 1973).

27. André Vauchez, "La notion de *Miles Christi* dans la spiritualité occidentale," in *Chevalerie et christianisme aux XIIᵉ et XIIIᵉ siècles*, ed. Martin Aurell and Catalina Girbea (Rennes: Presses universitaires de Rennes, 2011), 67–69.

The culmination of this movement has been seen in the First Crusade and its aftermath, where knights were offered the chance to use their violence in a legitimate way, to defend the Church and Christendom from external threat. Most famously, Bernard of Clairvaux published his own sermon on "modern knighthood" in the later 1120s as a way of drumming up support for his pet project, the Knights of the Temple, who were intended to entirely reform and sanctify the life of the knight by confronting him with a Christian hermeneutic for his all too secular life.[28]

The Instructional or Vernacular Tradition
The previous traditions are familiar enough from works on chivalric conduct. There is a third which has to be taken into account, and indeed has more relevance to the *Ordene*. It has not been brought into play much by students of medieval conduct to date. Yet it is the most significant of the three. This is the genre called in French the *enseignement*, or in the Occitan in which the classic twelfth-century examples are written, the *ensenhamen*. The genre is wider and older than the southern French examples however. It can be glimpsed in Germany in the eleventh century and the earliest examples are in Latin.

Enseignements are conduct books for the elite, generated within the circles of the social elite. They are not schoolroom products and have little of the theological or moral tinge of the Catonian or Salomonic tract in the twelfth-century examples. They are important for two reasons. Firstly they have the frank and open intention of teaching superior conduct to people who want to get on in life, and secondly the principal examples were written in the vernacular by lay authors addressing a lay audience on the sort of conduct which will get favourable notice.[29] They are all characterised by a particular format: a senior figure (male or female) encounters a confused young man or woman in

28. Malcolm Barber, *The New Knighthood: A History of the Order of the Temple* (Cambridge: Cambridge University Press, 1994), 44–51.
29. Alfred Monson, *Les ensenhamens occitans: essai de définition et délimitation du genre* (Paris: Klincksieck, 1981), and see the review of the genre in Martin Aurell, *Le chevalier lettré: savoir et conduite de l'aristocratie aux XIIe et XIIIe siècles* (Paris: Fayard, 2006), 328–32. The genre is more widespread than Occitania however: Book 5 of the late eleventh-century moral epic *Ruodlieb* incorporates a Latin example of such an *enseignement*, *The Ruodlieb*, ed. and trans. Christopher W. Grocock (Warminster: Aris & Philipps, 1985), 90–96. Undoubtedly the most significant early instance is Dhuoda's *Liber Manualis*, ed. and trans. Marcelle Thiebaux, Cambridge Medieval Classics 8 (Cambridge: Cambridge University Press, 1998).

need of instruction in the way of the world, which is promptly offered once the problem is explained. This is the same format employed by some of the early works associated with the teaching of chivalric ideals: the dialogues of Andrew the Chaplain's *De Amore*, the *Ordene de Chevalerie*, *Urbain le Cortois* and indeed it is found as late as Ramon Llull's *Libre del Orde de Cavalleria*. Much of chivalric literature owes its form, if not its sentiments, to this early vernacular genre.

Like the contemporary poetry of Marcarbru and Bertran de Born, *enseignements* can provide an insider's view of superior conduct in lay society two or three generations before the appearance of hyper-moral Chivalry. What we find from it is that, though twelfth century lay society had an idea of superior conduct, it did not lie entirely (or even at all) in the Christianised ethical conduct assigned to knighthood by the Salomonic tradition. The earliest of the Occitan examples is Garin lo Brun's *E·l termini d'estiu* addressed principally, though not entirely, to the conduct of aristocratic women. It is the work of a castellan-poet of the Auvergne and might very well date to deep within the first half of the twelfth century, as Garin was dead by 1162.[30] A second such insider's view is that of the Gascon baron, Arnaut-Guilhem de Marsan, a long poem of some 628 lines called *Qui comte vol apendre*. It dates to the 1170s. Here the author is again the conductor, this time offering his wisdom to a confused and depressed aristocratic youth he had encountered while out hawking.[31] The third, which can be firmly placed in the pre-chivalric canon, was the work of a troubadour addressed to aristocrats rather than a tract authored by one. This was *Rasos es e Mesura*, a poem of around 300 lines composed at some time between 1171 and 1190 by Arnaut de Mareuil, a professional poet who hailed from Périgord. Each of these *enseignements* is remarkable evidence of lay expectations of conduct in the twelfth century and have much to tell us about the question at issue here: when and how chivalry emerged.

30. Garin lo Brun, *L'Ensegnamen alla dama,* ed. and trans (It.) Laura Regina Bruno, Filologia occitanica Studi e testi 1 (Rome: Archivio Guido Izzi, 1996), 23–25.

31. Jacques De Cauna, *L'Ensenhamen ou Code du parfait chevalier du troubadour gascon d'Arnaut-Guilhem de Marsan* (Mounenh en Biarn: Editions Pyremonde, 2007), 64–95.

From *Cortesia* to Chivalry

When Garin lo Brun addresses his *amia*, his "dear lady friend" it is for the most part to give her gendered and pragmatic advice on her hygiene and dress, the selection of her maidservants; the way she should walk or ride her palfrey to church; her hospitality to her guests, however objectionable they may be, and how to gauge precisely the degree of effusiveness with which to treat men in her hall. But, most significantly for our purposes, at one point Garin altogether abandons gendered concerns and broaches the theme of *cortesia*, or as we might say "courtliness", in what is the earliest vernacular analysis of it as a conscious mode of superior conduct: "for," as he says, "the one who pursues it is respected by everyone so long as he demonstrates it." Courtliness is for Garin literally *savoir vivre*: a courtly person is one who knows what to say or do in any circumstance. Courtly people have address and poise, and tailor their behaviour to social advantage.[32] This is what makes his *ensenhamen* such an important text. It is an intelligent and independent insider's view of conduct amongst the twelfth-century aristocracy, which Garin regards as a body of skills which can be taught to the receptive. In Pierre Bourdieu's view of social conduct, Garin lo Brun was one who had the capacity consciously to exploit and orchestrate conduct within his social habitus. And Garin calls that conduct "courtliness" and does not approach it by way of any moral high ground.

Courtliness is a concept which has not been ignored by scholars; it was the subject of a celebrated essay by Stephen Jaeger published in 1985, which provided us for the first time with a model by which to assess the impact of the court on the choices and behaviour of its inhabitants. He also found evidence that such behaviour was codified in Germany as *curialitas* by the 1080s.[33] Jaeger's initial work found no evidence that courtliness affected the laity before the days of Chrétien de Troyes and the heyday of the court of Champagne.[34] But from

32. "Amia, si voleç / venir a mais de prez / de cortesia·us prec, / car cel qui la persec / n'a prez per tota gen, / s'en cortesia enten." Garin lo Brun, *L'Ensegnamen*, 86–87, lines 421–29.

33. C.Stephen Jaeger, *The Origins of Courtliness: Civilizing Trends and the Formation of Courtly Ideals, 939–1210* (Philadelphia: University of Pennsylvania Press, 1985), 152–61.

34. His views were revised subsequently, C. Stephen Jaeger, "Origins of Courtliness after 25 Years," *Haskins Society Journal* 11 (2009): 209–12.

Garin lo Brun's *E·l termini d'estiu* we learn that the vernacular equivalent *cortesia* was being applied by lay people in central and southern France to their own conduct in the same way a generation later, and Garin did not just use the word, he applied it to a code of taught conduct whose tenets he described. Garin was not writing in intellectual isolation in his tower at Veillac, for there is evidence that he was touching on a wider concern in his early twelfth-century society. Evidence for this can be found in the work of the more celebrated professional Gascon poet, Marcabru, Garin's contemporary, a man who was by his own account not an aristocrat. But he too felt qualified to reflect on *cortezia* in his sirventes *Cortesamen vuoill comenssar*.[35] Though it is a more lightweight composition of only seven stanzas, Marcabru is plainly dealing like Garin with a commonly understood concept of superior social conduct, which both men were attempting to define, teach and pin down, for Marcabru claimed he could instruct (*enseignar*) even the learned on the subject. Like Garin he thinks sober and restrained behaviour (*mesura*) is a large part of it, and that anyone who falls from that standard has strayed into low behaviour, *vilania*, which for him is defined by wild speech and silliness.

The Occitan material is then challenging evidence that we may have entirely misunderstood the subject of lay conduct before 1200. It is tempting to go with the drift of past scholarship and see it as further evidence of the cultural precocity of the Midi, but this would be a mistake. Occitania is only precocious in offering instances of lay writers who can describe courtliness as a code. I would suggest that we can find it outside southern France. A clear consciousness of lay *cortoisie* as superior conduct can be found in the Francophone England of the late 1130s in the ideals described in Geoffrey Gaimar's history of the English.[36] *Cortoisie, cortesia* or "courtliness" was by this evidence a conscious and didactic mode of superior lay conduct a century before

---

35. *Marcabru: a critical edition*, ed. Simon Gaunt, Ruth Harvey, and Linda Paterson (Cambridge: Cambridge University Press, 2000), 202–4. See also Joan M. Ferrante, "Cortes' Amor in Medieval Texts," *Speculum* 55 (1980): 690–91, for Bernart de Ventadorn's similar use of the concept of *cortezia*.

36. John Gillingham, "Kingship, Chivalry and Love: Political and Cultural Values in the Earliest History written in French: Geoffrey Gaimar's *Estoire des Engleis*," in *Anglo-Norman Political Culture and the Twelfth-Century Renaissance*, ed. C. Warren Hollister (Woodbridge: Boydell, 1997), 33–58. Gillingham's principal intent in his provocative study was to prove the existence of "chivalry" in the 1130s. He notes but underplays the significance of Gaimar's use of the words *curtesie* and *curteis*.

chivalry.[37] Garin lo Brun saw it and indeed taught it to his lady friend as a code to be known by those men and women who wished to be considered fit members of aristocratic society.

Tracts aside, the best evidence for the ideals and teaching of *cortoisie* is the omnipresence of the *prodom, probus homo* or *preudomme* in early twelfth-century (and indeed in eleventh-century) vernacular and (occasionally) Latin literature, as the model of a public man, whom all should emulate. He and (in due course) his female counterpart the *preudefemme* appear in twelfth-century sources from Iberia to the Rhineland. These avatars of superior conduct were themselves teaching aids, for what they did was by definition *cortois*.[38] The advice indeed of the first lines of the *Ordene de Chevalerie* to those who wanted to know what was good conduct was to go and talk to a *preudomme*.[39]

So how does this floodlight the seedbed of chivalry? Firstly it allows us to bury the Ultramontane Catholic view of chivalry as a moral-theological programme that centuries of preaching eventually imposed on the European social elite, which defined itself by a cult of military violence. This is for two reasons. That same aristocracy already by 1100 believed that it aspired to and practised a code of superior civil conduct suitable for public assemblies which would bring its practitioner on in the world, and it taught it as *cortesia* or courtliness. They called the graduate of this school of public performance in French the *preudomme*, or the *preudefemme*, a superior man or woman of consequence. Courtliness and the *preudomme* its practitioner can be found to be twelfth-century secular ideals from the Pyrenees to the Elbe, via Lombardy, Paris and London. It reveals them to be a feature of the pan-European thought world of the twelfth-century aristocrat and the courts and festivities they frequented. Hardly surprising then that the subsequent reframing of elite male conduct as "chivalry" should have travelled as far and as rapidly as it did across Europe at the end of the century. There was a pool of debate on which it could float, a friendly habitus.

---

37. For the dangers in failing to distinguish the two concepts, David Crouch, "Chivalry and Courtliness: Colliding Constructs," in *Soldiers, Nobles and Gentlemen: Essays in Honour of Maurice Keen*, ed. Peter Coss and Christopher Tyerman (Woodbridge: Boydell, 2009), 32–48.

38. Crouch, *Birth of Nobility*, 30–46.

39. *The Anonymous Ordene de Chevalerie*, 105, lines 1–4.

Conclusion: Chivalry as a Cultural Turn

This finally brings us back to that cultural turn which Maurice Keen identified with the appearance and dissemination of the *Ordene de Chevalerie* in the decade of the 1210s. It was a work which gained notice and currency; the Picard exemplar was soon copied by Anglo-Norman clerks across the Channel and helped inspire in thirteenth-century France a general respect for King Saladin as a virtuous *preudomme*.[40] Before the end of the Middle Ages the *Ordene* was to pass into Italian and Dutch vernacular versions and was one of the sources of Geoffrey de Charny's *Livre de Chevalerie*.[41]

The *Ordene* deserves its importance as one of the first treatises to identify the *chevaler* with the high moral standards demanded in the Salomonic tradition, as a superior order of society for which a quasi-liturgical ordinal is needed for admission. It is likely enough the work of a cleric, but much the same hyper-moral standards are demanded of the knight by the *Roman des Eles*, a roughly contemporary work by Raoul de Houdenc, a writer who can himself be identified as a literate knight. Catonian handbooks and his early reading must have formed Raoul's young mind to look at education as a moral discourse, a low-level *cultus virtutum* for the layman, which he took out into the world with him. The aristocracy which took up the idea of chivalry in his generation was doing no less than what had been going on for a century and more: relating public eminence to moral probity, as Cato and Boethius taught them it should be.

In this regard I think the most significant development is not so much the appearance of the *Ordene de Chevalerie*. It is when the early thirteenth-century Occitan *ensenhamen* loses its pragmatic secularity and adopts the same moral-theological outlook as the *Ordene* and the *Roman des Eles*. In fact the *ensenhamen* had already done so by 1210, and when it did the genre can be seen to have been changing in the face of a newly dominant ideology. So when between 1200 and 1210 Raimon Vidal de Besalú in his *Abril issi' e Mays intrava* writes that *cavayer* drew their social eminence from their moral excellence and the protection they offered lesser folk, then we clearly are dealing with

---

40. The idea of a courteous and moral Saracen was not new at that time, and had become a topos particularly notable in the romances inspired by themes from ancient Greece, see Catalina Girbea, *Le bon sarrasin dans le roman médiéval, 1100–1225* (Paris: Garnier, 2014).

41. Busby, "Three Anglo-Norman Redactions," 32–40.

knightliness as more than just knightly skills; it is being perceived as bound up with a moral ideology: "All good, honest and distinguished qualities are more pronounced in [knights] than in other people," Raimon blithely proclaims.[42]

Instead of virtue being urged on imperfect and corrupt knights, as the twelfth-century Salomonic tradition had done, exceptional virtue by 1200 is itself the qualification and badge of the order of knighthood, "which must be untainted by base conduct."[43] These last are the words Chrétien de Troyes around 1180 put in the mouth of the *prodome* Gornemant as he girded the sword on Perceval, and then offered the youth an *enseignement* as to how such a knight should properly conduct himself.[44]

In this way the figure of the knight became the repository of a distinct hyper-moral form of conduct associated with his order. We might as well accommodate it with the label "Chivalry" since it did focus on the knight and plainly was not *cortoisie*, which might apply to any social condition and either gender. This conclusion justifies Keen's idea of a cultural turn in aristocratic behaviour, and the evidence presented here sees the influences that produced it coalescing in the generation before 1200, somewhat earlier than Keen suggests. To me, it was fully accomplished by the time Raimon Vidal de Besalú completed his *Abril issi*. By 1210 any member of the male social elite was understood to be subject to higher ethical standards than others, and on that basis justified his social claims to leadership. These expectations were so generally felt that writers like Raimon Vidal and the author of the *Ordene de Chevalerie* took the representative figure of the knight as the subject of their new generation of *enseignements*. So much perhaps for *when* Chivalry came into existence. A rather less easy question to answer is *why* it did.

42. "E tug bon aip adreg onrat / son mielhs en lor qu'en autra gen." *Nouvelles occitanes du Moyen Âge*, ed. Jean-Charles Huchet (Paris: Flammarion, 1992), 130, lines 1635–36.

43. "qui doit estre sanz vilenie." Chrétien de Troyes, *Le Conte du Graal*, 1: 54, line 1636.

44. Ibid., 1: 54–55, lines 1631–68.

NOTES ON CONTRIBUTORS

Dominique BARTHÉLEMY is Professor at Sorbonne University and Director of Studies at the École pratique des hautes études (Paris). He is a member of the Académie des Inscriptions et Belles-lettres, and an honorary member of the Institut universitaire de France. He has studied French feudal society and published a series of monographs among which are *Chevaliers et miracles. La violence et le sacré dans la société féodale* (Armand Colin, 2004), *The Serf, the Knight and the Historian* (Cornell University Press, 2008), *La chevalerie: de la Germanie antique à la France du XIIe siècle* (Fayard, 2007; 2nd ed. Perrin, 2012), *Nouvelle histoire des Capétiens, 987–1214* (Seuil, 2012) and *La bataille de Bouvines, histoire et légendes* (Perrin, 2018). He is now completing a study of the so-called "Peace of God movement" to be published as *Histoire des paix diocésaines dans le royaume capétien* (Publications de l'École pratique des hautes études).

David CROUCH is former Professor of Medieval History at the University of Hull and a Fellow of the British Academy. Much of his work has been in the area of elite conduct before 1300, notably *The Image of Aristocracy in Britain, 1100–1300* (Routledge, 1992), *The Birth of Nobility. Constructing Aristocracy in England and France, 900–1300* (Pearson, 2005), and *The Chivalric Turn: Conduct and Hegemony in Europe before 1300* (Oxford University Press, 2019). He was involved in the project to edit the *History of William Marshal*, which was published by the Anglo-Norman Text Society in three volumes between 2002 and 2006. His biography of William Marshal (Routledge) was issued in its third edition in 2015.

Jeroen DEPLOIGE is Professor of Medieval History at Ghent University and member of the Belgian Royal Historical Commission. Specialised in the cultural history of the High Middle Ages, his most recent publications include *Manuscript and Memory in Religious Communities in the Medieval Low Countries* (ed. with R. Nip—Brepols, 2015) and the critical edition (with M. Embach *et al.*) of *Hildegardis Bingensis opera minora II* (Brepols, 2016). He also directs the historical database projects *The Narrative Sources from the Medieval Low Countries* (www.narrative-sources.be) and *Diplomata Belgica* (www.diplomata-belgica.be).

John D. Hosler is Professor of Military History at the U.S. Army Command and General Staff College (CGSC) at Fort Leavenworth, Kansas. A specialist on twelfth-century warfare in Europe and the Middle East, his books include *Henry II: A Medieval Soldier at War, 1147–1189* (Brill, 2007), *John of Salisbury: Military Authority of the Twelfth-Century Renaissance* (Brill, 2013), and *The Siege of Acre, 1189–1191: Saladin, Richard the Lionheart, and the Battle that Decided the Third Crusade* (Yale University Press, 2018; Spanish trans. Edhasa, 2019). He is the current president of *De Re Militari*, the Society for Medieval Military History.

Sara McDougall is Associate Professor of History at John Jay College of Criminal Justice of the City University of New York and is appointed to the doctoral faculty at the CUNY Graduate Center. She specialises in medieval French history and has broad interests in legal history, family history, and women's history. Recent publications include *Bigamy and Christian Identity in Late Medieval Champagne* (University of Pennsylvania Press, 2012), "The Making of Marriage in Medieval Europe," *Journal of Family History* 38:3 (2013), "The Transformation of Adultery in France at the End of the Middle Ages," *Law and History Review* 32:3 (2014), the *Gender & History 2017 Special Issue: Marriage's Global Past*, co-edited with Sarah Pearsall, and *Royal Bastards: The Birth of Illegitimacy, 800–1230* (Oxford University Press, 2017). She was a Mellon Fellow in Historical Studies at the Princeton Institute for Advanced Study in 2014–15 and was the Norman Freehling Visiting Professor at the University of Michigan Institute for the Humanities, Spring 2020.

Jean-François Nieus is senior research associate of the Belgian National Fund for Scientific Research (FNRS) and Professor of Medieval History at the University of Namur, where he teaches auxiliary sciences of medieval history and chairs the PraME—Pratiques médiévales de l'écrit research centre. His main focus is on secular governance in the High Middle Ages, primarily in northern France and the Low Countries, with a particular emphasis on the uses of literacy in the field of princely government and seigniorial administration. His academic responsibilities include membership of the editorial boards of the journal *Le Moyen Âge* and the *ARTEM—Atelier de recherche sur les textes médiévaux* series.

Eljas OKSANEN is a Marie Skłodowska-Curie Fellow at the University of Helsinki Department of Cultures. He received his PhD in History from the University of Cambridge for his dissertation on the relations across the English Channel in the Middle Ages, which was published as *Flanders and the Anglo-Norman World, 1066–1216* (Cambridge University Press, 2012). Oksanen's current research interests lie in interdisciplinary digital humanities-led work on medieval material culture as it relates to social and economic developments, and in studying the movement of people, goods and ideas between regions and realms in Europe through archaeological and historical sources.

Nicholas L. PAUL received his PhD in History at the University of Cambridge in 2005 and began teaching in the History Department at Fordham University in 2006. His primary areas of teaching and research are the crusades, the Latin East, and political culture in the Central Middle Ages. His first book, *To Follow in Their Footsteps: the Crusades and Family Memory in the High Middle Ages* (Cornell University Press, 2012) was co-winner of the John Nicholas Brown Prize of the Medieval Academy of America. At Fordham, he now serves as Director of the Center for Medieval Studies, where he has been involved in several Digital Humanities initiatives, including the *Oxford Outremer Map project*. He has also co-edited two volumes of essays arising from conferences at the Center, *Remembering the Crusades: Myth, Image, and Identity* (ed. with Suzanne Yeager—Johns Hopkins University Press, 2012) and *The French of Outremer: Communities and Communications in the Crusading Mediterranean* (ed. with Laura K. Morreale—Fordham University Press, 2018).

Jörg PELTZER is Professor of Comparative Regional History in a European Perspective at Heidelberg University and a British Academy Global Professor at the University of East Anglia, Norwich (2021–25). His research focuses on the political, social and legal history of the Central and Late Middle Ages. His publications include *Canon Law, Careers and Conquest. Episcopal Elections in Normandy and Greater Anjou, c.1140–c.1230* (Cambridge University Press, 2008), *Der Rang der Pfalzgrafen bei Rhein. Die Gestaltung der politisch-sozialen Ordnung des Reichs im 13. und 14. Jahrhundert* (Thorbecke, 2013), *1066. Der Kampf um Englands Krone* (Beck, 2016; 2nd ed. 2019), and *Fürst werden. Rangerhöhungen im 14. Jahrhundert—Das römisch-deutsche Reich und England im Vergleich* (De Gruyter, 2019).

Nicolas Ruffini-Ronzani is a postdoctoral researcher of the National Fund for Scientific Research (FNRS) at the University of Namur. His doctoral dissertation (Namur, 2014) was devoted to the aristocracy in the county of Cambrai in the High Middle Ages (*Église et aristocratie en Cambrésis (fin IXe–mil. XIIe siècle). Le pouvoir entre France et Empire au Moyen Âge central*). His current project deals with the building of the principality of Hainaut under the government of the Baldwins (1051–1205/6).

Louise Wilkinson is Professor of Medieval Studies at Lincoln University where she leads the Medieval Studies Research Group. Her research focuses on aristocratic and royal women in the thirteenth and early fourteenth centuries. Her publications include *Eleanor de Montfort: A Rebel Countess in Medieval England* (Continuum, 2012) and the critical edition and translation of *The Household Roll of Eleanor de Montfort, Countess of Leicester and Pembroke, 1265: British Library, Additional MS 8877* (Boydell, 2020). She is joint general editor of the Pipe Roll Society and was a co-investigator of the Henry III Fine Rolls Project and Magna Carta Project, both of which were funded by the Arts and Humanities Research Council of the United Kingdom.

Claudia Wittig studied German and English Philology and History at the University of Greifswald. In 2016, she got her PhD at the Centre for Medieval Literature of the University of Southern Denmark. She taught at the University of York and the University of Göttingen and was a visiting research fellow at the German Historical Institute in Paris. Since 2017, she has been a Marie Skłodowska-Curie Fellow at the Henri Pirenne Institute for Medieval Studies at Ghent University where she is working on a monograph on the moral education of the Western European nobility. Her publications include the volume *Prodesse et delectare. Fallstudien zur didaktischen Literatur des europäischen Mittalalters / Case Studies on Didactic Literature in the European Middle Ages* (ed. with N. Kössinger—De Gruyter, 2020) and several articles on medieval morality and historiography.

INDEX